Mary the Perfect CONTEMPLATIVE

Mary the Perfect CONTEMPLATIVE

CARMELITE INSIGHTS ON THE INTERIOR LIFE OF OUR LADY

BARBARA HUGHES, O.C.D.S.

ICS Publications
Institute of Carmelite Studies
Washington, D.C.

ICS Publications
2131 Lincoln Road NE
Washington, DC 20002-1199
www.icspublications.org

Published with Ecclesiastical Approval

Cover and text design and pagination by Rose Design
Printed in the United States of America

Sketch of Mary by Bill Angresano
Front cover painting, *Our Lady on Mount Carmel* by Bill Angresano

Library of Congress Cataloging-in-Publication Data

Names: Hughes, Barbara, author.
Title: Mary the perfect contemplative : Carmelite insights on the interior life of our lady / Barbara Hughes, O.C.D.S.
Description: Washington, D.C. : ICS Publications, [2022] | Includes bibliographical references and index. | Summary: “First edition. Reflections on the life of Mary from the perspective of the writings of the Carmelite saints”-- Provided by publisher.
Identifiers: LCCN 2022013587 (print) | LCCN 2022013588 (ebook) | ISBN 9781939272584 (pbk) | ISBN 9781939272591 (ebook)
Subjects: LCSH: Mary, Blessed Virgin, Saint--Biography. | Carmelites--Spiritual life.
Classification: LCC BT605.3 .H84 2022 (print) | LCC BT605.3 (ebook) | DDC
232.91--dc23/eng/20220407
LC record available at https://lccn.loc.gov/2022013587
LC ebook record available at https://lccn.loc.gov/2022013588

10 9 8 7 6 5 4 3

With appreciation to

Sister Carmela Marolda, O.C.D., of the Savannah Carmel

and

Father Kevin Culligan, O.C.D., of the Washington Province
for their wisdom and guidance through the years

Contents

Foreword

As brothers and sisters of our Lady, the Carmelite saints treasured Mary as the model contemplative when they wrote about the spiritual life. Looking merely at indexes and concordances of the writings of the Carmelite saints, one might get the wrong impression that these authors were not concerned about Mariology. This is indeed a false impression because their treatises concerning spiritual development towards union with God are always about Mary. What else is the aim of the spiritual life than union with God? And who better to model this union than the highly-favored daughter of the Father, the mother of the Son, and spouse of the Holy Spirit? Every soul seeking union with the Most Holy Trinity is seeking an end that was lived by Mary every day of her life.

Three saints of the Teresian Carmel—John of the Cross, Teresa of Jesus, and Thérèse of Lisieux—have been declared Doctors of the Church. Their spiritual doctrine, esteemed for its universal value for the church sheds light on the deep mysteries that occur within the human soul intent on seeking God. Mary is the perfect example of such a soul, and therefore the perfect model for all who journey toward union with God. While some find the writings of these great mystics difficult to understand, author Barbara Hughes has helped to bring the abstract to the real through the person of Mary, who while on earth, lived out her high calling as a wife and mother whose heart never strayed from God. In one way, *Mary the Perfect Contemplative* explores the full implications of the Marian character of Carmel, an order whose members profess "a life with Mary in allegiance to Jesus Christ." Yet, in another way, this book demonstrates not just what Mary has given to Carmel in her patronage and motherhood, but what she has given to the world.

As the Carmelite saints in past centuries were inspired by Mary, so the church in the twenty-first century needs the contemplative model of Mary's interior life. In her own age, Mary, with the Child Jesus and St. Joseph, fled to Egypt to escape the massacre of a ruler jealous for power. In our present age, replete with its own massacres and new Herods intent on domination, we are invited to follow Mary more closely, trusting in faith and seeking refuge in the promise of her son's redemption.

Today, on the Solemnity of the Annunciation, Pope Francis consecrated the whole world, and especially Russia and Ukraine, to the Immaculate Heart of Mary. May every heart be consecrated to this most blessed among women—she who walked by faith in union with God's will, even amid suffering and strife. The heart that contemplated the violence that humanity subjected her son is the same heart that prays for sinners, now and at the hour of our death. Our own hearts, so often turned away from God in sin, find a way back to him through our Lady's intercession. In his consecration prayer, Pope Francis spoke of humanity's weariness for sin and violence. Joining our mother at the foot of the cross, we stand with her whose fiat "opened the doors of history to the Prince of Peace." In a world that is desperate for the reign of peace, let us model ourselves after our mother. By becoming contemplatives after her Immaculate Heart, our hearts will be opened to the will of God, and the Kingdom of God will reign on earth.

Fr. Pier Giorgio Pacelli, O.C.D.
Solemnity of the Annunciation
March 25, 2022

Acknowledgments

NO BOOK IS EVER THE RESULT of one person's effort or inspiration. This was clearly the case when, at the suggestion of Father Kevin Culligan, O.C.D., I embarked upon this project. I began with minimal understanding of the direction it would take. However, once I began writing, I realized that the real genesis of this book had begun more than a year earlier when, for reasons I found difficult to explain, I felt impelled to pray the entire rosary every day. It was hard to understand this new urgency to pray and meditate daily on all the mysteries, but the ease with which I was able to accomplish this was a grace that I could neither ignore nor take lightly.

While I was reflecting on the events of Jesus's life through the eyes of Mary, new insights about the mysteries of God within the context of human history began to emerge. Through the rosary, Mary was opening my mind and heart to a deeper appreciation for her role in salvation history and in the life of the church. Drawing largely on the teachings of the Carmelite mystics, the book began to take shape, giving expression to the heights of union with God through the person of Mary, Bride of God's Love.

On a practical level, I am greatly indebted to Father Marc Foley, O.C.D., publisher at ICS Publications, for his support throughout the writing process. His positive response after reading each chapter provided the encouragement that kept me writing. Regarding the editing process, no words can express my appreciation for manuscript editor, Joanne Mosley, whose keen eye for detail, queries, and experience were invaluable. Thanks to her endless patience and her love for the Carmelite saints, what began as a purely professional relationship while working on this book, has evolved into a spiritual friendship that has been a gift, despite our being separated by the Atlantic Ocean.

To managing editor, Father Pier Giorgio Pacelli, O.C.D., who oversaw the project, ensuring that it was theologically sound, I am deeply grateful. Not unlike a piano tuner whose gentle touch perfects the tone and tenor that comes from a fine instrument, so his insight and expertise throughout the process have greatly enhanced this tribute to our Blessed Mother.

I am also edified and most appreciative of the work of artist, Bill Angresano for the sketch of Mary that appears in the front of the book. His ability to capture in art form the essence of this undertaking serves as a lovely complement to the prose and poetry of the Carmelite mystics. His enthusiastic participation in Carmel's tribute to Mary is also evident in his painting, *Our Lady on Mount Carmel*, which appears on the front cover of this book, and depicts Mary leading her sons and daughters in Carmel to the top of this mountain.

To the many friends who encouraged me along the way I am grateful, especially to Mike, my husband of more than fifty years and my companion in prayer. His continued support and encouragement were unwavering as they have been throughout our life together.

Writing this book has been more gift than effort, demonstrating the importance of teamwork. Each chapter was preceded by prayer, assuring me that this was Mary's project, not mine. As a mother and sister in faith, Mary has been and continues to be a source of inspiration and a true model for me, and it is a privilege to share my thoughts with a greater audience.

Abbreviations

St. John of the Cross

All quotations are taken from *The Collected Works of Saint John of the Cross*, trans. Kieran Kavanaugh, O.C.D., and Otilio Rodriguez, O.C.D. (Washington, D.C.: ICS Publications, 1991).

The abbreviations for John's works are as follows:

A	*The Ascent of Mount Carmel*
C	*The Spiritual Canticle*
LF	*The Living Flame of Love*
Lt	*Letters*
N	*The Dark Night*
P	*Poetry*
R	*Romances*
SLL	*The Sayings of Light and Love*

For *The Ascent of Mount Carmel* and *The Dark Night*, the first number refers to the book, the second to the chapter, the third to the paragraph. Thus, N 1.10.6 is a reference to book 1, chapter 10, paragraph 6 of *The Dark Night.* C 1.11 refers to chapter (stanza) 1, paragraph 11 of *The Spiritual Canticle.* C stanza 12, Redaction B refers to stanza 12 in John's second redaction of the poem "The Spiritual Canticle."

St. Teresa of Avila

All quotations are taken from *The Collected Works of St. Teresa of Avila*, 3 vols., trans. Kieran Kavanaugh, O.C.D., and Otilio

Rodriguez, O.C.D. (Washington, D.C.: ICS Publications, 1987, 1980 and 1985.

The abbreviations for St. Teresa's works are as follows:

F *The Foundations*
IC *The Interior Castle*
L *The Book of Her Life*
Ltr *Letters*
SS *Meditations on the Song of Songs*
ST *The Spiritual Testimonies*
W *The Way of Perfection*

For *The Life*, *The Way of Perfection*, and *The Foundations*, the first number refers to the chapter, the second number to the paragraph. Thus, L 3.5 refers to *The Book of Her Life*, chapter 3, paragraph 5. Regarding *The Interior Castle*, the first number refers to the dwelling place; the second number the chapter, the third number to the paragraph. Thus, IC 3.4.2 refers to the third dwelling place, chapter 4, paragraph 2. For *Letters,* Ltr is followed by the number of the letter and paragraph.

St. Thérèse of Lisieux

All quotations are taken from *Story of a Soul: The Autobiography of Saint Thérèse of Lisieux*, trans. John Clarke, O.C.D., 3rd edition (Washington, D.C.: ICS Publications, 1996).

The abbreviation for this work is as follows:

S *Story of a Soul*

Numbering refers to the page from this edition.

St. Elizabeth of the Trinity

All quotations of St. Elizabeth of the Trinity in *Heaven in Faith* are taken from *Complete Works of Elizabeth of the Trinity*, vol. 1, trans. Sister Aletheia Kane, O.C.D. (Washington, D.C.: ICS Publications, 1984), 94–120.

The abbreviation for this work is as follows:

HF *Heaven in Faith*

Numbering refers to the paragraph of this work.

Vatican Documents

CCC *Catechism of the Catholic Church* (Alexandria, Va.: Pauline Books & Media, 1994).

EG Pope Francis, *Evangelii Gaudium* (*On the Proclamation of the Gospel in Today's World*), November 24, 2013, *https://www.vatican.va/content/francesco/en/apost_exhortations/documents/papa-francesco_esortazione-ap_20131124_evangelii-gaudium.html*

GeE Pope Francis, *Gaudete et Exsultate* (*On the Call to Holiness in Today's World*), March 19, 2018, *https://www.vatican.va/content/francesco/en/apost_exhortations/documents/papa-francesco_esortazione-ap_20180319_gaudete-et-exsultate.html*

LG Vatican II, *Lumen Gentium* (*Dogmatic Constitution on the Church*) (November 21, 1964), *https://www.vatican.va/archive/hist_councils/ii_vatican_council/documents/vat-ii_const_19641121_lumen-gentium_en.html*

MC Pope Paul VI, *Marialis Cultus* (*For the Right Ordering and Development of Devotion to the Blessed Virgin Mary*), Apostolic Exhortation (February 2, 1974), *https://www.vatican.va/content/paul-vi/en/apost_exhortations/documents/hf_p-vi_exh_19740202_marialis-cultus.html*

MD Pope Pius XII, *Munificentissimus Deus*, Apostolic Constitution (November 1, 1950), *https://www.vatican.va/content/pius-xii/en/apost_constitutions/documents/hf_p-xii_apc_19501101_munificentissimus-deus.html*

NMI Pope John Paul II, *Novo Millennio Ineunte* (*At the Close of the Great Jubilee of the Year 2000*), January 6, 2001, *https://www.vatican.va/content/john-paul-ii/en/apost_letters/2001/documents/hf_jp-ii_apl_20010106_novo-millennio-ineunte.html/.*

OM Pope Leo XIII, *Octobri Mense* (*On the Rosary*), September 22, 1891, *https://www.vatican.va/content/leo-xiii/en/encyclicals/documents/hf_l-xiii_enc_22091891_octobri-mense.html*

RM Pope John Paul II, *Redemptoris Mater* (*On the Blessed Virgin Mary in the Life of the Pilgrim Church*), March 25, 1987, *https://www.vatican.va/content/john-paul-ii/en/encyclicals/documents/hf_jp-ii_enc_25031987_redemptoris-mater.html*

RVM Pope John Paul II, *Rosarium Virginis Mariae* (*On the Most Holy Rosary*), Apostolic Letter (October 16, 2002), *https://www.vatican.va/content/john-paul-ii/en/apost_letters/2002/documents/hf_jp-ii_apl_20021016_rosarium-virginis-mariae.html*

SD Pope John Paul II, *Salvifici Doloris* (*On the Christian Meaning of Human Suffering*), February 11, 1984, *https://www.vatican.va/content/john-paul-ii/en/apost_letters/1984/documents/hf_jp-ii_apl_11021984_salvifici-doloris.html*

Numbering refers to the paragraph number.

Scripture Quotations

Explanation of the Sketch of Mary

SO AS BETTER TO APPRECIATE the sketch of Mary by Bill Angresano, which appears opposite the title page, we might turn to St. John of the Cross for his description of the spiritual marriage as a transformation in God through love.[1] The saint explained that "in the union and transformation of love each gives possession of self to the other and each leaves and exchanges self for the other" (C 12.7). According to John, at this stage the soul "is like a sketch or the first draft of a drawing and calls out to the one who did this sketch to finish the painting and image" (C 12.1). Hence, the inked sketch of Mary in prayer, her eyes gazing upward, can be seen to represent the soul's transformation during its life on earth, which is but a sketch of the full image and an anticipation of the joy that awaits the soul in heaven. Faith is so enlightened at this point that, unable to know what else to do, the soul finds that her only recourse is to "turn to this very faith that contains and hides the image and the beauty of her Beloved and from which she also receives these sketches and tokens of love" (C 12.1), as this leads to the fullness of the soul's transformation in God.

As Queen of Apostles, Mary has a halo of twelve stars surrounding her head, signifying her ongoing mission to lead her children to God. With hands folded in prayer, the Flower of

1. For an explanation of "spiritual marriage" in relation to Mary, see the Glossary at the end of this book, beginning on p. 379.

Carmel stands in kinship with Elijah who stood in the presence of the living God (see 1 Kings 17:1). From her left wrist hangs the brown scapular—"for faith, as the theologians say, is an obscure habit" (C 12.2). It is like a crystal, about which John wrote:

> O spring like crystal!
> if only, on your silvered-over faces,
> you would suddenly form
> the eyes I have desired,
> which I bear sketched deep within my heart.
> (C stanza 12, Redaction B)

John is here describing faith as a crystal because it concerns Christ, the soul's Bridegroom, and because it is "pure in its truths, strong, clear, and cleansed of errors and natural forms" (C 12.3). The soul calls it a spring, because "from it the waters of all spiritual goods flow into the soul" (C 12.3).

Faith also engulfs the soul in living waters with *obscure* knowledge of God, which is why it has also been described as a veil. The crystal's "silvered-over faces" that John wrote about are the articles of faith and the substance of faith, which he compared to gold (see C 12.4). He writes, "In the next life, we shall see and enjoy openly this very substance that, clothed and covered with the silver of faith, we now believe" (C 12.4). So long as we are on this earth, faith is our guide on the path toward God, and Mary serves as the perfect example of how we might live out our faith within the context of our lives.

As Mary is our mother and sister in faith, her inclusivity toward the family of Carmel reflects the teaching of her son who declared, "Whoever does the will of my Father in heaven is my brother and sister and mother" (Mt 12:50). Through the gift of the brown scapular, Mary includes all who are "vowed to the service of Love . . . [and who] seek to experience love, to suffer love, and at last to be transformed in love."[2] For the brown scapular is a means of living "a life of allegiance to Jesus Christ," to borrow an important expression from the Carmelite *Rule*.[3]

From Mary's other wrist hangs the rosary, each bead an invitation to meditate on the sublime truths of the gospels, for the rosary is "a compendium of the Gospel that draws us into the Mystery of the Incarnation" (RVM 19).

As Mother of the Church, Mary stands atop the world, for even in heaven, her heart remains with her children on earth. An anchor, symbolizing the church, cradles the world much the way Mary cradled her infant son. Ever mindful of human frailty, her prayers of intercession are carried by angelic messengers who support and guard the church militant.

No longer bound by constraints of human mortality, our Mother pleads our cause. Her sole desire is for her children to discover that through the union of wills, they too will exclaim that "the eyes I have desired, which I bear sketched deep within my heart"[4] are but a foretaste of what is to come.

---

2. Paul-Marie of the Cross, O.C.D., *Carmelite Spirituality in the Teresian Tradition*, rev. ed., trans. Kathryn Sullivan, R.S.C.J. (Washington, D.C.: ICS Publications, 1997), 82.

3. *The Rule of Saint Albert*, para. 2 in *The Carmelite Rule*, Bruce Baker, O.Carm., and Gregory L. Klein, O.Carm., ed. (Totowa, N.J.: Catholic Book Publishing Company, 2000), 19.

4. C stanza 12, Redaction B.

Introduction

Writing a book about the Mother of God was not something I had planned to do. In fact, during much of my life, I hadn't been particularly devoted to Mary. I had wrongly assumed that, since she was free from original sin, it was easy for her to be perfect. When our children were teenagers and I read or listened to the gospel story about Mary and Joseph finding Jesus in the temple, I would recall the many nights that I spent looking at the clock, waiting and worrying because one of our kids was out past his or her curfew. How thrilled I would have been if they had come home to tell me they'd been in church praying and lost track of the time!

Although I admired the Holy Family, they seemed far too perfect to emulate. I couldn't see how they were relevant—that is, until a homily about Jesus remaining behind in the temple opened my eyes. The priest explained that the Holy Family was holy but not perfect. Like every family, they had plans and expectations that were not always communicated. The idea that Mary and Joseph were dealing with an adolescent, whose behavior unintentionally caused pain and anxiety, led me to reconsider my previous misconceptions.

After hearing a priest and a friend who is a theology professor share about the role that devotion to our Lady played in their lives, I began to wonder if I might be missing something. Not only was I intrigued, but I was also a bit envious of the confidence they placed in her. Since I knew they prayed the rosary every day, I decided to do the same to see if it made a difference. . . . And it did. That decision took place more than thirty years ago, and although I was motivated as much by curiosity as I was by devotion, it was the beginning of what has become a daily practice. It is but one example I have found of how Mary meets us where we are on the faith journey and then continues to surprise us. At the time I could not have known that some thirty years later I would feel impelled—for reasons I did not understand at the time—to pray all twenty decades of the rosary every day. Only in retrospect can I now say with a level of certainty that, through it all, I was being guided toward writing this book.

During those early days of praying the rosary, while meditating on the mysteries I began to understand that Mary was subject to the trials and tribulations that are part of human nature. Repeating the words of the Hail Mary slowly and intentionally, while reflecting on the life of Jesus through her eyes, was like opening the blinds on a sunny morning. Each phrase awakened me to Mary's singular role as mother, teacher, intercessor, and guide. The words "Hail Mary, full of grace, the Lord is with thee" revealed Mary's true identity in relation to God. She, who was full of grace, lovingly embraced the mission that God had chosen for her; and although she was free from sin, she was not free from suffering. As Mother of God, Mary was singularly favored, yet her life was anything but easy. The more I prayed and reflected on her role as wife, mother, and disciple, the more she became relevant in my own faith journey.

Reflecting on the mysteries of the rosary, I realized that no matter what our struggles, we can turn to our heavenly mother and she will understand. Mary knew how it feels to be the subject of gossip as an unwed mother in a small town, to give birth in a strange place away from family and friends, and to be a refugee in a foreign land. She knew the anguish of searching for a missing child, the loneliness of widowhood, and the struggles of being a single parent, only to watch her son leave the security of home and the family trade to embark on a path with no clear plan in sight. This gentlest of women knew the suffering endured by mothers who see their child misunderstood, threatened, arrested, and even executed as a common criminal. And finally, Mary knew how it feels to forgive and embrace, as mother, the very people who were responsible for her son's agony and death.

The more I ponder all that Mary endured during her life on earth, the more my devotion to this holy woman continues to grow. As the locus of God's activity through the mystery of the incarnation, Mary serves as the perfect model for all who wish to dwell in the house of the Lord. She, who is called "ark of the covenant" and "house of gold,"[1] was fashioned by the Father in God's own image and likeness. But unlike us, Mary wasn't broken by sin. We need redemption in order to be remolded toward a more perfect semblance of the image and likeness of God. However, she who was sinless was broken not to be refashioned, but to mirror through interior suffering her bruised and broken son who gave his life for the world. As Mother of God, Mary was privileged to participate in God's work of redemption. Through the incarnation, she brought Christ to the world, which makes her singularly qualified to be a perfect role model for all who seek to bring Christ to others by first deepening their own relationship with God. And yet many Christians, even Catholics, remain conflicted about Mary's role in the church. Some rely exclusively on recourse to Jesus and overlook Mary's role as mother and intercessor. They wonder why they should pray to Mary when they can speak directly to God, perhaps forgetting that she has been given to us to care for us as her children, who are members of her son's own Mystical Body. Others seemingly cling to Marian devotions with minimal biblical understanding of the magnitude of her role in salvation history and the

---

1. Two of the titles of Mary in the Litany of Loreto.

universal church. It was this realization, along with the wish to enter profoundly into Mary's interior life, so deeply rooted in her relationship with God, that led me to write this book.

The title, *Mary the Perfect Contemplative: Carmelite Insights on the Interior Life of Our Lady*, reflects the two strands that run through this book. The first represents Mary as she is portrayed in the gospels, a woman of faith living in the world within the context of her time. In her life on earth, Mary, who was the first disciple of Jesus, is a perfect role model, serving as an example of the Christian life. Her selfless love and perfect surrender to God were the embodiment of Christian faith, hope, and charity. As mother of the Son of God, Mary brought Christ to the world and wants nothing more than to bring the world to Christ. It is this latter desire that defines the second strand of this book, which presents Mary in light of the fullness of time as the embodiment of prayer, interiority, and contemplation—and ultimately of union with God.

As spouse of the Holy Spirit, living in union with the Holy Trinity, Mary was one with God and God was one with her; she exemplified what a life lived in union with God is like. Although she was singularly favored and free from original sin from the moment of her conception, Mary is not unapproachable. Rather, she invites us to draw near and learn what it means to be filled with the Holy Spirit, so that we too can mirror Christ's love and compassion in the world, bringing to fruition the Word of God that was planted in our soul at baptism. To be filled with the Holy Spirit is to be fully engaged in life as it contributes to building the kingdom of God on earth. Since no one exemplifies this more clearly than Mary, this book has evolved with a perspective of Mary on these three levels: it looks at Mary through *her human story* as it is recorded in the gospels; it examines *her interior life of union with God* in the context of family life; and it envisions *her conscious awareness of the unique mission that was entrusted to her*.

As we know from gospel accounts involving Mary, she was never a passive bystander with regard to the events of her life or those of her son. As spouse of the Holy Spirit, Mary was the epitome of fruitfulness throughout her life on earth. She gave birth to the infant Jesus; she was the vehicle that ushered in Jesus's public life when, at her request, he performed his first miracle; and she was present at the foot of the cross when the new Israel was born from the Israel of old. With the exception of the annunciation, whenever Mary is mentioned in Scripture, she is always in the company of others, illustrating for us the importance of social involvement and the communal dimension of a life lived in union with God. Mary was fully proactive, except when it came to receiving God's self-communication. Then she waited, trusting in God's initiative as she pondered in her heart what she did not understand, for nothing in her external life belied her interior disposition as handmaid of the Lord.

At the annunciation, God effected not only a marriage between humanity and divinity, but also a marriage between Mary's interior disposition and the external events of her life. Through her fiat, her oneness with God was consummated and she became the spouse of the Holy Spirit. Touched by mystery through the incarnation of the Son of God, this humble Virgin lived out her vocation as wife and mother within the context of what seemed to be a very ordinary life. Though her fiat changed forever the trajectory of the human race, only those to whom God revealed her high calling would know that she was the Mother of God. Mary was uniquely positioned for her role in salvation history. As daughter of the Father, mother of the Son of God, and spouse of the Holy Spirit, this thrice-favored bride of Love is the embodiment of infused participation in a trinitarian relationship.

Mary lived in the present with an eye to the future, in the light of eternity. Since only external events of Mary's life are recorded in Scripture, we cannot know with certainty the full extent of her conscious awareness of her future role. And yet, when we consider that Scripture is the living word of God, ongoing reflection and continued scholarship continue to deepen our awareness and appreciation of its many nuances.

Pope Benedict XVI noted that the evangelists were not speaking as private, self-contained subjects when they wrote the gospels, but from within a community, a living movement that was led by a power greater than itself. He explained that while reading the gospels within the context of the Hebrew Scriptures[2] and the audiences for which they were initially written is essential to understanding them, it doesn't necessarily foster a complete theological interpretation. He further explained: "It is necessary to keep in mind that any human utterance of a certain weight contains more than the author may have been immediately aware of at the time. When a word transcends the moment in which it is spoken, it carries within itself a 'deeper value.' This 'deeper value' pertains most of all to words that have matured in the course of faith-history. . . . The Scripture emerged from within the heart of a living subject—the pilgrim People of God—and lives within this same subject."[3]

In attributing to the people of God a deeper involvement in the creation of Scripture, Pope Benedict XVI acknowledged the ongoing presence of the Holy Spirit that continues to enlighten and guide the church. Since the church exists neither alone nor apart from God, theological understanding continues to emerge within the church even as it offers valuable insights for people of faith on a personal level. Therefore, it is important to engage

2. "Hebrew Scriptures" is used interchangeably with "the Old Testament" throughout this book.

3. Joseph Ratzinger/Pope Benedict XVI, *Jesus of Nazareth: From the Baptism in the Jordan to the Transfiguration*, trans. Adrian J. Walker (San Francisco: Ignatius Press, 2007), xix-xx.

both our head and our heart when we read and pray with Scripture, keeping in mind that the Holy Spirit engages the totality of our being, awakening the imagination even as it arouses within us a more empathic perspective.

As a mother, I find that engaging my heart while reading Scripture comes quite naturally. I recall rocking our children to sleep, their ear pressed to my heart as their breath seemed to become one with my own. When I imagine Mary holding the sleeping baby Jesus in her arms, I am mindful that when I read Scripture, I too am holding the Word of God on my lap or in my arms. I imagine how Mary looked upon Jesus, and then I try to let my eyes fall upon the words of Scripture with the same love and attention. Then I find I can easily spend an hour or more with one scene, sometimes with one word or sentence, as I simply listen to the breath of the Holy Spirit become one with my own. This is when *lectio divina*, listening to God's word, is at its finest. That's not to say that every time I read Scripture, I am aware of the breath of God in my soul, but it's a starting place that invites me to treasure the time I spend with God, even when I may be feeling tired, distracted, or preoccupied.

In trying to intuit Mary's awareness of her mission as the mother of the Son of God, the church has a treasure trove of enlightened authors on whom it can draw. One of them is St. John of the Cross, who offers insight into what this bride of the Holy Spirit may have perceived about her role among future generations. In the final paragraph of *The Spiritual Canticle*, John writes, "The bride [Mary] sets all this perfection and preparedness before her Beloved, the Son of God, with the desire that he transfer her from the spiritual marriage, to which he desired to bring her in this Church Militant, to the glorious marriage of the Triumphant" (C 40.7). From this, dare we conclude that St. John of the Cross saw in Mary's fiat an intuited anticipation of the birth of the church militant and the church triumphant that would be established through her son, the Bridegroom of the church? These and other questions and insights merit prayerful reflection and consideration and will be addressed throughout this book.

For anyone wishing to create a portrait of Mary, the first source is Sacred Scripture, primarily the gospels. Like an artist who, before applying paint to a canvas, begins by carefully considering the person to be represented, so the Holy Spirit inspired the evangelists to write their gospels, which form the realism of Mary's portrait. God could have revealed in the gospels all there is to know about his mother, thereby completing his portrait for us, but that has never been God's way. Throughout the Scriptures, God's word and works are shrouded in mystery, because in the absence of answers, people continue searching, collectively and as individuals. Just as the Holy Spirit continues to enlighten and guide the church's understanding of Scripture through the people of God, both through prayerful enlightenment and rigorous scholarship, so other works have emerged throughout the ages, along with new insights applied to ancient sources—all of this adding color and detail to the original "sketch" in the gospels and allowing the "painting" to emerge. And yet, as much as the creators of these sources—theologians, saints, and ordinary, holy men and women—have enhanced Mary's portrait over the centuries, the masterpiece remains unfinished. God has given us, his people, what we need to know in order to continue the ongoing discovery of Mary's hidden beauty within the gospels. And the Holy Spirit continues to guide our understanding of Mary, particularly regarding her role in the universal church.

Mary the Perfect Contemplative is an endeavor to enter into this sacred area and to contribute, in its own way, to the ever-developing portrait of Mary. This book takes as its starting point the accounts of Mary in the gospels, which are then enriched by relevant passages from the Hebrew Scriptures, early Christian texts, and church teachings, along with the insights of saints, scholars, and holy writers. In keeping with the deepening understanding of Mary's role as Mother of the Church and Queen of Heaven, which has evolved over time within the church, her portrait, as presented in this book, also draws on recent dogmas as well as many of the titles that have been attributed to Mary and prayers that have been written to honor her. Creating this portrait has been a graced opportunity to engage with the gospels and all these sources that provide subtle touches of color in various shades and hues, each enhancing the evolving portrait of Mary that is rendered ever more beautiful with the passing of time.

Among these radiant touches, few have graced God's masterpiece more dramatically than the dogma of Mary's immaculate conception. Although it was not declared a doctrine of faith until 1854, as early as the thirteenth century, Franciscan theologian Blessed John Duns Scotus argued, "Mary most holy is a daughter of Adam like all mankind, yet she did not contract original sin. . . . It is, in fact, a more perfect redemption than liberative redemption, because it is more perfect to preserve a person from a fall than to lift him up after falling. It is a more excellent benefit to preserve someone from evil, rather than permit him to sin and need to be freed from it."[4] To this passage we could add that Mary's holiness needs to be seen not just as the absence of sin but, in its more positive expression, as the continuous flow of divine life within the depths of her soul.

Just as a painting is affected by sunlight as its rays fall across a great work of art, so the writings of many mystics, most notably Sts. Teresa of Avila and John of the Cross, enlighten our understanding of the interior life of Mary. For this reason, they are frequently drawn on in this book. The works of these Carmelite Doctors of the Church are invaluable guides that help

4. Fr. Stefano M. Manelli, F.I., *Blessed John Duns Scotus: Marian Doctor* (New Bedford, Mass.: Academy of the Immaculate, 2011), 87.

us navigate the mystical waters of contemplation and union with God, which Mary exemplifies. John and Teresa also convey the importance of living mostly by faith, especially when God appears to be absent or when his plans are veiled to the eyes of even the holiest people such as Mary.[5] Through their writings, both Teresa and John explain the stages of deepening prayer, providing insight into the more profound stages of union such as "spiritual betrothal" and the "spiritual marriage,"[6] which would have been part of Mary's experience as spouse of the Holy Spirit and mother of the Son of God. Thus, their works are an incomparable source when it comes to understanding, if only in part, Mary's spiritual psyche, as it were.

In addition to the teachings of these great mystical writers, insights have also been gleaned from spiritual writers of more recent times, as well as from saints and other holy men and women whose lives were lived in union with God. Their contemplative experience, like soft light falling upon a canvas, offers a glimpse into the interior life of Mary, which we may not otherwise notice or understand. Only then are final touches added by incorporating secondary sources, those writers and scholars who have placed their lives at the service of the word of God. In all, these many-faceted layers are the valuable raw material that combine to

---

5. Lest anyone mistakenly assume that the writings of sixteenth-century mystics are too far removed from ordinary life, one Carmelite writer has this to say: "Carmelite psychology was always realistic. Under the reformer's [Teresa's] influence, it became more so. In fact, her prudence and supernatural wisdom made her require that contemplative life—and mystical experience when this is added—be made more and more dependent on [Christian doctrine], the sacraments, obedience to the church and to superiors, the practice of virtues, fidelity to the Rule. Only in this way can sentimentalism, illuminism, and quietism in any form whatsoever be avoided." Paul-Marie of the Cross, O.C.D., *Carmelite Spirituality in the Teresian Tradition*, 38.

6. See the Glossary, beginning on p. 379, for a presentation of these and other spiritual terms used in the book and how they relate to Mary.

bring Mary to life and to remind us that one can always penetrate ever more deeply into the mystery of the Mother of God.

As with any portrait, especially one with a subject as lovely and holy as the Mother of God, *Mary the Perfect Contemplative* is the fruit of a prayerful reading of Scripture and Marian sources. This book falls into two parts. Part I, which includes chapters 1 to 9, is entitled "Daughter of Zion: A Scriptural Portrait of Mary" and follows Mary through the relevant passages of the Bible. It covers the main episodes of Mary's life, often juxtaposed with spiritual themes in the writings of Teresa, John of the Cross, and Thérèse of Lisieux.

Chapter 1 introduces Mary's role within the plan of salvation and centers on the annunciation as it looks at the preparation for the coming of the Messiah.

Chapter 2 reflects on Mary's stay with Elizabeth and Zechariah as the three of them, together with the infant in Mary's womb and the unborn John the Baptist in Elizabeth's, form the first Christian community. It also reflects on the deep faith and compassion of St. Joseph, the man God had chosen to be Mary's husband and guardian of the Child Jesus.

Chapters 3 to 5 cover the infancy narratives as described in the Gospel of Luke and Gospel of Matthew, with a focus on the humility and hospitality of Mary and how she reflects those same virtues that are inherent in God. It also reflects on how the journey of the magi and their being welcomed by Mary relates to our own personal faith journey and the role Mary plays in it.

Chapter 6 and 7 are concerned with two aspects of the ministry of Jesus in which Mary is involved: the wedding feast at Cana, in which the intervention of Mary leads to Jesus being revealed as Bridegroom; and the episode that involves Jesus redefining his family to include all who follow him and keep his word as his brothers, sisters, and mother, which sheds light on Mary as the perfect disciple of her son.

Chapter 8 is a portrayal of Jesus's passion and his death and of Mary alongside him on Calvary as she experienced her own interior suffering and death, during which she became our mother when Jesus bequeathed her to us from the cross.

Chapter 9 focuses on the events following the resurrection, where we see Mary supporting the apostles in prayer as they await the coming of the Holy Spirit, during which we see her in her role as Mother of the Church.

Part II of the book, which includes chapters 10 to 17, is entitled "Blessed Virgin Mary: Mother, Model, and Intercessor." With an emphasis, once more, on both Scripture and spiritual writings, this section covers aspects of Marian prayer and devotion to Mary.

Chapter 10 presents Mary as the road to Jesus.

Chapter 11 focuses on the rosary, the Marian prayer par excellence: its historical development, its role in the life of the church, and a prayer formula that Mary has repeatedly asked the faithful to pray.

Chapter 12 examines the role of mystery in the life of the church and how Mary exemplifies one who approaches mystery not as a problem to be solved but as a reality into which we are all invited to enter.

Chapters 13 to 16 explore the depth of meaning within the four sets of mysteries of the rosary while offering thoughts for meditation on these scenes from the lives of Jesus and Mary.

Chapter 17 provides a history of the brown scapular of Our Lady of Mount Carmel and its meaning and place in the Catholic Church and in popular devotion as a tangible sign of belonging to Mary.

An Epilogue, concluding the chapters, offers a tribute to Mary and her role not only as mother of Jesus but as mother of people of every race, color, and creed. Each individual chapter concludes with a Marian prayer, as a way to maintain a prayerful ambiance for readers throughout.

Following the Epilogue are two Appendixes. The first contains questions that can be used for personal reflection or for discussion in a group setting. The second provides passages that could be used as a source for *lectio divina.* They are arranged in pairs, with one passage from Scripture on Mary and the other from Carmelite writings on prayer and contemplation, to help readers gain deeper insight as to how each enriches the other. As Christians seek to deepen their relationship with God, there are no better guides than Mary, Mother of the Church, and her Carmelite sons and daughters to lead the way for all who hope to scale the heights of divine intimacy through prayer.

Other sections include a Glossary of spiritual terms that have been used throughout the book, as they relate to Mary; a Bibliography of works on Mary; and, as we have seen, an Explanation of the Sketch of Mary that Bill Angresano drew, which appears—symbolically and aptly—in the opening pages: a sketch waiting to be filled in with the spiritual layers that make up this literary portrait and with the colors that comprise the same artist's painting on the cover of this book.

Mary, who is called ark of the covenant, carried the infant God in her womb for nine months, held him in her arms, and enthroned him in her heart. As our spiritual mother, Mary not only carries us in her heart but also bequeaths this privileged role to us, too, so that the Word of God planted within us might be carried to the world in which we live. Just as many parents discover, almost unconsciously, that their approach to parenting frequently models that of their own parents, so the more we learn about our dear mother, the more she can serve as model and guide as we strive to emulate her and journey ever more deeply into the heart of God.

PART I

DAUGHTER OF ZION: A SCRIPTURAL PORTRAIT OF MARY

Nazareth:

Preparing the Way for Christ's Coming

LONG BEFORE THE ANNUNCIATION, words like *covenant*, *daughter*, and nuptial language such as *beloved*, *bride*, and *bridegroom* permeated the Hebrew Scriptures.[1] From the moment of creation and every step along the way, before the Son of God became incarnate of a woman, God's loving presence was evident. The God of Israel was neither distant nor uninvolved, for no sooner had Adam and Eve sinned than God promised to send a redeemer. Seeing in them his own image, Love's only recourse was to save his children from the death they had brought upon themselves. Responding with mercy and compassion—though not without justice—God instructed and guided the chosen people. Such a response has inspired some to refer to Scripture as "God's love letter" to his people.[2] Both the Old and the New Testaments provide a continuous narrative of

---

1. Nuptial language, such as *spiritual betrothal*, *spiritual marriage*, and *bride* are some of the terms used by Carmelite writers, especially St. John of the Cross, in their teachings on the spiritual journey and union with God. For an explanation of these and other spiritual terms used in this book, and how they relate to Mary, see the Glossary, beginning on p. 379.

2. This term was first used by the late Rev. Billy Graham and since then has become almost part of the American Christian lexicon.

the God who broke into human history, initially through the law, prophets, patriarchs, and kings—and finally through Mary.

The spotless Virgin is God's epiphany to the world. As a living proclamation of God's faithfulness to a sinful race, Mary represents divinity's original plan, for she alone is God's masterpiece, unmarred by the stain of sin. Shining forth in the world, Mary is the ideal image of what God intended for every person before the fall. Ever respectful of the gift of free will, God interacts with his people in a way that is characterized by divine initiative and human response, divine giving and human receiving. Although Mary was in the mind of God before the foundation of the world, the history of the Israelite nation is a lesson in the importance of preparation. Only when conditions for the coming of the promised Messiah were in place did God effect his plan.

The divine timeline is not like ours. As a metaphysical reality, God's perfect timing is measured neither in months nor in years, but as opportune occasions for us to grow in faith so that like the psalmist we, too, can exclaim, "I trust in you, O Lord; / I say, 'You are my God.' / My times are in your hand" (Ps 31:14–15a). God sees deeply into the soul of each person and event, has knowledge of all our needs, and provides a remedy when they reach him. As John of the Cross explains: "Not all the affections and desires reach him, but only those that go out through true love" (C 2.2). As our love deepens, our faith and trust in God increase, quickening our prayer with an urgency that reaches the heart of God.

The Israelites had been enslaved in Egypt for four hundred years before God intervened through Moses. But when the affections, desires, and true love of the spotless Virgin, whom God had fashioned as the new Eve, could be contained no longer, her soul was ready to cry out, in union with the will of God, "The time is fulfilled" (Mk 1:15). And so began the marriage between heaven and earth as foretold: "Faithfulness will spring up from the ground, / and righteousness will look down from the sky" (Ps 85:11). The act of the incarnation reflects the deepest yearning of Mary, and the humility and poverty of God. And so it is that when contemplatives embark upon the purgative path—"purging" their attraction to sin and pursuing a life of virtue—they look to Mary as the perfect model of surrender.

Understandably, the journey toward union with God is long and arduous, but with Mary as mother, teacher, and intercessor, we take heart, knowing that her story is our story, her journey our journey. Beginning with the Father in the Garden of Eden, the story of our salvation reached its climax through the dying and rising of the Son and its new birth in the church through the power of the Holy Spirit. The timeline, neither linear nor static, invites us to proclaim with confidence that Christ has come, Christ is with us, and Christ will come again.

MARY, THE NEW EVE AND MODEL OF OBEDIENCE

Mary's unique relationship with God and humankind has given her a special place in salvation history, a role validated by several church fathers and esteemed throughout the church, not least by Carmelites. As early as the second century, church fathers contrasted Mary's annunciation with Eve's encounter with the serpent. Following the fall of Adam and Eve, God hinted at the role of Mary when responding to the serpent with the words:

> I will put enmity between you and the woman,
> and between your offspring and hers;
> he will strike your head,
> and you will strike his heel. (Gen 3:15)

Expanding on this text in his dialogue with Trypho, Justin Martyr explained:

> He is born of the Virgin, in order that the disobedience caused by the serpent might be destroyed in the same manner in which it had originated. For Eve, an undefiled virgin, conceived the word of the serpent, and brought forth disobedience and death. But the Virgin Mary, filled with faith and joy, when the angel Gabriel announced to her the good tidings that the Spirit of the Lord would come upon her, and the power of the Highest would overshadow her, and therefore the Holy One born of her would be the Son of God, answered: "Be it done unto me according to Thy word." And, indeed, she gave birth to Him.[3]

Who could doubt the importance of obedience, since it was through Mary's fiat that Christ became the new Adam and Mary became the new Eve? The full weight of such profound mysteries can be appreciated only when contemplative hearts understand and embrace humble obedience to the Word of God as a life imperative. Teresa considered unconditional obedience a prerequisite for all who seek union with God. In counseling her nuns, she wrote: "I say that I don't know why a nun under obedience by vow is in the monastery, if she doesn't make every effort to practice this obedience with greater perfection. At least I can assure her that as long as she fails in obedience, she will never attain to being a contemplative. . . . Even though a person may not have this obligation of the vow, if he decides or aims after contemplation, it is necessary for him in order to proceed correctly to give up his will" (W 18.8). Under the patronage of Mary, Teresa's insistence on obedience as essential for the nuns of her reform is a direct descendant, as it were, of Mary's fiat—a sure disposition that brings us closer to God.

---

3. Justin Martyr, "Dialogue with Trypho" in *Saint Justin Martyr*, trans. Thomas B. Falls, vol. 6 of *The Fathers of the Church* (Washington, D.C.: CUA Press, 1948), 304–5.

Justin noted that when the angel announced the Good News to Mary, she received "faith and joy." As the first person to receive the Good News and believe, Mary ushered in the dawning of a new day. Upon receiving the Word of God in her womb, she was filled with the joy of salvation, a living example of the joy Jesus brings. It is the same joy Jesus was referring to when he prayed to his Father, "Now I am coming to you, and I speak these things in the world so that they may have my joy made complete in themselves" (Jn 17:13). Regarding this joy, St. Teresa wrote, "The soul as well, I think, can say these words [Ph 1:21] now because this state [of more perfect union with Christ] is the place where the little butterfly we mentioned dies, and with the greatest joy because its life is now in Christ" (IC 7.2.5). The transformation of the butterfly, for Teresa, represents the transformation from death through sin to new life centered in Christ. Mary was perfectly centered in Christ, and as spouse of the Holy Spirit, Mary's mission was her joy, and her joy was complete. She held nothing back, teaching by example that the more complete our surrender to God, the greater our joy. Therefore, it is only fitting that Mary is called "Cause of Our Joy," for as she opened her soul to God, our salvation was brought forth through her.[4]

In his apostolic exhortation *Evangelii Gaudium* (The Joy of the Gospel), Pope Francis explains that all who receive the Gospel share in this joy and that no one exemplifies this joy more perfectly than the woman who bore God in her womb. Invoking Mary as "Mother of the living Gospel, wellspring of happiness,"

---

4. The title "Cause of Our Joy" is associated with the Litany of Loreto, which has been prayed in the sanctuary of Loreto (Italy) since at least 1531 and was officially approved in 1587 by Pope Sixtus V. Its origin is believed to be a medieval rhymed litany influenced by Eastern Marian devotion, in particular by the famous *Hymnos Akathistos*; see *https://udayton.edu/imri/mary/l/litany-of-loreto-in-context.php*.

who brought the Word of God to the world, the Holy Father described her as "brimming over with joy" as she "sang of the great things" God had done for her (EG 288). Mary's rejoicing (see Lk 1:47) is a reminder that Jesus is the greatest source of our joy.

Words have power, but no word can compare with the Word made flesh. Only the Word of God can move beyond the superficial sentries of the senses and the mind, kiss the soul, and fill hearts with unspeakable joy. Breathing spirit and life into a broken world, the Word of God enlightens minds while entering the portals of the soul, heals wounds, and binds up the broken places of our lives. This blessed union remains ever ancient yet ever new, because "in the beginning was the Word, and the Word was with God, and the Word was God" (Jn 1:1). If the words of mere mortals have the power to heal, lift spirits, and make us feel loved, how much more powerful is the Word that enlightens, heals, and transforms souls. Guigo II, a twelfth-century Carthusian credited with first describing the four-step practice of *lectio divina*, wrote, "Seek in reading and you will find in meditation; knock in prayer and it will be opened to you in contemplation."[5] Inevitably, what we are seeking is Jesus, revealed in his word of Scripture.

In the parable of the seed, which appears in all three Synoptic Gospels (see Mt 13:1–23, Mk 4:1–20, and Lk 8:1–15), Jesus compared the word of God to seeds sown in human hearts. Some fall on the path, others on rocky soil, and still others sprout only to be strangled by thorns. Only seed that falls on fertile soil survives and bears fruit. St. Thérèse was fond of imagining her soul as a garden and herself a tiny flower. But rather than allow the harsh conditions to choke the word of God, she

5. Guigo II, *Scala Paradisi*, ch. 2, in *Patrologia Latina*, 40, 988; also quoted in John of the Cross, SLL 158.

embraced every slight and humiliation as a way to grow in virtue to give glory to God (see S 206). Similarly, St. Teresa of Jesus described the soul as a garden that requires water, noting that the gardener "will rejoice and be consoled and consider it the greatest favor to be able to work in the garden of so great an Emperor" (L 11.10). When we reflect on the incarnation of the Word of God in Mary against the backdrop of the parable of the seed, this mystery becomes personal. Through the sacrament of baptism, the Word of God is planted in the soul: a tiny seed that, when nurtured and cared for, eventually bears fruit. We are the gardeners who, like our first mother, Eve—and our new mother, Mary—and like Teresa and Thérèse, have a choice, though it may not always be easy. For as St. John Paul II writes in his encyclical on Mary, "This is the beginning of the Gospel, the joyful Good News. However, it is not difficult to see in that beginning a particular heaviness of heart, linked with a sort of 'night of faith'—to use the words of St. John of the Cross—a kind of 'veil' through which one has to draw near to the Invisible One and to live in intimacy with the mystery. And this is the way that Mary, for many years, lived in intimacy with the mystery of her Son, and went forward in her 'pilgrimage of faith'" (RM 17).

As we can see, not even Mary—so united with her son on this earth—was spared the unknowing that a pilgrimage of faith demands. As St. John of the Cross suggests, the darker the night, the closer one comes to God himself. During this pilgrimage of faith, it is imperative to trust that God supplies what is needed for seeds to bear fruit and that as a person's life in God deepens, so does the soul's joy. This does not negate the presence of suffering, because joy does not depend on external circumstance but is an inner disposition of serenity that is the fruit of the presence of God.

While the miracle of the incarnation is celebrated by the church throughout the liturgical year, at no time does it seem as paradoxical as during the season of Advent, when we are directed to prepare for the coming of God who is already with us. However, for contemplatives, the reality is more mystery than paradox, perceived as an invitation to behold the secret of Christ's veiled presence, even as we await his coming. All who long to see the face of God can take comfort in the words of the prophet Balaam who proclaimed what contemplative hearts behold:

> The oracle of one who hears the words of God,
> and knows the knowledge of the Most High,
> who sees the vision of the Almighty,
> who falls down, but with his eyes uncovered:
> I see him, but not now;
> I behold him, but not near—
> a star shall come out of Jacob. (Num 24:16–17)

The words of Balaam ring as true today as when they were spoken. The God of Abraham, Isaac, and Jacob came as the Father's self-revelation in the person of the incarnate Word. With longing, we behold the Messiah from afar through eyes veiled and unseeing, until our hearts infused with love discover that love creates an ever-increasing sight. As the veil progressively disappears, the soul is alerted to the presence of God within. It is a passing phenomenon while the soul undergoes a metamorphosis, until all that remains is a cloud of unknowing in the mist of uncertainty. With our minds obscured and senses confounded, we seek role models within the communion of saints, where none shines as brightly as the woman who is aware that, like the moon that reflects the light of the sun into our night sky, the only light she has to give is the light that is reflected by her from her son. Perhaps overwhelmed by the light of Christ and mindful of their sins, seekers turn to Mary, their mother, who echoes the greeting she heard from Gabriel, "Do not be afraid" (Lk 1:30), as she lovingly bids us draw near. Then, directing our attention to the Word of God, she guides her children by word and example.

THE ANNUNCIATION

Chronologically, according to Luke, Gabriel's visit to Zechariah occurred before the angel's visit to Mary. However, since the annunciation to Mary is pivotal to our understanding of the role of Mary as Mother of God and our mother, Luke's account of the annunciation is a good place to begin:

> In the sixth month the angel Gabriel was sent by God to a town in Galilee called Nazareth, to a virgin engaged to a man whose name was Joseph, of the house of David. The virgin's name was Mary. And he came to her and said, "Greetings, favored one! The Lord is with you." But she was much perplexed by his words and pondered what sort of greeting this might be. The angel said to her, "Do not be afraid, Mary, for you have found favor with God. And now, you will conceive in your womb and bear a son, and you will name him Jesus. He will be great, and will be called the Son of the Most High, and the Lord God will give to him the throne of his ancestor David. He will reign over the house of Jacob forever, and of his kingdom there will be no end." (Lk 1:26–33)

Luke sets the stage with a narrative that situates the timing of Gabriel's visit to Mary within the context of Elizabeth's pregnancy. He names the place and identifies Mary as a virgin who is betrothed to Joseph of the lineage of King David, thereby establishing a link to the Old Testament. Like that of all women in Jewish culture of her time and place, Mary's lineage was considered unimportant; but for Jewish Christians, connecting Joseph's ancestral roots to the royal lineage of King David—from whom the Messiah was expected—was essential. Yet even more important than Joseph's lineage was Mary's virginity, which had been foretold: "The Lord himself will give you a sign. Look, the young woman is with child and shall bear a son, and shall name him Immanuel" (Isa 7:14). This prophecy evokes for us other examples of exceptional announcements of births in the Hebrew Scriptures.

God's intervention in Mary's pregnancy links it to the pregnancies of Sarah who gave birth to Isaac, Hannah who gave birth to Samuel, and Elizabeth who was pregnant with John the Baptist. Yet, even more notable than the similarities are the striking differences. The other three women were thought to be sterile and conceived a child only after God intervened. In each case the conceptions were accomplished through human sexual relations. Not so with Mary, whose virginity sets her apart from other childless women in Scripture. Furthermore, the pregnancies of the other three women were an answer to prayer, whereas for Mary it was an unexpected occurrence. Similarly, anyone who travels the path of prayer understands that God is a God of surprises and reveals himself in unexpected ways, often when least anticipated. While we can prepare ourselves for the gift of infused prayer, we are not the cause of it. Therefore, when God grants such favors, we are to receive them joyfully and to respond like Mary with grateful and heartfelt thanksgiving.

As both Matthew and Luke point out, Mary became pregnant when she was betrothed to Joseph before they were living together. Scripture tells us nothing about Mary prior to the angel's visit. But the non-canonical *Protoevangelium of James*, a second-century text, claims that Mary was taken to the temple in Jerusalem by her parents, Anna and Joachim, at the age of three and consecrated to the Lord as a holy virgin. This ancient work also posits that she remained at the temple until she was twelve.[6] Much of this legend, which is regarded as pious devotion, has never received official recognition by the church. However, the feast of the Presentation of Mary in the Temple has been celebrated in the East since the sixth century and was added to the church calendar in the West in the fifteenth century. Theologically, the consecration of Mary offering herself to God as a holy virgin at a young age fits well with the doctrine of the immaculate conception, which proclaims that Mary had been chosen by God, a most-pure vessel through whom the Son of God would enter the world.

At any rate, the teaching of the Catholic Church is clear that Mary was a virgin before the birth of Jesus and remained a virgin throughout her life (see CCC 496–507). Her virginity was fundamental to her being chosen to be the Mother of God and is clearly implied by Matthew's gospel: "Now the birth of Jesus the Messiah took place in this way. When his mother Mary had been engaged to Joseph, but before they lived together, she was found to be with child from the Holy Spirit" (Mt 1:18). This provides much that is enriching for our spiritual life.

According to the thirteenth/fourteenth-century Dominican theologian and mystic Meister Eckhart, Mary's virginity has a deeper meaning for contemplatives. He posited that the word "'virgin' designates a human being who is devoid of all foreign images and so it was necessary that Jesus was received in the womb of a virgin."[7] Not only was Mary's womb physically empty, but her virginal emptiness was a spiritual reality. Just as her womb was an empty vessel that God filled, so her heart and

---

6. Cf. *Protoevangelium of James*, 7–8, *https://www.newadvent.org/fathers/0847.htm.*

7. Reiner Schürmann, ed. and trans., *Wandering Joy: Meister Eckhart's Mystical Philosophy* (Great Barrington, Mass.: Lindisfarne Books, 2001), 9.

mind were empty of all that was not of God, making Mary a perfect model for contemplatives.[8]

Not all are called to biological motherhood or to a life of celibacy, but all are called to empty their hearts so that they may be filled with God. As Mother of the Incarnate Word, Mary's every impulse was directed toward God. In anticipation of her role as mother of Jesus, Mary was betrothed to God before she was betrothed to Joseph; her whole being was turned toward God, desiring to do his will and receptive to his action. She waited on God.

This is in keeping with what Carmelites have always taught regarding prayer. Like the prophet Elijah, Carmelites strive to wait on the Lord who is revealed in the gentlest of breezes. Aware of their own impotence regarding infused prayer, those who travel the path of interior prayer prepare themselves to receive what only God can give. In humble anticipation, contemplatives await the kiss of the Bridegroom, echoing the words of the Song of Songs: "Let him kiss me with the kisses of his mouth!" (Song 1:2). In her *Meditations on the Song of Songs*, St. Teresa counseled her nuns about "the kisses of his mouth," explaining: "You must keep in mind one point: the Lord has heard your petition that He kiss you with the kisses of His mouth. For if you know through the effects of His having done so, there is no reason to delay in anything; but forget yourself so as to please this most sweet Bridegroom. . . . O Lord of heaven and earth, how is it possible that even while in this mortal life one can enjoy You with so special a friendship that the Holy Spirit says this so clearly" (SS 3.2, 14).

Despite Teresa's certitude about her experience of the fruits of the Bridegroom's kisses, she struggled when trying to explain

8. "The reception of Jesus by a virgin can be compared to that of an image by the intellect. If the intellect is to receive the image, it is necessary that it be empty." Schürmann, *Wandering Joy*, 11.

this great mystery from a theological perspective. Fortunately, the writing of St. Bernard of Clairvaux, a thirteenth-century Cistercian monk who wrote more than eighty sermons on the Song of Songs, offers the following insight:

> The mouth that kisses signifies the Word who assumes human nature; the nature assumed receives the kiss; the kiss however, that takes its being both from the giver and the receiver, is a person that is formed by both, none other than "the one mediator between God and mankind, himself a man, Christ Jesus" [1 Tim 2:5]. It is for this reason that none of the saints dared say: "let him kiss me with his mouth," but rather, "with the kiss of his mouth." . . . Normally the touch of lip on lip is the sign of the loving embrace of hearts, but this conjoining of natures brings together the human and divine, shows God reconciling "to himself all things, whether on earth or in heaven" [Col 1:20].[9]

Given Mary's privileged place in her relationship with the triune God, the "mouth that kisses" signifies the Word and credits the Holy Spirit as the origin of the kiss, thereby establishing Mary's unique identity as spouse of the Holy Spirit. In the Song of Songs, the bride declares, "I am a rose of Sharon, / a lily of the valleys" (Song 2:1). To which the bridegroom responds, "As a lily among brambles, / so is my love among maidens" (Song 2:2). The dialogue that continues is a mutual expression of love in full bloom, and Mary is the perfect example of a love consummated through the spiritual marriage. This most precious "flower of Carmel" was raised by God above every other human being, and Carmelites are privileged to refer to her not only as mother but as sister in faith.

---

9. Bernard of Clairvaux, "Sermon 2" in *Song of Songs I*, vol. 2 of *The Works of Bernard of Clairvaux*, trans. Kilian Walsh, O.C.S.O. (Collegeville, Minn.: Liturgical Press, 2008), 10.

Mary's entire being was open to be filled by God, an interior disposition that is particularly meaningful for contemplatives. Given the Carmelite approach toward self-emptying through detachment from worldly concerns, Mary's waiting on the Lord is a perfect example of this spiritual imperative. John of the Cross counseled those who are striving toward union with God through prayer to set aside all that stands in the way of a deepening relationship with God, be it on a sensory or a spiritual level. In a letter to the Carmelite nuns at Beas, the Mystical Doctor wrote, "One must open toward heaven the mouth of desire empty of all other fullness, that thus it may not be reduced or restricted by some mouthful of another pleasure, but truly empty and open toward him who says: '*Open your mouth wide and I will fill it*'" (Lt 7; cf. Ps 81:10). In this way, Mary's dispositions at the annunciation are the perfect response to God in both life and prayer.

HIGHLY FAVORED DAUGHTER

In Luke's gospel, Mary is greeted by her cousin Elizabeth as "blessed . . . among women" (Lk 1:42) and, in one translation, by the angel Gabriel as "highly favored daughter" (Lk 1:28, NAB). The *New American Bible's* use of the translation *daughter*[10] conveys the sense that Mary was free from original sin, since it implies that Mary was already part of the intimate family of God. In the Hebrew Scriptures, *daughter* often refers to Zion and to Jerusalem, the city that housed the ark of the covenant. In addressing Mary as favored daughter, the greeting anticipates her becoming the Ark of the New Covenant.

10. The Greek word, κεχαριτωμένη (kecharitomene), conveys something that no single English word can convey. The selection of "daughter" by the translators of the *New American Bible* communicates the feminine aspect of the word and finds a traditional analog in the Old Testament prophets.

Therefore, it is fitting that the vessel chosen to house the Son of God was also an archetype of the sacramental life of the church, through which Christians encounter Christ and become, through baptism, part of the intimate family of God. The prophet Zephaniah's oracle on the reproach and promise for Jerusalem could easily be applied to Mary as Ark of the New Covenant:

> Sing aloud, O daughter Zion;
>   shout, O Israel!
> Rejoice and exult with all your heart,
>   O daughter Jerusalem!
> The LORD has taken away the judgments against you,
>   he has turned away your enemies.
> The king of Israel, the LORD, is in your midst;
>   you shall fear disaster no more.
> On that day it shall be said to Jerusalem:
> Do not fear, O Zion;
>   do not let your hands grow weak. (Zeph 3:14–16)

Mary is thus a sign and a song that sings of the presence of God both among us and within each of us.

In addressing Mary as highly favored and blessed among women, the angel and Elizabeth signaled that redemption was near. Yet who could have imagined that God's indictment of the serpent—"I will put enmity between you and the woman, / and between your offspring and hers" (Gen 3:15a)—would be accomplished through this young Jewish woman? No one could have known, least of all Mary, which explains why, upon hearing the angel's greeting, Mary was deeply troubled (see Lk 1:29). She didn't understand what the words meant, causing the angel to respond, "Do not be afraid, Mary" (Lk 1:30).

In Hebrew literature, the presence of an angel signifies the sacredness of an event, so it is not surprising that Mary's first response was fear. On a human level, this is a natural reaction. Writing about supernatural experiences, Rudolf Otto, an influential thinker about religion in the first half of the twentieth century, referred to fear in the presence of the holy as "*mysterium tremendum et fascinans.*" In his book *The Idea of the Holy*, Otto explained that the initial reaction to what he termed a "numinous experience" is silence, followed by terror in the presence of an overwhelming power. Finally, he explained that there is a sense of *fascination with what is perceived as being both merciful and gracious.*[11]

St. Teresa of Jesus could certainly have related to Otto's description. In her autobiography she wrote extensively about her reaction to visions and locutions. The dual presence of fear and fascination led her to seek counsel from spiritual directors, several of whom were uninformed and served as poor spiritual guides. However, according to the saint, supernatural experiences are also accompanied by a level of certainty that remains even after the experience has passed. When Teresa was wrongly told that it was the devil, not God, who was the cause of her experiences, she was greatly distressed. Years later, it led her to caution her nuns about the directors from whom they sought counsel, even as she reassured them that God can and does favor souls with supernatural phenomena.

Given Mary's age and the magnitude of the grace that was bestowed upon her, she was understandably troubled by the angel's greeting. After reassuring her that she had found favor with God: "The angel said to her, 'Do not be afraid, Mary, for

---

11. Rudolf Otto, *The Idea of the Holy*, trans. John W. Harvey (London: Oxford University Press, 1923); see especially his Chapter IV, "Mysterium Tremendum." (This work first appeared in German in 1917.)

you have found favor with God. And now, you will conceive in your womb and bear a son, and you will name him Jesus. He will be great, and will be called the Son of the Most High, and the Lord God will give to him the throne of his ancestor David. He will reign over the house of Jacob forever, and of his kingdom there will be no end.' Mary said to the angel, 'How can this be, since I am a virgin?'" (Lk 1:30–34).

Unlike Zechariah, who asked for proof, since both he and his wife were advanced in age, Mary accepted on faith what the angel told her and simply inquired how this would happen. Her question tells us two important things about Mary. First, her faith in God was unwavering; and second, her decision was an informed decision. We do Mary a great disservice when we think that she was led by blind obedience, for there would be no merit in that. One of the gifts of the Holy Spirit is knowledge, which also involves human participation. Since grace operates within the human process through our response to God's initiative, we have a responsibility to be informed when faced with decisions. Mary's question was thoughtful, reflective of an inquiring mind, not a doubting one. In response, the angel answered her question, proclaiming, "The Holy Spirit will come upon you, and the power of the Most High will overshadow you; therefore the child to be born will be holy; he will be called Son of God" (Lk 1:35).

Just as important as the explanation regarding how the incarnation of the Son of God would take place is the mystery revealed at the heart of the angel's response. In bearing witness to the presence and involvement of the Trinity, he shows us that the act that would change the world and transform humanity's relationship with God forever confirms the oneness of will that defines the relationship within the triune God. The only thing needed to set this wondrous miracle in motion was the consent from the woman God had chosen. "Then Mary said, 'Here am

I, the servant of the Lord; let it be with me according to your word.' Then the angel departed from her" (Lk 1:38).

With Mary's fiat, the state of her soul went from betrothal to God to espousal with God. The moment the Word entered her womb through the power of the Holy Spirit, her relationship with the triune God was consummated. God was made incarnate in her womb, dwelling in her both physically and spiritually, and Mary's new identity was born. She became the Mother of God; she was indeed "full of grace," as the angel proclaimed. To be full of grace is to know the depths of God's love from within the deepest center of the soul, a state represented by a trinitarian communication, which Teresa explains:

> In the seventh dwelling place, the union comes about in a different way: our good God now desires to remove the scales from the soul's eyes and let it see and understand, although in a strange way, something of the favor He grants it. When the soul is brought into that dwelling place, the Most Blessed Trinity, all three Persons, through an intellectual vision, is revealed to it through a certain representation of the truth. First there comes an enkindling in the spirit in the manner of a cloud of magnificent splendor; and these Persons are distinct, and through an admirable knowledge the soul understands as a most profound truth that all three Persons are one substance and one power and one knowledge and one God alone. . . . Here all three Persons communicate themselves to it, speak to it, and explain those words of the Lord in the Gospel: that He and the Father and the Holy Spirit will come to dwell with the soul that loves Him and keeps his commandments. (IC 7.1.6)

We can never know if Mary experienced the presence of the Trinity in exactly this way, but perhaps the annunciation would have made her conscious of the action of the three divine Persons relating to her personally.

Adding further insight, John of the Cross describes the union of love in *The Spiritual Canticle*:

> When there is union of love the image of the Beloved is so sketched in the will, and drawn so intimately and vividly, that it is true to say that the Beloved lives in the lover and the lover in the Beloved. Love produces such likeness in this transformation of lovers that one can say each is the other and both are one. The reason is that in the union and transformation of love, each gives possession of self to the other and each leaves and exchanges self for the other. Thus each lives in the other and is the other, and both are one in the transformation of love. (C 12.7)

In this light, Mary's surrender to God led to a tremendous receptivity for God to live in her and for her to live in God.

What St. Paul said of himself can be said of Mary just as truly: "It is no longer I who live, but it is Christ who lives in me. And the life I now live in the flesh I live by faith in the Son of God, who loved me and gave himself for me" (Gal 2:20). In the case of the Blessed Virgin, from the moment Mary gave her consent, Christ was physically present in her. This is not to minimize her being continually transformed interiorly throughout her life. Some might wonder whether Mary could have been brought to the state of spiritual marriage from the moment of her conception, since she was free from sin. It doesn't seem likely, since the highest state of union involves an act of the will that is freely made. Mary, as the only sinless human being, was not in need of purification, but a certain level of emotional and spiritual maturity was needed. It was true for Jesus, since Scripture tells us, "Jesus increased in wisdom and in years, and in divine and human favor" (Lk 2:52). The same would hold true for Mary.

As knowledge of God and knowledge of herself developed, Mary was continually being formed in the ways of God for the role she would play in salvation history. Prior to her fiat, she was lawfully betrothed to Joseph and spiritually betrothed to God. Spiritual betrothal and spiritual marriage are distinct realities, yet the closeness between them is significant. Teresa addressed this when she explained that the door between the sixth and seventh dwelling places remains open. She divided them while writing about these dwelling places because, as she noted, "there are things in the last [dwelling place] that are not revealed to those who have not yet reached it" (IC 6.4.4). The pinnacle of union requires a human willingness to die to self; and Mary, like every human being, had to learn what it meant to live for God before she was ready to die for God. When she was ready, and according to God's plan, she gave her consent and remained ever faithful to the will of God.

SELF-KNOWLEDGE AND HUMILITY

Mary's response to the angel personifies the virtue of humility, which goes hand in hand with knowledge of God and knowledge of self. Early spiritual masters such as St. Benedict and St. Bernard of Clairvaux identified humility as the first rung on the ladder of the spiritual life. This is not to infer that humility comes easily, but that it is essential to developing a relationship with God. In counseling her nuns, Teresa stressed the importance of humility more often than any other virtue, pointing to Mary as the perfect model. In *The Way of Perfection*, she said: "Let us, my daughters, imitate in some way the great humility of the Blessed Virgin, whose habit we wear . . . However much it seems to us that we humble ourselves, we fall short of being the daughters of such a mother and the brides of such a Spouse" (W 13.3). What Teresa is saying so rightly is that if we are to be truly humble, we can take for ourselves no greater model than Mary in the gospels.

True humility cannot exist in the absence of knowledge of God or knowledge of self, since both incline the soul to see itself in relation to God. St. Teresa wrote, "In my opinion we shall never completely know ourselves if we don't strive to know God" (IC 1.2.9). The more perfect the union of self-knowledge and knowledge of God becomes, the more the virtue of humility is present. Recall St. Teresa's insistence that self-knowledge was essential during the beginning stages of the spiritual life, which she addresses in relation to the second dwelling places: "Let [the soul] walk through these dwelling places which are above, down below and to the sides, since God has given it such great dignity. Don't force it to stay a long time in one room alone. Oh, but if it is the room of self-knowledge! How necessary this room is—see that you understand me. . . . Here it will discover its lowliness better than by thinking of itself" (IC 1.2.8).

This discovery comes from knowing the truth about oneself in three significant areas.

First, the human person is utterly nothing without God. Second, persons are inclined toward sin because of original sin. And third, despite our nothingness and our sinful nature, God loves us unconditionally. Humility born of self-knowledge is neither self-exalting nor self-deprecating. Rather, the soul sees herself as she is in relation to God. We see this in Mary when she responded to the angel by first identifying herself accordingly as "servant of the Lord." Mary's entire being was centered in God. She saw herself only as she existed in and for God, in whom she had found her identity. This resulted in her responding, "Let it be with me according to your word" (Lk 1:38). Mary surrendered her will to God completely, allowing God to do with her whatever God willed, thus charting a path for contemplatives. As we journey through the deepening stages of prayer, we discover our truest identity as a beloved daughter or son of God and as spouse of Jesus. The degree with which we allow our true identity to guide us parallels our ability to bear fruit, since nothing empowers us more than knowing that we are loved by God who enables us to do all things through him and in him.

THE ROLE OF GRACE

Given the wondrous things that God brought about in Mary, we may wonder how one who was so perfectly without sin can be a model for ordinary people. But Mary is more than a role model. She is our mother and intercessor who prays for us before the throne of God. We honor Mary because she was singularly chosen for a mission for which God had ordained and prepared her. Like us, she was free to follow the will of God or cling to her own will. The same holds true for every person. Adam and Eve were also born without original sin, but they chose to follow their own will over the will of God. To imagine that Mary was not tempted is to place her above her son. Jesus was tempted in the desert and endured the physical and emotional discomfort and challenges that are part of being human. Throughout his life he remained steadfast in doing the Father's will, and Mary did the same. Mary was a human being. She endured the joys, sorrows and challenges that are part of everyday life, just as we all do. In writing about sanctity and grace, Father Gabriel of St. Mary Magdalen, O.C.D., sheds light on the call to holiness, noting that we are all called to be saints: "This does not mean, however, that we are all called to the same degree and kind of sanctity. Beside those we call the 'great saints,' those who had a special mission to accomplish and therefore received singular gifts of nature and grace, there have been the humble and hidden saints, who were sanctified in obscurity and silence. Sanctity does not consist in the greatness of the works accomplished or of the gifts received, but in the degree of sanctifying grace and charity to which the soul has attained by faithful correspondence with God's invitation."[12]

Following the example of Mary, we travel the path to Christian maturity by faithfully seeking to know, love, and serve God. We seek his will as it appears within the context of our life and pray for the wisdom and strength to respond to God's grace. Luke ends the account of the annunciation with the words, "Then the angel departed from her" (Lk 1:38). Guided only by the flame that burned within her heart, Mary's mission was just beginning.

In many ways, so is our own mission just beginning. Every day is a new opportunity to grow more deeply in love with God. We never know where life will take us or what will be asked of us, but with Mary as model and guide, we take comfort in knowing that she can lead us ever deeper into the heart of God. Mary, called "Theotokos," is God-bearer, whom we could also call God-sharer, for her first impulse was to share the gift of Jesus that she had received. Continually other-centered, Mary was first centered in God and then directed toward her neighbor. Her life was an ongoing testimony to the two greatest commandments: "You shall love the Lord your God with all your heart, and with all your soul, and with all your mind" and "You shall love your neighbor as yourself" (Mt 22:37, 39). With Mary as guide and intercessor, we can all find in her the way to perfection and union with God.

---

12. Father Gabriel of St. Mary Magdalen, O.C.D., *Divine Intimacy: Meditations on the Interior Life for Every Day of the Liturgical Year*, trans. the Discalced Carmelite Nuns of Boston (London: Baronius Press, 2008), 9.

INVITATION TO PRAYER

As we continue our faith journey, let us turn to Mary and pray the words that are rich in mystery, more precious than gold, and belong to her alone. As a tribute to the Mother of God, these words, which are sweeter than honey, have been prayed and sung in every language and in every land. So let us lift our hearts as we join the chorus of voices throughout the world and pray:

HAIL MARY, FULL OF GRACE, THE LORD IS WITH YOU.
BLESSED ARE YOU AMONG WOMEN AND BLESSED IS THE FRUIT
OF YOUR WOMB, JESUS. HOLY MARY, MOTHER OF GOD,
PRAY FOR US SINNERS NOW AND AT THE HOUR
OF OUR DEATH. AMEN.

2

A Town of Judah:

Crossing a Threshold

In those days Mary set out and went with haste to a Judean town in the hill country, where she entered the house of Zechariah and greeted Elizabeth. When Elizabeth heard Mary's greeting, the child leaped in her womb. And Elizabeth was filled with the Holy Spirit and exclaimed with a loud cry, "Blessed are you among women, and blessed is the fruit of your womb. And why has this happened to me, that the mother of my Lord comes to me? For as soon as I heard the sound of your greeting, the child in my womb leaped for joy." And blessed is she who believed that there would be a fulfillment of what was spoken to her by the Lord."
(Lk 1:39–45)

How much time elapsed between Gabriel's departure and Mary's visit to Elizabeth is unknown, but Luke tells us that Mary proceeded in haste. Her response to the angel's message about Elizabeth's pregnancy triggered an action that was executed quickly and without hesitation, offering a perfect example of Teresa's description of persons in the seventh dwelling places: "This is the reason for prayer, my daughters, the purpose of this spiritual marriage, the birth always of good works, good works" (IC 7.4.6). Teresa explains that during the spiritual marriage, all three Persons communicate themselves to the soul and that, in some inexplicable way, the soul perceives this divine companionship within its deepest center, even when it is occupied with work: "You may think that as a result, the soul will be outside itself and so absorbed that it will be unable to be occupied with anything else. On the contrary, the soul is much more occupied than before with everything pertaining to the service of God; and once its duties are over, it remains with that enjoyable company" (IC 7.1.8). Mary's perpetual disposition of action flowing from contemplation exemplifies this perfectly, as her every thought, word, and action was directed toward God and in service to God.

In *The Interior Castle,* Teresa ends with the seventh dwelling places, but to view them as a goal that has been reached falls short of its meaning. The spiritual marriage is a new beginning. Just as the love between a husband and wife who are committed to each other deepens through the years, so those who have been brought to the spiritual marriage continually deepen their knowledge and love for God. Mary's life is a living portrait of a life lived in communion with God. In *The Living Flame of Love,* John of the Cross explains how this knowledge leads to a growing awakening within these souls: "And here lies the remarkable delight of this awakening: The soul knows creatures through God and not God through creatures. This amounts to knowing the effects through their cause and not the cause through its effects. The latter is knowledge a posteriori [equivalent to knowing the back of God, rather than his face] and the former is essential knowledge" (LF 4.5). This goes to the heart of the matter: that knowledge of God needs to be experiential knowledge—and from this, all else follows and we keep the right perspective on all of creation.

Mary's union with God allowed her to know the will of God immediately; and for Mary, to know God's will was to do God's will. As she was the perfect contemplative, Mary's actions were not her actions, but God acting through her. All her actions flowed from and were an expression of her knowledge of God, and they were the result of her spousal union. Her obedience and charity were one with God, which makes Mary the embodiment of perfect discipleship. There was no need for Gabriel to direct Mary to help Elizabeth because, through her union with God, Mary was perfectly attuned to and obedient to the will of God. As Scripture reminds us: "So we have known and believe the love that God has for us. God is love, and those who abide in love abide in God, and God abides in them" (1 Jn 4:16). The mere mention of the elderly woman's pregnancy was enough to alert Mary to Elizabeth's need, causing Mary to rush to the aid of her kinswoman. John of the Cross explains how the inflamed soul is united with the Flame of Love, which is the Holy Spirit (cf. LF 1.3): "Thus in this state the soul cannot make acts because the Holy Spirit makes them all and moves it toward them. As a result all the acts of love are divine, since both the movement to these acts and their execution stem from God. . . . since it raises them up to the activity of God in God" (LF 1.4). John may well have been thinking here of Mary, of whom he wrote that she was always moved by the Holy Spirit (see A 3.2.10).

Like all mystics, Mary didn't dwell on a mountaintop. When the Holy Spirit came upon her and the incarnate Word entered her womb, her experience of God created a sense of urgency, causing her to go "with haste" (Lk 1:39). The word *haste*, though small, has huge implications for anyone seeking God. From a Carmelite perspective, Mary proceeding in haste reflects the urgency that, according to John of the Cross, impels the soul forward. "I will not gather flowers, nor fear wild beasts; / I will go beyond strong men and frontiers" (C 3.8). John's poetry describes a soul totally inflamed with love of God, so that it is neither delayed by worldly distractions nor detained by the devil's attempts to lure the soul from God. Mary reflects John's words that "the soul that truly loves God is not slothful" (C 3.1). With eyes fixed on God alone, Mary's immediacy offers a clear message for those who fall prey to the distractions of worldly pleasures, who are enamored of spiritual consolations, or who allow doubts and uncertainty to delay their willingness to take up the cross. Nothing could deter Mary in serving God, for as Teresa wrote concerning such souls, "It has strong confidence that since God has granted this favor He will not allow it to lose the favor" (IC 7.1.8). This applies perfectly to Mary's courage.

Although Luke makes no reference to whether Mary traveled alone or was in the company of others, traveling in a land that was occupied by Rome was dangerous. Yet just as Mary had not allowed concern about her honor deter her from uttering her fiat and accepting pregnancy outside marriage, so she did not allow temporal risks or difficulties deter her from hurrying to assist Elizabeth. Her response to the news of Elizabeth's pregnancy exemplifies Teresa's words, "O my sisters! How forgetful this soul, in which the Lord dwells in so particular a way, should be of its own rest, how little it should care for its honor and how far it should be from wanting esteem. . . . It should think little about itself" (IC 7.4.6). Such is the demeanor of one whose soul is transformed in God. According to John, "In this transformation the eye of the soul's feeling is so illumined and agreeable to God that we can say God's light and that of the soul are one. The natural light of the soul is united with the supernatural light of God so that only the supernatural light is shining; just as the light God created was united to the light of the sun and now only the sun shines even though the other light is not lacking" (LF 3.71).

Such was the interior light that surely shone in Mary as she hurried to the aid of Elizabeth. Just as Elijah's zeal for the Lord flowed from his contemplative spirit, so the light within Mary was made manifest by the urgency of her apostolic zeal which flowed from her communion with God. She was, and remains, the model of the apostolic charism of Carmelite spirituality.

So powerful was the presence of God in Mary that Luke tells us that the moment Elizabeth heard Mary's greeting, the baby in her womb leapt with joy. Reminiscent of David dancing before the Lord when the ark of the covenant was returned to Jerusalem (see 2 Sam 6:5, 14), the infant John leapt at the arrival of Mary, the Ark of the New Covenant. "When Elizabeth heard Mary's greeting, the child leaped in her womb. And Elizabeth was filled with the Holy Spirit and exclaimed with a loud cry, 'Blessed are you among women, and blessed is the fruit of your womb. And why has this happened to me, that the mother of my Lord comes to me?'" (Lk 1:41–43). The theological implications of Elizabeth's greeting are as illuminating as they are edifying. Having pondered the miracles surrounding her own pregnancy, Elizabeth was infused with supernatural insight, so that when the infant in her womb leaped, she immediately recognized Mary as the mother of the Lord. Like Elijah who recognized God in the gentlest of breezes, Elizabeth knew that she stood in the presence of the living God, for to know Jesus is to know God. Housed within the body of this gentle virgin was the fulfillment of the long-awaited promise.

Inspired by Mary's privileged relationship with God, we must not lose sight of her humanity. Mary was divinely favored, but she was not divine. She was subject to the same emotions that are part of human nature, which may give rise to questions that merit reflection. As she hurried to visit Elizabeth, we might wonder whether she was tempted to question if the appearance of Gabriel was just a dream? Whether it was factually possible that the inconceivable God had been conceived within her womb, or whether she had been deceived. If such questions entered Mary's mind, they neither delayed nor deterred her from her mission. The faith of this highly favored daughter didn't require reassurances or proof for her to continue the journey. Transformed in love, Mary was "inclined in God toward God" (LF 3.77). Her feelings would have been what John describes as hidden caverns deep within the soul: "having become enkindled lamps within the splendors of the divine lamps, they render the Beloved the same light and heat they receive" (LF 3.77).

Unlike Teresa, who was comforted when knowledgeable men reassured her that her visions were from God, Mary did not seek such reassurances. Yet, we know that at Elizabeth's proclamation, Mary was filled with joy. As Mary was the recipient of supernatural knowledge both through the angel's message and from deep within, her joy was complete, inspiring her song of praise:

> My soul magnifies the Lord,
>   and my spirit rejoices in God my Savior,
> for he has looked with favor on the lowliness of his servant.
>   Surely, from now on all generations will call me blessed;
> for the Mighty One has done great things for me,
>   and holy is his name.
> His mercy is for those who fear him
>   from generation to generation.
> He has shown strength with his arm;
>   he has scattered the proud in the thoughts of their hearts.
> He has brought down the powerful from their thrones,
>   and lifted up the lowly;
> he has filled the hungry with good things,
>   and sent the rich away empty.
> He has helped his servant Israel,
>   in remembrance of his mercy,

according to the promise he made to our ancestors,
to Abraham and to his descendants forever.
(Lk 1:46–55)

Inspired by the Holy Spirit, Mary's song of praise and gratitude offers an example of perfect humility as she attributes to God all that is being accomplished through her.

As she was always led by the Holy Spirit, Mary's first impulse in response to Elizabeth's praise was directed toward God, for God is always the first objective of a soul who abides in him through the union of wills. The Book of Psalms, the Song of Songs, and various prayers and hymns in the Hebrew Scriptures testify to the promptings of the Holy Spirit, resulting in the composition of those hymns, prayers, and poetic verses that have set hearts aflame throughout the ages. Similarly, the poetry of Sts. Teresa, John of the Cross, Thérèse, and others are examples of divine outpourings. While Teresa's poetry is not as well known as the poetry of John of the Cross, she considered it a supernatural favor from God, which she described in her autobiography: "What is the soul like when it is in this state! It would want to be all tongues so as to praise the Lord. . . . I know a person who though not a poet suddenly composed some deeply-felt verses well expressing her pain. They were not composed by the use of her intellect; rather, in order that she enjoy the glory so delightful a distress gave to her" (L 16.4).

In his introduction to Teresa's Poetry, Kieran Kavanaugh, O.C.D., writes, "Teresa was not interested in writing poems for their own sake; she wrote them as a release for the mystical fire she could no longer contain in her heart."[1] Similarly, Mary's *Magnificat* was an outpouring of ecstatic joy, an

1. Kieran Kavanaugh, O.C.D., "Poetry – Introduction," in *The Collected Works of St. Teresa of Avila*, vol. 3, trans. Kieran Kavanaugh, O.C.D., and Otilio Rodriguez, O.C.D. (Washington, D.C.: ICS Publications, 1985), 371.

outward manifestation of interior joy and supernatural wisdom. Recognizing that she had been singularly favored, not because of anything she had done, but because of what God had done through her, Mary immediately attributed her joy to God, whom she called Savior. She understood that as the mother of the Messiah, her identity would be forever linked with salvation history. Yet, despite this great blessing, there was no hint of pride in her proclamation. Immediately, she turned her attention to the mercy of God, adding: "His mercy is for those who fear him" (Lk 1:50).

In keeping with the biblical prophets, Mary reminds us how different are God's ways from our ways. Declaring that God, with the might of his arm, demonstrates a preference for the poor, confuses the proud, and deposes the mighty, Mary rejoices because God lifts up the lowly, fills the hungry with good things, and sends the rich away empty. Ever mindful of God's mercy, Mary declares God true to his word, her pregnancy being proof that God has upheld his servant Israel and fulfilled the promises made to Abraham and to his descendants.

Bearing the Good News physically and verbally, Mary, in her visit to Elizabeth, serves as a prototype for the church. In his apostolic exhortation on the proclamation of the Gospel, Pope Francis writes: "The Church which 'goes forth' is a community of missionary disciples who take the first step, who are involved and supportive, who bear fruit and rejoice. An evangelizing community knows that the Lord has taken the initiative; he has first loved us (Jn 4:19), and therefore we can move forward, boldly take the initiative, [and] go out to others" (EG 24).

In going forth to visit her cousin, Mary didn't simply repeat the Good News she heard from Gabriel; she interpreted it. As we read in *The Living Flame of Love*: "Corresponding to the exquisite quality with which the intellect receives divine Wisdom, being made one with God's intellect is the quality with which the soul gives this wisdom, for it cannot give it save according to the mode in which it was given" (LF 3.78). Evangelization requires someone to receive and share the Good News, which makes Mary the perfect model of apostolic zeal because she shared the Good News she had received. Thus, it could be said that Mary was the first evangelist. Through Mary, Elizabeth and Zechariah were able to receive the Good News and appreciate the fullness of the events that were taking place within their midst.

At the same time, Mary's interpretation of the fullness of God's presence established a precedent that all who receive the Good News are to share it, a practice that has been inherent in Carmelite spirituality from its beginning: "Conscious of their own imperfection, the hermits of Mount Carmel remained long in solitude. But because they desired to be in some way useful to their neighbor, and lest on this point they incur inner guilt, at times, yet very rarely, they left their hermitage. And as it was with the scythe of contemplation that they harvested in the desert so now in preaching they will scatter the grain on the threshing floor and with open hands they will sow the seed."[2] This beautiful image invites us to ponder the many ways in which charitable actions like those of Mary and the early Carmelite hermits can be likened to hands that sow seeds of the Good News.

In crossing the threshold to enter the home of Zechariah, Mary served as a bridge between the old and the new covenant, and between the old and the new priesthood that would be established through her son. The meeting between Mary and Elizabeth was the personification of divine goodness, their exchange an echo of the psalmist's prophecy:

---

2. Nicholas of Narbonne, *The Flaming Arrow*, Vineyard Series 2, trans. Michael Edwards (Durham, England: Teresian Press, 1985), in Paul-Marie of the Cross, *Carmelite Spirituality in the Teresian Tradition*, 22.

> Steadfast love and faithfulness will meet;
> righteousness and peace will kiss each other.
> Faithfulness will spring up from the ground,
> and righteousness will look down from the sky.
> (Ps 85:10–11)

Remaining faithful to the old, they rejoiced over what was new, knowing: "At an acceptable time I have listened to you, / and on a day of salvation I have helped you" (2 Cor 6:2). This glimpse into the transition between the old and the new covenants reminds us that Jesus did not come to destroy the old law but to build on it (see Mt 5:17).

THE FIRST CHRISTIAN COMMUNITY

During the three months when Mary remained in the home of Elizabeth and Zechariah, their dwelling place was transformed into a birthing center for human and divine activity, their home an adoration chapel that housed the first tabernacle on earth. Jesus was physically present in Mary, though veiled from human eyes, not unlike his presence in tabernacles throughout the world, where he is seen only through the eyes of faith. Hidden from the rest of the world, Mary, Elizabeth, and Zechariah were the first Christian community: "For where two or three are gathered in my name, I am there among them" (Mt 18:20). With Jesus in their midst, Mary, Elizabeth, and Zechariah formed the nucleus of what would become the church, a reality that can be appreciated only in retrospect.

As the sacred mysteries unfolded in their midst, a sense of awe and wonder surely dominated the conversation between Mary and Elizabeth, while Zechariah, a privileged bystander unable to speak, reflected on all that was happening. "Awakened from the sleep of natural vision to supernatural vision"

(LF 4.6), he was transformed from doubter to believer. Not only were these saintly people witnessing supernatural events that would change the world, but they were also participants in the divine activity as it was taking place. Centuries later, we understand that such divine awakenings are not limited to biblical characters but are available to all to whom God grants infused knowledge. As John of the Cross writes: "Yet God always acts in this way—as the soul is able to see—moving, governing, bestowing being, power, graces, and gifts on all creatures, bearing them all in himself by his power, presence, and substance. And the soul sees what God is in himself and what he is in his creatures in only one view, just as one who in opening the door of a palace beholds in one act the eminence of the person who dwells inside together with what that sovereign is doing" (LF 4.7).

To experience God's activity in the manner described here, we need to wait on God in prayer. Like Zechariah, we must persevere in silence, with an open heart, since it is always God who decides to whom and when to grant such favors.

While remaining with Elizabeth, Mary most likely performed household chores that Elizabeth, advanced in age and in the final months of her pregnancy, would have found difficult. Being young, healthy, and filled with joy at the child growing within, Mary would have carried out ordinary tasks of daily life with little effort and an extraordinary amount of love. Mindful of the child within, she could easily do whatever was needed, since far from impeding a woman's physical capabilities, pregnancy can energize her. Spiritual writer Caryll Houselander offers food for thought about pregnancy: "When a woman is carrying a child, she develops a certain instinct of self-defense. It is not selfishness; it is not egoism. It is an absorption into the life within, a folding of self like a little tent around the child's frailty, a God-like instinct to cherish and some day to bring forth the life. A closing upon it like the petals of a flower, closing upon the dew that shines in its heart."[3]

Houselander's words are a beautiful tribute to Carmel's precious flower as she imagines what Mary experienced deep within, knowing that the Son of God was housed within her womb. Continuing with the same theme, Houselander muses that Mary went about her work with intentions more exalted than those of ordinary people. She contrasts Mary's intentions with the intentions of those who, while scrubbing the floor for a tired friend, dressing a wound for a patient in a hospital, or setting the table with a feeling of self-congratulation, might think that such activities are making them more perfect, more unselfish, or more kind. Houselander notes that this would not have been Mary's disposition because, as handmaid of the Lord, Mary regarded herself as serving Christ and understood that by serving Elizabeth, she was bringing Christ into the world.[4]

John of the Cross warned against the danger of practicing works of mercy that unwittingly led to "vanity, pride, vainglory, and presumption" (A 3.28.2). Unlike Mary, who walked securely in humility and joy, we are prone to esteem the work of our hands, thereby tainting the good we do. Not so with Mary, who was free from the ravages of pride. This humble servant of God was literally one with the humility of God as she carried Jesus in her womb. "He could go nowhere but where she chose to take Him; He could not speak; her breathing was His breath; His heartbeat in the beating of her heart."[5] Her every thought, word, and action were rooted in the presence of God who was present in her body and in her soul.

---

3. Caryll Houselander, *The Reed of God* (Notre Dame, Ind.: Ave Maria Press, 2006), 58.

4. See Houselander, *The Reed of God*, 59.

5. Houselander, *The Reed of God*, 59.

Only Mary has enjoyed, or will ever enjoy, the unique privilege of carrying and giving birth to the infant God. Yet John of the Cross assures us that souls transformed in love experience similar awakenings, often extremely subtle, which God communicates in secret to the soul. In his poem "The Living Flame of Love," John writes:

> How gently and lovingly
> you awake in my heart,
> where in secret you dwell alone;
> and in your sweet breathing,
> filled with good and glory,
> how tenderly you swell my heart with love. (LF stanza 4)

John explains that the substance of the soul experiences "the voice of a multitude of excellences, of thousands of virtues in God, infinite in number." And he continues: "The soul is established in them, terribly and solidly set in array in them like an army, and made gentle and charming with all the gentleness and charm of creatures" (LF 4.10). His choice of words suggests that the humble Carmelite friar had the image of the Blessed Virgin Mary in mind when he penned those lines, for they offer a perfect description of this fair lady.

TRUSTING IN GOD

To complete the biblical portrait of Mary during her pregnancy, we turn to the Gospel of Matthew, which begins with the genealogy of Joseph. Since Jesus is both Son of God and Son of Man, Matthew addressed the significance of Joseph as guardian and foster father of Jesus in the beginning of the text, immediately after the genealogy:

> Now the birth of Jesus the Messiah took place in this way. When his mother Mary had been engaged to Joseph, but before they lived together, she was found to be with child from the Holy Spirit. Her husband Joseph, being a righteous man and unwilling to expose her to public disgrace, planned to dismiss her quietly. But just when he had resolved to do this, an angel of the Lord appeared to him in a dream and said, "Joseph, son of David, do not be afraid to take Mary as your wife, for the child conceived in her is from the Holy Spirit. She will bear a son, and you are to name him Jesus, for he will save his people from their sins." All this took place to fulfill what had been spoken by the Lord through the prophet:
>
> > "Look, the virgin shall conceive and bear a son,
> > and they shall name him Emmanuel,"
>
> which means, "God is with us." When Joseph awoke from sleep, he did as the angel of the Lord commanded him; he took her as his wife, but had no marital relations with her until she had borne a son; and he named him Jesus. (Mt 1:18–25)

This passage from Matthew's gospel informs us that Joseph was an upright man, that Mary was pregnant, and that Joseph was not the biological father. The compassion of Joseph, unwilling to cause his wife public shame, is recognized by Matthew, though nothing is said about Mary's character. Only Luke records what took place in Mary's life prior to Joseph's dream. However, when read side by side, the two gospels complete a portrait of Mary's holiness that is rooted in her privileged relationship with God. From Matthew we learn that Mary made no effort to defend her virginity, despite the cloud of suspicion that surrounded her pregnancy. St. Teresa saw Mary's silence as a sign of perfect humility, a virtue that she said goes hand in hand with charity and love and serves as the ground for all other virtues. Teresa repeatedly instructed her nuns in the importance of the virtue of humility, even when one's good name is at stake. "Indeed, it calls for great humility to be silent at seeing oneself condemned without fault. . . . The truly humble person must in fact desire to be held in little esteem, persecuted and condemned without fault even in serious matters. If she is to imitate the Lord, in what better way can she do so?" (W 15.1–2). To remain silent when unjustly accused, especially if this puts us at risk, also requires a serene heart that flows from complete trust in God, which was surely true of Mary.

The silence of this daughter of Zion exemplifies humble restraint, regardless of the cost of discipleship. In surrendering her will to the will of God, she was infused with loving knowledge, which John of the Cross explains is experienced through suffering that is followed by the delight of love. Elucidating how this loving knowledge is communicated, John of the Cross writes, "If as I say—and it is true—this loving knowledge is received passively in the soul according to the supernatural mode of God, and not according to the natural mode of the soul; individuals, if they want to receive it, should be very annihilated in their natural operations, unhampered, idle, quiet, peaceful and serene, according to the mode of God" (LF 3.34). He further explains, "God infuses this love in the will when it is empty and detached from other particular earthly or heavenly pleasures and affections" (LF 3.51). And he cautions readers: "If individuals should, then, desire to act on their own through an attitude different from the passive loving attention . . . , they would utterly hinder the goods God communicates supernaturally to them in the loving knowledge" (LF 3.34). For to receive this knowledge, it is vital to remain still, under the action of God, so as not to disturb it in any way.

Although John is writing about prayer, Mary's silence exemplifies perfect consistency regarding the interior disposition and external demeanor of persons in the spiritual marriage. Her spirit of detachment was continuous as she waited on the Lord's initiative for her every movement. According to St. Thomas Aquinas, virtue is not a habit but an act, and every act follows a choice.[6] Mary, who saw herself as handmaid of the Lord, habitually chose God's will over self-interest or natural inclinations. Her interests were God's interests, and her inclinations were inspired by the Holy Spirit, which made her not only the first, but the most perfect disciple.

As Mary was ever conscious of the infant God in her womb and of her oneness with the triune God, her thoughts and actions were continually informed by her desire to imitate the humility of God, which, Teresa wrote, "drew the King from heaven to the womb of the Virgin" (W 16.2). This explains why Mary chose to remain silent, even as she observed the dilemma her pregnancy posed for Joseph. Understanding that the divine mystery taking place within her resulted from God's initiative, she waited on God, trusting that he would see events through according to his plan. Her faith was complete, her trust in God unwavering, and her patience edifying.

Mary is unlike any other being, her light reflecting the light of her Beloved, who looks upon her and sees himself in her every action and interior movement. So John could well have been inspired by his love for Mary, the immaculate spouse of the Holy Spirit, when he wrote about the exquisite warmth and light that accompany the higher stages of perfection:

---

6. Cf. *Summa Theologiae* I-II, q. 55, a. 1, ad. 2. See also this passage: "For a man to do a good deed, it is required not only that his reason be well disposed by means of a habit of intellectual virtue, but also that his appetites be well disposed by means of a habit of moral virtue.": in *Summa Theologiae* I-II, q. 58, a. 2, ad. 4.

> O lamps of fire!
> in whose splendors
> the deep caverns of feeling,
> once obscure and blind,
> now give forth, so rarely, so exquisitely,
> both warmth and light to their Beloved. (LF stanza 3)

Surely no one shone with the borrowed light of Christ more perfectly than she, who is called "Morning Star."[7]

Returning to Matthew's gospel, Joseph certainly recognized this light in Mary, which accounts for his desire to protect her from public disgrace. After suffering through the darkness of unknowing, Joseph, enlightened by an angel while asleep, received Mary into his home as his wife according to the angel's directive. Joseph's heart was at peace, for like Joseph in the Old Testament, whose name he bears, the saint received more than information: he received the wisdom of God, which according to John of the Cross "descends from God through the first hierarchies of angels unto the last, and from these last to humans. It is rightly and truly said in Scripture that all the works of the angels and the inspirations they impart are also accomplished or granted by God" (N 2.12.3). This can also be seen by the fruits of God's action when Joseph awoke. Confident that the message he received from the angel was from God, he was resolute to do God's will.

According to John, persons are afflicted until they are sufficiently refined, purified, and capable of receiving this loving inflow (cf. N 2.12.4). With the will inflamed, the intellect is illumined with knowledge and light. Whether the communication comes through an angel in a dream or through a more

---

7. From the Litany of Loreto.

secret communication in the depths of the soul, divine Wisdom enkindles within the person a fervor like a living flame. Having been enlightened, Joseph embraced the role for which he had been chosen, thereby becoming a collaborator in the act of redemption. Responding to his vocation as paternal guardian of Jesus and protector of Mary, this humble man of God enjoyed a unique privilege, and his relationship with Mary and the Child Jesus is to be highly esteemed. Although Joseph never had sexual relations with Mary, he was legally her husband. He had been told to name the child Jesus, an act that, according to Jewish custom, meant publicly acknowledging that he was the father of Mary's son. Thus Joseph further protected Mary from public humiliation while still obeying the law of Moses.

Joseph's obedience to the angel's words and his compassion for Mary over strict observance of the law signaled the teaching that Jesus would one day offer regarding the spirit of the law. Mary understood that Joseph's naming the child gave legitimacy to Jesus's birth. Under Jewish law, Mary and Joseph were legally married, and together they shared the responsibility of parenting the Child Jesus. Despite the significance of the role Joseph played in the lives of Jesus and Mary, not one of his words is recorded in Scripture. If anything, his silence tells us more about the strength of this humble, self-effacing man, of whom it could be said "that he who clings to God in his distress / wins with the weapons of his nothingness."[8]

St. Joseph's exalted position as head of the Holy Family led Teresa, like Mary, to place herself under the protection of this noble saint. Incorporating community into her unique style of travel inside the covered wagon, Teresa included a

8. Jessica Powers (Sister Miriam of the Holy Spirit, O.C.D.), "Israel Again," in *The Selected Poetry of Jessica Powers*, ed. Regina Siegfried, A.S.C. and Robert F. Morneau (Washington, D.C.: ICS Publications, 1999), 93.

prayer schedule, clock, bell, breviaries, holy water, a crucifix, and a statue of our Lady and St. Joseph. She could scarcely think of Mary and the Child Jesus without thinking of St. Joseph, as evidenced by her naming eleven of her seventeen enclosed houses of prayer after the saint. When she decided on the number of nuns in her foundations, she initially decided to limit the number to thirteen, in honor of the twelve apostles, with the mother prioress like Jesus as the head. Then she expanded it to fourteen, to include our Lady, and finally she decided on fifteen, to add St. Joseph, thus including the entire Holy Family. Teresa's love for St. Joseph is well documented, and she claimed that she never sought his intercession without receiving what she had asked.

Like Mary, St. Joseph is a perfect model of obedience. Together, this holy couple serves as a model for all the faithful, but especially for married couples. Mary and Joseph surely took comfort in knowing that Emmanuel ("God with us") was in their midst, an assurance they had both received through the message of an angel. Each encountered the living God individually as every married person does, but their life together added a communal dimension, just as the sacrament of matrimony does for every couple who lives the biblical mandate to be "fruitful and multiply" (Gen 1:28). However, fruitfulness has many layers and dimensions. It implies not only physical fecundity but the birthing of spiritual and corporal works of mercy in the world in answer to the universal call to holiness. Scripture exhorts us: "You shall be holy, for I am holy" (1 Pet 1:16, cf. Lev 11:44, 19:2). According to the *Dogmatic Constitution on the Church* from the Second Vatican Council, all are called to be saints:

> By reason of their state and rank in life they have their own special gift among the people of God. From the wedlock of Christians there comes the family, in which new citizens of

> human society are born, who by the grace of the Holy Spirit received in baptism are made children of God, thus perpetuating the people of God through the centuries. The family is, so to speak, the domestic church. In it parents should, by their word and example, be the first preachers of the faith to their children; they should encourage them in the vocation which is proper to each of them, fostering with special care vocation to a sacred state.
>
> Fortified by so many and such powerful means of salvation, all the faithful, whatever their condition or state, are called by the Lord, each in his own way, to that perfect holiness whereby the Father Himself is perfect. (LG 9–11)

Reflecting on the life of Holy Family as it is portrayed in the gospels provides us with a model of holiness, not only for married couples but for all who desire to live their life in union with God according to the graces within their chosen state of life.

Mary and Joseph serve as perfect models not only for contemplatives but also for parents, who, though falling short of perfection, fulfill their responsibilities with perseverance and joy. In his apostolic exhortation on the call to holiness in today's world, Pope Francis refers to persons who strive to be holy as "the middle class of holiness." He calls them "the saints 'next door,'" whose holiness often goes unnoticed (GeE 7). Notably, this document—an exhortation that all can embrace, as it calls everyone to recognize that holiness flows from our relationship with God—was issued on March 19, the feast of St. Joseph. In it, the Holy Father makes significant references to the Carmelite saints Teresa of Jesus, John of the Cross, Thérèse of the Child Jesus, and Teresa Benedicta of the Cross as companions on the journey, thus confirming the universal appeal of Carmelite spirituality for all who seek to become saints. Pope Francis concludes with the example of Mary: "I would like these reflections to be crowned by Mary, because she lived the Beatitudes of Jesus as none other. . . . She teaches us the way of holiness and she walks ever at our side" (GeE 176).

INVITATION TO PRAYER

As the first Christian pilgrim, Mary traveled with the Son of God in her womb from her home in Nazareth to the home of Elizabeth and Zechariah. Inspired by her role as Theotokos ("God-bearer"), we can turn to her in confidence, trusting that she will carry our prayer to the throne of God in heaven:

ACT OF ENTRUSTMENT OF THE HOME TO MARY HELP OF CHRISTIANS

(by Venerable Luisa Piccarreta)

MOST HOLY VIRGIN MARY, APPOINTED BY GOD TO BE THE HELP OF CHRISTIANS, WE CHOOSE YOU AS THE MOTHER AND PROTECTRESS OF OUR HOME. WE ASK YOU TO FAVOR US WITH YOUR POWERFUL PROTECTION. PRESERVE OUR HOME FROM EVERY DANGER: FROM FIRE, FLOOD, LIGHTNING, STORM, EARTHQUAKE, THIEVES, VANDALS, AND FROM EVERY OTHER DANGER. BLESS US. PROTECT US. DEFEND US. KEEP AS YOUR OWN ALL THE PEOPLE WHO DWELL IN THIS HOME. PROTECT THEM FROM ALL ACCIDENTS AND MISFORTUNES, BUT ABOVE ALL OBTAIN FOR THEM THE MOST IMPORTANT GRACE OF AVOIDING SIN. MARY HELP OF CHRISTIANS, PRAY FOR ALL THOSE WHO LIVE IN THIS HOME, WHICH IS ENTRUSTED TO YOU FOR ALL TIME. AMEN.

3

Bethlehem:

The Birth of Jesus

One of the fruits of the highest stages of the spiritual life, referred to as the "spiritual marriage,"[1] is an ongoing awareness of the presence of God (see IC 7.1.6–7). Given Mary's unique role, God was present in her spiritually and physically, thus making her the embodiment of theological and spiritual assimilation. For Carmelites, whose rule enjoins them to meditate on the law of the Lord day and night, Mary represents the essence of Carmelite spirituality; indeed, no one, after Christ, mirrors the law as spirit and life better than Mary. With Scripture informing much of what John of the Cross taught, he surely recognized in Mary glimpses of a life transformed in God. The image of the infant Jesus moving within Mary's womb, igniting the living flame while tenderly wounding her in the deepest center of her soul, seems to parallel John's final work. In describing the living flame of love, the Carmelite mystic wrote, "Such is the glory this living flame imparts that each time it absorbs and attacks, it seems that it is about to give eternal life and tear the veil of mortal life" (LF 1.1). This could be read as a description of Mary's interior life, especially in the weeks leading up to the birth of Jesus.

1. See the discussion of this important concept in the Introduction.

During the final days of pregnancy, a mother usually experiences a growing sense of urgency to be delivered of the child in her womb. The desire finally to hold the newborn infant in her arms overpowers any natural apprehension she may feel regarding the pains of childbirth. However, for Mary, knowing that the birth of Jesus was imminent and the veil of the divine mystery about to be rent, a deep, supernatural longing within her soul surely added to this natural sense of urgency; "that the whole creation has been groaning in labor pains until now" (Rom 8:22) would not have escaped the woman God had chosen to deliver his Son.

Concomitant with this longing would have been flames of love, which John of the Cross attributed to the presence of the "Spirit of [the soul's] Bridegroom, who is the Holy Spirit" (LF 1.3). To express the soul's experiences in encountering these flames and emphasize the intensity of the longing they provoke, John uses the exclamations *O* and *how*; he notes that "each time they are uttered they reveal more about the interior than the tongue expresses" (LF 1.2). At the conclusion of the first stanza of his poem "The Living Flame of Love," the bride pleads, "If it be your will: tear through the veil of this sweet encounter!" One could well read this in relation to Mary, as her longing intensified during her pregnancy, not just for herself but for all who would be the beneficiaries of the redemption that was at hand with her son's birth.

Understandably, when John was asked to describe the sublime communion that takes place within a soul transformed in God, he hesitated. Only after finding support in Sacred Scripture was he willing to take up the task and then only while he was in a deeply recollected state. Confident that God doesn't limit his gifts to those consecrated in religious life, John wrote his commentary for a lay woman, which offers reassurance to all who embark upon the path of interior prayer. The Mystical

Doctor explained, "There is no reason to marvel at God's granting such sublime and strange gifts to souls he decides to favor. If we consider that he is God, and that he bestows them as God, with infinite love and goodness, it does not seem unreasonable. For he declared that the Father, the Son, and the Holy Spirit would take up their abode in those who love him by making them live the life of God and dwell in the Father, the Son, and the Holy Spirit, as the soul points out in these stanzas" (LF Prol. 2; cf. Jn 14:23). This promise in the gospels is addressed to all of us, so that all might understand that even what is most sublime and lofty is not beyond our reach.

Teresa experienced a similar reluctance in writing about the spiritual marriage, where the soul is in perfect union with God. However, finally, and with considerable uncertainty, she did so under obedience, exclaiming: "O great God! It seems that a creature as miserable as I should tremble to deal with a thing so foreign to what I deserve to understand. And indeed, I have been covered with confusion wondering if it might not be better to conclude my discussion of this dwelling place with just a few words" (IC 7.1.2).

The reluctance of these great mystics to describe the heightened stages of prayer and of the interior life helps us appreciate the ineffable grace of the spiritual marriage. Despite their taking up the task, both John and Teresa inevitably resort to the use of metaphors when trying to describe the inner workings of divine action in souls of mere human beings. This makes Mary the perfect model for contemplatives. For she herself did not allude to what she experienced interiorly. Rather, she exemplified the spiritual marriage through her life, and in a most admirable manner. Regardless of the cost, Mary's every word and action was guided by her willingness to surrender her entire being to God. Thus, her life remains an ongoing testimony to the interior disposition of a soul who has been brought to this state of union with God. We could easily think of Mary and of all that she endured in these words of Teresa: "That there are trials and sufferings and that at the same time the soul is in peace is a difficult thing to explain" (IC 7.2.10). In the Gospel of John, Jesus reassures us that his peace is not the peace that the world gives.[2] His peace is the serenity that comes from union with the will of God and therefore is not dependent on external circumstances. Rather, the peace that God gives exists deep within a person's soul, even in the midst of external trials and suffering.

Mary's constancy in her oneness with the will of God offers a perfect example of a person who is wedded to God. Her life speaks for itself, but lest we wrongly conclude that the highest stages of the interior life are reserved only for the Mother of God, John of the Cross cites the Samaritan woman, St. Peter, and David as having experienced "the words that God speaks in souls that are purged, cleansed, and all enkindled" (LF 1.5–6). These words by the Carmelite saint encourage seekers to trust that the heights of union are possible even for sinners. For God draws whomever he chooses, though not without the agony and ecstasy of purification and illumination that typically precede the deepening stages of union with God.

THE INFANCY NARRATIVES

In examining the infancy narratives, it is worth noting that distinctions in the Gospels of Matthew and Luke have recently led some biblical scholars to question whether Jesus's birth in Bethlehem was more symbolic than factual. In his book on the infancy narratives (a personal rather than official work), Pope

---

2. "Peace I leave with you; my peace I give to you. I do not give to you as the world gives. Do not let your hearts be troubled, and do not let them be afraid" (Jn 14:27).

Benedict XVI refutes such claims.[3] He suggests that it is more likely that Matthew didn't know that Joseph and Mary were from Nazareth, which would account for his depiction of Joseph intending to return to Bethlehem after leaving Egypt. However, on learning that Herod's son, who was even more brutal, was on the throne of Judea, the Holy Family returned to Galilee.

Luke, on the other hand, associates Jesus's early life primarily with Nazareth, which may explain the evangelist's account that the family returned there after the birth. However, as Pope Benedict notes, "The two different strands of tradition agree on the fact that Bethlehem was Jesus' birthplace. If we abide by the sources, it is clear that Jesus was born in Bethlehem and grew up in Nazareth."[4] More important than any distinctions or discrepancies regarding details is that the Gospels of Matthew, Luke, and John enrich our understanding of the nativity event spiritually and theologically. Furthermore, all three Gospels, when viewed together, serve as conduits to a deeper appreciation of Mary's role in salvation history, from which our relationship with her flows.

Beginning with Luke's account, Mary is once again en route, this time traveling to Bethlehem. A census had been ordered by Caesar Augustus requiring everyone to register in the town of their birth: "Joseph also went from the town of Nazareth in Galilee to Judea, to the city of David called Bethlehem, because he was descended from the house and family of David. He went to be registered with Mary, to whom he was engaged and who was expecting a child. While they were there, the time came for her to deliver her child. And she gave birth to her firstborn son and wrapped him in bands of cloth, and laid him in a manger, because there was no place for them in the inn" (Lk 2:4–7).

---

3. See Joseph Ratzinger/Pope Benedict XVI, *Jesus of Nazareth: The Infancy Narratives*, trans. Philip J. Whitmore (New York: Image Books, 2012), 65.

4. Ratzinger/Benedict XVI, *Jesus of Nazareth: The Infancy Narratives*, 66.

The journey of Mary and Joseph to Bethlehem is a clear example of God's plan intersecting with world events, fulfilling the prophecy that the Messiah would be born in Bethlehem.

> But you, O Bethlehem of Ephrathah,
> who are one of the little clans of Judah,
> from you shall come forth for me
> one who is to rule in Israel,
> whose origin is from of old,
> from ancient days. (Mic 5:2)

Throughout the history of the Jewish people, God chose the smallest and least significant people to accomplish his works. That Mary was a "young woman" (cf. Isa 7:14) when she was chosen to be the Mother of God is in keeping with God's seeming penchant for choosing those least important or esteemed to implement his plans:[5] from the youthful Jeremiah, who was sent as a prophet to the nations, to David, a mere shepherd boy who became king of Israel, up to St. Thérèse of the Child Jesus in our own time.

Thérèse's Christmas conversion, just before she turned fourteen, led her to enter Carmel when she was fifteen. Not only has her little way of spiritual childhood garnered international acclaim, but it won for her the distinction of being named Doctor of the Church. While we might look at such souls as privileged, she, like every saint, underwent purification by way of suffering as described by John of the Cross in *The Ascent* and *The Dark Night*, which all who seek union with God must do.

5. The *Protoevangelium of James* speaks of Mary's young age, given as sixteen years, and suggests the low esteem accorded to her mother, Anna, who is said to have been "driven. . . . in derision out of the temple of the Lord" as a reproach for her childlessness, before the conception and birth of Mary. See *Protoevangelium of James*, 12 and 3 respectively, *https://www.newadvent.org/fathers/0847.htm.*

Although Mary was exempt from original sin, she was never exempt from suffering. She left Nazareth in her final month of pregnancy, aware that her time of delivery was imminent, yet she accompanied Joseph to Bethlehem, trusting in Divine Providence. Her unwavering faith may well have served as inspiration for John of the Cross as he described his own journey into the dark night of faith as a solitary one:

> On that glad night,
> in secret, for no one saw me,
> nor did I look at anything,
> with no other light or guide
> than the one that burned in my heart. (N stanza 3)

Indeed, it would have been the flame burning deep within the heart of Mary that enabled her to endure the trials and sufferings that were part of her mission as mother of the Redeemer.

It is erroneous to assume that once the soul has passed through the nights of sense and spirit, like crossing a river, currents that threaten life are never experienced again. Teresa wisely reminded her sisters that they were not angels, and therefore trials and suffering were to be expected. However, once the appetites of sense have been put to death—that is, once our nature has been unconditionally oriented toward God—the practice of virtue becomes more normative, even habitual. The allure of physical, emotional, and spiritual comforts will always be present—though they have less power—for there would be no merit in choosing God's will over our own if it were the only path before us.[6] Surely Mary experienced sadness on a human level

---

6. It should perhaps be mentioned also that when there is no choice, in practical terms, there is still the choice (and the merit) of embracing God's will, in faith and trust, even though it may seem to run counter to our own will.

when she left the home where she and Joseph began their life together. Being young and pregnant, she would have been able to expect more experienced women in Nazareth to help her through the birthing process, but suddenly everything changed. Yet, once again, the humble spouse of the Holy Spirit was able to set aside personal comfort and temporal security in deference to the will of God.

Through Mary, we come to understand that suffering remains part of life, even for those closest to God. Like braided streams, suffering and life's events are woven together throughout the landscape of our story. Rapids and currents threaten to upend what has been gained, but at the more advanced stages of the interior life, they no longer disturb the soul's interior peace. This imagery of water suggests the flow and oneness of spirit and life as proclaimed by the psalmist: "He sends out his word, and melts them; / he makes his wind blow, and the waters flow" (Ps 147:18). Water is also a metaphor used by mystical writers to convey the flow of God's grace welling up in us, as employed by Teresa who described the stages of prayer by likening them to four waters (see L 11.7).[7]

Like John of the Cross, contemplative souls cry out: "That eternal spring is hidden, / for I know well where it has its rise, / *although it is night*" (P 8.1). In a similar manner, Teresa explained, "Here an abundance of water is given to this deer that was wounded. Here one delights in God's tabernacle" (IC 7.3.13). Since Mary was God's tabernacle, we can rightly conclude that God delighted in her. Continuing the theme—this time, with the image of water representing the storm of trials—Teresa wrote, "I tell you, sisters, that the cross is not wanting, but it doesn't disquiet

7. "It seems to me the garden can be watered in four ways" (L 11.7). See the explanation in this paragraph of the *Life*, as well as the treatment of this theme in L 11–18.

or make them lose peace. For the storms, like a wave, pass quickly. And the fair weather returns, because the presence of the Lord they experience makes them soon forget everything" (IC 7.3.15). In a similar manner, Mary could both suffer these trials and also accept them with perfect hope and serenity.

When Mary realized that the Son of God would be born in a borrowed cave[8] where animals were lodged, she accepted what she could not change, her acquiescence a love song of praise before God that we might imagine analogous to the words of John of the Cross: "With regard to love, the soul's presence before God is of rare and exquisite excellence, and so too in regard to this vestige of fruition, and also in regard to praise and to gratitude" (LF 3.81). Though an unseemly place for the birth of God, the humble cave outside the city provided a welcoming environment for the couple away from the noise and crowds that inhabited the inns, foreshadowing the evangelist's proclamation: "He came to what was his own, and his own people did not accept him" (Jn 1:11). The cave outside the city that served as the birthing place for Jesus was not only symbolic but could be regarded as an archetype of the rejection that Jesus would experience during his life on earth.

As Joseph prepared the cave to receive the infant God, we imagine Mary looking on prayerfully, awaiting Jesus's entrance into the world, and we wonder: Did her thoughts travel to the cave on Mount Horeb where Elijah sought shelter? As she waited for her deliverance, did she recall how the holy prophet of Carmel waited for God to pass by and how the Almighty revealed himself as a tiny whispering sound? On this holiest of nights, as she waited for God to reveal himself as a tiny babe, did she wonder if, like Elijah, she would respond by hiding her face?

---

8. See Ratzinger/Benedict XVI, *Jesus of Nazareth: The Infancy Narratives*, 67. Note also that some early sources interpret the birth of the Lord to have taken place in a cave, a premise that is reflected in Eastern iconography.

Or was this most-pure bride of the Holy Spirit so caught up in what was about to unfold that she was lost in ecstasy? Such intimate details about the holy birth remain hidden. All we are told is: "She gave birth to her firstborn son" (Lk 2:7). Some events are too solemn for words, and silence can be the only response. Yet that doesn't deter inquiring minds from speculating.

In the popular 1977 television miniseries *Jesus of Nazareth*, Mary is portrayed as experiencing all the physical pain that accompanies the natural process of labor and delivery. However, this may be contradicted by what the prophet Isaiah foretold:

> Before she was in labor
>   she gave birth;
> before her pain came upon her
>   she delivered a son.
> Who has heard such a thing?
>   Who has seen such things? (Isa 66:7–8)

Whether or not we can imagine Mary's labor as painless, the church nevertheless speaks of a miraculous birth. The essential miracle is the church's dogma of Mary's perpetual virginity. Pope John Paul II expressed this clearly in a general audience in 1987: "Mary was . . . a 'virgin' before the birth of Jesus and she remained a virgin at the moment of giving birth and after the birth. This is the truth which is presented by the texts of the New Testament, and which was expressed . . . by the Fifth Ecumenical Council held in Constantinople in 553, which speaks of Mary as '*ever virgin.*'"[9]

---

9. Pope John Paul II, "Udienza Generale," January 28, 1987, *https://www.vatican.va/content/john-paul-ii/it/audiences/1987/documents/hf_jp-ii_aud_19870128.html/*. See also the statement of St. Augustine: "[Mary] remained a virgin in conceiving her Son, a virgin in giving birth to him, . . . always a virgin." *Sermon 186*, 1 (PL 38:999), quoted in CCC 510.

The notion of Mary's virginity at the moment of giving birth (and a related lack of pain) has been explained well by John Saward, who sums up church tradition on this matter: "The God-Man leaves His Mother's womb without opening it . . . , without inflecting any injury to her bodily virginity . . . , and therefore without causing her any pain."[10] It is in this light that the passage from Isaiah, quoted above, may be seen to apply perfectly to the virginal birth of Jesus (alongside any further elements of prophecy contained in Isaiah's words).

The virginal birth contains implications about the identity of Mary and of Jesus. On the birth of God in human form—after a conception that itself had been miraculous—Tertullian wrote succinctly, "It was necessary for the author of a new birth to be born in a new way."[11] With regard to Mary, her virginity before, during and after giving birth is a sign of her virginal identity, as expressed in the *Catechism of the Catholic Church* (with words from Vatican II's *Dogmatic Constitution on the Church* quoted within): "The deepening of faith in the virginal motherhood led the Church to confess Mary's real and perpetual virginity even in the act of giving birth to the Son of God made man. In fact, Christ's birth 'did not diminish his mother's virginal integrity but sanctified it'" (CCC 499).

Concomitant with the virginal birth is, as mentioned, the lack of pain in childbirth, which is a sign of Mary's role as the new Eve. In the Genesis account of original sin, after the fall of Adam and Eve, God says to Eve, "I will greatly increase your pangs in childbearing; / in pain you shall bring

---

10. John Saward, *Cradle of Redeeming Love: The Theology of the Christmas Mystery* (San Francisco: Ignatius Press, 2002), 206.

11. Tertullian, *De Carne Christi*, 17. See the website of Monsignor Arthur Burton Calkins, *https://www.piercedhearts.org/hearts_jesus_mary/christology/virginal_conception_birth_calkins.htm#_ftnref63/.*

forth children" (Gen 3:16). The pain was a consequence of sin, and since Mary was sinless, it is entirely logical that she was spared the pain of childbirth that other women must endure. This does not, of course, mean that Mary was spared pain in her life—we have only to think of the martyrdom of heart that she suffered on Calvary—but that the virginal birth contains a significant weight of meaning in light of the incarnation of Christ.

Standing in sharp contrast to Isaiah's prophecy—it might at first seem—is that of Micah who proclaimed,

> Therefore he shall give them up until the time
> when she who is in labor has brought forth;
> then the rest of his kindred shall return
> to the people of Israel. (Mic 5:3)

The imagery of a woman in labor has long been a symbol of intense suffering in the Hebrew Scriptures. If what Micah describes are the pangs of childbirth, this could also apply to the Israelites, but they could also be viewed as an archetype of Mary's suffering at the foot of the cross and of the woman in Revelation (see Rev 12:1–2), representing the birthing of the church. Thus, it could be said that the church that was born through the passion and death of Christ was mirrored in the pain and anguish born by Mary, who is called Mother of the Church.

Regarding the virginal birth of Jesus, seventeenth-century mystic Venerable Mary of Agreda (whose cause for beatification was reopened by Pope Francis in 2015) described Jesus's entry into the world as a supernatural event. She wrote that Mary was caught up in ecstasy prior to the birth. After coming to her senses, she became aware of the child moving within her, but without any pain or discomfort, when the supernatural delivery of the infant Jesus occurred. "He did not divide, but penetrated the virginal chamber as the rays of the sun penetrate the crystal shrine, lighting it up in prismatic beauty."[12] According to the nun, Jesus was transfigured, and the Virgin Mary beheld the infant Jesus in all his glory, much the way he appeared on Mount Tabor.

As with all private revelations, Catholics are not obliged to believe what they portend, even when they bear an imprimatur certifying that they contain nothing contrary to Scripture or to church teaching. Mary of Agreda's description expands but does not contradict what the church teaches about the birth; since it says that her womb was left intact, it supports the doctrine of Mary's perpetual virginity. God grants mystical wisdom and supernatural favors to certain people, so as to benefit the faithful by reassuring them of God's continued presence in the world. And if such spiritual insights increase our devotion and love for God and his holy mother, they arguably merit respect and thoughtful consideration.

John of the Cross offers a beautiful interpretation of Christ's birth, in his poetry, which shines a light both on the humanity of Jesus and on Mary's contemplative disposition as she beholds her son:

> When the time had come
> for Him to be born,
> he went forth like the bridegroom
> from his bridal chamber,
> embracing his bride,
> holding her in his arms,

---

12. Mother Mary of Agreda, *The Mystical City of God: Popular Abridgment of the Divine History and Life of the Virgin Mother of God*, trans. Fiscar Marison (Rev. George J. Blatter) (Charlotte, N.C.: Saint Benedict Press/TAN Books, 2012), 229.

whom the gracious Mother
laid in a manger
among some animals
that were there at the time.
Men sang songs
and angels melodies
celebrating the marriage
of Two such as these.
But God there in the manger
cried and moaned;
and these tears were jewels
the bride brought to the wedding.
The Mother gazed in sheer wonder
on such an exchange:
in God, man's weeping,
and in man, gladness,
to the one and the other
things usually so strange. (R 9)

As we shall see, these lines give us much on which to reflect.

John writes that the God in the manger "cried and moaned," while he says of Mary that she "gazed in sheer wonder." That God held Mary in his arms even as she held him represents the mutual exchange of love between the bride and the Bridegroom, and her joy would have been complete. It is notable that John speaks of Jesus going forth "like the bridegroom from his bridal chamber." In doing so, he echoes the words of the psalmist (Ps 19:5) and of John Damascene, who wrote, "For the eternal light, which came into existence out of eternal light before the ages, the immaterial and bodiless One, takes a body from this [woman] and comes forth from the bridal chamber as

Bridegroom although he is God."[13] This inspiring description alludes to the incarnation as being the birth of a Savior who also takes us to himself as his bride. It echoes the words of Jesus himself, when he responded to a question from the people of Capernaum about why the disciples of John the Baptist did not fast. Referring to himself, he told them, "The wedding guests cannot fast while the bridegroom is with them, can they? As long as they have the bridegroom with them, they cannot fast" (Mk 2:19). As Mary could see, with the eyes of contemplation, this was the joy and glory of God made manifest on earth.

The incarnate God as Bridegroom of the soul can be understood only through the eyes of faith. Once the notion of God as our Bridegroom has been embraced, it becomes the heart song that reflects the inexplicable joy and wonder that both Mary and Joseph experienced. The belief that God cried and suffered so that a sinful race could be glad seems like sheer madness, but then who can explain a God who heaps miracle upon miracle on the very people who turned against him? How could it be that the God who would become Bread for the world was placed in a feeding trough for animals, or that an ox and an ass would be among the first to look upon the face of God? Did they represent the blindness of humanity that looks but does not see?

Luke tells us that Mary pondered all these things in her heart (see Lk 2:19). Overwhelmed by the gravity of all that took place, Mary remained silent as her gaze met the gaze of her son. This encounter is reflected in the experience of John of the Cross when he writes:

---

13. St. John of Damascus, "An Oration on the Nativity of the Holy Theotokos Mary," in *Wider than Heaven: Eighth-Century Homilies on the Mother of God*, trans. Mary B. Cunningham (Crestwood, N.Y.: St. Vladimir's Seminary Press, 2008), 56.

When you looked at me
your eyes imprinted your grace in me;
for this you loved me ardently;
and thus my eyes deserved
to adore what they beheld in you. (C stanza 32, Redaction B)

To look at God looking at us is a profoundly Carmelite perspective; in this light, we once more see Mary as the perfect contemplative.

GLORY TO GOD IN THE HIGHEST

On the night of Jesus's birth, Luke's gospel tells us, an angel appeared to shepherds who were keeping watch by night:

> An angel of the Lord stood before them, and the glory of the Lord shone around them, and they were terrified. But the angel said to them, "Do not be afraid; for see—I am bringing you good news of great joy for all the people: to you is born this day in the city of David a Savior, who is the Messiah, the Lord. This will be a sign for you: you will find a child wrapped in bands of cloth and lying in a manger." And suddenly there was with the angel a multitude of the heavenly host, praising God and saying,
>
> "Glory to God in the highest heaven,
> and on earth peace among those whom he favors!"
> (Lk 2:9–14)

Once again, God singled out the lowest and most unlikely for the greatest of privileges. Shepherds were poor, uneducated men living in the fields among animals. They were among the marginalized of society, who sometimes stole what was needed to survive. While others enjoyed the luxury of nighttime sleep, no such comfort was afforded to shepherds who had to remain awake and alert. Luke tells us that no sooner had Mary and Joseph knelt in adoration before the infant God than an angel appeared to the shepherds. "So they went with haste and found Mary and Joseph, and the child lying in the manger. When they saw this, they made known what had been told them about this child" (Lk 2:16–17).

This brings us to important questions: What exactly did the shepherds see? How could the sight of an infant lying in a manger be a sign, and why would it bring them to their knees? The real sign that the shepherds witnessed was the poverty of God, and on a deeply personal level these poor men could relate. Their poverty and lowly standing in the community captured the heart of God, and nothing, neither the wealth nor the prestige of the entire world, could compare with what they received. Their eyes had been opened and their lives changed. The poor shepherds, chosen by God, understood what many fail to grasp and what John of the Cross articulated so profoundly:

> To reach satisfaction in all
> desire satisfaction in nothing.
> To come to possess all
> desire the possession of nothing.
> To arrive at being all
> desire to be nothing.
> To come to the knowledge of all
> desire the knowledge of nothing.
> To come to enjoy what you have not
> you must go by a way in which you enjoy not.
> To come to the knowledge you have not
> you must go by a way in which you know not. (A 1.13.11)

Truly, those who are poor in spirit are rich in the eyes of God. That God granted so lofty a favor to shepherds reflects what Teresa had to say when writing about the unexpected spiritual favors that God may grant to those who are only beginning the journey toward union with God:

> It will seem that to reach these dwelling places one will have to live in the others for a long while. Although it is usual that a person will have to have stayed in those already spoken about, there is no certain rule, as you will have often heard. For the Lord gives when He desires, as He desires, and to whom He desires. Since these blessings belong to Him, He does no injustice to anyone. (IC 4.1.2)

In this respect, the invitation to the shepherds on Christmas night is a source of encouragement for us all and reinforces the fact that extraordinary favors are gifts from God rather than something that we merit.

Regardless of their state in life or purity of heart, God favors those whom he chooses. Mary understood this, just as Teresa did when she wrote that "anyone who has experience, especially when there is a lot of it, will understand very well" (IC 4.1.2). Like the Bridegroom, Mary had a special place in her heart for the poor. Welcoming the shepherds, her smile surely dispelled fears, as only a mother's can. As she bid them draw near to her son, did her smile have for them a healing effect that was not unlike the healing St. Thérèse experienced when, on seeing the smile of the Virgin, she was cured of a life-threatening illness? The most-pure Virgin Mother's assimilation in God became a mirror that reflected the hospitality of God, which draws souls to all that is beauty and truth. To help us better understand these secret ways of God, we turn to John of the Cross who writes: "This secret ladder of love assimilates the soul to God completely because of the clear vision of God that a person possesses at once on reaching it. . . . St. John says: *We know that we shall be like him*, not because the soul will have as much capacity as God—this is impossible—but because all it is will become like God. Thus, it will be called, and shall be, God through participation" (N 2.20.5; cf. 1 Jn 3:2).

It is difficult to imagine that John of the Cross did not have the Blessed Virgin, the most Godlike of all creatures, in mind when he penned those words. Mary's welcome to the shepherds would, then, have been like God welcoming them. We might wonder if, in these men, she recognized those whom her son would one day reach out to and heal—the poor, the lame, the blind, and the marginalized. Did she know that Jesus would refer to himself as the Good Shepherd who would leave the righteous to rescue the lost sheep? The answer is obviously "no," for to imply that Mary knew about events prior to their taking place would diminish the presence of the theological virtues of faith, hope, and charity present within her soul, which are essential elements of the Christian journey.

John referred to the jewel of faith as "an inner tunic of such pure whiteness that it blinds the sight of every intellect. . . . *Without faith*, as the Apostle says, *it is impossible to please God* [Heb 11:6]" (N 2.21.4). Mary was also clothed with the robe of hope, for "without this green livery of hope in God alone, it would not behoove anyone to go out toward this goal of love; a person would obtain nothing, since what moves and conquers is unrelenting hope" (N 2.21.8). But the perfection and finishing touch, according to John, was the precious garment of charity, which "not only adds elegance to the other two colors but so elevates the soul as to place her near God" (N 2.21.10).

As the spouse of the Holy Spirit, Mary's every impulse was fired by love's urgent longings. Her privileged communication with the Trinity assured her of God's presence as her life, transformed in love, unfolded day by day. However, it did not give her extraordinary or superhuman powers. Clothed with perfect faith, hope, and love, Jesus's mother welcomed the shepherds. Seeing the Beloved in them, she surely watched in awe as she witnessed the effects of their encounter with Jesus.

According to Luke's gospel, all who heard the shepherds' account "were amazed at what the shepherds told them. But Mary treasured all these words and pondered them in her heart" (Lk 2:18–19), a most fitting response for souls in this exalted state. "And with unspeakable delight she thanks and loves the Father again through his Son Jesus. She does this united with Christ, together with Christ. And the savor of this praise is so delicate as to be totally beyond words" (C 37.6). Here, John of the Cross is writing of the soul transformed in the love of God—a description that is eminently applicable to Mary. For not only was Mary transformed in love, but she also gave birth to Love. The God who was wrapped in mystery lay swaddled in her arms and nursed at her breast. When the shepherds left and the stillness of the night enfolded this gentle woman, did the silence cause her to marvel at what God was doing through these humble herdsmen? We know only what Scripture tells us, which is that she continued to ponder their words in her heart.

"The shepherds returned, glorifying and praising God for all they had heard and seen, as it had been told them" (Lk 2:20). Despite their lowly status, they could not contain the Good News. Just as the Samaritan woman, reputed as a sinner, returned to the village proclaiming that she had seen the Messiah, the shepherds similarly shared what they had seen. Having been chosen to be the first to see the Savior of the world, the shepherds are a reminder that God's ways are not our ways. Or, as St. Thérèse wrote in the opening lines of the story of her life: "He does not call those who are worthy but those whom He pleases" (S 13). Perhaps St. Paul said it best when he wrote, "For we do not proclaim ourselves; we proclaim Jesus Christ as Lord and ourselves as your slaves for Jesus's sake. For it is the God who said, 'Let light shine out of darkness,' who has shone in our hearts to give the light of the knowledge of the glory of God in the face of Christ" (2 Cor 4:5–6). The proclamation to the shepherds is, par excellence, the light of the knowledge of the glory of God.

JESUS, THE NEW ISRAEL

"After eight days had passed, it was time to circumcise the child; and he was called Jesus, the name given by the angel before he was conceived in the womb" (Lk 2:21). In accordance with Mosaic Law, Jesus was presented formally to the community. In naming Jesus, Joseph became his legal father, and through the ritual of circumcision, Jesus became a legal member of the Israelite nation. The shedding of his blood at the circumcision was proof that Jesus would not be exempt from suffering—he

> who, though he was in the form of God,
> did not regard equality with God
> as something to be exploited,
> but emptied himself,
> taking the form of a slave,
> being born in human likeness. (Phil 2:6–7)

The Holy Family was not exempt from obedience to the law of Moses, and Mary's sole desire was to do the will of God, which meant bearing with patience and compassion the suffering that would accompany the God-made-human. Her obedience to the Father's will filled her with joy, even as the knife cut through her infant son's flesh—perhaps the first wounding of her soul.

The desire to do the will of God is one of the most important fruits of prayer, though often not without pain or suffering. While the teachings of John and Teresa provide insight, by way of their own experience in prayer, those less experienced have difficulty understanding the more advanced and paradoxical nature of the heights of divine union, where pain and joy can be concomitant. In Mary, whose life was the embodiment of prayer, we look at her and we understand. One who understood the will of the triune God, Mary saw beyond the pain. Every aspect of her life was viewed by her through the eyes of her heavenly spouse. Her union with her divine spouse facilitated her total surrender to the will of the Father in all things concerning her son.

THE PRESENTATION OF JESUS IN THE TEMPLE

> When the time came for their purification according to the law of Moses, they brought him up to Jerusalem to present him to the Lord (as it is written in the law of the Lord, "Every firstborn male shall be designated as holy to the Lord"), and they offered a sacrifice according to what is stated in the law of the Lord, "a pair of turtledoves or two young pigeons."
>
> Now there was a man in Jerusalem whose name was Simeon; this man was righteous and devout, looking forward to the consolation of Israel, and the Holy Spirit rested on him. It had been revealed to him by the Holy Spirit that he would not see death before he had seen the Lord's Messiah. Guided by the Spirit, Simeon came into the temple; and when the parents brought in the child Jesus, to do for him what was customary under the law, Simeon took him in his arms and praised God, saying,
>
> "Master, now you are dismissing your servant in peace,
> according to your word;
> for my eyes have seen your salvation,
> which you have prepared in the presence of all peoples,
> a light for revelation to the Gentiles
> and for glory to your people Israel." (Lk 2:22–32)

Although the Mother of God did not require purification, Mary's action ushered in the purification of the world. Her obedience in handing her son over to God in the temple foreshadowed Jesus being handed over as the sacrifice that would redeem the world. The significance of the occasion was not lost on Simeon, whose joy was celebrated in song. In the sixth century, St. Romanos reflected on this moment: "Wondrous and marvelous, incomprehensible, ineffable are the things we now see, for the One who created Adam is being carried as a babe. The uncontainable is contained in the arms of the elder."[14] Filled with the Holy Spirit and having proclaimed his song of praise, Simeon concluded with the prophecy: "This child is destined for the falling and the rising of many in Israel, and to be a sign that will be opposed so that the inner thoughts of many will be revealed—and a sword will pierce your own soul too" (Lk 2:34–35). We cannot know what transpired in the heart of Mary as she listened to Simeon's words. As Rwandan-American author Immaculée Ilibagiza has written, "The Blessed Mother knew that she had given birth to the Savior of humankind, so she immediately understood and accepted Simeon's prophecy. Although her heart was deeply touched by this favor of bearing the baby Jesus, her heart remained heavy and troubled, for she knew what had been written about the ordeals and subsequent death of the Savior."[15]

---

14. St. Romanos the Melodist, *On the Life of Christ*, trans. Ephrem Lash (San Francisco: HarperCollins, 1998), 28. The Mother of God appeared to the sixth-century youth, presented him with a scroll and told him to eat it. Thus he was given the gifts of understanding, composition, and hymnography.

15. Immaculée Ilibagiza with Steve Erwin, *Our Lady of Kibeho: Mary Speaks to the World from the Heart of Africa* (Carlsbad, Calif.: Hay House, 2008), 188. On July 2, 2001, the Holy See released the declaration of Bishop Augustin Misago of Gikongoro that the Marian apparitions which took place in Kibeho from 1981 to 1983 were authentic.

From the moment when Mary heard Simeon's pronouncement, she knew that the road ahead would involve suffering for herself and her son. This would be their shared experience on the journey, a union of purpose in the service of Christ's mission as Savior of the world. And this is the blessed irony where joy and pain become concomitant realities. Simeon's prophecy to Mary serves as an archetype of the trials facing all who journey toward union with God. The soul's personal, mystical selection by God can take place only within the experience of the God-man whose total gift of self to the Father was received and realized on the cross. Scripture tells us nothing about Mary's or Joseph's reactions to the prophecies of Simeon and Anna—only that "when they had finished everything required by the law of the Lord, they returned to Galilee, to their own town of Nazareth" (Lk 2:39). Outwardly, perhaps, nothing about Mary's demeanor had changed, but the confirmation of what awaited her brought her further along her mystical journey as her life became more deeply immersed in the trinitarian love of God.

When we reflect on the person of Mary, her purity of heart, the constancy of her virtues, and the surrender of her entire being to God in all things, we are quickly humbled and predisposed to plead for her protection against the sin of pride or presumption. Yet rather than distance her from us, her love for God encourages us to seek her counsel and motherly wisdom as we make our own journey in life, and in prayer, to her son. We will never reach on earth the level of union that was Mary's singular privilege, yet we look to her and find, in her life, inspiration for our own lives, and we are given reassurance in Jesus's words, which were a hallmark of Mary's own life: "for God all things are possible" (Mt 19:26).

INVITATION TO PRAYER

Only our Lady was privileged to bear and nurture the Son of God in her womb, but as Christians we are also bearers of the Word of God. This precious seed which was planted in our soul at baptism has been entrusted to us so that, through the grace of God, it may be nurtured and incarnated in the world in which we live. To be spiritually pregnant is to be filled with God, which is the goal of all who travel the road to union with God. Therefore, it seems fitting to turn to the one who suckled the Son of God at her breast and ask her to nourish us on our faith journey. Mindful of her motherly love, let us invoke Our Lady of La Leche—Mary, the nursing mother—so that, through her intercession, she who nursed the infant Jesus at her breast may succor all who call upon her name:

LOVELY LADY OF LA LECHE, MOST LOVING MOTHER OF THE CHILD JESUS, AND MY MOTHER, LISTEN TO MY HUMBLE PRAYER. YOUR MOTHERLY HEART KNOWS MY EVERY WISH, MY EVERY NEED. TO YOU ONLY, HIS SPOTLESS VIRGIN MOTHER, HAS YOUR DIVINE SON GIVEN TO UNDERSTAND THE SENTIMENTS WHICH FILL MY SOUL. YOURS WAS THE SACRED PRIVILEGE OF BEING THE MOTHER OF THE SAVIOR. INTERCEDE WITH HIM NOW, MY LOVING MOTHER, THAT, IN ACCORDANCE WITH HIS WILL, I MAY BECOME THE MOTHER OF THE CHILDREN OF OUR HEAVENLY FATHER [FOR THERE ARE MANY WAYS TO BE A MOTHER]. THIS I ASK, O LADY OF LA LECHE, IN THE NAME OF YOUR DIVINE SON, MY LORD AND REDEEMER. AMEN.[16]

---

16. Mission of Nombre de Dios and Shrine of Our Lady of La Leche, St. Augustine, Florida; see *https://www.catholicculture.org/culture/liturgicalyear/prayers/view.cfm?id=1099.* The shrine is the first ever to be dedicated to the Blessed Virgin Mary in the United States, in 1620. It includes a statue of the Virgin Mother nursing the infant Jesus.

4

Distant Lands:

Offering a Light to the Nations

NO CHRISTMAS CRÈCHE WOULD BE complete without statues of the three wise men as portrayed in Matthew's gospel. Although it would have taken months, perhaps even years, for travelers from distant lands to arrive at the place where the Holy Family lodged, neither timing nor details surrounding the birth of Jesus seem to have concerned the evangelist. Gentiles were being baptized when Matthew wrote his gospel, and his intention was to assure Christian Jews that Jesus's mission was universal. Devoting only one sentence to the birth of Jesus, he immediately moved on to offer an account of the visit of the magi: "In the time of King Herod, after Jesus was born in Bethlehem of Judea, wise men from the East came to Jerusalem, asking, 'Where is the child who has been born king of the Jews? For we observed his star at its rising, and have come to pay him homage.' When King Herod heard this, he was frightened, and all Jerusalem with him; and calling together all the chief priests and scribes of the people, he inquired of them where the Messiah was to be born" (Mt 2:1–4).

Matthew highlights the circumstances of Jesus's birth within the context of Herod's reign, but the theological significance of pagans traveling from distant lands to worship the infant God of the Israelites had more far-reaching implications. With the coming of the magi, the Messiah no longer belonged exclusively to the Jews, as foretold by the prophet:

> Lo, these shall come from far away,
>   and lo, these from the north and from the west,
>   and these from the land of Syene.
> Sing for joy, O heavens, and exult, O earth;
>   break forth, O mountains, into singing!
> For the LORD has comforted his people,
>   and will have compassion on his suffering ones.
> (Isa 49:12–13)

The star that guided the wise men was not only a sign of divine intervention, but it signaled the universal dimension of the Messiah's birth. For Jews, the involvement of a heavenly body portended the deeper reality that God's salvific action was intended for all people: "When they had heard the king, they set out; and there, ahead of them, went the star that they had seen at its rising, until it stopped over the place where the child was. When they saw that the star had stopped, they were overwhelmed with joy. On entering the house, they saw the child with Mary his mother; and they knelt down and paid him homage. Then, opening their treasure chests, they offered him gifts of gold, frankincense, and myrrh" (Mt 2:9–11).

The worship of Jesus by the magi was an act of sheer faith. There were no external trappings that would distinguish the infant or his mother as royalty, and yet they understood instantly what the evangelist later wrote: "And the Word became flesh and lived among us, and we have seen his glory, the glory as of a father's only son, full of grace and truth" (Jn 1:14). Guided by an interior light that John of the Cross called "the artificer of all, who is Wisdom" (A 3.2.12), they were filled with joy.

There is no mention of Joseph's presence, and so we can imagine—at least from the details we are given—that it was perhaps Mary who opened the door (literally or figuratively) to welcome the travelers. In her serving as doorkeeper, as it were, to the magi, Mary's action symbolizes her opening the door for all who journey to her son by way of faith. As our heavenly mother, Mary not only opens the door and bids us welcome, but she also invites us to enter so that she may lead us to the place of our deepest longing. Just as the Son of God pitched his tent among us, so Mary meets us where we are. She is the Morning Star that points the way to her son, the *Janua Cœli* who opens the door to heaven. As a loving mother, she listens to our story and then shares with us her story and the story of her son, inviting each of us to take from it what we need to remain faithful as we travel the path to union with God. The wise men gained access to the Son of God through Mary, just as the world gained access to him through her when the he entered her womb.

A STORY WITHIN A STORY

In keeping with Jewish customs of hospitality, we can imagine that after worshipping the Child Jesus, the men were offered something to eat and drink. Mary, being attentive and welcoming, would surely have asked them about their journey and how they came to know about her son's birth. She must have listened with awe as the strangers shared their story and marveled at how the God of the universe engages mere mortals to accomplish his work.

In an article on religious experience, Father Joseph Chorpenning, O.S.F.S., notes, "Theology takes as its starting-point human experience, which has an intrinsically narrative or story quality to it. The story, then, is the most common and universal means of communicating human experience, and human beings are essentially storylistening and storytelling human beings."[1] Consequently, every account in Scripture bears, within the main story, multiple stories that, when unpacked, lead us to a deeper awareness of divine activity within human history. Therefore, we can rightly conclude that the journey of the wise men is also a story about the soul's interior journey toward transformation, and that their journey is also our journey, their story, our story.

Up to this point, the focus has been on Mary as the perfect contemplative. While it is imperative to keep the goal in sight, no one begins the journey at the end. Mary, who watched the events of Scripture unfold in real time, invites us to reflect on the many ways God is present in the events of our lives and in those of others.

In framing his writing, John of the Cross declared that Scripture was his help in writing about matters difficult to understand: "Taking Scripture as our guide, we do not err since the Holy Spirit speaks to us through it" (A 1.Prol. 2). Similarly, we are on safe ground when we examine the story of the magi as an analogy. Reading it alongside the writings of the mystics can help guide us in understanding our own faith journey.

Although little is known about the magi, it is safe to assume that as they studied the night skies in search of truth, their sojourn had as much to do with their interior disposition as it did with physical travel. Without an inner restlessness, they could easily have waited to learn about the birth while studying its meaning from a distance. Instead, they committed to the journey, not knowing where it would lead, or what the cost to themselves might involve. Trusting that the star would lead them to the newborn king, their journey to the Christ Child

---

1. Joseph Chorpenning, "St. Teresa's Presentation of Her Religious Experience," in *Carmelite Studies*, vol. 3: *Centenary of St. Teresa*, ed. John Sullivan, O.C.D. (Washington, D.C.: ICS Publications, 1984), 167.

parallels, in many ways, the interior journey of those who travel the path to union with God.

Matthew's account of the visit of the magi and the flight of the Holy Family that followed is replete with images of the journey, meriting exploration in tandem with the teachings of the Carmelite saints. All who travel the path of interior prayer can relate to the trials and tribulations that assail the soul, but they can also understand the joy and know firsthand the invisible grace that propels them forward, which John of the Cross described when he wrote:

> One dark night,
> fired with love's urgent longings
> —ah the sheer grace!—
> I went out unseen,
> my house being now all stilled. (N stanza 1)

These lines shed light on the interior experience of the adventurous journey to God. Such a journey may be accompanied by risk and danger; yet as we have seen with the magi and with the Holy Family, grace propels them onward.

Impelled by a sense of self-transcendence, the magi were willing to leave behind all that was familiar. Crossing desert and mountainous terrain, and guided by a star "more surely than the light of noon to where he was awaiting me" (N stanza 4), the wise men entered the night, filled with hope in search of the newborn King of the Jews. As with all who embark upon the path of prayer, "it was also fortunate the departure took place at night; that is, that God took from the soul all these things through a privation that was a night to it" (A 1.1.4).

According to John, crossing the desert purges beginners of sensory appetites, delights of the flesh, and gratifications of the will. Its hostile environment often causes sojourners to travel by night to avoid the glaring heat of day, and although nighttime travel entails challenges, it is laden with hidden blessings. Like the star that guided the wise men, love's urgent longings become more defined, offering a metaphor for the dynamics of souls entering the night of sense. Adapting to forces beyond their control, the magi surrendered to the darkness, trusting the star that shone in the midnight hour, and in the process sensory pleasures lost their appeal. In his poem "Journey of the Magi," T. S. Eliot captured the nighttime experience of the magi, to which anyone who travels in the nights of sense and spirit can relate:

> And the cities hostile and the towns unfriendly
> And the villages dirty and charging high prices:
> A hard time we had of it.
> At the end we preferred to travel by night,
> Sleeping in snatches,
> With the voices singing in our ears, saying
> That this was all folly.[2]

Here, Eliot focuses mostly on the externals of the journey, thus complementing the lines, seen earlier, by John of the Cross. Yet he also hones in on difficulties and doubts that are characteristic of journeying in faith, all of which at some stage suggest that the undertaking may all be "folly." At such times, it is faith alone that keeps one steadily moving forward.

While John used the metaphor of night, Teresa's image of the castle is also applicable. She explained that the soul who practices prayer should not hold itself back. "Let it walk through these dwelling places which are up above, down below, and to the sides, since God has given it such great dignity" (IC 1.2.8). As

---

2. T. S. Eliot, "Journey of the Magi," in *T.S. Eliot: The Complete Poems and Plays, 1909–1950* (Orlando: Harcourt Brace & Company, 1967), 68.

the magi traveled through friendly and unfriendly terrain, and the solitude and monotony became a pilgrimage of the heart, whereby they would have entered the rooms of self-knowledge, confronting their fears while discovering personal limitations. The same holds true in regard to prayer, as Teresa writes: "Along this path of prayer, self-knowledge and the thought of one's sins is the bread with which all palates must be fed, no matter how delicate they may be for they cannot be sustained without this bread" (L 13.15). Just as the purgative stage helps souls grow in humility, so the illuminative stage offers enlightenment and assurance, even in the early stages of self-discovery, as Teresa explains: "But let's remember that the bee doesn't fail to leave the beehive and fly about gathering nectar from the flowers. So it is with the soul in the room of self-knowledge; let it believe me and fly sometimes to ponder the grandeur and majesty of its God. Here it will discover its lowliness better than by thinking of itself" (IC 1.2.8).

This itself is a voyage of discovery, and a journey like that of the magi is an embodiment of the going out of oneself in the quest to find God.

GOD'S SECRET COMMUNICATION

Anyone gazing at the night skies while in a solitary place, away from the lights of the city, will appreciate how heavenly bodies reveal the grandeur of God in ways few other sights can. This, too, was part of the wise men's journey, just as it is for all who seek to know and experience the glory of God. Experiences of illumination, though transient, restore hope and renew spirits. God grants supernatural favors to souls when most needed, to prepare them for trials that lie ahead. And so it was for the magi. Along the way, doubts surely plagued them; yet deep within, a sense of certitude prevailed, which John of the Cross identified as faith: "Though faith brings certitude to the intellect, it does not produce clarity, only darkness" (A 2.6.2). When the star disappeared, the magi sought counsel—as should souls who find themselves in uncharted waters when it comes to prayer.

At this stage of the spiritual journey, John cautions against the temptation to seek consolation by returning to earlier prayer practices. He also stresses the importance of seeking spiritual direction, even as he alerts seekers to be wary of blind guides. Teresa offers similar advice regarding the importance of seeking a spiritual director at this stage. She advises that a spiritual director who is both learned and a person of prayer is ideal, yet she cautions: "My opinion has always been and will be that every Christian strive to speak if possible to someone who has gone through studies; and the more learned the person the better. Those who walk the path of prayer have a greater need for this counsel; and the more spiritual they are, the greater their need" (L 13.17).

And she warns, "Let not the spiritual person be misled by saying that learned men without prayer are unsuitable for those who practice it" (L 13.18). Here again, the example of the magi offers valuable reflection: even though they did not know Christ before setting out on their journey, it was their learning—submitted in humility to the truth of something greater—that led them to Jesus.

When the magi sought directions from Herod, perhaps they thought they were addressing a man who knew the Scriptures and who could direct them. However, Herod was neither a man of prayer nor learned in Scripture, but he was clever enough to seek help from those who were. After informing the magi that the Messiah was to be born in Bethlehem, he compounded his ignorance with lies when he asked the magi to let him know where the child could be found so that he could honor him. Although the magi listened, they made no commitment to return. Guided by divine Wisdom, they exemplified the warning which one day Jesus would give: "Be wise as serpents and innocent as doves" (Mt 10:16). Such is the wisdom that comes from God, which John of the Cross attributes to "the Spirit of the Lord, who abides in us and aids our weakness" (C Prol.1). He refers to such insights as "mystical theology, which is known through love and by which these truths are not only known but at the same time enjoyed" (C Prol. 3). We can immediately think of the supernatural love that would have filled the hearts of the magi as divine Wisdom impelled them onward to Christ.

No sooner had the magi left than the star reappeared. As often happens when a person seeks God, the felt presence of God is not a constant but is granted when needed most. Then, like the star that reappeared unexpectedly to guide the wise men, clarity and purpose become one's guides. And as John explains, concerns and apprehensions disappear as people allow God to lead them: "The faculties are at rest and do not work actively, but passively, by receiving what God is effecting in them. If at times the soul puts the faculties to work, it should not use excessive efforts or studied reasonings, but it should proceed with gentleness of love, moved more by God than by its own abilities" (A 2.12.8). This is a most helpful reminder that it is God who initiates our journey in faith and that he will give us all the help we need.

"On entering the house, they saw the child with Mary his mother; and they knelt down and paid him homage" (Mt 2:11). In this intimate setting, the magi experienced in person what Carmelites experience in "contemplation," which John of the Cross explains is an infused gift, a secret knowing (cf. N 1.10.6). We might even say that when the magi saw Jesus with their very eyes, faith told them that this was no ordinary child. The result of faith, contemplation also offers a fitting analogy for what the wise men experienced when the star reappeared as they continued their journey to Bethlehem. Having placed their faith in the Word of God, they were filled with joy; they had led "the faculties of the soul to these three virtues [faith, hope and charity]" (A 2.6.6). Then Mary welcomed these travelers who had come from afar and watched as they prostrated themselves before the infant God. As a witness to this wondrous event, her heart surely overflowed with joy, perhaps calling to mind the prayer of thanksgiving recorded in the Hebrew Scriptures:

> A bright light will shine to all the ends of the earth;
> many nations will come to you from far away,
> the inhabitants of the remotest parts of the earth to your holy name,
> bearing gifts in their hands for the King of heaven.
> (Tob 13:11)

As the handmaid of the Lord, this young mother regarded herself as servant to all—to whomever she encountered—exemplifying the teaching of Teresa who wrote, "You . . . must concentrate on those who are in your company. . . . Such service will not be small but very great and very pleasing to the Lord" (IC 7.4.14). This is an important insight, which can show the value of an apparently small and overlooked aspect of the infancy narratives: Mary's simple welcoming of those who came to visit her son.

"Then, opening their treasure chests, they offered him gifts of gold, frankincense, and myrrh" (Mt 2:11). Imagine Mary's response when they laid their precious gifts before her son. Though unimpressed by material wealth, she was surely touched by the generosity of these humble men. And yet as Mary accepted their gifts on behalf of the Giver of every good gift, she could not have known that the full meaning of these gifts would be revealed only when Jesus offered his life on the altar of the cross. As we reflect on the person of Mary, who with a mother's tenderness contemplated the scene before her, the words of the prophet Isaiah ring true:

> Enlarge the site of your tent,
>   and let the curtains of your habitations be stretched out;
> do not hold back; lengthen your cords
>   and strengthen your stakes.
> For you will spread out to the right and to the left,
>   and your descendants will possess the nations
>   and will settle the desolate towns. (Isa 54:2–3)

In keeping with this, the magi represent the nations coming to Christ, whose descendants will one day be spread throughout the world.

"And having been warned in a dream not to return to Herod, they left for their own country by another road" (Mt 2:12). Through the centuries, the significance of the visit of the magi has grown, and eventually they were assigned origins reflecting the continents of Asia, Africa, and Europe. Not only can the magi be said to represent missionary efforts of the Christian community, but in our present day, when interreligious dialogue has become an important part of the church's mission, the love with which these wise men were surely embraced by the Mother of God extends far beyond the Christmas season.

Many regard Mary as a meeting ground for dialogue among the Abrahamic religions. Jews hold her in high regard as a devout Jewish woman and as the mother of a great teacher; among Muslims, she is revered as the virgin who gave birth to a great prophet. Concerning Mary's role in interreligious dialogue, Cardinal William Keeler explained that while Muslims do not believe that Mary is the Mother of God, they hold her in "esteem and honor"; and although a radical difference in faith separates us, regarding Mary, the difference "paradoxically also holds us forever in conversation with one another."[3]

As the history of the church continues to be written, Mary's role is expanding. Recognized as a model of goodness, she is respected among the Abrahamic faiths and prominently positioned to open the door to dialogue. Given Teresa's Jewish roots, recent strides to engage in dialogue among religions would surely have brought joy to her heart. Interreligious dialogue is also in keeping with the spirit of Elijah, who befriended the widow at Zarephath, and Elisha, who cured Naaman the Syrian of his leprosy. The prophetic mission of Carmel has a long history of inclusivity, which surely makes Mary, under her title of Our Lady of Mount Carmel, a perfect guide.[4]

THE FLIGHT INTO EGYPT

> Now after they had left, an angel of the Lord appeared to Joseph in a dream and said, "Get up, take the child and his mother, and flee to Egypt, and remain there until I tell you; for Herod is about to search for the child, to destroy him." Then Joseph got up, took the child and his mother by night,

---

3. Cardinal William Keeler, "How Mary Holds Christians and Muslims in Conversation," in *Origins* 25, 36 (February 29, 1996), reproduced on the website of the United States Conference of Catholic Bishops, *https://www.usccb.org/committees/ecumenical-interreligious-affairs/how-mary-holds-christians-and-muslims-conversation/*.

4. It is worth noting the Jewish or Palestinian roots of some of the Carmelite saints and leading figures. Both St. Teresa and St. John of the Cross had Jewish ancestry; St. Edith Stein and Venerable Hermann Cohen were both Jewish; and the Carmels of Bethlehem and Nazareth were founded by St. Mary of Jesus Crucified, perhaps better known as Mariam, "the little Arab," who came from Galilee. The order, most importantly, has its origins in the Holy Land and is under the patronage of Our Lady of Mount Carmel, with Elijah as "father of Carmel."

> and went to Egypt, and remained there until the death of Herod. This was to fulfill what had been spoken by the Lord through the prophet, "Out of Egypt I have called my son." (Mt 2:13–15)

Once again, we see that Joseph is instructed through a dream and immediately acts on the angel's message. His fear for the safety of Mary and the child was valid. Herod's reputation as a ruthless tyrant was well known; he had executed his own sons because he feared they were a threat to his power. Ever obedient to the will of God, the couple quickly gathered what was needed for the journey, praying for God's protection. Unlike the Israelites who had been pursued by Pharaoh's army upon leaving Egypt, Mary and Joseph were told to flee to Egypt. What did it all mean? Where would it lead? With the Child Jesus concealed under her mantle and held close to her breast, we can imagine Mary speaking softly, singing a lullaby to her son, the words of Simeon echoing in her soul as it was being pierced by a sword.

Even if she had, as John of the Cross suggests, "supreme knowledge of the divinity" (C 7.4), Mary did not understand fully all that was taking place. Surely, both she and Joseph were plagued by questions. Perhaps especially disconcerting would have been the instruction to seek asylum in Egypt, the very land where the Israelites had been enslaved for over four hundred years. To understand Mary's suffering, we turn once again to John of the Cross:

> How do you endure
> O life, not living where you live,
> and being brought near death
> by the arrows you receive
> from that which you conceive of your Beloved? (C stanza 8)

These lines evoke an experience of exile—most profoundly, that of our life in this body while we long to live fully in God. In Mary's life on earth, this has a particular and unique resonance, for she was taking God himself into exile.

Mary's heart was pierced by a two-edged sword, suffering "from two contraries: natural life in the body and spiritual life in God. They are contraries insofar as one wars against the other" (C 8.3). On a natural level, Mary wanted only what was good for her son. At the same time, she understood that there were forces beyond her control and that she must surrender her will again and again to the Father. For the first time, Mary would have felt the full weight of the suffering that would be hers as the mother of Jesus and spouse of God. In anticipation of her son's mission for the salvation of the world, and later in offering her son on the cross, Mary would become both victim and priest.

MARY, THE NEW RACHEL

When Herod saw that he had been tricked by the wise men, he had all the male children in Bethlehem who were two years old or under massacred. Then was fulfilled what was spoken by the prophet Jeremiah:

> A voice was heard in Ramah,
> wailing and loud lamentation,
> Rachel weeping for her children;
> she refused to be consoled, because they are no more.
> (Mt 2:18; cf. Jer 31:15)

According to Scripture scholar Brant Pitre, the link between Mary and Rachel in the Old Testament is often overlooked, though similarities abound. As the mother of Joseph, who was sold and taken into Egypt, Rachel is considered the mother of

Israel. Her firstborn son saved the Israelites from famine. Mary, whose firstborn son saved the world from death, is known as the mother of the new Israel. According to Pitre, if Jesus is the new Adam, the new Moses, and the new Joseph, then Mary, the new Eve, is also the new Rachel.

Rachel was buried on the road to Bethlehem; Jeremiah's claim, "Rachel is weeping for her children" (Jer 31:15), implies that even from the grave, she was aware of the suffering of her children as they passed her grave on their way to Babylon where they would live in exile. As the new Rachel, Mary, aware of the massacre of the innocents that was about to take place in Bethlehem and the surrounding region, surely wept for the infants who would be slain. Continuing the comparison between Mary and Rachel, Pitre further identifies Rachel as an archetype of Mary as mother and intercessor for the people of God.[5]

To this day Jews, Muslims and Christians visit Rachel's tomb, pouring out their heart to the mother who dwells in a lonely grave to be near her suffering children. We don't know if Mary and Joseph passed the actual site of Rachel's tomb during their flight to Egypt, but we can be sure their hearts were grieving, for when a loved one dies, words cannot console; as the prophet exclaimed, "Why do you cry out over your hurt? / Your pain is incurable" (Jer 30:15). Yet as Mary, through the eyes of her soul, could see the light of redemption, so we can find new meaning in her constancy as model and intercessor, in the words of John of the Cross:

> Extinguish these miseries,
> since no one else can stamp them out;

---

5. Brant Pitre, *Jesus and the Jewish Roots of Mary: Unveiling the Mother of the Messiah* (New York: Image Books, 2018), 163–69.

and may my eyes behold you,
because you are their light,
and I would open them to you alone. (C stanza 10)

Even in the midst of danger and the wrench of leaving their homeland, Mary and Joseph would have found, gazing upon the infant Jesus, delight and consolation.

How long the Holy Family remained in Egypt is not known, but once again Joseph was instructed by an angel: they were to return to Israel, specifically to Galilee. "There he made his home in a town called Nazareth, so that what had been spoken through the prophets might be fulfilled, 'He will be called a Nazorean'" (Mt 2:23).

We know the end of the story; the gospels have been written, the Good News preached. But Mary was living in the moment with all the dangers and uncertainties that being the Mother of God entailed. As with all seekers who travel by faith and surrender their life to God, her knowledge was veiled. As with every disciple, her understanding of events evolved and was revealed only at the proper time. The prophet's words, "When Israel was a child, I loved him, / and out of Egypt I called my son" (Hos 11:1), identified Jesus as the new Moses, but only by walking with Jesus and witnessing the events of his life would Mary come to understand the fullness of the prophet's words: "The more I called them, / the more they went from me" (Hos 11:2). Although the words of prophecy rang true at the appointed time, Dominican priest Albert Nolan explains: "A prophecy is not a prediction, it is a warning or a promise. The prophet warns Israel about God's judgment and promises God's salvation. Both the warning and the promise are conditional. They depend upon the free response of the people of Israel. If Israel does not change, the consequences will be disastrous. If Israel does change, there will be an abundance of blessings.

The practical purpose of a prophecy is to persuade the people to change or repent. Every prophet appealed for a conversion."[6]

More and more, Mary would realize that the fate of her son was linked to a refusal of the people to accept him. This was already strikingly clear in the persecution of Jesus while he was still an infant. Perhaps, on the long road to Egypt, Mary would have understood something of the events—something essential, at any rate, even if she could not yet know the details—that would unfold as her son's identity was gradually revealed as the Suffering Servant in Isaiah (see Isa 52:13–53:12).

Among Mary's many titles, "Queen of Prophets" is one of several that bear the mark of Carmelite spirituality. Through her many apparitions, she continues to call her children to conversion of heart and to a return to God through prayer. Like Elijah on Mount Carmel, who proved to the Israelites that the Lord was the true God, Mary's many miracles draw the attention of believers and unbelievers alike. The miracle of the sun at Fatima, the roses and her portrait on the *tilma* of St. Juan Diego, and the countless miraculous healings at Lourdes testify to her supernatural intervention, but they are not the reason Mary visits her children. Like Elijah, who discovered and proclaimed the presence of God not in the sensational aspects of nature but in the gentle breeze, so Mary draws willing hearts to look beyond the miraculous and discover their true identity as the beloved of God through union with her son.

Teresa called prayer the entrance to the interior castle. And what is the interior castle if not the place where seekers meet God who awaits their return? As John of the Cross wrote, "In order that God lift the soul from the extreme of its low state to the other extreme of the high state of divine union, he must

---

6. Albert Nolan, O.P., *Jesus Before Christianity* (Maryknoll, N.Y.: Orbis, 1992), 19.

obviously, in view of these fundamental principles, do so with order, gently and according to the mode of the soul" (A 2.17.3). Surely, there could be no one gentler than our mother Mary, who stands ready to open the castle door so that, like the wise men of the East, we too can fall on our knees and worship the incarnate God, the Bridegroom, that our souls may be transformed in God through love.

INVITATION TO PRAYER

In welcoming the magi, Mary welcomed strangers from distant lands. She became a refugee when the Holy Family fled to Egypt to save Jesus from the violence of Herod. In our present world, where war and violence cause many people to flee their homeland, where strangers are in need of welcome, and where the plight of refugees is dire, let us turn to our heavenly mother, whose love knows no bounds, to open hearts so that we might look upon people of every nation and every race as children of God and brothers and sisters in Christ. And so we turn to our dear mother and ask her to intercede for us as we pray:

MEMORARE

REMEMBER, O MOST GRACIOUS VIRGIN MARY, THAT NEVER WAS IT KNOWN THAT ANYONE WHO FLED TO THY PROTECTION, IMPLORED THY HELP, OR SOUGHT THY INTERCESSION WAS LEFT UNAIDED. INSPIRED WITH THIS CONFIDENCE, I FLY TO THEE, O VIRGIN OF VIRGINS, MY MOTHER; TO THEE DO I COME; BEFORE THEE I STAND, SINFUL AND SORROWFUL. O MOTHER OF THE WORD INCARNATE, DESPISE NOT MY PETITIONS, BUT IN THY MERCY HEAR AND ANSWER ME. AMEN.[7]

7. The *Memorare* first appeared as part of a longer fifteenth-century prayer, "Ad sanctitatis tuae pedes, dulcissima Virgo Maria." Although traditionally attributed to St. Bernard of Clairvaux, the author is unknown.

Jerusalem:

Finding Jesus in the Father's House

ALTHOUGH SCRIPTURE IS SILENT about the Holy Family during the time they spent in Egypt until their return to Nazareth, it would be shortsighted to suggest that those years were insignificant. The same could be said about the hidden years of Jesus after the Holy Family returned to Nazareth until they traveled to the temple when Jesus was twelve years of age, for as St. Louis de Montfort noted: "There is, then, in Jesus a dynamic 'becoming' in his presence as the Kingdom of God. Having taken on the opaqueness of our humanity, which was in rebellion against the Creator, he becomes more and more transparent of who he is from the first moment of his conception: the reign of God."[1] The episode of Jesus in the temple at the age of twelve breaks the silence of his hidden years and is the first sign given by Jesus himself of his destiny which would become more and more transparent.

And yet the silence that surrounded those hidden years, as well as those that would follow, amplifies the importance of

1. Stefano De Fiores and J. Patrick Gaffney, eds., *Jesus Living in Mary: Handbook of the Spirituality of St. Louis Marie de Montfort* (Bay Shore, N.Y.: Montfort Publications, 1994), 1029.

human growth and development, even for Jesus. It was during those hidden years that Jesus grew in experience toward his future role as teacher and redeemer. Like the hidden communication that takes place within the soul, the hidden years were a time of grace and self-discovery, not only for Jesus but for the entire Holy Family. Trusting that God's plan would be revealed within the context of their lives, the Holy Family exemplified the importance of patience and prayerful listening as a prelude to action.

As the Son of God, Jesus was both human and divine, but neither his divine nature nor his human nature negated the existence of the other. As St. Thomas Aquinas explained, "Christ did not know everything from the beginning, but step by step, and after a time, i.e., in His perfect age; and this is plain from what the Evangelist says, viz. that He increased in *knowledge and age* together [Lk 2:52]."[2] We are not God, but we are called to be Godlike. And for those who are baptized, we have within us the Father, who is the Lover; the Son, whom the Father called his Beloved; and the Holy Spirit who is the Love between them. Therefore, we discover the person that God is calling us to be most often through reflection and prayerful listening to the hidden communication of the Holy Spirit, who loves us into becoming the image of the Son. Mary is an ongoing testimony to this truth, her life a continual state of communion with the Trinity. Yet despite her privileged state, or perhaps because of it, she continued to grow in wisdom and understanding through silent prayer, thus offering a perfect example for all who seek to know, love, and serve God.

Whether knowingly or unknowingly, each of us—every man, woman, and child—is impelled by the quest for wisdom and truth to seek and return to our place of origin, which is the heart of God. Repentance and grace are the means, but the

---

2. St. Thomas Aquinas, *Summa Theologiae* III, q. 12, a. 2, ad. 1.

choice to embark on the quest is ours. To better understand our own faith journey, reflecting on the hidden years of the Holy Family and their journey to and from Jerusalem, we can begin with the words from Matthew's infancy narrative, "Out of Egypt have I called my son" (Mt 2:15), which set the stage.

While the implied reference to Moses delivering the Israelites from Egypt is significant, equally important is the term *son*, because it indicates a paradigm shift. Throughout the Hebrew Scriptures, God's love relationship with the Israelites was mostly symbolized by conjugal love.[3] When Israel was faithful, Isaiah and Ezekiel referred to the people of God as a bride (Isa 54, Ezek 16:8), but when they turned away from God, the prophets addressed Israel as "harlot" (see Hos 2:5, Isa 1:4, Ezek 16:16). In the Song of Songs, the symbolism that accompanies the bride as she journeys toward union with the Bridegroom is erotic enough that it has been a source of embarrassment for some. However, given the intimate nature of God's relationship with his people, analogies, metaphors, and poetic imagery of conjugal love are the storyteller's only recourse. As theologian Christopher West points out, "Heaven's music is simply too much for mortals. Like the pitch that shatters glass, human beings simply cannot handle the infinitely transcendent melody of the Song that has been sung throughout eternity among the Father, the Son, and the Holy Spirit."[4] St. Teresa was shocked when a sermon by a priest, who spoke admirably about the Song of Songs, was met with laughter (see SS 1.5) and advised her nuns against such a response or listening in an uninformed manner: "It will seem to

---

3. On occasion, as will be seen, Israel is depicted as a child: see Ezek 16:4–6 and Hos 11:1–4, the latter of which includes the words quoted in Mt 2:15.

4. Christopher West, *Heaven's Song: Sexual Love as it was Meant to Be* (West Chester, Penn.: Ascension Press, 2008), 2.

you that there are some words in the *Song of Songs* that could have been said in another style. In light of our dullness such an opinion doesn't surprise me. I have heard some persons say that they avoid listening to them. Oh, God help me, how great is our misery! Just as poisonous creatures turn everything they eat into poison, so do we" (SS 1.3).

Although the beauty of the language eludes some, there is no better way to describe the love relationship between an omnipotent God and a sinful human race. Only the language of lovers bridges the chasm that separates humanity from divinity. Explanations are rendered meaningless when we try to account for God's faithfulness in response to humanity's penchant to stray. Only when plunged into the mystery of the Trinity do we find a community of love so infinite that it could not be contained in heaven yet embraces our life on earth. Even then, it remains beyond the ability of mortals to understand fully that "God so loved the world that he gave his only Son, so that everyone who believes in him may not perish but may have eternal life" (Jn 3:16). Only in the Trinity can we account for the variation in how God relates to us, from Bridegroom to Parent, as in this moving passage by the prophet:

> When Israel was a child, I loved him,
> and out of Egypt I called my son.
> The more I called them,
> the more they went from me;
> they kept sacrificing to the Baals,
> and offering incense to idols.
> Yet it was I who taught Ephraim to walk,
> I took them up in my arms;
> but they did not know that I healed them.
> I led them with cords of human kindness,

with bands of love.
I was to them like those who lift infants to their cheeks.
I bent down to them and fed them. (Hos 11:1–4)

Hosea's oracle is the story of a Father's love, which only makes sense within the life-giving divine communion of the Trinity. Only in the divine Three-in-One can God be Lover, Beloved, and Love. The shift from conjugal to parental love can best be understood through what Pope Benedict refers to as the "Messianic trilogy" from Isaiah:[5] "A shoot shall come out from the stock of Jesse" (Isa 11:1), "the virgin shall conceive, and bear a son" (Isa 7:14, English Standard Version), and "For a child has been born for us" (Isa 9:6). Pope Benedict explains that in the prophecy from Isaiah, the promise extends beyond David back to Jesse. From a stump that seemed to be dead, God launches a new beginning, in the person of Jesus of Nazareth. Though profoundly connected with God's promise and historical events, God intervenes, and the fruit of Mary's womb is brought about through her espousal to the Holy Spirit.

There has also been a development in the interpretation of the Song of Songs over the centuries, from understanding it as an image of God's love relationship with the Israelites to one of Christ's love for his church and finally as the love relationship between Christ and the individual soul. St. Bernard of Clairvaux, attempting to explain the divine love relationship intimated in the Song of Songs, wrote eighty sermons on it before death interrupted his continued reflections. The level of intimacy between God and humanity, even the erotic language, is essential to our understanding of Mary's relationship with the

5. Ratzinger/Benedict XVI, *Jesus of Nazareth: The Infancy Narratives*, 117. Note that in the quotation that follows this from Isaiah 7:14, *virgin* is the reading from the Greek given in the ESV and other translations as an alternative to *young woman*, which is used in the NRSV.

Father, Son, and Holy Spirit. Only in the Trinity can we understand the depth of Mary's pain when her heart was pierced, first by the sword that Simeon prophesied (see Lk 2:35), then as she and Joseph fled with Jesus into Egypt, fearing for their child's life, and now, years later, as they searched for Jesus when they discovered he was missing. Only in the Trinity can we appreciate the continual deepening of Mary's relationship with God and humanity as she followed her son every step along the way.

THE FINDING OF JESUS IN THE TEMPLE

> Now every year his parents went to Jerusalem for the festival of the Passover. And when he was twelve years old, they went up as usual for the festival. When the festival was ended and they started to return, the boy Jesus stayed behind in Jerusalem, but his parents did not know it. Assuming that he was in the group of travelers, they went a day's journey. Then they started to look for him among their relatives and friends. When they did not find him, they returned to Jerusalem to search for him. (Lk 2:41–45)

When Jewish boys reached the end of their thirteenth year, they were obligated by Jewish law to make a pilgrimage to the temple on these three major festivals: Passover, Pentecost, and the Feast of Tabernacles. In preparation for this obligation, it was not unusual for boys to be eased into adulthood by learning the commandments and traveling to the temple at the age of twelve. That the Holy Family had gone every year, and that Mary also went (it is believed by many scholars that women were not required to do so by law),[6] is indicative of their piety and of

6. See Ratzinger/Benedict XVI, *Jesus of Nazareth: The Infancy Narratives*, 121.

the importance the Holy Family placed on observing the law of Moses. However, since women were not allowed beyond the Court of Women in the temple, it is conceivable that Mary and Joseph would have agreed to meet at a designated place after the Passover celebration.[7]

Since Jesus was not yet considered an adult, for him to be with the women would have been as likely as his being with the men. And when we consider that the population in Jerusalem swelled during the time of festivals, it was entirely understandable that Mary and Joseph could have gone a whole day's journey before realizing that Jesus was missing (see Lk 2:44). That Jesus took it upon himself to remain in the temple is significant. Neither an act of disobedience nor a lack of consideration for his parents, the choice can be understood as an expression of his maturing self-understanding of his humanity and divinity—that is, who he was in relation to God, whom he then understood was his Father.

Just as Mary who, as a young girl, identified herself at the annunciation as the handmaid of the Lord, so Jesus seems to identify himself as he stood on the cusp of adulthood. That the testimony to his identity took place in the temple during the festival of Passover had additional significance, for Jesus was to become the Passover victim that would free the world from the bondage of sin. How much of this he understood at the time is unknown, though surely none of this was known to Mary or Joseph. All they knew was that Jesus was missing, and they were deeply alarmed.

The implications and nuances of Mary's grief as she searched for Jesus are so profound that the depth of her anguish can be appreciated only within the context of her union with the

---

7. "Josephus speaks in four places of the space on the temple mount which women. . . . were allowed to enter, and about the boundary beyond which they dared not go." Adolf Büchler, "The Fore-Court of Women and the Brass Gate in the Temple of Jerusalem," *The Jewish Quarterly Review* 10, no. 4 (July 1898): 683, *https://www.jstor.org/stable/1450393?seq=1#metadata_info_tab_contents/.*

triune God. By means of her privileged role as spouse of the Holy Spirit and mother of the Son of God, Mary had experienced the bond of love within the Trinity, yet she did not always understand the meaning of events as they unfolded. Like us, she had to live by faith. Nonetheless, her experience at the annunciation had given her a glimpse of the interaction of the three divine Persons. St. Teresa's explanation of the seventh dwelling places may shed light on this profound state: "When the soul is brought into that dwelling place, the Most Blessed Trinity, all three Persons, through an intellectual vision, is revealed to it through a certain representation of the truth. These three Persons are distinct, and through an admirable knowledge the soul understands as a most profound truth that all three Persons are one substance and one power and one knowledge and one God alone. It knows in such a way that what we hold by faith" (IC 7.1.6).

Teresa's description gives us an idea of what Mary experienced at the annunciation—relating personally to each of the three divine Persons, while also glimpsing the relationship within the triune God. Such a supernatural glimpse is indeed to "know," more than to believe, but once that experience is over, the necessity of living by the ordinary way of faith resumes.

John of the Cross provides additional insight regarding souls who reach this exalted state. In his poetic version of John's gospel about the Blessed Trinity, he wrote:

As the lover in the beloved
each lived in the other,
and the Love that unites them
is one with them,
their equal, excellent as
the One and the Other:
Three Persons, and one Beloved among all three. (R 1)

These were the divine realities that would have echoed in Mary's heart, ever since the unforgettable visit of the angel Gabriel, announcing that she would bear a son—the Son of God.

Mary's relationship to her son was also unique. In *Love of Eternal Wisdom*, St. Louis de Montfort noted that although the Son reigns as the Wisdom of the Father, the infinite and eternal Word being spoken through the incarnation, the Second Person of the Trinity is personally externalized in the humanity of Jesus.[8] The mystery of Jesus's humanity and divinity is beyond our ability to fully comprehend, but as we follow Mary through the gospel narratives, knowing what we know about the spiritual marriage, we see that her life on earth was a lived example of a person in communion with the Most Blessed Trinity. As John of the Cross explained: "It is not secret to the soul itself that has attained this perfection, for within itself it has the experience of this intimate embrace. It does not, however, always experience these awakenings; for when the Beloved produces them, it seems to the soul that he is awakening in its heart, where before he remained as though asleep. Although it was experiencing and enjoying him, this took place as with a loved one who is asleep, for knowledge and love are not communicated mutually while one is still asleep" (LF 4.14). And yet when it seems as though God is asleep, that, too, is a gift: for it entails waiting on God in faith and unknowing.

This absence of supernatural knowledge and awareness of God can perhaps help us to understand Mary's sense of utter loss when she discovered that Jesus was not among relatives or with the other pilgrims. His disappearance inflicted more than the human sorrow that would afflict any parent whose child has gone missing. Jesus was more than her son: he was the Son of

---

8. See De Fiores and Gaffney, *Jesus Living in Mary*, 1258.

God, the Word Incarnate. In the absence of the child of her womb, who had been entrusted to her care for the redemption of the world, the interior anguish of Mary's soul would have made her inconsolable. Her silent plea seemingly echoed the cry of David, "My God, my God, why have you forsaken me? / Why are you so far from helping me, from the words of my groaning?" (Ps 22:1). It was the cry that her son, feeling abandoned by God, would repeat from the cross (see Mt 27:46).

Teresa's explanation of what souls in the seventh dwelling places experience helps us understand Mary's anguish: "[The soul] has strong confidence that since God has granted this favor He will not allow it to lose the favor. Though the soul thinks this, it goes about with greater care than ever not to displease Him in anything" (IC 7.1.8).

As she and Joseph searched for Jesus, Mary surely feared not only for her son's safety but also that she had offended God by failing in the mission that had been entrusted to her. As the daytime sky became night and the darkness reflected the night within her soul, the heartfelt cry of the psalmist, "O my God, I cry by day, but you do not answer; / and by night, but find no rest" (Ps 22:2), became her personal agony. And as she sought Jesus among her fellow pilgrims, the psalmist's lament, "My tears have been my food / day and night" (Ps 42:3), became her own. Nothing, it is easy to imagine, could assuage her heart, torn like the veil of the temple that would one day be rent in two. Her continuous questioning of her family and fellow travelers—"Have you seen Jesus?"—and each negative response it brought would have convicted her soul. Yet despite the agony of this seeming absence of God, she trod the road that led back to Jerusalem, unaware that the fear and bitter anguish that stripped her soul of human esteem were but a foretaste of what would come to pass as she followed her son to Calvary.

"After three days they found him in the temple, sitting among the teachers, listening to them and asking them questions. And all who heard him were amazed at his understanding and his answers" (Lk 2:46–47). At the time, Jesus's listening audience didn't consider him a threat. After all, he was only a boy. Their fear and rejection of him would come later. But what did Mary and Joseph make of the sight before them? Luke tells us that they "were astonished" (Lk 2:48) And why not? Hidden from them was the divine mission that drew Jesus to the Father, a relationship that not even Mary, with all her loving knowledge, was able to fathom.

Relieved and exhausted, Mary responded on a very human level and did what any mother who was distraught would do. She confronted her son by reminding him of the pain he had caused his parents. Yet her words, "Child, why have you treated us like this? Look, your father and I have been searching for you in great anxiety" (Lk 2:48), were seemingly turned against her. "Why were you searching for me? Did you not know that I must be in my Father's house?" (Lk 2:49). In what seems like an unsympathetic response to his mother's anguish, Jesus declared in no uncertain terms that God is his Father, not Joseph. Just as Mary saw her identity in terms of her relationship to God, wishing only to carry out his will, so Jesus was making the same public proclamation. The declaration of his divine sonship justified his actions, making it clear that he must be about his Father's business, and that the Father's will must always take precedence over all other matters and relationships. Later in Jesus's public life, we hear echoes of this defining moment when he said, "Whoever loves father or mother more than me is not worthy of me; and whoever loves son or daughter more than me is not worthy of me" (Mt 10:37).

With the revealing of his identity as being one with his Father in heaven, Jesus's relationship with the Father parallels his mission, and so he remains in the temple despite the pain this would inflict on his earthly parents. Throughout the search and when Jesus was found, Joseph remained silent, even as Jesus seemed to dismiss his role as his father in a very public manner. Like Joseph, Mary also remained silent following Jesus's announcement. Although their hearts were filled with joy at finding their son, they were simultaneously broken; their silence was the only response to their felt solitude of absence, as described by Mary Paul Cutri, O.C.D.: "The *felt experience* of God's absence is *abandonment*. The solitude is felt not merely as aloneness, but as abandoned aloneness. . . . It feels as if God, who was once there for me, has left me. I am then taken to a more profound depth of solitude by the realization that what I once 'possessed' is no longer my possession. The truth I learn in solitude is that God never was and never can be my possession in the sense of power control."[9]

These words express the powerlessness and lack of control that we all must experience when we accept that God is in charge. With this realization, though, comes trust and a willingness to give God complete freedom over our lives. It also engenders a healthy knowledge of our own limitations.

The holiness of Mary and Joseph, whose entire lives were for and in God, was exemplary; and yet, they were mere human beings. Their sorrow was not a consequence of sin, but a consequence of human nature. Even the most perfect souls continue to be led into a deeper abandonment of self in God while they are housed within the confines of human nature.

As noted in the previous chapters, the spiritual marriage does not eradicate pain and suffering. The more advanced souls become, the more Christlike they become, and no one becomes

---

9. Mary Paul Cutri, O.C.D., *Sounding Solitude: An Approach to Transformation in Christ by Love* (Washington, D.C.: ICS Publications, 2010), 48.

like Christ without the cross. Many admirers of Mother Teresa of Calcutta were shocked when her letters and journal entries were made public in 2007, a decade after her death, because they exposed a depth of anguish they had not expected. One of her most striking journal entries testifies to the depth of her darkness, which she maintains lasted for more than fifty years: "Lord, my God, who am I that You should forsake me? The child of your love—and now become as the most hated one—the one You have thrown away as unwanted—unloved. I call, I cling, I want—and there is no One to answer—no One on Whom I can cling—no, No One—Alone. The darkness is so dark—and I am alone—Unwanted, forsaken—The loneliness of the heart that wants love is unbearable."[10] This outpouring may provide insight into the interior life of Mary, as well. Indeed, the more one has experienced God, the more devastating the subsequent confusion and darkness can appear.

The words of Jesus, "Whoever does not take up the cross and follow me is not worthy of me" (Mt 10:38), are not mere hyperbole. No one would experience Jesus's cross more acutely in their lifetime than Mary. The mother of Jesus was being prepared for the cross even before the cross became a Christian symbol of victory over death. Every event in Mary's life served as preparation and promise of what awaited her. Each event conveyed a message and meaning, and although both eluded her understanding at the time, the fullness of meaning would be revealed over time as she continued to journey with her son. From Mary, we learn that regardless of our relationship with God, the nearness of his love will always blind us because the price of love is faith, and the cost of discipleship is the cross.

---

10. Mother Teresa of Calcutta, *The Writings of Mother Teresa of Calcutta*, Mother Teresa Center. Used with permission.

This is the paradox of the night of spirit that pierces only to gladden the heart, as John of the Cross explained: "It remains to be said, then, that even though this happy night darkens the spirit, it does so to impart light concerning all things; and even though it humbles individuals and reveals their miseries, it does so only to exalt them; and even though it impoverishes and empties them of all possessions and natural affection, it does so only that they may reach out divinely to the enjoyment of all earthly and heavenly things, with a general freedom of spirit in them all" (N 2.9.1). What Mary and Joseph would have faced, on finding Jesus in the temple, was a stark reminder that he did not belong to them—that the only proper response was to hand him back, day after day, to the Father.

"Then he went down with them and came to Nazareth, and was obedient to them. His mother treasured all these things in her heart. And Jesus increased in wisdom and in years, and in divine and human favor" (Lk 2:51–52). Mary's silence following such momentous events resembles the repeated refrain "*I-don't-know-what*" in John of the Cross's poem "Not for all of beauty":

> For when once the will
> is touched by God himself,
> it cannot find contentment
> except in the Divinity;
> but since his Beauty is open
> to faith alone, the will
> *tastes him in I-don't-know-what*
> *which is so gladly found.* (P 12.5)

As in these beautiful, profound lines, much of what Mary experienced remained veiled in mystery. When words fail and clarity is withheld, some might stammer, attempting to explain the unexplainable, but Mary chose to remain silent, holding within her heart all that had transpired during the previous days. Her quiet acceptance of what was beyond her ability to understand exemplifies what John of the Cross describes in the above verses.

We can imagine Mary reflecting prayerfully on these mysterious events, just as we ponder, in prayer, significant events in our own lives. Unlike us, Mary was living the gospel events in real time, before they were revealed or written. Yet she trusted that God would disclose, in due time, the significance of all that transpired. Her life was an ongoing act of faith, shining like the stars in the nighttime sky. When coming face to face with unknowing, Mary acquiesced to God without attempting to find words to explain what God was accomplishing through her and through the life of her son, for she knew that words would always fall short. When her heart was gladdened as at Jesus's birth or troubled by the prophecy of Simeon, her silence assures us that God speaks in the silence of a listening heart in God's time, not ours.

Reminiscent of the boy Samuel who "continued to grow both in stature and in favor with the LORD and with the people" (1 Sam 2:26), Jesus returned to Nazareth awaiting the time for the inauguration of his public mission. The hidden years remind us of the importance of prayerful preparation as each person is called to further the kingdom of God. How and when this happens is not for us to know. We look to Mary, who returned to Nazareth in the company of Jesus and Joseph, caring for her family while engaged in the ordinary tasks that fell to women at the time.

When Teresa counseled her nuns that Jesus can be found amid the pots and pans as well as in the chapel (see F 5.8), she may have had Mary in mind. Her words remind us that all work is holy when done for the honor and glory of God. Even Jesus, the Son of God, modeled the importance of waiting on God's initiative, while he remained at home until he felt the call to begin his public ministry. When we are tempted to rush in and accomplish what we perceive as important work, even if the work involves furthering the kingdom of God, we do well to heed John's counsel in this regard: "Let those, who are singularly active, who think they can win the world with their preaching and exterior works, observe here that they would profit the Church and please God much more, not to mention the good example they would give, were they to spend at least half of this time with God in prayer, even though they might not have reached a prayer as sublime as this" (C 29.3). This is the right perspective, and it is especially necessary to cultivate when our work is in the service of furthering the kingdom of God. Only when our apostolic actions flow from an ever-deepening relationship with God will our work bear fruit. This means that God's call to union with himself always take precedence over and above any mission he may give us (see Jn 15:5).

Mother Teresa of Calcutta likewise stressed the importance of waiting on God in prayer, explaining that whatever work her nuns do is God's work, not theirs. To ensure their primacy of mission—to convey the love of God in whatever they do—she insisted that her nuns spend an hour in prayer before the Blessed Sacrament prior to beginning their day's work. For as she noted: "The work is God's work, the poor are God's poor. Let us put ourselves completely under the power and influence of Jesus, so that He may think with our minds, work with our hands, for we can do all things if His strength is with us. Our mission is to convey the love of God, who is not a dead God, but a living God."[11] Here, the saint of Calcutta intuits the lived experience that Mary was privileged to enjoy while living with Jesus.

---

11. Mother Teresa of Calcutta, *The Writings of Mother Teresa of Calcutta*, Mother Teresa Center. Used with permission.

Mary's intimate knowledge of her son, rooted in their day-to-day life, is almost more than we can imagine. The full reality of those hidden years can only be guessed at as we prayerfully ponder the love that was present not only between Mary and Jesus but within the Holy Family. Thus, the lived experience of Jesus, Mary, and Joseph serves as a model for all families. As an analogy of the perfect love that exists within the communion of the triune God, the Holy Family, like all families, is an apt image of the Trinity.[12] And yet, as with every earthly family, their physical situation was altered when Joseph died.[13]

It seems only natural that Joseph's death would have left a considerable void in the life of Mary. More than a husband, he had been her partner and protector. Together they had faced trials and crises, as well as a myriad of joys. Joseph had been her companion, a man of unwavering faith whom God had chosen for her. How her heart must have ached, as she watched his life slip away! And yet, she would have trusted that Joseph's physical death was not the end. We can imagine how Mary would have turned to Jesus for reassurance and support during her time of grief. Seeing his mother's grief at this time may account, in part, for the sensitivity that Jesus showed to the widow of Nain whose daughter had died (see Lk 7:11–14) or for the tears he shed when he saw Mary and Martha grieve over their brother's death (see Jn 11:35–36).

---

12. See Pope Francis, *Amoris Laetitia* (The Joy of Love) 29–30.

13. We may well suppose that Jesus's foster-father died before the beginning of the Savior's public life. In several circumstances, the gospels speak of the latter's mother and brothers (see Mt 12:46; Mk 3:31; Lk 8:19; Jn 7:3), but never do they speak of his father in connection with the rest of the family. See Charles Souvay, "St. Joseph," in *The Catholic Encyclopedia*, vol. 8 (New York: Robert Appleton Company, 1910), *https://www.newadvent.org/cathen/08504a.htm.*

Being a widow would change more than Mary's marital status. During the time of Jesus, carpenters occupied a middle place in social status, since they were trained and considered artisans, though less so in Galilee than in Judea. After Joseph's death, Mary would have lost this status and Joseph's income. The popular assumption that Jesus was trained as a carpenter by his father seems to give credence to a familiar maxim at the time of Jesus: that anyone who does not teach his son a craft teaches him robbery.[14] And yet the words spoken by the people in the synagogue, "Is not this the carpenter's son? Is not his mother called Mary?" (Mt 13:55), could cast doubt on the assumption. While it is possible that Jesus was not sufficiently skilled in carpentry before Joseph's death, the fact is that we simply don't know. Like most Jews in Galilee, Jesus would have had to eke out a living any way he could. If he had a trade, he would have been better off than some, though less so than the peasants who owned a small piece of land.[15]

The status of Mary and Jesus and the ordinary circumstances of their life in Nazareth remind us that outward appearances or success according to worldly standards are not reliable indicators when it comes to doing God's work. We see evidence of this again and again in the lives of the saints, and what often appears as a setback is actually an opportunity that prepares persons for the work that God has in mind for them to accomplish. St. Thérèse knew, from the age of nine (see S 58–59), that she wanted to enter Carmel, but it took another six years until she was granted admittance. Still, the years of waiting were far from wasted. Her love for God deepened, and she learned a great deal

14. See, for example, Rabbi Pesach Feldman, ed., "Outlines of Halachos from the DAF," at *https://dafyomi.co.il/kidushin/halachah/kd-hl-082.htm/*.

15. See William Barry, S.J., *Who Do You Say I Am? Meeting the Historical Jesus in Prayer* (Notre Dame, Ind.: Ave Maria Press, 1996), 31.

about herself. Once admitted, she was better able to devote herself to God with her whole heart. As with Mary and Jesus, the full meaning and scope of one's mission may not be recognized until after one's death.

After Thérèse died, *Story of a Soul* gained international renown, eventually leading to her being proclaimed Patroness of Missions and Doctor of the Church. Acting on the advice of his spiritual director, Gerard Manley Hopkins burned all his poetry. He was told it was too worldly. When a subsequent director advised him to continue writing, he compromised by allowing publication only after his death.[16] Similarly, the world discovered *Markings* by Dag Hammarskjöld only after his death in a suspicious plane crash while he was trying to broker a peaceful solution to a horrible war in the Congo. The esteemed peacemaker experienced his own dark night, concealing an intense spiritual life which he recorded over several decades in a journal of poems and meditations, left to be published after his death.

Neither Teresa nor John expected to reform the Carmelite Order when they entered religious life. God's plan unfolded over time. In one of her soliloquies, Teresa lamented, "It seems I want to be completely occupied in Your service, and when I consider well my own misery, I see I can do nothing good, unless You give me this good" (Sol 1.1). Later, realizing the folly of her complaining, she reminded herself that God was within her and that what matters is not what we do, but what God does.

---

16. Apart from a few uncharacteristic poems scattered in periodicals, Hopkins (1844–1889) was not published during his own lifetime. His good friend Robert Bridges (1844–1930), whom he met at Oxford and who became Poet Laureate of the United Kingdom in 1913, served as his literary caretaker. Hopkins sent him copies of his poems, and Bridges arranged for their publication in 1918. See Glenn Everett, Ph.D., "Gerard Manley Hopkins: A Brief Biography," The Victorian Web, *https://victorianweb.org/authors/hopkins/hopkins12.html.*

To suggest that hidden years are unproductive years is to undervalue the interior action of the Holy Spirit who is continually at work, loving us into becoming the person we are called to be. When we entrust our life to God, God meets us where are and then takes us where we could never venture on our own. This is the beauty of the contemplative life and validates the importance of the dark night. Prayerful listening is about waiting on God's initiative, then following God's will wherever it takes us.

The return of the Holy Family to their hidden life in Nazareth did not disrupt Jesus's mission; it advanced it. Grace and communion with God would have taught Mary that there is gain within purposeful sacrifice and that any loss is neither an absurdity nor a delusion, since for her loss was her gain just as loss would become infinite gain for her son, who died carrying out the will of his Father. When Mary accepted God's invitation to become the Mother of God, she couldn't have known that it would lead her to Calvary. Yet, paradoxically, although communion with the Trinity was her greatest consolation, it wasn't completely accessible. Some things remain veiled, even for those in the spiritual marriage, as Teresa explains:

> It should be understood that this presence is not felt so fully. I mean so clearly, as when revealed the first time or at other times when God grants the soul this gift. For if the presence were felt so clearly, the soul would find it impossible to be engaged in anything else or even to live among people. But even though the presence is not perceived with this very clear light, the soul finds itself in this company every time it takes notice. . . . To see [the three Persons of the Trinity] does not lie in its power, but depends on when our Lord desires that the window of the intellect be opened. (IC 7.1.9)

Once the shutters are closed, the light goes out and the room of the soul finds itself in darkness. And yet it is the night of faith that will eventually lead those who trust in God to the light. As we travel the path to union with God, we continue to look to our Blessed Mother who shows us the way.

Wishing to reaffirm her sisters in the role that Mary plays in our spiritual life, Mother Teresa of Calcutta wrote to them, "Mary is Queen of Heaven mainly because under her Divine Son, she has sovereign dominion in the administration of supernatural graces and benefits of God's kingdom. She is our mother because in her love she cooperated in our spiritual rebirth. . . . She continues to be our mother by nourishing the life of Christ in us . . . Holiness increases in proportion to the devotion that one professes for Mary. The way back to God is through the sinlessness and purity of life. Mary the Immaculate one is the way. She, our life, our sweetness, and our hope is the way to peace."[17] These words are a testimony to how Mary, whose life on earth was focused on her son, continues that mission today by directing all of us to Jesus as she embraces us as her children too.

Our work and our love become perfect when we do everything for Jesus, who alone can turn our sorrow into joy, darkness into light, and the cross into a sign of triumph. It was so for our mother, Mary, and so it is for all who journey to the new Jerusalem by way of Calvary. Surely, there could be no better guide than the handmaid of the Lord, who made the journey to Calvary not once but each time her heart was pierced as if by a sword.

---

17. Mother Teresa of Calcutta, *The Writings of Mother Teresa of Calcutta*, Mother Teresa Center. Used with permission.

INVITATION TO PRAYER

Not unlike the gospel account of Mary and Joseph who searched for the Child Jesus, our faith journey is fraught with trials, questions, and suffering. Yet their example shows us that trusting in the providence of God can enable us, as it did them, to move beyond natural deterrents and to surrender to the unknown, confident that God is with us. As we continue our pilgrimage toward union with God, we turn with confidence to our Lady, whose example inspires and guides us along the way. Just as Mary was kept safe from bodily harm throughout her travels, we ask her to keep us safe so that we may better serve God and reach our eternal destination where she lives and reigns with Jesus, her son. And so we make this prayer:

PRAYER TO OUR LADY OF THE HIGHWAY

O LADY OF THE HIGHWAY, BE WITH US ON OUR JOURNEY,
FOR ALL YOUR WAYS ARE BEAUTIFUL AND ALL YOUR PATHS ARE PEACE.
O GOD, WHO WITH UNSPEAKABLE PROVIDENCE DOES RULE AND GOVERN THE WORLD, GRANT UNTO US, YOUR SERVANTS, THROUGH THE INTERCESSION OF OUR WATCHFUL MOTHER, TO BE PROTECTED FROM ALL DANGER AND BROUGHT SAFELY TO THE END OF OUR JOURNEY. AMEN.[18]

---

18. "Prayer To Our Lady Of The Highway," The National Shrine of the Cross in the Woods, *http://www.crossinthewoods.com/our-lady-of-the-highway-shrine/*. Different statues and stained-glass murals depicting Our Lady of the Highway can be found in parishes throughout the United States in various forms, watching over cars and their passengers. A shrine of Our Lady of the Highway is located at the National Shrine of the Cross in the Woods in Indian River, Michigan.

6

Cana:

Looking to Christ, the True Bridegroom

JESUS'S HUMAN SELF-IDENTITY developed as he grew in age and stature. At the age of twelve, he proclaimed his sonship to the Father when he remained behind in the temple. During the wedding feast in Cana, he assumed the role of bridegroom. This identity makes sense only when viewed in conjunction with the prologue to John's gospel, which identified Jesus not only as the Son of God, but *as* God: "In the beginning was the Word, and the Word was with God, and the Word was God. He was in the beginning with God" (Jn 1:1–2).

At about the age of thirty, Jesus emerged from Nazareth, and from then on, his life took on a sense of urgency amid quickly moving events. He was baptized, identified as the Lamb of God, led into the desert where he was tempted, and emerged with a clear understanding of his mission. But it was Jesus's first miracle, at the wedding feast in Cana, that signaled the coming of a new covenant that would be accomplished through the Son of God on the marriage bed of the cross. As his public life began, not only did Jesus's life change, but Mary's did as well. Although Jesus's role as bridegroom didn't negate his role as son of Mary, it altered it, which happens when any son reaches adulthood and leaves home in search of a bride.

With Jesus gone from their home in Nazareth, Mary was left alone to contemplate in silence yet another transition. What did it mean? Where would it lead? Once again facing the unknown, silence became Mary's most precious adornment. Her heart became her cloister. Watching and praying, Mary kept vigil. Ever attentive to the mystery of divine love, her solitude shattered every voice except the voice of her spouse. The consummate contemplative, she whom we invoke as "Mystical Rose" showed by example that only within the felt absence of God, as she would have felt in the absence of her son, can we experience the gentle breeze of the Beloved. Eager to glean the dew that falls from the petals of this precious Flower of God, we draw close: her sweet whispers, barely audible, emerge from within the cell of her wounded soul. For although she had felt the absence of God, her heart was secretly gladdened.

As a deeper understanding of her son's mission closed in around her, Mary went forth. Writing about the soul's felt absence of the Beloved, John of the Cross says: "Through this love she went out from all creatures and from herself, and yet she must suffer her Beloved's absence, for she is not freed from mortal flesh as the enjoyment of him in the glory of eternity requires" (C 1.2). Mary's unique calling never caused her to retreat into isolation; rather, it drew her out into the world just as it drew her son. Once again, she was traveling, this time to a wedding feast in Cana, a seemingly ordinary event that would reveal an extraordinary mission. Little could she have known that her words and the actions of her son on that "third day" (cf. Jn 2:1) would be proclaimed and studied through millennia, the meaning so far-reaching that the boundaries of Cana would encircle the globe.

Only in retrospect can we appreciate the continuum of events that characterized Mary's life as building blocks, preparing the way for her son who would become the cornerstone.[1] As she traveled the roads of Galilee, her knowledge of all that would take place was piecemeal at best. Yet as she silently recalled all that had taken place, her life became an ongoing act of faith, based largely on remembering, which is not so different from our own faith journey.

As pilgrims seeking the God in whose image we have been created, we are inclined like Mary to pause and remember, for somewhere in the hidden recesses of our mind, perhaps on a preconscious level, we remember a time when our first parents walked with God in Eden. The memory is etched so deeply in our heart that to ignore it is impossible. Regardless of our religious upbringing (or lack of it), the search for wholeness is part of the human psyche, calling us to seek the transcendent. St. Elizabeth of the Trinity turned to Ruysbroeck to capture the underlying theology behind this profound reality, which she included in her work *Heaven in Faith*: "God in His eternal solitude already carried us in His thought. 'The Father contemplates Himself' 'in the abyss of His fecundity, and by the very act of contemplating Himself He engendered another person, the Son, His eternal Word. The archetype of all creatures who had not yet issued out of the void eternally dwelt in Him, and God saw them and contemplated them in their type in himself. This eternal life which our archetypes possessed without us in God, is the cause of our creation'" (HF 22).

The theological insight of this profound passage unearths a wealth of meaning hidden within the story that began in the Garden of Eden. Our understanding of the Genesis account, which explains humanity's deepest hunger for God despite the

1. See in particular these texts: "The stone that the builders rejected / has become the chief cornerstone" (Ps 118:22); "He looked at them and said, 'What then does this text mean: "The stone that the builders rejected / has become the cornerstone"?'" (Lk 20:17).

loss of our original innocence, continues to evolve. As we mine Scripture's hidden treasures, the same can be said of every biblical account, thereby confirming the word of God as the living word. Similarly, as our understanding of Mary evolves, our attraction to her is rooted in the promise of the woman destined to house the Word Incarnate. For only through the Son could the kingdom of God reign on earth as it does in heaven.

According to St. Louis de Montfort, "It is through Mary that Christ must become known and through Mary that he must come to reign more and more because it is through her that he came into the world."[2] It was his belief that Jesus does not fully reign until he is fully known and loved by all.

St. Louis de Montfort's claim highlights the role that we all play in bringing about the reign of God as we journey toward Christian maturity. Understandably, we turn to our heavenly mother for wise counsel so that, with God's grace, our intellect, memory, and will can be formed according to their purpose, which is to discover our identity in God. As we seek to become the person that God is calling us to be, Mary has a role to play, leading us to the Bridegroom of the church and of our soul.

THE WEDDING FEAST AT CANA

> On the third day there was a wedding in Cana of Galilee, and the mother of Jesus was there. Jesus and his disciples had also been invited to the wedding. When the wine gave out, the mother of Jesus said to him, "They have no wine." And Jesus said to her, "Woman, what concern is that to you and to me? My hour has not yet come." His mother said to the servants, "Do whatever he tells you." (Jn 2:1–5)

---

2. De Fiores and Gaffney, *Jesus Living in Mary*, 1216.

The account of the wedding feast at Cana appears in only one gospel, yet its preeminence as a sign of what is to come cannot be overstated. The Hebrew Scriptures are replete with images of the marriage covenant that describe the relationship between God and the Israelites. "Your Maker is your husband, / the LORD of hosts is his name" (Isa 54:5); "I will make for you a new covenant on that day. . . . And I will take you for my wife forever" (Hos 2:18–19).

A wedding celebration was a perfect setting for Jesus's first miracle, for the miraculous changing of water into wine portended more than merely rescuing the newlyweds from an embarrassing situation. It signified the beginning of the new and eternal covenant in the person of Jesus Christ as foretold by the prophets of old:

> The LORD of hosts will make for all peoples
> a feast of rich foods, a feast of well-aged wines. . . .
> It will be said on that day,
> Lo, this is our God; we have waited for him, so that he might save us. (Isa 25:6, 9)

The poignancy of this human-divine love relationship, though captured in the Song of Songs, left the Israelites with unanswered questions. What did it mean when lovers in the Song pine for each other, yet repeatedly fail to take opportunities to meet? Why does the bride search for her lover and then conceal herself? And why does the lover yearn for the bride and then hide? The unrequited love represents the ongoing journey of the soul's search for God. Although we often seek our heart's deepest desire in the wrong places, our misguided steps do not deter a God who reveals himself in the seeking and the yearning. Jewish philosopher Rabbi Joseph B. Soloveitchik attributes this interior conflict to what he characterizes as "Adam I" and "Adam II," who represent man in the two creation stories in Genesis. Adam I seeks to dominate, while Adam II seeks companionship. As a man of faith, Soloveitchik confesses that he is lonely but not alone, and that his experience of loneliness is invigorating, keeps him searching, and presses him into the service of God.[3] The rabbi's feelings of endless searching can be understood in view of what Scripture scholar Brant Pitre posits regarding the Jewish people: "If we follow the lead of ancient Jewish tradition and see the bridegroom in the Song of Songs as God, and the bride as the people of Jerusalem, then the Song of Songs does not end with a wedding, but with the bride (Israel) waiting for the bridegroom (God) to come."[4] The search for the Messiah continues in our own hearts, too, as he is ever elusive yet ever coming to us as if in an eternal Advent.

The Song of Songs can be understood on many levels. It has long been viewed by the Jewish people as the story of Israel's exile and return. For Christians, it is the story of paradise lost and found. But for the mystic, it is also about the soul's journey toward spiritual marriage. Only through the person of Jesus as Bridegroom can this marriage be consummated. We might understand that Mary, who is uniquely favored as spouse of the Holy Spirit, experienced the spiritual marriage of the mystics, and can give credence to the plea of the bride: "Let him kiss me with the kisses of his mouth! / For your love is better than wine" (Song 1:2). As a bride, Mary experienced the kiss of the Holy Spirit,[5] gracing her as "a lily among brambles" (Song 2:2).

---

3. See Rabbi Joseph Soloveitchik, *The Lonely Man of Faith* (New York: Doubleday, 2006), 2–13.

4. Brant Pitre, *Jesus the Bridegroom: The Greatest Love Story Ever Told* (New York: Image, 2014), 27.

5. "When the bride asks for a kiss therefore, she asks to be filled with the grace of this threefold knowledge [the Father and Son, and the Holy Spirit, of whom she has knowledge through the kiss]. . . . And it is certain that he makes this revelation through the kiss, that is the Holy Spirit.": Bernard of Clairvaux, *Sermons on the Song of Songs*, 35.

Ironically, the bride is also mother of the Bridegroom, an epiphany that will be revealed at Cana: not in words, but in the deepest center of her soul through the hidden communication of the Holy Spirit.

In the account of the wedding feast, Mary is introduced immediately: "On the third day there was a wedding in Cana of Galilee, and the mother of Jesus was there" (Jn 2:1). This signals that she has an important role to play. That the evangelist John notes that the event took place "on the third day" (presumably after John the Baptist's encounter with the priests and Levites in Bethany, when he identified himself as one sent to prepare the way for a greater one who would come after [see Jn 1:19–28]) is also significant, as Pope Benedict explains: "In the Old Testament, the third day is the time for theophany, as, for example, in the central account of the meeting between God and Israel on Sinai: 'On the morning of the third day there were thunders and lightnings. . . . The Lord descended upon it in fire' (Ex 19:16–18). At the same time what we have here is a prefiguring of history's final and decisive theophany: the Resurrection of Christ on the third day."[6] The wedding at Cana is likewise a theophany but in a domestic setting, which gives us much food for thought about the presence of the transcendent God in the ordinary circumstances of our lives.

Just as prototypes in the Old Testament contain more than is immediately understood, so Mary's interaction with Jesus at the wedding feast contains meanings that were only understood after Jesus's death and resurrection. On a natural level, Mary was attentive enough to notice that the wine was in short supply, but given her interior communion with the Holy Trinity, her request contained a profound insight, the full import of which may even have

---

6. Ratzinger/Benedict XVI, *Jesus of Nazareth: From the Baptism in the Jordan to the Transfiguration*, 250.

been veiled from her. Ordinarily, a lack of wine would be brought to the attention of the host of the celebration, who was the bridegroom. Instead, Mary brought the problem to Jesus, who was a guest at the wedding. This may suggest that she had a deeper understanding of Jesus's role and that the lack of wine at the wedding feast seemed an appropriate time for Jesus to reveal his mission. It certainly lends a better understanding of Jesus's response, "Woman, what concern is that to you and to me? My hour has not yet come" (Jn 2:4). His words bear a striking resemblance to those in the Song of Songs, where the bridegroom warns:

> I adjure you, O daughters of Jerusalem,
> by the gazelles or the wild does:
> do not stir up or awaken love
> until it is ready! (Song 3:5)

Undeterred by Jesus's reminder that his time was not for her to decide, Mary immediately turned her attention to the practical matter at hand, which was a lack of wine for the wedding guests. Without losing a moment or nursing feelings of rejection, Mary's focus remained on Jesus. Knowing his compassion for those in need, she was confident that he would intervene, and so she directed the servants: "Do whatever he tells you" (Jn 2:5). Mary's directive is significant not only for the servants but for all who wish to follow Jesus. Her instruction has been echoed through the centuries by saints and spiritual guides. St. Teresa's thinking was certainly in harmony with Mary's action, offering the following insight about souls whom God brings to the union of wills: "It is a union not based on words or desires alone, but a union proved by deeds. Thus, when the bride knows she is serving the Bridegroom in something, there is so much love and desire to please Him that she doesn't listen to the reason the intellect will give her or to the fears it will propose. But she lets faith so work that she doesn't look for her own profit or rest, rather she succeeds now in understanding that in this service lies all her profit" (SS 3.1). Once again, we see Mary serving, in her quiet way, as "the handmaid of the Lord."

Similarly, John of the Cross stressed the importance of action in addition to prayer and good intentions, for those who seek union with the bridegroom: "The soul is aware that neither her sighs and prayers nor the help of intermediaries. .. are sufficient for her to find her Beloved. The soul that truly loves God is not slothful in doing all she can to find the Son of God, her Beloved. . . . She must practice the virtues and engage in the spiritual exercises of both the active and contemplative life. As a result she must tolerate no delights or comforts" (C 3.1). This is not a call to hardship for its own sake but to an asceticism that aids us in finding the Lord and serving him more fruitfully in whatever situations we may find ourselves.

Mary not only directed the servants, but she informed them that Jesus was the one who would tell them what they were to do. Having gleaned from Jesus's response that his revelation as bridegroom would be accomplished by him when the Father willed it, she knew that the designated time was beyond her purview. She, who brought the Son of God into the world, assumed the role of intercessor. Believing in the divine nature of Jesus with unwavering faith, she aligned herself with the prophets who awaited the manifestation of salvation that would take place through him. After telling the servants to do whatever Jesus told them, Mary remained silent. As always, her focus remained on her son, the absence of words serving to amplify her wisdom for all time. Her humble surrender remains a model of discipleship, for "when the soul has departed from the house of her own will and the bed of her own satisfaction, outside she will find divine Wisdom" (C 3.3). Mary's pronouncement—her last-recorded words in the gospels—became her final proclamation, and her silence a manifestation of her contemplative spirit as her role in salvation history became more defined. The ever-humble virgin was a living example of the directive of John of the Cross who wrote: "You do very well, O soul, to seek him ever as one hidden, for you exalt God and approach very near him when you consider him higher and deeper than anything you can reach. Hence pay no attention, neither partially nor entirely, to anything your faculties can grasp. I mean that you should never seek satisfaction in what you understand about God, but in what you do not understand about him" (C 1.12).

Just as God is hidden, so the closer we come to approaching him, the more God draws us into the secret places of his heart, known only to him. This is evidenced in Mary, who from now on is effaced in the gospels insofar as her words are no longer recorded. Yet she remained a continual and vital presence by the side of Jesus, right up to Calvary.

According to Jewish tradition, the marriage of God and the Israelites was consummated through sacrifice and worship.[7] Understanding that the Lamb of God must be sacrificed, Jesus knew that his "hour" had not yet come. His priesthood remained in the future, at a time ordained by the Father who alone knew the final hour.

WATER CHANGED INTO WINE

> Now standing there were six stone water jars for the Jewish rites of purification, each holding twenty or thirty gallons. Jesus said to them, "Fill the jars with water." And they filled them up to the brim. He said to them, "Now draw some out, and take it to the chief steward." So they took it. (Jn 2:6–8)

---

7. See Kaufmann Kohler, et al., "Covenant," in *The Jewish Encyclopedia*, *https://www.jewishencyclopedia.com/articles/4714-covenant/*.

Six jars—one less than seven, which Jews regarded as the perfect number—can be seen as one more indication that the manifestation of Jesus's glory had not yet arrived. "On the seventh day God finished the work that he had done, and he rested on the seventh day from all the work that he had done" (Gen 2:2). It was left to Jesus to accomplish the work that would finally be complete when the Son of God with his final breath would utter, "It is finished" (Jn 19:30). According to the *Catechism of the Catholic Church*: "Justification is the *most excellent work of God's love* made manifest in Christ Jesus and granted by the Holy Spirit. It is the opinion of St. Augustine that 'the justification of the wicked is a greater work than the creation of heaven and earth,' because 'heaven and earth will pass away but the salvation and justification of the elect. . . . will not pass away.' He holds also that the justification of sinners surpasses the creation of the angels in justice, in that it bears witness to a greater mercy." (CCC 1994). Already Mary, aware of the sword that would pierce her heart, may have intuited that the road from Cana (and indeed from Bethlehem) would one day lead to Calvary.

Jesus, who would declare himself the source of living water, commanded that the purification jars be filled with water—a foreshadowing of his words to the Samaritan woman: "Those who drink of the water that I will give them will never be thirsty. The water that I will give will become in them a spring of water gushing up to eternal life." (Jn 4:14). The account of the miracle at Cana is slight on details, offering only the directives by Jesus to fill the jars to the brim, draw out some of the water, and take it to the wine steward. Did Jesus pronounce a blessing? Was there a visible change in the appearance of the water? We don't know, but the underlying message is clear: faith requires obedience, not proof.

John's narrative continues: "When the steward tasted the water that had become wine, and did not know where it came from (though the servants who had drawn the water knew), the steward called the bridegroom and said to him, 'Everyone serves the good wine first, and then the inferior wine after the guests have become drunk. But you have kept the good wine until now.' Jesus did this, the first of his signs, in Cana of Galilee, and revealed his glory; and his disciples believed in him" (Jn 2:9–11).

The water that Jesus changed into wine was most exquisite in taste, a manifestation of the extraordinary quality of miraculous wine, both then and in the future. Six jars holding twenty to thirty gallons each produced a huge quantity of wine, representing the abundance of God's love for us. Pope Benedict XVI, noting the significance of God's overflowing generosity, explains, "The superabundance of Cana is therefore a sign that God's feast with humanity, his self-giving for men, has begun. The framework of the event, the wedding, thus becomes an image that points beyond itself to the messianic hour: The hour of God's marriage feast with his people has begun in the coming of Jesus. The promise of the last days enters into the Now."[8] This statement goes to the heart of the episode at Cana, and it points to Calvary, not just as the inexorable destination in Jesus's life, but also as the wedding feast of the Lamb (see Rev 19:7).

The miracle at Cana was a manifestation of Jesus's divinity, but its meaning eluded the disciples. They couldn't have known that it was a sign of the wine that would be offered in anticipation of the final Passover, a sign that would be repeated during the celebration of the Eucharist for ages to come. Jesus's first miracle at Cana caused the disciples to believe in him, a belief that would be shattered when the wine of the Bridegroom would become a sacrificial offering, in the form of blood from the Lamb of God. All that would come later. For now, they were

8. Ratzinger/Benedict XVI, *Jesus of Nazareth: From the Baptism in the Jordan to the Transfiguration*, 252.

like souls in the second dwelling places of the interior castle, who Teresa insisted should not be undervalued: "However lukewarm these moments may be, God esteems them highly. And you, sisters, don't underestimate this first favor, nor should you become disconsolate if you don't respond at once to the Lord. His Majesty knows well how to wait many days and years, especially when He sees perseverance and good desires. This perseverance is most necessary here" (IC 2.1.3).

It is easy to look back, with the benefit of hindsight, on the early delights of the disciples. Jesus himself—and most possibly his mother, too—knew that these days would eventually be overshadowed by his ultimate destiny, and throughout his ministry, Jesus showed great patience with the disciples, despite their inability to understand. Yet the early rejoicing, as for beginners in prayer, is also an important stage, bonding us to the Lord no matter where we happen to be on our faith journey.

"After this he went down to Capernaum with his mother, his brothers, and his disciples; and they remained there a few days" (Jn 2:12). All that Mary had witnessed in Cana surely filled her soul with gladness. Remaining in the company of the bridegroom, like the bride in the Song of Songs, she sat down under the shadow of him whom the bride compares to the apple tree (see Song 2:3). Or as John of the Cross wrote:

> Beneath the apple tree:
> there I took you for my own,
> there I offered you my hand,
> and restored you,
> where your mother was corrupted. (C stanza 23, Redaction B)

Reference to the apple tree highlights the role of Mary as the new Eve. Her obedience to God set in motion the events that would set the world aright after the fall. She is the woman in Genesis, the bride whose fiat would facilitate the marriage between God and humanity and lead to her crowning glory. About the shade in this garden of delight, Teresa explained, "Oh, what heavenly shade this is! And who could say what the Lord reveals from it! I recall what the angel said to the most Blessed Virgin, our Lady: *the power of the Most High will overshadow you.* How fortified will a soul be when the Lord places it in this grandeur!" (SS 5.2; cf. Lk 1:35). Moving on in her *Meditation on the Song of Songs*, Teresa described how different wine is given to different souls, each producing a different effect according to the Lord's plan (cf. SS 6.2).

Given Mary's relationship with the Trinity, she was the recipient of precious wine, which she would have savored during those days in Capernaum. Should anyone misinterpret the words Jesus spoke to Mary at Cana as a rebuke, the days following the wedding feast, spent with his mother and his disciples, refute such thinking.[9] The days they spent in the company of each other testify to the deep affection Jesus had for his mother. That precious time was gift and grace, during which Mary drank in the sweet wine of his love, reserved especially for her. Here, we could lend her the words of the bride in John's *Spiritual Canticle*:

> In the inner wine cellar
> I drank of my Beloved, and, when I went abroad
> through all this valley,
> I no longer knew anything,
> and lost the herd that I was following.
>
> There he gave me his breast;
> there he taught me a sweet and living knowledge;

---

9. This is, of course, not the only evidence refuting the idea of a rebuke. Whenever Jesus addresses Mary as "Woman" in the Gospels, it evokes the great dignity and mission of Mary as the new Eve.

> and I gave myself to him,
> keeping nothing back;
> there I promised to be his bride.
>
> Now I occupy my soul
> and all my energy in his service;
> I no longer tend the herd,
> nor have I any other work
> now that my every act is love. (C stanzas 26–28, Redaction B)

This could be applied as a beautiful description of the life of Mary, the perfect disciple of her son. The years in which she had taught and formed him had passed, and now he was giving her a "living knowledge" as she occupied herself in his service.

Mary, spouse of the Holy Spirit, now in anticipation of the consummation of the marriage of Jesus with humankind that would take place on Calvary, surrendered herself to the service of her son. Teresa helps us appreciate what Mary experienced in the center of her being, where the abundance of God's love affected every element of her life:

> A greater or less amount can be given a person to drink, a good or better wine, and the wine will leave him more or less inebriated and intoxicated. So with the favors of the Lord; to one He gives a little wine of devotion, to another more, with another He increases it in such a way that the person begins to go out from himself, from his sensuality, and from all earthly things; to some he gives great fervor in His service; to others, impulses of His love; to others, great charity toward their neighbors. . . . He brings [the bride] into the wine cellar so that she may come out more abundantly enriched. It doesn't seem the King wants to keep anything from her. (SS 6.3)

Mary gave everything, and in return, Jesus made known to her everything he had heard from the Father (see Jn 15:15)—holding nothing back, especially from Mary, his mother and most perfect disciple.

The superabundance of grace with which Mary was blessed is evident in her great fervor in God's service, the divine impulses of love she received, and the perfect charity with which she was bestowed. Nothing in terms of grace was withheld from this precious daughter of Zion.

Just as Mary witnessed the patience and compassion of Jesus toward his disciples, so she accompanies us on the journey with the same patience and understanding, meeting us at whatever stage we find ourselves, even as she invites us to journey more deeply in faith toward her son. As a mother, knowing that infants cannot tolerate solid food, Mary offers the sweet milk of her loving counsel so that like the apostles we will persevere until our faith no longer depends on signs and wonders. She knows we must learn to walk before we can run—even though, like the apostles, we often run away when put to the test.

Like her son, Mary loves unconditionally. She is not only both bride and mother of the Bridegroom, she is also Mother of the Church and of every soul who longs for union with God. Uniquely positioned to come to our aid, she comforts and encourages us on our journey to her son, her sole advice being: "Do whatever he tells you" (Jn 2:5). When we falter and consider ourselves lost, forever falling short of her perfection, Mary reminds us of the many saints who struggled and overcame similar obstacles. These words of St. Thérèse, whose spirituality of childhood offers hope, are an invitation to pray as she did: "O my Jesus! what is your answer to all my follies? Is there a soul more *little*, more powerless than mine? Nevertheless even because of my weakness, it has pleased You, O Lord, to grant my *little childish desires* and You desire, today, to grant other desires that are *greater* than the universe" (S 193).

We do not have to achieve great exploits. On the contrary, we simply need to make ourselves little and receptive, and God will enable us to do what we could not do of our own efforts. The perfect disposition would be to embrace the vocation of servant of the Lord, as Mary did.

THE BRIDEGROOM REVEALED

John the Baptist identified Jesus as Bridegroom and referred to himself as friend of the Bridegroom, which—given that the episode of Cana occurred around the beginning of Jesus's ministry—was almost certainly after Jesus turned water into wine during the wedding at Cana: "I am not the Messiah, but I have been sent ahead of him. He who has the bride is the bridegroom. The friend of the bridegroom, who stands and hears him, rejoices greatly at the bridegroom's voice" (Jn 3:28–29).

In our contemporary American terminology, John would have been the best man. Could we not, then, refer to Mary as the maid of honor at the wedding feast, since it is the duty of the maid of honor to assist the bride before and during the wedding ceremony? More importantly, however, we should see Mary as the bride of Christ, for it was her vocation to stand by his side, accompanying him in his ministry, which would culminate in standing at the foot of the cross, wedded to the Lamb of God. It was Mary who told the servants to do whatever Jesus told them to do, and is this not the role that Mary fulfills for all her children—the bride of Christ, the church?

The evangelist Mark writes, "Now John's disciples and the Pharisees were fasting; and people came and said to him, 'Why do John's disciples and the disciples of the Pharisees fast, but your disciples do not fast?' And Jesus said to them, 'The wedding guests cannot fast while the bridegroom is with them, can they? As long as they have the bridegroom with them, they cannot fast. The days will come, when the bridegroom is taken away from them, and then they will fast on that day'" (Mk 2:18–20). Jesus declared himself the Bridegroom, thus acknowledging that it was a favored time, but that it would not last. In veiled language, he was already alluding to his death and departure. During times of spiritual consolation, we too can bask in the experience of God's presence, but all the mystics counsel that God's grace and efficacy are greater during those times when we do not feel the presence of God. As Teresa warned, a life of prayer cannot exist in the presence of self-indulgence (see W 4.2), and John of the Cross taught that there are many ways to fast, which he referred to as detachment: "In order to be united with him, the will must consequently be emptied of and detached from all disordered appetite and satisfaction with respect to every particular thing in which it can rejoice, whether earthly or heavenly, temporal or spiritual, so that purged and cleansed of all disordinate satisfactions, joys, and appetites it might be wholly occupied in loving God with its affections" (Lt 13).

Once more, Mary is our perfect model. On the road with Jesus, she had nothing: no place to rest her head (see Lk 9:58). Detached from everything, she had only Jesus—which means that she had everything.

Jesus, the Lamb of God, died for all; but the salvation that he brought about does not eliminate the responsibility of each soul to worship the Father in Jesus's name or to sacrifice personal gratification for the reign of God. During these troubled times, when it seems much of the world has lost sight of the Bridegroom, the experience of Mary reminds us that he is with us, especially during times of felt absence, and that prayer and fasting remain the entrance through the narrow gate. Mary's call to fast and pray, in some of her apparitions, remains perhaps her signature plea today, one that we can all take to heart. Like the bride in the Song of Songs, we await the wedding feast that will be celebrated at the heavenly banquet table with the bridegroom. We take comfort in knowing that, as the Gate of Heaven, Mary—who is in the company of the angels and saints—will greet us with sweet words of welcome when at last, purified and justified through faith, we hear: "My dove, my perfect one, is the only one, / the darling of her mother" (Song 6:9).

INVITATION TO PRAYER

As we continue our pilgrimage on earth, we can hold fast to the words that our dear mother spoke to the servants at Cana, "Do whatever he tells you." Yet, ever mindful of our weakness, we turn to Mary, confident that just as Jesus did not refuse her when she told him that the wine was in short supply, so he will not refuse to grant the petitions that she places before him on our behalf. And so we pray:

A PRAYER TO THE HEART OF MARY

O Heart of Mary, Mother of God, and our Mother, most amiable Heart, object of the complacency of the most adorable Trinity, and worthy of all the veneration and affection of angels and men; Heart most conformable to that of Jesus, of which Thou art the most perfect likeness; Heart full of goodness and compassion for our miseries, vouchsafe to melt our frozen hearts, and grant that they may be entirely turned toward the Heart of our Divine Savior. Infuse into them the love of thy virtues; inflame them with that sacred fire with which thou continually burnest. Take under thy protection the Holy Catholic Church; defend it, and be always its consolation, its asylum

Continued

INVITATION TO PRAYER *Continued*

AND ITS INVINCIBLE FORTRESS AGAINST EVERY ASSAULT OF ITS ENEMIES. BE THOU OUR WAY TO COME TO JESUS, AND THE CHANNEL THROUGH WHICH WE RECEIVE ALL GRACES NECESSARY FOR OUR SALVATION. BE THOU OUR HELP IN OUR WANTS, OUR RELIEF UNDER AFFLICTIONS, OUR COMFORT IN TEMPTATIONS, OUR REFUGE IN PERSECUTIONS, AND OUR SUPPORT IN ALL DANGERS; BUT ESPECIALLY IN OUR LAST CONFLICT AT THE TIME OF DEATH, WHEN ALL THE POWERS OF HELL WILL USE THEIR UTMOST ENDEAVORS TO SEIZE OUR SOULS IN THAT AWFUL MOMENT, IN THAT TERRIBLE CRISIS, ON WHICH DEPENDS OUR ETERNAL LOT. DO THOU, AT THAT TIME, O MOST PIOUS VIRGIN, MAKE US EXPERIENCE THE SWEETNESS OF THY MATERNAL HEART, AND THE EFFICACY OF THINE INFLUENCE WITH JESUS, THINE ALL-POWERFUL SON, BY OPENING UNTO US, A SECURE REFUGE IN THE SOURCE ITSELF OF MERCY, A SECURE REFUGE, THAT WE MAY ENJOY THE HAPPINESS OF BLESSING HIM IN HEAVEN FOR ALL ETERNITY. AMEN.

7

Galilee:

God's Family Redefined

MARY IS MENTIONED IN SEVERAL gospel accounts during Jesus's public ministry, but after the wedding feast in Cana, none of her words have been recorded. And yet it's unlikely that Mary would not have been aware of Jesus's activities, teachings, miracles, and frequent confrontations with religious leaders as they became more widespread. Early in his ministry, Jesus returned to Nazareth, entered the synagogue, and, reading from Scripture, announced:

> The Spirit of the Lord is upon me,
> because he has anointed me to preach good news to the poor.
> He has sent me to proclaim release to the captives
> and recovery of sight to the blind,
> to let the oppressed go free,
> to proclaim the year of the Lord's favor.
> (Lk 4:18–19; cf. Isa 61:1–2)

After Jesus read aloud the passage from Isaiah, he told the people that today the words of the prophet were fulfilled. At first the listeners were astonished. But then, as he began to preach the inclusivity of God's kingdom, they rose against him, intending to hurl him over the edge of a cliff, but he slipped away. We do not know if Mary was in the synagogue that day, but since it was the Sabbath (Lk 4:16), it seems likely that she was. And even if she was not, she surely heard about what took place, because Nazareth was a small village, where everyone was known and synagogue worship was a central aspect of the lives of most people there; news about something like this would certainly have found its way quickly to Mary. Like any mother whose child had put himself in danger, Mary would have been concerned for Jesus's safety. And yet on another level, she understood that following the will of God would involve risks that would lead to suffering. Once again, we can imagine her holding these things in her heart as she sensed that Jesus's mission would be fraught with danger. Mary's knowledge of her son's mission was intuited, due to her close relationship with him, but there was much that she could not know; she still had to wait until more was revealed in God's time. There is a parallel in the life of prayer, as when John of the Cross speaks about the knowledge of souls transformed in God through love. According to John, this secret or hidden knowledge of God, which he refers to as mystical theology, takes place in darkness and without our knowing. John explained, "This contemplation, in which the soul, by means of her transformation, has sublime knowledge in this life of the divine grove and its living beauty, is consequently called 'night.' Yet however sublime this knowledge may be, it is still a dark night when compared with the beatific knowledge she asks for here" (C 39.13).

Speaking for the soul, the Mystical Doctor continues, "When I shall delight in the essential vision of God, then the night of contemplation will have changed into day and light for my intellect" (C 39.13). As theologian Elizabeth Johnson writes, "For human beings today the ideal of perfection is not knowledge but *freedom*: for the twentieth-century person, the ideal person is someone who is free in a very deep way rather than someone who knows everything. . . . In genuine, true free human decisions, the future is veiled for us in some significant way, so that we sum ourselves up and hand ourselves over in real commitment without full realization of what the outcome will be."[1] Many people and saints, reflecting the attitude of Mary, have committed themselves in faith without any knowledge of where this will lead them.

For contemplatives, the inner work of discernment involves interpreting external events within the context of the transcendent. It requires moving beyond the senses to allow the Holy Spirit to enlighten and create a new way of seeing. "There is a way both to know and not to know what is outside of ourselves, both at the same time."[2] Mary herself stood at the crossroads of knowing and not knowing, traveling ahead—step by step, at times in darkness—as she embarked on her new role in the life of Jesus, accompanying him on his ministry.

Since Mary's entire life was an assimilation of her human experience with her life in God, she would have taken nothing at merely face value. Therefore, as news about Jesus's ministry traveled throughout the region of Galilee, where Jesus spent most of his time, Mary would naturally have been concerned about his safety. However, on a deeper level, she accepted what she knew was Jesus's response to the Father's will.

Much has been made about the gospel account of Mary and family members requesting to see Jesus. Deemed important enough to be described in all three synoptic gospels, the event could be misconstrued by a casual observer as a slight by Jesus toward his mother. However, a closer look reveals that

---

1. Elizabeth A. Johnson, *Consider Jesus: Waves of Renewal in Christology* (New York: Crossroad Publishing, 1994), 40.

2. Johnson, *Consider Jesus*, 39.

Jesus's response was not about Mary, but about the kingdom of God. According to the Gospel of Matthew: "While he was still speaking to the crowds, his mother and his brothers were standing outside, wanting to speak to him. Someone told him, 'Look, your mother and your brothers are standing outside, wanting to speak to you.' But to the one who had told him this, Jesus replied, 'Who is my mother, and who are my brothers?' And pointing to his disciples, he said, 'Here are my mother and my brothers! For whoever does the will of my Father in heaven is my brother and sister and mother'" (Mt 12:46–50).

Although this event is sometimes interpreted as though Mary and Jesus's relatives were trying to dissuade him from his mission, it seems inconceivable that Mary would try to do this. While his relatives may have been so inclined, it is likely that Mary agreed to accompany them, not to discourage Jesus, but to meet her kinspeople where they were on their spiritual journey, supporting them as she supports every person who seeks her help. On a natural level, Mary would not have missed an opportunity to see Jesus, whom she must have missed terribly ever since he left home.

Just as Mary surely used life events as teachable moments for Jesus when he was growing up, so Jesus, who grew to maturity at his mother's knee, would do the same with his followers. Indeed, Mary's influence on her son during Jesus's formative years would have been manifest in his words and teachings as an adult. When he was told that his mother and brothers were outside, wanting to speak to him, the occasion became an opportunity to teach the crowd about the inclusivity of the reign of God. To better understand the fullness of this Scripture passage, we need to examine it within the context of first-century Jewish culture.

From the beginning, the Jewish people saw themselves as a collective unit. When Abraham was called, he was told that his descendants would be as numerous as the stars in the sky. And later, Moses was called to free the Israelites from Egypt as a nation: "Then the Lord said, 'I have observed the misery of my people who are in Egypt; I have heard their cry on account of their taskmasters. Indeed, I know their sufferings'" (Ex 3:7). Over the years, the collective nature of the chosen people continued to be fostered, but they were also being formed as an exclusive body.

Under the kingship of David and of Solomon after him, Israel became a dominant force in the ancient Near East. The Israelites had been blessed as a people, a nation, and a great kingdom. When, during the time of Jesus, the Jews found themselves under Roman occupation, it reinforced their solidarity as a nation against the Gentiles. This solidarity reaffirmed their national identity and set them apart as a unique religious group that had been favored by the Lord. This explains the importance they had always placed on the law of Moses, for it was the law that bound them together as a people. Ties within Jewish families were blood ties, not just with the immediate family but, through marriage, to include the extended family. Dominican theologian Albert Nolan points out: "Not only were all members of one's family regarded as brothers and sisters, mothers and fathers to one another, but they identified themselves with one another. The harm done to one member of the family was felt by all. The shame of one affected all. Any man could say to an outsider, 'whatever you do to the least of my brothers, you do to me.' To his own kinsmen he could say, 'Whoever welcomes you, welcomes me; whoever is ashamed of you is ashamed of me.' Not that it was necessary to say it. It was taken for granted."[3] This gives us a helpful insight into the sense of belonging that Jesus would have had toward his family and kinsmen, and it invites

3. Nolan, *Jesus Before Christianity*, 74.

us to see the true meaning of family bonds in the way that we relate to other people within the Christian—and indeed the human—family.

Group solidarity is not unique to the Jews. Sayings such as "Blood is thicker than water" or a warning against "airing the family's dirty laundry in public" testify to the human tendency to protect those to whom we feel connected, regardless of the times or culture. Fierce loyalty to national boundaries, ideologies, ethnicity, or religious beliefs have led to an unrelenting series of wars throughout human history, but this was not how God envisioned his family. However, something even more insidious than family loyalties was being challenged when Jesus said, "Here are my mother and my brothers! For whoever does the will of my Father in heaven is my brother and sister and mother" (Mt 12:49–50).

Jesus was confronting the basic Jewish dynamic of separateness. First-century Jews understood that the only way they could survive Roman occupation was through unconditional loyalty to the law and to the temple, thereby separating themselves from everything pagan. Paying tithes and first-fruit offerings, keeping the Sabbath, and adhering strictly to the purity code became for many the way to separate all that was impure from those who were considered pure or righteous. As for those who taught and enforced this purity code, Jesus admonished them in no uncertain terms, saying, "Woe to you, scribes and Pharisees, hypocrites! For you cross sea and land to make a single convert, and you make the new convert twice as much a child of hell as yourselves" (Mt 23:15).

Anyone who could not meet their standard of approval was automatically discriminated against. Albert Nolan explains that the word *poor* extended beyond economic status to include all the oppressed and anyone who depended on the mercy of others. Further elaborating, he notes: "Sinners were social outcasts.

Anyone who for any reason deviated from the law and the traditional customs of the middle class (the educated and the virtuous, the scribes and the Pharisees) was treated as inferior, as low class. The sinners were a well-defined social class, the same social class as the poor in the broader sense of the word. . . . The laws and customs on these matters were so complicated that the uneducated were quite incapable of understanding what was expected of them."[4]

By contrast, Jesus's identifying the people in the crowds that followed him as his mother and brothers was meant as a teaching about the mercy and compassion of God, which was extended to everyone. He wanted the Jewish people to understand that it is not blood ties, health, economic status, or even religion that unites people. Holiness lies in doing the will of God, who is Father of all. Jesus was telling them that God wants all people to live together as a family, united by the desire to do God's will.

When we consider Matthew's account within the context of the events that took place prior to Jesus's teaching, the intention of Jesus is clear. Prior to declaring that all those who do God's will are his mother and brothers, he had told the Pharisees that "the Son of Man is lord of the Sabbath" (Mt 12:8). Next, he cured the man with a withered hand (see Mt 12:9–14), then a man who was blind and mute (see Mt 12:22) and many others who were coming to him. All this took place on the Sabbath and was followed by another confrontation with the Pharisees, who accused Jesus of casting out demons by the power of Beelzebul (see Mt 12:22–32). As often happened when Jesus was confronted by the Pharisees, he responded by questioning them. "If I cast out demons by Beelzebul, by whom do your own exorcists cast them out? . . . But if it is by the

4. Nolan, *Jesus Before Christianity*, 29.

Spirit of God that I cast out demons, then the kingdom of God has come to you" (Mt 12:27–28). At this stage of his public ministry, Jesus was identifying himself with the kingdom of God, and also acknowledging his oneness with the Father: "All things have been handed over to me by my Father; and no one knows the Son except the Father, and no one knows the Father except the Son and anyone to whom the Son chooses to reveal him" (Mt 11:27). Here, in giving thanks to the Father for revealing to infants what he had hidden from the wise and intelligent (see Mt 11:25), Jesus was acknowledging that patriarchal authority resides only in the Father, whose reign will come about through forgiveness, humble service, and compassion for the least among them. When we examine Jesus's response about his mother and brothers within this context, we can better appreciate the radical nature of his message.

If anyone could have understood Jesus's idea of the family of God, it would have been Mary. Her song of praise in response to Elizabeth's greeting praised the God of mercy who scatters the proud, lifts up the lowly, casts down the mighty, fills the hungry with good things, and sends the rich away empty (see Lk 1:41–55). Rather than taking offense at Jesus's new characterization of the family of God, Mary would have rejoiced, grateful that she was able to witness Jesus proclaiming the vision of a kingdom which she was privileged to understand.

DISCIPLESHIP AND THE CROSS

> Now large crowds were traveling with [Jesus]; and he turned and said to them, "Whoever comes to me and does not hate father and mother, wife and children, brothers and sisters, yes, and even life itself, cannot be my disciple. Whoever does not carry the cross and follow me cannot be my disciple." (Lk 14:25–27)

Jesus's teaching about hating family members may seem like a contradiction of his message about compassion and inclusivity, but it is really a teaching about priorities. The passage is frequently cited in reference to priests and religious who have given up family members in order to dedicate their lives to the kingdom of God. The decision by some to sacrifice the possibility of a biological family in fact expands their sense of family by embracing as family the people they are called to serve. In religious communities, members of their order or congregation become their family, since they support and assist each other in spiritual and temporal matters.

One ancient source suggests that Mary experienced this at an early age when she was taken to the temple at the age of three by her parents, Anna and Joachim. According to the non-canonical *Protoevangelium of James* (c. AD 145), Mary was left in the temple to fulfill a promise that her mother had made, which was to dedicate the child in her womb to the Lord. While most three-year-old children would cry if left behind by their parents, Mary's parents seemed to be aware of her unusual maturity, prompting them to wait until she was old enough to accept and at least partially understand what was taking place.

> Anna said: Let us wait for the third year, in order that the child may not seek for father or mother. And Joachim said: So let us wait. . . . And the priest received her, and kissed her, and blessed her, saying: The Lord has magnified your name in all generations. In you, on the last of the days, the Lord will manifest His redemption to the sons of Israel. And he set her down upon the third step of the altar, and the Lord God sent grace upon her; and she danced with her feet, and all the house of Israel loved her. And her parents went down marveling, and praising the Lord God, because the child had not turned back.[5]

---

5. *Protoevangelium of James*, 7–8, *https://www.newadvent.org/fathers/0847.htm.*

Although this source is apocryphal, and we can never know if the details are a historical account, it seems most likely that it contains, at the very least, the essence of Mary's trusting relationship with her parents, her piety, and her love of God.

Holding to the right perspective, Mary loved her parents, but her gaze upon the Lord superseded the natural love she had for Anna and Joachim. We see evidence of this same level of desire in those who dedicate their life to God when we read the lives of the saints. Early on in life, Thérèse knew that God was calling her to Carmel. For years she nursed her desire in secret, knowing she was too young. When she finally decided it was time to share her heart's desire with her father, it was not without great pain. In *Story of a Soul*, Thérèse shared the account, a prime example of the cost that both she and her father paid:

> I didn't know what steps to take to announce it to Papa. How should I speak to him about parting from his Queen, he who'd just sacrificed his three eldest? Ah! what interior struggles I went through before feeling courageous enough to speak! . . . Without saying a word, I sat down by his side, my eyes already wet with tears. He gazed at me tenderly, and taking my head he placed it on his heart, saying: "What's the matter, my little Queen? Tell me." . . . Through my tears, I confided my desire to enter Carmel and soon his tears mingled with mine. (S 107–8)

It is a privilege for us to have such a vivid firsthand account of this exchange; the dispositions of Thérèse, knowing that she would be leaving her beloved father, may well evoke the way in which Mary gave herself to God, loving him above all others.

St. Teresa of Jesus described her own interior struggle upon leaving her father when she decided to enter Carmel:

> I remember clearly, and truly, that when I left my father's house I felt that separation so keenly that the feeling will not be greater, I think, when I die. For it seemed that every bone in my body was being sundered. Since there was no love of God to take away my love for my father and relatives, everything so constrained me that if the Lord hadn't helped me, my reflections would not have been enough for me to continue on. In this situation, He gave me such courage against myself that I was able to carry out the task. (L 4.1)

Teresa's account is more striking concerning the inner struggles and shows the spiritual combat that can precede and accompany the gift of oneself. Again, this may shed some light on the experience of Mary possibly when leaving her parents at a very young age to serve God and certainly when accepting the message of the angel Gabriel, which could have led to her being repudiated by Joseph.

Like Mary, neither Thérèse nor Teresa turned back from their resolve, but not all parents are at the level of self-giving that Anna and Joachim were. In the case of St. Elizabeth of the Trinity, it was her mother who resisted the saint's continued pleas to enter Carmel. Her mother came to her, crying, "Why do you want to leave me?" To which Elizabeth responded, "Darling Mother, how can I resist the voice of God calling me? He is holding out his arms to me, telling me he is despised, scorned, forsaken. Shall I abandon him as well? He wants my sacrifice. I have to go however much it hurts me to leave you and cause you such heartbreak. I have to answer his call."[6]

---

6. Carmel of Dijon, *Elisabeth de la Trinité: Souvenirs* (Paris: Éditions St-Paul, 1945), 76, in Jennifer Moorcroft, *He Is My Heaven: The Life of Elizabeth of the Trinity* (Washington, D.C.: ICS Publications, 2001), 64.

At one point her mother gave her permission to enter Carmel, only to rescind it a few days later. Eventually, she told Elizabeth that she could enter when she turned twenty-one. Yet rather than discourage her, the delays strengthened Elizabeth's resolve, gifting her with a deeper understanding of her vocation, as recorded in a recent biographical account: "This time of uncertainty about being able to enter Carmel was valuable; she was able to penetrate to the inner heart of the Carmelite life that was union with God by love, rather than pining for the externals. She realized a true Carmelite spirit was not something that could be taken away from her; she could be a genuine Carmelite wherever she was."[7] Elizabeth's interior disposition offers hope to contemplatives, regardless of their state of life, knowing that the soul can become a cell of enclosure for those who are married, single, divorced, or widowed—saints and sinners alike.

God's family has no boundaries that can separate seeking hearts from union with the Divine. Jesus's radical summons is extended to all. His dining with sinners and Pharisees alike was a sign of respect for them, for no one was excluded from God's banquet table. Tax collectors, prostitutes, and those possessed by evil spirits were all invited. Jesus imagined God's family as one of unity, not of division. All who followed in his footsteps were to proclaim the reign of God to the world. Yet, knowing that not everyone would accept the invitation to take up their cross, Jesus predicted what the future would hold for his followers, when he said:

> I have come to set a man against his father,
> and a daughter against her mother,
> and a daughter-in-law against her mother-in-law;
> and one's foes will be members of one's own household.

7. Moorcroft, *He Is My Heaven*, 34.

> Whoever loves father or mother more than me is not worthy of me; and whoever loves son or daughter more than me is not worthy of me. (Mt 10:35–37)

Jesus knew that his disciples would have to be firm in heart in following him; without that resolve, which St. Teresa calls "resolute determination" (W 21:2), it is all too easy to turn back in the face of opposition.

Human beings create division, not God. We are free either to accept or to refuse Jesus's vision of the kingdom, but if we accept, there will be suffering. Edith Stein, born in 1891 to a German Jewish family, was not a religious person. Highly educated, she devoted her life to philosophy as an alternative to faith—that is, until she picked up a copy of St. Teresa of Avila's autobiography, *The Book of Her Life*. So taken was she with the saint's description of life in God that she read the book in one sitting, and after she finished it, declared, "This is the truth." Six months later, Edith was baptized a Catholic. Her mother never understood Edith's conversion, nor her entrance into Carmel, which took place twelve years later: "These decisions of Edith's pained her deeply, and it pained Edith deeply as well to witness her mother's grief over the matter."[8]

Sister Teresa Benedicta of the Cross (Edith's name in religious life) understood well Jesus's words: "'Servants are not greater than their master.' If they persecuted me, they will persecute you; if they kept my word, they will keep yours also" (Jn 15:20). In the last eighteen months of her life, she wrote *The Science of the Cross*, on the teachings of John of the Cross, the master of the dark night of the soul. As a member of the Jewish people, Sister Teresa Benedicta knew that death at the hands of

---

8. "I.C.S. Introduction," in Edith Stein, *The Science of the Cross*, trans. Josephine Koeppel, O.C.D. (Washington, D.C.: ICS Publications, 2002), xiv, xvii.

the Nazis could well be her destiny, but she remained faithful to the end. Like Mary at the foot of the cross, she held fast to the belief that the cross was a sign of victory, not defeat.

Heroic sacrifices are asked not only of men and women who are called to religious life. In modern times, Dorothy Day provided a striking example of how God's invitation to experience his love through union is extended to believers and non-believers alike. As a young adult, Dorothy had been an atheist, had an abortion, and had a child with a man who was not her husband. But it was her encounter with a Catholic nun, who instructed Dorothy in the Catholic faith, that led to her decision to be baptized.[9] Responding to God's gentle nudging, she renounced her former way of life, was baptized a Catholic, and dedicated herself to living with and ministering to the poor and marginalized in society. Eventually, it led to her founding the Catholic Worker movement, which is still thriving today. A single mother, she was nonetheless inspired by St. Thérèse of Lisieux. An irony to some, Thérèse's influence is an example of the expansive walls of the cloister, for in the end both Thérèse and Dorothy were led along the long and lonely road to Calvary.

At the age of thirty, when Dorothy first read the life of St. Thérèse of Lisieux, she wondered what this French bourgeois saint had to offer. However, after several readings of *Story of a Soul,* her understanding gradually shifted, leading her eventually to write a biography of the saint, eventually published in 1960. In the preface of her book, Dorothy explained the reason she undertook the project:

> My purpose in writing this book in the first place was to reach the 65,000 subscribers to the *Catholic Worker*, many of whom

---

9. Kate Hennessy, *Dorothy Day: The World Will Be Saved by Beauty: An Intimate Portrait of My Grandmother* (New York: Simon & Schuster, 2017), 48.

> are not Catholic and not even "believers," to introduce them to a saint of our day. . . . Also I wrote to overcome the sense of futility in Catholics, men, women and youths, married and single, who feel hopeless and useless, less than the dust, ineffectual, wasted, powerless. On the one hand Thérèse was "the little grain of sand" and on the other hand "her name was written in heaven"; she was beloved by her heavenly Father, she was the bride of Christ, she was little less than the angels. And so are we all.[10]

It is worth noting that Dorothy Day devoted several chapters of her biography of St. Thérèse to the saint's parents, Louis and Zélie Martin, who were canonized by Pope Francis in 2015. She described their love for God, the church, and one another, evidenced in some of the letters she included. She also recorded their daughter Pauline's testimony at their beatification: "My parents always seemed to me to be saints. We were filled with respect and admiration for them. Sometimes I asked myself if there could be others like them on earth, I never saw any such around me."[11] In the end, all five of their daughters gave their lives to God. Although Zélie Martin never lived to see four of her daughters enter Carmel, she must have rejoiced at their generosity. When the Martins began their life together, they could not have imagined that from behind the cloister grille, their daughters, especially Thérèse, would be known and esteemed around the world.

Saints come from every walk of life. Like Mary, they understood the cost of discipleship. They embraced a road that was fraught with personal pain, yet in the deepest center of their

---

10. Dorothy Day, *Thérèse* (Springfield, Ill.: Templegate Publishing, 1991), xii.

11. Day, *Thérèse*, 34.

being, they experienced the peace and joy that only God can give. As the life of every saint testifies, that which is indescribable from a natural perspective is accompanied by an interior experience of serenity. Those who practice the two most important commandments, which are in fact the one great commandment—to love God with one's whole heart and soul and mind and strength, and to love one's neighbor as oneself (see Mk 12:30–31)—find the actual road to intimacy and union with God a small price to pay when compared with the love of the Bridegroom. Sacrificing the earthly support of those closest to them for the sake of the kingdom, ironically, gifts souls with incredible spiritual support, which John of the Cross captured in his poem, "A gloss (with spiritual meaning)":

> My soul is disentangled
> from every created thing
> and lifted above itself
> in a life of gladness
> supported only by God.
> So now it can be said
> that I most value this:
> My soul now sees itself
> *without support yet with support.* (P 11.1)

Here, John expresses rightly that putting God in first place—understanding, like Mary, the cost of discipleship—creates strength through one's detachment and even greater strength through the support received from God himself coming to meet and sustain the person who gives up everything for him.

THE WORD OF GOD

Everything that relates to the incarnate Son of God bears the hallmark of the Holy Spirit and is an expression of the Father's gift to us. No one was more aware of this during Jesus's life on earth than Mary, in whom the Word of God had been conceived. And yet it remained her secret, even when "a woman in the crowd raised her voice and said to him, 'Blessed is the womb that bore you and the breasts that nursed you!'" (Lk 11:27). Jesus's response to the woman—"Blessed rather are those who hear the word of God and obey it!" (Lk 11:28)—would have been sweet music to Mary's ears. Carmelite Sister Mary Paul Cutri perhaps helps us understand Mary's disposition when she writes, "Solitude's savorings are transformative, like the sun's rays that change whatever they rest upon. Some effects burn profoundly, deep with lasting gifts of true joy, genuine humility, quiet peace, and gentle love. The human heart expands in inclusive compassion for others, nonintrusive understanding, and holy wisdom, as manifest in the gift of poverty of spirit."[12]

These words offer a perfect description of Mary, who kept her most precious secrets hidden well within the confines of her heart. The joy that accompanies perfect humility and detachment from all that God had accomplished through her was savored in the solitude of her heart, where God would reward her. Her delight existed in learning from the one whom she had nursed at her breast, for the language of the nuptial bed is not to be shared in the marketplace. Once again, John's poetry sheds light on the topic:

> There he gave me his breast;
> there he taught me sweet and living knowledge;

---

12. Cutri, *Sounding Solitude*, 82.

and I gave myself to him,
keeping nothing back;
there I promised to be his bride. (C stanza 27, Redaction B)

As Jesus and his companions lived out their long journey of ministry that would eventually end in Jerusalem, Mary's familial relationship to Jesus would evolve from being the mother of the young Jesus to being his bride at the foot of the cross. There, the full import of her motherhood would be completely realized, and she would become Mother of the Church, mother of the Mystical Body of Christ.

Of necessity, the mystics turned to metaphors when attempting to describe the state of a soul that is unable to do anything but quietly receive the superabundance of God's love, a love that is impossible to resist. As the psalmist wrote, "But I have calmed and quieted my soul, / like a weaned child with its mother; / my soul is like the weaned child that is with me" (Ps 131:2). St. Francis de Sales used the analogy of the breast when describing God's love for us, comparing it to a mother's breast engorged from milk that begins to flow at the sight of the infant, even before the child grasps hold of it: "Children may sometimes hold onto their mother's breast. . . . They may begin eagerly. . . . After a while, the milk eases their urgency and begins to lull them to sleep. Still, they do not let go of the breast. Their lips continue to make a slow and gentle movement. They swallow with the slightest motion. They do this without thinking about it, but it brings them pleasure. It is the same way with a soul that is at rest in God's presence."[13]

In line with this imagery, Catherine of Siena referred to the blood of Christ as essential milk that flows from the breast of

13. St. Francis de Sales, *Treatise on the Love of God* (Brewster, Mass.: Paraclete Press, 2011), 55–56.

the crucified Christ like mother's milk, nourishment that intoxicates the soul. This is the experience of intimate love for which we were created, and no one personifies this level of intimacy more perfectly than Mary. Her love is completely reciprocal in that everything she received she gave back to God in both word and deed. She credited nothing to herself and in giving her all to God became the richest human being of all. Her soul became a perfect vessel in which to receive God's love. Her sole desire was and remains that all may hear the word of God and keep it. Though all are invited to hear the word of God, not all will do so. Mary understood this, as did the saints, who therefore offered their lives as Christ did on the cross for the salvation of souls.

PARADOX OF LOVE

Sister Bridget Edman's play, *St. Thérèse of Lisieux: Nietzsche is My Brother*, portrays an imaginary dialogue between St. Thérèse of Lisieux and Friedrich Nietzsche. Thérèse appears to the atheist philosopher and invites him to come and pick roses with her, roses that have no thorns. Nietzsche replies, "I will only pick roses with thorns," at which Thérèse asks, "Why do you want to hurt yourself?"[14] This is the great irony of souls who long for happiness and wholeness yet reject God and hurt only themselves. Further into the dialogue, Thérèse tells Nietzsche that she loves him, but he refuses to believe her. The saint looks at him and calls him poor, which riles him because he needs to be seen as strong. Yet it is Thérèse with her childlike simplicity who reflects serene and gentle strength.

Throughout the gospels, this serene and gentle strength is visible in Mary as the first fruit of perfect poverty of spirit.

---

14. Bridget Edman, O.C.D., *St. Thérèse of Lisieux: Nietzsche is My Brother: A Play* (Washington, D.C.: ICS Publications, 2010), 84.

She is the image of grace. Free from all things, her disposition is empty of all concerns, except to please God and to do his will, for when God communicates himself silently and secretly, as he did in Mary, souls transformed in love cannot do other than please God and do his will: "As Christ lives in us more fully, we are bonded more strongly to others. The mystery of solitude reaches everyone and unites with every human emotion and experience. Within the ravages of human struggle and pain, communion erupts where every person incorporated in Christ Jesus is my mother and my brother and my sister."[15]

In this lies the fulfillment of Jesus's words: "The glory that you [Father] have given me I have given them, so that they may be one, as we are one" (Jn 17:22). Through Mary's relationship with the triune God, we are better able to embrace (though we will never fully understand) the mystery of Mary as daughter of the Father, mother of the Son, and spouse of the Holy Spirit. Mary can be seen as the continuous thread of God's love, beginning with the people of Israel, accompanying the Messiah, and reigning in God's kingdom as Queen of Heaven. St. Louis de Montfort taught that through Mary, people progress in the love of Christ more in one month than they would in a year through their own efforts. Mary is Queen of Heaven, but we could also give her the title of Queen of Heaven and Earth because God's family is her family.

On October 31, 1942, the consecration of the world to the Immaculate Heart of Mary was made by Pope Pius XII during a live radio broadcast from the Cathedral of Saint Mary Major in Lisbon, where the bishops from Portugal gathered for the celebration of the silver jubilee of Fatima. The consecration was renewed in St. Peter's Square on December 8 of the same year. The pope prayed on that occasion:

---

15. Cutri, *Sounding Solitude*, 122.

> To you, to your Immaculate Heart, We, as universal Father of the great Christian family, as Vicar of Him to Whom has been given all power over Heaven and earth, and from Whom we have received the care of all souls redeemed by His Blood, who inhabit the world; to you, to your Immaculate Heart, in this tragic hour of human history, we entrust, we offer, we consecrate, not only Holy Church, the Mystical Body of your Son Jesus, which suffers and bleeds in so many places and in so many ways, but also the whole world torn by strife, ablaze with hate and victim of its own sin. Give peace to the peoples separated from us by error or by schism, and especially to those who profess such singular devotion to you and in whose homes an honored place was ever accorded your venerable icon (today perhaps often kept hidden to await better days); bring them back to the one true fold of Christ under the one Shepherd.[16]

The consecration of the world to the Immaculate Heart of Mary was repeated by Pope John Paul II, on March 25, 1984. The act is always timely, because there was never an age when there was not one crisis or another. Yet we remain hopeful. Mary surrendered her life to God, guided by the Holy Spirit on a journey of faith toward service and fruitfulness, and she will help us do the same. The consecration of the world to Mary by a head of the church continues in our times the fulfillment of her role as mother—Mother of the Church, mother of us all. If we were all to live in peace, looking to Mary our mother to guide us to union with each other and with her son, that would be the family life "on earth as in heaven" that Jesus desires for his church.

---

16. In Timothy Tindal-Robertson, *Fatima, Russia and Pope John Paul II: How Mary Intervened to Deliver Marxist Russia from Atheism* (Still River, Mass.: Ravengate Press, 1991), 232–33.

INVITATION TO PRAYER

Just as we have seen Mary accompany Jesus beyond his early life into his public ministry, so Mary continues to accompany us, regardless of our age or status. As our mother and Mother of the Church, she lovingly watches over us, sees our struggles, and responds to our needs. No one is excluded from her maternal care, for she wants only what is best for us, as she pleads with her children to turn away from sin. Reminded of the many saints who have sought her intercession and found solace in her motherly love, we offer this prayer for the conversion of the world:

PRAYER TO OUR LADY, HELP OF CHRISTIANS

(*by St. John Bosco*)

Most Holy Virgin Mary, Help of Christians
how sweet it is to come to your feet
imploring your perpetual help.
If earthly mothers cease not to remember their children,
how can you, the most loving of all mothers forget me?
Grant then to me, I implore you,
your perpetual help in all my necessities,
in every sorrow, and especially in all my temptations.
I ask for your unceasing help for all who are now suffering.
Help the weak, cure the sick, convert sinners.
Grant through your intercessions many vocations
to the religious life.
Obtain for us, O Mary, Help of Christians,
that having invoked you on earth we may love and eternally
thank you in heaven.

8

Calvary:

At the Foot of the Cross

LIKE DARK CLOUDS THAT PRECIPITATED an afternoon thunderstorm, danger was in the air, and Jesus's disciples were growing increasingly uneasy. Dreams about an earthly kingdom that fueled imaginations during the early days of Jesus's ministry had worn thin, and talk about a cross with predictions of persecution and death made them fearful. Jesus's regular confrontations with the Pharisees were on the rise, and to make matters worse, his overturning the tables of the moneychangers in the temple area caused no small disturbance. Nothing was going as they had expected. But then, the ways of God rarely do.

How could Jesus's disciples have known that it was better "to have one man die for the people than to have the whole nation destroyed?" (Jn 11:50). Only Mary comprehended the magnitude of what was happening. She understood that obedience to the will of God would involve suffering as foretold by Simeon: "This child is destined for the falling and the rising of many in Israel, and to be a sign that will be opposed . . . and a sword will pierce your own soul too" (Lk 2:34–35). For thirty years, the prophetic words of this holy man had resided deep within Mary's heart, but they were never far from her mind whenever the forces of evil gathered.

The dueling emotions that Mary experienced during much of her life were revealed to St. Teresa during a vision of our Lord regarding consolations. He admonished the saint, saying, "When you see My Mother holding Me in her arms, don't think she enjoyed those consolations without heavy torment. From the time Simeon spoke those words to her, My Father gave her clear light to see what I was to suffer" (ST 32:1). Teresa's words help us to realize that Mary was carrying her cross daily, with Jesus, long before Calvary.

Years before St. Paul developed his theology of the cross, Mary lived it. During Jesus's ministry, the meaning of the words he had spoken to her at Cana became increasingly clear. The hour of her son's glorification would be accomplished not through wonders and miracles, but through faithful obedience to the Father. Yet Mary intuited that the Father never willed for the Son to suffer and die. Having tasted the depth of his love through her relationship with the triune God, Mary understood Jesus's words: "For this reason the Father loves me, because I lay down my life in order to take it up again. No one takes it from me, but I lay it down of my own accord. I have power to lay it down, and I have power to take it up again. I have received this command from my Father" (Jn 10:17–18). As Thomas Merton explained: "The Father willed the salvation of man, but left Jesus entirely free to specify the means. What is pleasing to the Father is not that the Son dies, but that he uses his free will fully to choose what he deems best in saving man. And Jesus out of love for the Father chose the way of total renunciation of power. At the same time, the will of the Father is in fact the will of God, i.e., of the three divine Persons. Christ chose to save man by renunciation of power, by total poverty, annihilation, and death."[1] The command

1. Thomas Merton, *Dancing in the Water of Life: Seeking Peace in the Hermitage*, ed. Robert E. Daggy (New York: Harper Collins, 1997), 53.

Jesus received was something he chose freely, out of love, and was not something imposed on him by the Father.

Jesus became one of us because he loves us. His way is a way of peace and compassion, but the cross is inevitable when justice intersects with injustice. Edith Stein described the cross as "the symbol of all that is difficult and oppressive and so against human nature that taking it upon oneself is like a journey to death."[2] How is it, then, that Christians are told that unless they take up their cross daily, they cannot be disciples of the Lord? The answer lies in the greatest paradox of all, which is that in taking up the cross, Christians choose life, not death. To view the cross apart from sin is to deprive the cross of its meaning, for the roots of the tree on which Jesus died reach all the way back to the Garden of Eden. Sin entered the world as "an abuse of the freedom that God gives to created persons so that they are capable of loving him and one another" (CCC 387). By contrast, Jesus's free choice of the cross was an expression of obedience and love and a testimony to the union of wills within the Holy Trinity.

The disobedience of Adam and Eve severed humanity's original communion with God. What sin had destroyed could be restored only through perfect obedience. So when the hour had come, the Son handed himself over to the Father and willingly laid down his life. Expanding on this gift of Jesus's self-offering, St. Paul wrote, "For you know the generous act of our Lord Jesus Christ, that though he was rich, yet for your sakes he became poor, so that by his poverty you might become rich" (2 Cor 8:9). As the new Adam, Christ restored humankind to the Father so that we might become "participants in the divine nature" (2 Pet 1:4). By the side of the new Adam, standing at the foot of the cross, was the new Eve, who participated freely in the birthing of the church, her fiat at the annunciation extending

2. Stein, *The Science of the Cross*, 17.

all the way to Calvary. Mary's gift of total self-giving to God initiated the untying of the knot that had bound humankind to sin. As the first and most faithful disciple of Jesus, Mary labored in the company of her son who, through his life, death, and resurrection, opened the gates of heaven—and death was no more.

There has been some discussion in recent decades about whether Mary's role in salvation history merits her being called by the title "co-redemptrix." Pope Francis, at his general audience on March 24, 2021, clarified that this title should not be used, as Jesus alone is the Redeemer.[3] What we can say, though, is that Mary, to a preeminent degree, cooperated with Jesus in his mission of salvation and that his passion was accompanied by Mary's "compassion" as she "suffered with" him on Calvary.

According to St. Thomas Aquinas, "God, in his omnipotence, could have redeemed the human race in many ways, but He chose to become man by being conceived and born of a woman. He saw this as the most fitting or appropriate means for redeeming the human race."[4] Mary was part of God's plan of salvation from the beginning. Through her fiat and throughout her entire life, Mary honored the human-divine partnership to which she had been called in a most singular and highly favored way. She cooperated in every way and accompanied Jesus throughout his life from the crib to the cross, regardless of the cost to herself. Therefore, it is impossible to consider salvation history without affirming the role that Mary played from the moment of her fiat to the agony she endured at the foot of the cross and beyond.

In 2004, when Mel Gibson's feature film *The Passion of the Christ* was released, it was criticized by some for its violent

---

3. Pope Francis, "General Audience," March 24, 2021, *https://www.vatican.va/content/francesco/en/audiences/2021/documents/papa-francesco_20210324_udienza-generale.html/*.

4. *Summa Theologiae* III, q. 1, a. 2.

portrayal of the crucifixion. Many people reported they closed their eyes during many of the scenes because they found that the sufferings that Jesus was forced to endure were too difficult to watch. Though it was only a movie, it speaks of Mary's courage and of the level of suffering that she herself endured as she watched her son being nailed to the cross. As he hung from the cross at the hands of his executioners, she remained for three long hours watching and waiting, faithful to the end. Mary's suffering on that day was unimaginable and reminds us of the prophet's lamentation:

> What can I say for you, to what compare you,
> O daughter Jerusalem?
> To what can I liken you, that I may comfort you,
> O virgin daughter Zion? (Lam 2:13)

In these moving words, it is easy to recognize a prefiguration of Mary on Calvary.

Christian tradition maintains that Mary accompanied Jesus on the road to Calvary. Her presence on Golgotha (see Jn 19:25–27) gives credence to the long-held tradition that she followed Jesus along the *Via Dolorosa*. Although nothing is recorded about the interior wounds she suffered, they were, surely, no less real and harrowing. In order to gain even partial access to the torment of a heart so assaulted and wounded, we turn to St. John of the Cross, who was gifted with an ongoing desire to suffer with Jesus.

John was born into a life of severe poverty, his life characterized by suffering and deprivation from early on. However, rather than embitter him, it increased his desire to unite his pain with that of the crucified Lord. While he was presiding at his first Mass, the Carmelite friar asked God, during the moment of consecration, to protect him from ever offending God mortally, and he heard the words, "I grant you what you ask of me." According to one of his biographers, "From then on, he is confirmed in grace and has a two-year-old child's purity of heart."[5] On a rare occasion of self-disclosure, John confided to his brother Francisco the following account:

> We had in the monastery a crucifix, and one day, as I stood before it, it occurred to me that it would be more suitable to have it in the church. It was my wish that not only the friars but those outside could also venerate it. And I did what I had thought of doing. After I put it up in the church as fittingly as I was able to do, I was standing before it one day in prayer—and then he spoke to me: Brother John, ask of me whatever I should grant you for the favor you have done me here! And on my part I said to him: Lord, what I wish from you is suffering which I may bear for you, and that I may be despised and disdained.[6]

This request of John's was granted, and the rest of his life became a crucifixion, inflaming his heart so completely that through his poetry and prose the church has reaped the benefits of his graced relationship with God. Without mentioning Mary by name, his lyrical account to his brother, opens a window for those who dare to gaze into the soul of this highly favored daughter of Zion. Like Mary who stood silently at the foot of the cross, John did not disclose all the inner workings of his heart—only enough to guide souls by way of a night that is sheer grace. Given his purity of heart and his desire to suffer, who better to guide souls through the suffering of Mary than St. John of the Cross? Only one who has gone through severe

---

5. Père Bruno de Jésus-Marie, O.C.D., *St. John of the Cross* (New York: Sheed & Ward, 1932), 53f.

6. Recorded by Thomas Perez de Molina, quoted in Stein, *The Science of the Cross*, 25.

trials can understand souls whose interior workings seem to thrive amid external suffering. To know that the cross carries within it—though hidden from outward appearance—a transformative grace and blessing is no small favor. John's biographers agree that his greatest experience of the cross took place while he was imprisoned in Toledo. Though he suffered mightily in body and soul, what he received in return was true self-knowledge and a heightened degree of enlightenment that has been a gift to the church and to the world. John emerged from his prison cell purified in soul and adorned with the highest level of virtue. His disposition was so inclined toward charity that when he spoke about his tormentors, it was as though they were great benefactors. His unfailing love of God and of neighbor gives new meaning to his words: "My Beloved, all that is rugged and toilsome I desire for myself, and all that is sweet and delightful I desire for you" (SLL 131). This is characteristic of his Christlike generosity of spirit.

MY "HOUR" HAS COME

Throughout John's gospel, Jesus alludes to his "hour" as a time when he would be lifted up and glorified, but it was always in the future. Before changing water into wine during the wedding feast at Cana, he told his mother that his hour had not yet come. However, during his final discourse, his language, though veiled, indicated that the future was *now*. In instituting the Eucharist on the night before he died, Jesus did so in anticipation of his passion and death, carrying the eucharistic reality into his suffering. According to the Swiss mystic Adrienne von Speyr, Jesus's plan for the church was for it to be his bride free from sin—and by implication, we could say, his helpmate in redemption:

> He wants [the church] to be his gift to men as the place in the world that is as free from sin as possible. He wants to

> make her his spotless bride, as a continual grace flowing from him, as the filial response to the eternal act of the Father's begetting. And now at the time when she is still with him, protected by him, in the act of becoming reality through him, he sees how sin accumulates around her. The first projection of the Church outside of him is a failure. . . . He will always remain the center of the Church even though she is in the world. He will give her to the world as something of himself: which makes it all the more terrible that already now she looks as she does.[7]

This passage also suggests the pain of Jesus in knowing how we fall short in his desires for us.

Darkness did not deter Jesus, the Bridegroom of the church. From the Upper Room he went forth into the night, knowing that his marriage to humankind would be consummated through his death on the cross. His hour of glorification was upon him, and somewhere in the dark of night, his mother would surely have wept tears he was no longer able to shed. Having surrendered himself to the Father, he was surrounded by night, not as a symbol or as an invisible, formless perception, but as a threatening force of evil that defies the light and all that is good. Having been thrust into the forces of evil during the Nazi regime, Edith Stein provides a graphic description of the dynamics of the spiritual "night" that can accompany the darkness of evil that surrounds it: "Just as light allows things to step forward with their visible qualities, so night *devours* them and threatens to devour us also. Whatever sinks into it is not simply nothing; it continues to exist but as indeterminate, invisible, and formless as night itself or shadowy, ghostlike, and therefore threatening.

---

7. Adrienne von Speyr, *The Passion from Within*, trans. Lucia Wiedenhöver, O.C.D. (San Francisco: Ignatius Press, 1998), 110.

Moreover, not only is our own being threatened through external dangers hidden by the night, but it is shocked interiorly by night itself."[8]

While Edith Stein warned her readers not to confuse this mystical night with the cosmic night—the sharp edges of which are muted by the soft glow of a moonlit cosmos—they both point to a fullness of meaning to be discovered. Edith's focus here is on the mystical night as she describes the effects it has on our interior life: "It casts the soul into loneliness, desolation, and emptiness, stops the activity of all her faculties, frightens her by threatening horrors it conceals within itself. . . . Night, however, the cosmic as well as the mystic, is something shapeless and something comprehensive whose fullness of meaning can only be indicated but not exhausted."[9]

This mystical night reflects something of the horrors into which Mary was thrust, along with her son, from the moment of his arrest to his death on Calvary. His physical pain became her inner pain as the sword that Simeon had foretold pierced her soul during the darkest hours of her suffering on Calvary. Who can explain love that deepens when afflicted or the anguish that strengthens the mind even as it wounds the soul?

Over the years, human sensibilities have sanitized the cross, depicting only the wounds where the nails and sword entered the body of Christ. The amount of blood is scant compared with what the scourging and the tearing of flesh would have produced. When the crown of thorns was placed on Jesus's head, it dug deeply into his scalp, causing copious amounts of blood to flow from his sacred head down into his eyes and upon his cheeks. This was the face and the body that Mary looked upon as she stood by the cross along with Mary the wife of Clopas and

8. Stein, *The Science of the Cross*, 39–40.

9. Stein, *The Science of the Cross*, 41.

Mary Magdalene. In utter disbelief at all that was taking place, their hearts would surely have echoed the voice of the prophet:

> Who has believed what we have heard?
> And to whom has the arm of the LORD been revealed?
> For he grew up before him like a young plant,
> and like a root out of dry ground;
> he had no form or majesty that we should look at him,
> nothing in his appearance that we should desire him.
> He was despised and rejected by others;
> a man of suffering and acquainted with infirmity;
> and as one from whom others hide their faces
> he was despised, and we held him of no account.
> (Isa 53:1–3)

Thus, the time had come for the great prophetic "Song of the Suffering Servant" to be fulfilled.

Throughout the ordeal, Mary stood by, watching her son stripped of his garments, perhaps the very ones she had woven with loving care. With his wounds reopened and the bones of his body laid bare, Jesus stood naked and humiliated, the scorn of his executioners. How could this gentle woman endure such horror and pain as she gazed upon her son? We find the answer in John's description of a person who has completely forgotten herself and now resides within the heart and the wounds of the crucified Savior. The consummate union sustains and liberates the soul, even as it wounds it, for in this spiritual marriage, as John of the Cross writes, "each surrenders the entire possession of self to the other with a certain consummation of love. The soul thereby becomes divine, God through participation, insofar as is possible in this life" (C 22.3). Mary's strength thus became God's strength, her soul, again in John's words, "all cauterized with the fire of [God's] love" that "dispatches its wounds like most tender flares of delicate love" (LF 1.8). John knew the fire of love at the heart of suffering.

We could conclude that the apostle John, Mary the wife of Clopas, and Mary Magdalene were also beneficiaries of these tender flares of love as they looked upon their Master, holding fast to their love for him. Looking about, did they wonder what had happened to Peter, James, and the others? Why were they not here? It was only days earlier that they had all watched Jesus lamenting outside the city, wanting to gather Jerusalem's "children together as a hen gathers her brood under her wings" (Mt 23:37). Now, even his closest friends had deserted him, except for John and a few women.

These faithful women, though unable to intervene, were surely grateful for John's presence. Despite any fear of the Roman soldiers, he led Mary close to the cross. As she bore the weight of Jesus's suffering in her heart, the composure and dignity of Jesus's grieving mother gave them the strength they needed to remain steadfast. Rather than allowing her grief to consume her with anger, Mary united her pain with that of her son as a first-fruit offering for the salvation of the world.

Denial, betrayal, fear, and hatred were nothing new in this world, nor would they end at the cross. This is the reason God's sacrifice on Calvary transcends time. Jesus's final hour on earth would last into eternity as the Lamb of God became the eternal now. Immersed in the heart of God, Mary's heart, blessed and broken, was offered on the altar of the cross as the beat of her heart became one with the beat of God's own heart. As Mother of the Church, Mary understood what was revealed to Adrienne von Speyr: "The Eucharist is instituted before the passion so that the Church will never have to suffer for one minute without a eucharistic consciousness. The Lord as Bridegroom sends his bride, the Church, consciously into suffering. He takes her with him; he makes the decision to suffer for both together . . . and when the time is right, he will send his Church into suffering with the same suddenness and anguish, so that she can participate with him."[10]

Just as Mary, in anticipation of what the church would suffer, lived this fully on Calvary, so we as church and members of the Body of Christ are called to live this as we take up our cross daily and follow Jesus, the Lamb of God.

MARY BECOMES OUR MOTHER

> When Jesus saw his mother and the disciple whom he loved standing beside her, he said to his mother, "Woman, here is your son." Then he said to the disciple, "Here is your mother." And from that hour the disciple took her into his own home. (Jn 19:26–27)

Addressing Mary as "Woman" can be understood as a reference to Eve in Genesis (cf. Gen 2:23). Jesus was not simply telling Mary to return with John to his home. His choice of words was never limited to temporal matters but reflected the wisdom of an all-knowing God. Aware that he was about to breathe his last and having only one more gift to give, he gave his mother to the world. He looked upon her as one whose soul had been pierced with a sword again and again, but whose love for God never wavered.

Having donned human nature, the Son of God understood the important role that mothers play in the lives of their children, though no mother is perfect. In giving us his own mother, Jesus was providing us with a spiritual mother as tender comforter, wise teacher, powerful intercessor, and ideal role model. Even before

10. von Speyr, *The Passion from Within*, 119.

Mary was born and became an example of perfect maternal love, the Hebrew Scriptures characterized the love God bore for humankind as motherly in nature. Knowing how crucial such love was for human survival, God spoke through the prophet:

> Can a woman forget her nursing child,
> or show no compassion for the child of her womb?
> Even these may forget,
> yet I will not forget you. (Isa 49:15)

This maternal love of God was made visible from the cross when Jesus bequeathed to us his mother. All this, so that we might have a mother to love—a mother who would nurture and protect, teach and guide us so that we might enter the kingdom of heaven when our hour comes. Jesus didn't wait for a response from his mother; there was no need. Mary's fiat at his conception was unconditional and beyond the constraints of time. Once addressed as "favored one," her "yes" to God was as everlasting as her love.

Jesus's gift of his mother to the world has served many who have lost their biological mothers early in life. Both St. Teresa of Jesus and St. Thérèse fled to Mary upon the death of their natural mothers. They sought her wisdom and guidance, but most of all they looked to her for motherly comfort during times when they each were deprived of the presence of their own mother. Mary reciprocated by giving them the succor and peace of mind they needed during so critical a time in their lives. The lengths to which Mary will go for her children have been demonstrated through her dramatic intervention in the life of the Palestinian Carmelite mystic St. Mary of Jesus Crucified, Mariam Baouardy, also known as "the Little Arab."

Born in Galilee in 1846 and orphaned before the age of three, Mariam was graced early in life with an interior voice from the Lord, asking her to devote her life to him. Mariam never forgot the Lord's request, and when, at the age of thirteen and now living in Egypt, she learned that a marriage was arranged for her by relatives, she resisted by cutting off her hair and refused to marry the man chosen for her. In response, she received a severe beating from her uncle. Months later, when she refused the pressure of a young Muslim man to renounce her faith and convert to Islam, he too attacked her, slashing her throat with a knife. Her assailant, believing she was dead, rolled her in a sheet and threw her out into a deserted street. Years later, under obedience as a Carmelite nun, she related that she had indeed been dead, saw heaven, and was bidden to return to earth as her "book was not yet finished." This is how one writer recounts the events that followed:

> With these words, the vision ended and Mariam found herself lying in a grotto, with an "unknown religious" by her side who said she had picked her up on the way, carried her to this grotto and sewn the wound on her neck. The habit and veil of the religious was as blue as the sky and unlike any of any other religious she knew. She spoke very little, moistened the lips of the sick child with a "sponge as soft as cotton" and made her sleep almost constantly. Mariam thought that she was in that grotto nearly four weeks. When she was well enough to go out, the religious took her to a church and asked for a confessor for her. On leaving the confessional the orphan did not find her benefactress. She was alone, deprived of all earthly protection.[11]

Later, she realized that this unknown religious had been Mary herself.

---

11. D. Buzy, S.C.J., *Thoughts: Blessed Mary of Jesus Crucified* (*Mariam Baouardy*) (Bethlehem, Palestine: Carmel of Bethlehem, 1997), 13.

After nine years that included work as a domestic and many hardships, "the Little Arab" entered Carmel in 1867. Throughout her life as a Carmelite nun, she was illumined by extraordinary lights of grace. Despite her fragile health, she founded Carmels in Mangalore (India), Bethlehem, and Nazareth. Suffering was her constant companion. While in India she heard Christ say to her, "I don't want you to remain one moment without suffering; if no one makes you suffer, I will change the minds of men to make you suffer. I want you always to suffer."[12] Once again, we are faced with the mystery of redemptive suffering. Jesus's words to Mariam only make sense when we consider suffering both in terms of the particular vocation of Mariam and also in terms of our redemption and as a manifestation of Christ's glory on the cross. In the words of St. Paul: "For the message about the cross is foolishness to those who are perishing, but to us who are being saved it is the power of God" (1 Cor 1:18). Citing with appreciation the invaluable insights that many saints have given us, Pope John Paul II wrote: "The saints offer us precious insights which enable us to understand more easily the intuition of faith, thanks to the special enlightenment which some of them have received from the Holy Spirit, or even through their personal experience of those terrible states of trial which the mystical tradition describes as the 'dark night.' Not infrequently the saints have undergone *something akin to Jesus's experience on the Cross* in the paradoxical blending of bliss and pain" (NMI 27).

In the light of this paradox, we may say that John's prison cell became a symphony hall giving voice to heaven's song in poetic verse, the sick bed of Thérèse became the nursery for her "little way," and Calvary became Mary's Mount Tabor. To help us understand the depth of such a complete transformation in

12. Buzy, *Thoughts*, 13–19.

love, we turn to John of the Cross, who cried out as if in ecstasy: "What you gave me (that weight of glory in which you predestined me, O my Spouse, on the day of your eternity when you considered it good to decree my creation), you will give me then on the day of my espousals and nuptials and on my day of gladness of heart, when loosed from the flesh and within the high caverns of your chamber, gloriously transformed in you, I shall drink with you the juice of sweet pomegranates" (C 38.9).

These "pomegranates"—the divine knowledge (cf. C 37.8)—thus inebriated John, whose heart song rejoices at the words of Jesus during his final discourse, when he prayed, "Father, I desire that those also, whom you have given me, may be with me where I am, to see my glory, which you have given me because you loved me before the foundation of the world" (Jn 17:24). To be "with" Jesus—already on this earth—and to live in union with God is the reason we were created, though the path will be different for every person according to God's unique plan for each of us.

God often plants the desire for a work in our heart before he asks it of us. We can see this from the life of the Discalced Carmelite friar Père Jacques Bunel, also known as Père Jacques de Jésus. While serving as headmaster of a boarding school run by his order, he preached a retreat to Discalced Carmelite nuns about Mary. Marveling at the privilege she enjoyed in bringing God into the world—she whom God made "full of grace" and called "Mama"—Père Jacques commented:

> God always prepares the being to whom he would confide a great mission. Each one of us has been and will remain chosen by God. He has given us a special mission to be the saviors of the world. Because we have this mission, we are chosen before others for his service of love. . . . Let us do as the Virgin Mary did. When the moment arrived, the angel came to reveal God's plan, saying: "Do you wish to accept the role

> of mother of the savior of the world?" She replied: "Fiat. . . ." She knew neither how this could take place nor how she would be able to reconcile it with her vow [of virginity]. Still she surrendered herself to God's will for her. And what do we do? What have we done with God's preparation in us?[13]

The following year, his words became a reality as he lived out his "special mission" to the end. After the Nazi invasion, he had taken in several Jewish refugees, for which he was arrested and sent to a series of four different camps. His heroic charity and tireless ministry there won him the esteem of prisoners and the wrath of the prison guards, who delighted in degrading the priest. When the prison camp where he was held was liberated, his health was so frail that he died less than a month later. Accounts about the heroic virtue that led to his torture began to surface after his death, as in this account of his carrying a beam of wood like the cross: "[One of his fellow prisoners] vividly described the mock processions in which Père Jacques was compelled to lead the weakest prisoners in feeble formation around the central pool for hours on end. Father Barbier, a survivor of the camp, later revealed how his brother priest had been stripped of his Carmelite habit and forced, nude, to carry an eighteen-foot beam on his shoulders as he circled the pool in a blasphemous parody of Christ's Passion."[14]

Reminiscent of her son's walk to Calvary, the sight of this holy priest bearing the wooden beam on his shoulder must have captivated the heart of the Mother of God. Just as the flares of divine love engulfed her heart when she gazed upon her son, so

---

13. Francis J. Murphy, ed. and trans., *Listen to the Silence: A Retreat with Père Jacques* (Washington, D.C.: ICS Publications, 2005), 35.

14. Philippe de la Trinité, *Le Père Jacques: Martyr de la Charité* (Paris: Desclée de Brouwer, 1947), 387, cited in Francis J. Murphy, *Père Jacques: Resplendent in Victory* (Washington, D.C.: ICS Publications, 1998), 102–3.

the same flame of love was transmitted to the heart of this humble friar. Though stripped of his Carmelite habit, under her mantle he would bear forever the mark of a Carmelite priest on his soul. In every way he had accepted her son's mandate when from the cross he said to John, "Here is your mother" (Jn 19:27). Like Mary, Père Jacques de Jésus—whose cause for canonization was opened in 1990—died the slow martyrdom of love. And with the same loving care that the beloved disciple showed toward Mary after Jesus's death, he exhibited loving care for the prisoners in the Nazi concentration camps, attending to their needs in whatever way was possible under such dire circumstances.

If our personal failures and sins lead to feelings of discouragement when reflecting on the lives of saints who exhibited such heroic virtue, we are not alone. Early in her life, St. Thérèse was likewise puzzled, musing over how the Lord seems to caress some souls from early in life, granting them such favors of grace that their baptismal robes are never soiled, while others never even hear about Jesus or the name of God. In answer to her dilemma she wrote:

> Jesus deigned to teach me this mystery. He set before me the book of nature; I understood how all the flowers He has created are beautiful, how the splendor of the rose and the whiteness of the Lily do not take away the perfume of the little violet or the delightful simplicity of the daisy. I understood that if all flowers wanted to be roses, nature would lose her springtime beauty, and the fields would no longer be decked out with little wild flowers. And so it is in the world of souls, Jesus's garden. He willed to create great souls comparable to Lilies and roses, but He has created smaller ones and these must be content to be daisies or violets destined to give joy to God's glances when He looks down at His feet. Perfection consists in doing His will, in being what He wills us to be. (S 14)

This understanding of the differences between souls may be one reason why Thérèse was not discouraged at not seeing herself as one of the heroic souls.

Yet even Thérèse, with all her simplicity and childlike confidence, did not escape her personal agony and dark night. When her body was slowly succumbing to death, her physical suffering and spiritual anguish led her by the way of abandonment as her solitary trials drew her into the garden of Gethsemane where darkness enveloped her. This is the mystery of suffering that Edith Stein termed the "science of the cross," which she explains in this way:

> When we speak of a *science of the cross*, this is not to be understood in the usual meaning of *science*; we are not dealing merely with a theory, that is, with a body of—really or presumably—true propositions. Neither are we dealing with a structure built of ideas laid out in reasoned steps. We are dealing with a well-recognized truth—a theology of the cross—but a living, real, and effective truth. It is buried in the soul like a seed that takes root there and grows, making a distinct impression on the soul, determining what it does and omits, and by shining outwardly is recognized in this very doing and omitting. . . . From this living form and strength in one's innermost depths, a perspective of life arises, the image one has of God and of the world.[15]

For Edith, as for John of the Cross about whom she is writing, that perspective of life was formed by the mystery of the cross.

"The *cross* is the *emblem* of all that has causal and historical connection with the cross of Christ."[16] Edith is writing here of the cross as symbol but also as reality. She further explains a

15. Stein, *The Science of the Cross*, 9–10.

16. Stein, *The Science of the Cross*, 42.

form of realism that she terms "holy realism." This, she tells us, is an "inner receptivity of the soul reborn in the Holy Spirit" and seen when one is "joyfully led and molded by that which it has received, unhampered by any mistaken inhibitions and rigidity."[17] Suffering in union with Christ can lead to this open receptivity to the cross and thus to spiritual transformation.

Regarding a soul transformed in God through love, John of the Cross commented, "it does not enjoy eternal life perfectly since the conditions of this life do not allow it" (LF 1.6). Like the Master in whose footsteps we follow, we live in an imperfect world where goodness exists side by side with evil. Yet, we know that good is victorious over evil, and this is ultimately made manifest in the glory of Jesus's resurrection from the dead.

THE GIFT OF OUR MOTHER

Jesus's bequeathing his mother to us as he was dying, and entrusting us to her, was not simply a symbolic gesture. It was his last will and testament by which we have been adopted into the family of God from which we had been estranged. Not only was the gift of Mary to us in accord with the Father's will, but it was in keeping with the Father's image of family, to include us all in union with his son. On being given his mother, "our tainted nature's solitary boast,"[18] the Virgin Mother of God became mother of us all. Therefore, we rightly proclaim that Mary leads her children to the Father through Jesus, her son, in union with the Holy Spirit, her spouse for all eternity. Mary, who is called "Seat of Wisdom," has shown by example what

17. Stein, *The Science of the Cross*, 10–11.

18. William Wordsworth, "The Virgin." See *https://allpoetry.com/The-Virgin.*

Edith Stein termed "holy realism," for throughout her life, Mary received and responded to grace with uninhibited, childlike simplicity. While on earth, Jesus invited children to come near, and he warned his followers that unless they became like little children, they could not enter the kingdom of heaven. At the same time, he knew that if we are to follow in his footsteps, we need a mother—*his* mother—so that we might become the person we are called to be.

Not all are called to heroic lives as reformers or martyrs, great prophets or priests. When St. Thérèse reflected on the First Letter of St. Paul to the Corinthians, not finding herself in any of the roles the apostle had mentioned, her discouragement turned to joy when she discovered that the greatest gift of all was love. This led her to exclaim:

> I finally had rest. Considering the Mystical Body of the Church, I had not recognized myself in any of the members described by St. Paul, or rather I desired to see myself in them *all. Charity* gave me the *key* to my *vocation.* I understood that if the Church had a body composed of different members, the most necessary and most noble of all could not be lacking to it, and so I understood that the Church *had* a *Heart and that this Heart was BURNING WITH LOVE. I understood it was Love alone* that made the Church's members act. . . . I understood that LOVE COMPRISED ALL VOCATIONS, THAT LOVE WAS EVERYTHING, THAT IT EMBRACED ALL TIMES AND PLACES. . . . IN A WORD, THAT IT WAS ETERNAL! (S 194)

Thérèse had discovered, with every fiber of her being, the truth that there is nothing greater than love. And there is also no greater sign of love than the sign of the cross: "For God so loved the world that he gave his only Son" (Jn 3:16).

As we travel the path to Christian maturity, an adage among spiritual guides warns seekers not to confuse the map with the territory. Scripture, the sacraments, and the teachings of the church serve as a road map for the journey. They are signposts that direct us along the way. They help keep us on the right path, guiding and strengthening us so that we will remain faithful and not lose sight of our destination. However, the territory is the unique landscape of each person's soul, where the cross intersects with life. We can look to the saints for inspiration, but while they are a help, their journey is not our journey. Only God knows the person we have been created to be. We are formed within the unique context of our life, for there are no carbon copies in God's creation.

The cross will always be a part of life, but the cross no longer stands on Calvary. It is embedded within the events of every person's life. It may take the form of the death of a loved one, the loss of a job, serious illness, war, poverty, or racial prejudice. Whenever and wherever injustice and pride intersect with truth and justice, the cross will follow, but so does the promise of the resurrection. Through Jesus, we have learned that in this life, death will always precede life as a means of reaching eternal life, but never as an end.

Surely, we have no better example of this truth than Mary, whose love for her son was so great and so deeply experienced that his suffering became her interior suffering. She, who was sinless, accepted suffering as she stood on Calvary in our behalf, sinners though we are. Through her communion with the triune God, Mary understood that through the death and resurrection of her son, eternal life would be ours.

INVITATION TO PRAYER

No one can fully appreciate all that Mary suffered as she accompanied her son during his final hours on earth, but neither can hearts remain untouched by all she endured. One of the most moving attempts to capture in verse the pain of our dear mother at the foot of the cross is the Stabat Mater, believed to have been written by a Franciscan friar named Jacopone da Todi in the thirteenth century, though some scholars have attributed it to Pope Innocent III, among others. This hymn focuses on the pain Mary endured (stanzas 1–8), followed by a prayerful response (stanzas 9–20). Mindful of all that Mary suffered, let us ask her to touch our hearts as we pray the response from this beautiful hymn, as a consolation to Mary that her son did not die in vain.

O thou Mother: fount of love!
Touch my spirit from above,
Make my heart with thine accord.

Make me feel as thou hast felt
Make my soul to glow and melt
With the love of Christ my Lord.

Holy Mother, pierce me through;
In my heart each wound renew
Of my Savior crucified.

Let me share with thee His pain,
Who for all my sins was slain,
Who for me in torment died.

Let me mingle tears with thee,
Mourning Him who mourned for me,
All the days that I may live.

Continued

INVITATION TO PRAYER *Continued*

By the Cross with thee to stay;
There with thee to weep and pray,
Is all I ask of thee to give.

Virgin of all virgins best,
Listen to my fond request:
Let me share thy grief divine.

Let me to my latest breath,
In my body bear the death
Of that dying Son of thine.

Wounded with His every wound,
Steep my soul till it hath swooned
In His very blood away.

Be to me, O Virgin, nigh,
Lest in flames I burn and die,
In His awful Judgment day.

Christ, when Thou shalt call me hence,
Be Thy Mother my defense,
Be Thy Cross my victory.

While my body here decays,
May my soul Thy goodness praise,
Safe in Paradise with Thee. Amen.[19]

---

19. Excerpt from the *Stabat Mater*, stanzas 9–20, trans. Edward Caswall; see *https://www.ourcatholicprayers.com/stabat-mater.html.*

The Upper Room:

Mother of the Church

JUST AS JOHN OF THE CROSS PROVIDED insight into the suffering of Mary during the passion and crucifixion of her son, so Teresa of Jesus provides insight to what may have transpired in the depths of Mary's soul during the post-resurrection days leading to Pentecost and beyond. Teresa's *Spiritual Testimonies*, in which the saint recounts graces she received, provide a window through which we can view the work of the Holy Spirit in souls who are united to God through the spiritual marriage and thus gain a further glimpse into the soul of Mary. As with Teresa, Mary's experience of the Holy Trinity within her soul would have resulted in complete consistency between her inner life and her outer deeds. Every brushstroke of the triune God revealed the work of the master artist who was transforming her soul.

This is not to suggest, of course, that Teresa's experiences were like those of Mary. During a vision of the Lord, Teresa was given to understand that "there couldn't be any fixed rule about the favors He grants us because sometimes it was fitting that they take place in one way and at other times in another way" (ST 12.5). So if the Lord chooses not to duplicate experiences in the life of any one person, how much more infinitely varied are the graces he grants to different persons according to their need and God's plan for them! That the Lord grants to every soul what is most helpful is one example of the infinite goodness and omnipotence of God, who favors each person according to God's generosity and the soul's interior disposition. God's investment of himself in every person and the extent to which he takes care of us were evident during Jesus's interactions with others, both before and after his resurrection. During the many appearances to his disciples after he rose from the dead, Jesus continued to meet the disciples where they were personally on the spiritual path. Jesus restored hope to Mary Magdalene as she wept by the empty tomb, offered his wounded hands and side to Thomas to dispel his doubts, and revealed himself on the road to Emmaus first by breaking open the Scriptures and then in the breaking of the bread. He asked his disciples—his friends—for a piece of fish to eat, proving that he was not a ghost. And he singled out Peter, not to chastise him for having denied him three times, but to invite him to profess his love—not once but three times. Then, despite Peter's penchant for missteps, Jesus entrusted him with the task of feeding his sheep. Through his actions, Jesus showed himself to be the manifestation and self-revelation of God's unconditional love and mercy. Mindful of human weakness and our heart's deepest concerns, God responds accordingly, providing for our every need.

Given that Jesus had deep regard and love, even for sinners, his love for his most-pure mother would surely have prompted him to appear to her and console her after all she had endured for him throughout his life, especially at the foot of the cross. Although no such event is recorded in Scripture, Teresa learned of the appearance during the following exchange with our Lord: "He told me that immediately after His resurrection He went to see our Lady because she then had great need and that the pain she experienced so absorbed and transpierced her soul that she did not return immediately to herself to rejoice in that joy. By this I understood how different was this other transpiercing, [than the] one transpiercing my soul. But what must have been that transpiercing of the Blessed Mother's soul! He also said that He remained a long time with her because it was necessary in order to console her" (ST 12.6).

This revelation of Jesus to Teresa about his appearance to Mary seems plausible. Having watched Mary suffer at the foot of the cross, Jesus felt her pain as surely as his own, and he knew that her suffering didn't end when his body was laid in the tomb. While images of the previous days played themselves out in Mary's mind, what was taking place in the depths of her soul? According to Teresa's description of a soul so united with the Trinity, Mary would have understood "as a most profound truth that all three Persons are one substance and one power and one knowledge and one God alone" (IC 7.1.6). Teresa further explains that through a mystical vision or an awareness of the Trinity, "all three Persons communicate themselves to [the soul], speak to it" (IC 7.1.6), and she adds that "in the extreme interior, in some place very deep within itself, . . . [the soul] perceives this divine company" (IC 7.1.7.). Thus it could be said that from deep within the cell of Mary's soul, she who is spouse of the Holy Spirit, mother of the Son and daughter of the Father would have experienced the presence of the Trinity and that it coexisted with the pain in her heart because of all that Jesus had endured. Reflecting on Mary's privileged state, we might wonder: Did the divine interior whisperings within the Trinity offer solace by revealing to her the depth of meaning in Jesus's words, such as in his prayer to the Father: "I made your name known to them, and I will make it known, so that the love with which you have loved me may be in them, and I in them" (Jn 17:26)? Or did she hear divine lamentations that eventually gave voice to the solemn reproaches that have echoed in the church throughout the centuries?

> My people, what have I done to you? Or how have I grieved you? Answer me! Because I led you out of the land of Egypt, you have prepared a Cross for your Savior. . . . Because I led you out through the desert forty years and fed you with manna and brought you into a land of plenty, you have prepared a Cross for your Savior. . . . What more should I have done for you and have not done? Indeed, I planted you as my most beautiful chosen vine and you have turned very bitter for me, for in my thirst you gave me vinegar to drink and with a lance you pierced the Savior's side. . . . My people, what have I done to you? Or how have I grieved you? Answer me![1]

Indeed, given all that she had experienced, how could Mary's heart not echo intimately the inner sighs of the triune God?

Jesus's death did not alleviate the pain that had pierced Mary's soul during his passion. Rather, it extended it into the hours following his burial, creating an invisible wound that would not or could not stop bleeding. As Teresa learned through the transverberation of her soul, the spiritual marriage is not devoid of pain. In the course of a subsequent vision, she was led to understand better the fullness of what had transpired. Once she was able to reconcile the coexistence of pain and deep interior joy, she immediately saw the connection with Mary:

> I have understood better what our Lady experienced, for until today—as I say—I did not understand the nature of the transpiercing. The body remains so torn apart that even what I write today causes suffering, for my hands are as though

1. "The Reproaches," taken from the liturgy of Good Friday in *The Roman Missal*, Third Typical Edition (Washington, D.C.: USCCB, 2011), 331–36.

> disjoined and in pain. . . . Even this morning I felt the pain, for while in prayer I experienced a great rapture. And it seemed that our Lord brought my spirit next to His Father and said to Him: "This soul You have given to Me, I give to You." And it seemed the Father took me to Himself. (ST 12.1, 3)

Considering these words and how wondrously Jesus consoled Teresa after her heart had been pierced, he would surely have bestowed even greater consolation on his mother for all she had suffered for love of him and the Father.

A revelation to Venerable Mary of Agreda, regarding the appearance of Jesus to Mary after he rose from the dead, takes us beyond Mary's pain and into the mystery of redemption by means of an ecstatic encounter with her resurrected son in his glorified body. Describing in greater detail what she saw as transpiring between Jesus and Mary during this encounter, the seventeenth-century mystic wrote:

> The glorious body of the Son so closely united itself to that of His purest Mother, that He penetrated into it or she into His, as when, for instance, a crystal globe takes up within itself the light of the sun and is saturated with the splendor and beauty of its light. In the same way the body of the most holy Mary entered into that of her divine Son by this heavenly embrace. . . . For some hours the heavenly Princess continued to enjoy the essence of God with her divine Son, participating now in His triumph as she had in His torments. Then by similar degrees she descended from this vision.[2]

While we cannot know to what extent Mary of Agreda's vision reflected historical events, her stress on the unity between Jesus and his mother conveys a profound reality.

---

2. Venerable Mary Agreda, *The Mystical City of God*, 453–54.

We needn't, however, depend solely on private revelation to suppose that Jesus would have appeared to his mother before making known his presence to the disciples. Early Christian writers intimated the likelihood of such an encounter between Jesus and Mary. Given the supernatural conception of Jesus and the church's teaching regarding the virginal birth, several church fathers have pointed to the resurrection as a sign that links Mary's womb with Jesus's tomb. They agreed that Jesus, the new Adam, and Mary, the new Eve, gave birth to the new Israel through their mutually shared pain, Jesus's physical and Mary's spiritual. Given this association, Jesus appearing to his mother, not only to comfort her but also to confirm her as the new Eve, seems plausible. One of the strongest pronouncements in this regard came from St. Ephrem the Syrian in the fourth century: "In your Resurrection you made your birth comprehensible, since the womb was sealed, and the sepulcher closed up.. . The womb and the sepulcher being sealed were witnesses unto you. The womb of the mother and hell cried aloud of your Resurrection: The womb conceived you, which was sealed; the tomb let you go forth which was closed up."[3]

St. Ephrem is making a connection between Mary's womb, which in her perpetual virginity remained sealed before and after the birth of Jesus, and the tomb of Jesus, sealed before and after his resurrection (Mt 28:2). The gospels proclaim only that

---

3. Ephrem, *Hymns on the Nativity*, 10.6–8, in Brant Pitre, *Jesus and the Jewish Roots of Mary* (New York: Image, 2011), 157. See also these words of Pope John Paul II in a discourse he gave in Capua on May 24, 1992: "It is known that some Church Fathers set up a significant parallelism between the begetting of Christ *ex intacta Virgine* [from the untouched Virgin] and his resurrection *ex intacto sepulcro* [from the intact sepulchre]": "Discorso di Giovanni Paulo II ai Partecipanti al Convegno Internazionale di Studi per il XVI Centenario del Concilio di Capua," *https://www.vatican.va/content/john-paul-ii/it/speeches/1992/may/documents/hf_jp-ii_spe_19920524_concilio-capua.html.*

the tomb was empty when Jesus rose from the dead. There were no witnesses to the resurrection, which in one scholar's mind confirms the ancient symbolism of the sealed womb and the sealed tomb from which Jesus miraculously exited.[4] Mary's virginal womb remained intact and empty following the birth of Jesus, an archetype of the empty tomb from which Jesus would miraculously escape death.

Jesus as the new Adam appearing to the new Eve is a cause for our rejoicing. From the moment of her fiat to her agony at the foot of the cross, Mary cooperated in the spiritual redemption of humankind. She accompanied the Son of God from womb to tomb. Pope St. John Paul II often highlighted Mary's role in salvation history and her participation in the redemptive work of Christ. What is surely her most profound title, "Mother of God," is acknowledged and invoked each time the "Hail Mary" is prayed.

The gratitude that Jesus must have felt toward his mother for all she had endured would not have gone unrewarded by him. When he was on earth, Jesus promised eternal life to those who give water or food to the needy or who perform acts of kindness in his name. How much more would he wish to reward his mother in this life and in the life to come for her participation in the act of redemption and the salvation of the world in his name? After she had witnessed her son's passion and death, the image of his suffering was preserved forever in Mary's heart, and yet coexisting with her pain was the ability to rejoice in what God had done. Mary, as mother of the suffering Christ, understood the ravages of sin on the human race and the price her son paid to restore humanity's communion with God. Having lived her entire life from within her soul's deepest center, in union with the Trinity, Mary exemplified the fullness of what

---

4. Pitre, *Jesus and the Jewish Roots of Mary*, 157–58.

persons can experience on this side of physical death. Her experiential wisdom and knowledge of God exceeded that of every other living creature and positioned her perfectly for her role as "Comforter of the Afflicted" and "Help of Christians."[5]

According to Scripture, Mary remained with the disciples after Jesus ascended into heaven. Her presence would have been a source of reassurance, since even after Jesus's resurrection, he remained an enigma for them. The many appearances of Jesus to his disciples did little to dispel their confusion concerning their Master's mission and the role they were to play. And his resurrection seemed to revive old expectations of an earthly kingdom: "When they had come together, they asked him, 'Lord, is this the time when you will restore the kingdom to Israel?'" (Acts 1:6). Trusting that the apostles would understand and receive the grace needed to continue her son's mission, Mary continued to hold them in her heart. Praying for them and with them, she remained confident that Jesus had not called them in vain. Lest her presence among them fill them with shame—their guilt standing in sharp contrast with the courage of this gentle woman—Mary would have been the wounded healer in their midst. When the twelve-year-old Jesus had been lost for three days, Mary, believing she had failed God, knew the pain that accompanies human weakness. And so, her immaculate heart ached for them. Like her son who was wounded for our sins, she looked upon them with love, knowing they had already been forgiven.

When the time came, the apostles would be called upon to prove their love for their Master, but for the time being, Mary took her place among them as consoler. Knowing that her mission on earth was nearing completion while theirs was only beginning, the Mother of God, with childlike humility, was able

---

5. Titles from the Litany of Loretto, approved in 1587 by Pope Sixtus V. See *https://www.ewtn.com/catholicism/devotions/litany-of-loreto-246/*.

to rest in the maternal heart of the Father. Satisfied that she had been fed by God himself, she was content to be a mother and feed those whom her son had chosen to lay the foundation for his kingdom on earth. Her willingness to overlook their sins and weaknesses was not unlike that of God, which is reflected when he chose David, about whom was said, "the LORD has sought out a man after his own heart" (1 Sam 13:14). David, like everyone but Mary, was a sinner. Yet so closely was her soul united with the humility of God that her actions became the personification of the psalmist's prayer:

> O LORD, my heart is not lifted up,
> my eyes are not raised too high;
> I do not occupy myself with things
> too great and too marvelous for me. (Ps 131:1)

Although Mary's soul was united with the Trinity, she neither raised her eyes too high, nor was she so absorbed in the presence of God that she overlooked the needs of this world. As Teresa reminds us, "You may think that as a result the soul will be outside itself and so absorbed that it will be unable to be occupied with anything else. On the contrary, the soul is much more occupied than before with everything pertaining to the service of God" (IC 7:1.8). This description of the soul that has reached the spiritual marriage applies perfectly to Mary.

THE ASCENSION OF JESUS AND THE COMING OF THE SPIRIT

Forty days after his resurrection from the dead, Jesus, having prepared the apostles for their mission, gathered them on Mount Olivet and instructed them to wait in Jerusalem for the coming of the Advocate whom the Father would send. "As they were watching, he was lifted up, and a cloud took him out of their sight" (Acts 1:9). Once again, the apostles were deprived of the physical presence of their Lord. Confounded and awe-struck by what they had witnessed, they could not have known the wondrous events that lay ahead. Nor could they have envisioned the price they would pay when they heeded the Master's call: "Follow me."

Luke writes: "Then they returned to Jerusalem from the mount called Olivet, which is near Jerusalem, a sabbath day's journey away. When they had entered the city, they went to the room upstairs where they were staying, Peter and John and James and Andrew, Philip and Thomas, Bartholomew and Matthew, James the son of Alphaeus and Simon the Zealot, and Judas, son of James. All these were constantly devoting themselves to prayer, together with certain women, including Mary the mother of Jesus, as well as his brothers" (Acts 1:12–14). As we can see, Mary was there, right from the beginning, at the heart of the church, praying with the church and for the church.

With Jesus taken from them, did the apostles look at Mary and wonder, "Who is this that looks forth like the dawn, / fair as the moon, bright as the sun, / terrible as an army with banners" (Song 6:10)? Unbeknown to them, she who had waited for nine months to cradle the infant God in her arms was now waiting to cradle the infant church as it was being born. Mary's entire life was a preparation for this moment, when once again "she was pregnant and was crying out in birth pangs, in the agony of giving birth" (Rev 12:2).

In the absence of her son and in anticipation of the coming of the promised advocate, Mary's role was to reassure and prepare Jesus's apostles for the event that would transform their hearts, not unlike the way the Holy Spirit had transformed her body: just as her womb had become the tabernacle that housed the incarnate Son of God, so their souls would become temples of the Holy Spirit who would guide, enlighten, and strengthen them for the journey that would change the world. With Mary in their midst, the nine days of prayer preceding the coming of the Holy Spirit were a time of grace for those gathered in the Upper Room, but this was also a source of joy for Mary as she joined her son's followers in prayer.

We might understand Mary's role as that of a presider during the first Pentecost novena. St. Teresa imagined Mary's role this way when she placed a statue of the Blessed Mother in the prioress's choir stall in the Monastery of the Incarnation. The visible representation of the Mother of God presiding over the nuns as they prayed became a graced time for Teresa, who was rewarded with a vision in which Mary said to her, "You were indeed right in placing me here; I shall be present in the praises they give my Son, and I shall offer praises to Him" (ST 21.1).

Mary's presence among the apostles was a continual act of praise for all that God had accomplished through her son. Only after the coming of the Holy Spirit would they understand that Jesus's legacy was mercy, his lesson was truth, and his weapon was love. Although his physical presence was taken from them, Jesus the Christ continued to be present in the world, his life and death an ongoing testimony to the humility of God. Just as Mary had taught her son to pray when he was a child, so she taught the apostles by example that every work undertaken in the Lord's name must be preceded by prayer and prepared for by sacred listening. She would have reminded them of all they had learned about prayer from Jesus, perhaps reiterating that prayer is a dialogue, an act of intimate communication between humanity and divinity, and ought never to be a one-sided conversation where the only voice they heard was their own. The experience of the Carmelite saints can help us better understand some of the aspects of prayer.

When Teresa was considering her first discalced foundation, she was conflicted, because she was perfectly content in the house where she was currently living. Nevertheless, she and the lady companion with whom she had been conversing about the foundation decided to pray fervently over the matter. One day after Communion, their prayers were answered as Teresa heard the Lord's voice. "His Majesty earnestly commanded me to strive for this new monastery with all my powers, and He made great promises that it would be founded and that He would be highly served in it" (L 32.11). Here Teresa teaches us by example to turn to God in prayer when we are seeking answers or conflicted about a decision we may be facing. God may not speak to us as directly as he did to Teresa, but if we persevere, we will find inner peace and a sense of direction, all in God's time.

More than an answer to a dilemma or a desire, however, prayer attributes ownership of every good work to God where it rightly belongs, as St. Thérèse so aptly explained:

> If a piece of canvas painted on by an artist could think and speak, it certainly would not complain at being constantly touched and retouched by the *brush*, and would not envy the lot of that instrument, for it would realize it was not to the brush but to the artist using it that it owed the beauty with which it had been clothed. The brush too, would not be able to boast of the masterpiece produced with it as it knows that artists are not at a loss; they play with difficulties, and are pleased to choose at times weak and defective instruments. (S 235)

As we can see, to be an apostle is to know oneself, acknowledge our weakness, and depend on God. Furthermore, we need to be open to whatever the Lord asks of us, as Teresa wrote: "We must be like soldiers who even though they may not have served a great deal must always be ready for any duty the captain commands them to undertake, since it is he who gives them their salary. And how much better the pay our king gives than the pay of earthly kings. Since the captain sees his soldiers present and eager to serve and has understood the capability of each one, he distributes the duties according to the strength he sees" (W 18.3–4). This passage could certainly be applied to Jesus, looking lovingly on the apostles before Pentecost and knowing what he has in mind for them.

As Mary looked lovingly on the apostles gathered in the Upper Room, she herself knew that great things would be asked of them. Her task was to recommend them to God. As they awaited the coming of her heavenly spouse, Mary's presence among them assured them that God had not abandoned them. Now they, too, were her sons, the beloved of God, whom she viewed as "a heritage from the LORD," for "the fruit of the womb [is] a reward" (Ps 127:3) that would continue to nourish the church. The old covenant that God made with Abraham, having been fulfilled through Mary's son on the cross, now awaited consummation as the new covenant through the descent of the Holy Spirit. As Mother of the Church, Mary waited and prayed with the apostles, for the coming of the Holy Spirit who would descend upon the earth and would remain with them as promised (see Jn 14:16).

"So when the day of Pentecost had come, they were all together in one place. And suddenly from heaven there came like the rush of a violent wind, and it filled the entire house where they were sitting. Divided tongues, as of fire, appeared among them, and a tongue rested on each of them" (Acts 2:1–3). As a witness to this awe-inspiring scene and to the fulfillment of God's plan of salvation, Mary watched in awe as the apostles were transformed in love by Love. In silent wonder, she succumbed to the rushing of the mighty wind, so different from the Spirit's gentle arrival at her home in Nazareth when the Word was made flesh. This time, the Holy Spirit descended not as a seed planted in her womb, but as tongues of fire overhead, and with this came a deeper knowledge in her soul of the triune God. Once again, we can learn from Teresa of Jesus, whose experience of the Trinity may help us understand, in part, something of what Mary was privileged to know. Describing her experience, Teresa wrote: "What was represented to me were three distinct Persons. Well, if each one is by Himself, how is it that we say all three are one essence. . . . These Persons love, communicate with, and know each other. In all three Persons there is no more than one will, one power, and one dominion, in such a way that one cannot do anything without the others" (ST 29.3).

Concluding this description, Teresa admits there is much she doesn't understand, but she affirms through faith: "And when I understand less, I believe more; and this belief gives me greater devotion" (ST 29.3). Teresa's insight offers a template for all who seek God, which is that believing is more important than knowing. God gives each person what is needed as they journey deeper into the heart of God. The experiences of the mystics provide a glimpse of the heavenly favors given to some during their lifetime, but none was brought to the heights of what Mary experienced while on earth. And so we, like Teresa, can accept in faith all that God puts before us, satisfied that believing is more important than knowing.

A BOLD NEW BEGINNING

"All of them were filled with the Holy Spirit and began to speak in other languages, as the Spirit gave them ability" (Acts 2:4). According to an ancient Jewish legend, after the fall of Adam and Eve, night descended at the end of the world's first Sabbath, and the two became fearful and wept. Then God showed Adam that he could make a fire that would dispel darkness and the terror of the night. Kindling flame is a symbol of our first labor on earth. Then the Sabbath ended, and the workday began. Adam thanked God for the fire, which turned earth's raw stuff into a thing of beauty, and dread of night disappeared.[6]

When viewed through a Christian lens, the story takes on a prophetic dimension, clearly pointing to the incarnation of Christ, who is the Light of the world. The conclusion of the Sabbath prefigures the fallen world of sin into which Jesus descended, but which he overcame by his death on the cross. In rising from the dead, Jesus brought a new light to renew the face of the earth through the Holy Spirit, which was made visible through tongues of fire. Salvation was not our doing but the work of God. While on earth, Jesus said, "I came to bring fire to the earth, and how I wish it were already kindled!" (Lk 12:49). With the coming of the Holy Spirit, the fire on earth became a reality. Enkindled by the coming of the promised Advocate, the apostles responded by proclaiming the resurrection of Jesus and began baptizing in the name of the Father, and of the Son, and of the Holy Spirit.

THE FINAL YEARS OF MARY'S LIFE ON EARTH

The Scriptures are silent regarding the life of Mary after Pentecost and her role during the early years of the church. Christian tradition holds that she lived with the apostle John in Jerusalem. When the persecution of Christians made living in Jerusalem too dangerous, it is presumed that John, to whom Jesus had entrusted his mother from the cross, took Mary with him to Ephesus, probably around AD 40 or possibly after James was beheaded in AD 44. At the time, the Christian community in Ephesus was flourishing and was considered a safe place to live.[7] It is not known how

---

6. Jerome Machar, O.C.S.O., *Cross of Death, Tree of Life: A Sacred Reading of the Story of Redemption* (Notre Dame, Ind.: Ave Maria Press, 1996), 120.

7. See V. Antony J. Alaharasan, *Home of the Assumption: Reconstructing Mary's Life in Ephesus* (Worcester, Mass.: Ambassador Books, 2002), 13–23.

long Mary remained there. Some traditions claim that she died in Jerusalem; others have promoted the theory that she remained in Ephesus for the duration of her life on earth. However, less important than where Mary spent the last days of her life is knowing that her presence on earth, though largely hidden and for the most part unknown, exemplifies the quiet strength of this indispensable mother, who brought Jesus into the world.

As Mary's life on earth was slowly coming to an end, she would have lived the remaining years of her life, like the earlier ones, in continual communion with God. She whom we call Mother of the Church had witnessed both the glory and the persecution of the bride of Christ on earth. Her role as the "woman" foretold in Genesis, a role to which Jesus alluded at the wedding feast in Cana and at the foot of the cross, had been fulfilled. The title "bride of Christ" now belongs to the church—this church which honors Mary's role in salvation history. Like the Son of God, who hung on the cross and rose from the dead, his bride would also undergo the crucifixion and triumph of the cross, as described in the book of Revelation: "But the woman was given the two wings of the great eagle, so that she could fly from the serpent into the wilderness, to her place where she is nourished for a time, and times, and half a time. Then from his mouth the serpent poured water like a river after the woman, to sweep her away with the flood. But the earth came to the help of the woman; it opened its mouth and swallowed the river that the dragon had poured from his mouth" (Rev 12:14–16).

This Scripture passage is a powerful statement regarding the persecutions that the church was undergoing, at the time Revelation was written, and would continue to undergo, even to this present age. Yet Mary understood that, despite persecutions and attacks from both inside and outside the church, this bride of Christ would flourish. Knowing that it was watered by the blood of martyrs, who died in imitation of her son, Mary remained confident that the souls of the just were being sent to God and that

> he will wipe away every tear from their eyes.
> Death shall be no more,
> mourning and crying and pain will be no more,
> for the first things have passed away. (Rev 21:4)

Her steadfast confidence remains an example even today, for as Mother of the Church, she continues to draw us to her son.

How long Mary remained on earth before being assumed into heaven is unknown. Legends regarding what the church refers to as the "dormition of Mary" abound. As early as the second century, an apocryphal work called the *Transitus Mariae* (the passage of Mary) tells us that Mary died in the presence of the apostles in Jerusalem and that her body then just disappeared—or was buried and then disappeared.[8] In the sixth century, Gregory of Tours wrote, "At daybreak, however, the apostles took up her body on a bier and placed it in a tomb; and they guarded it, expecting the Lord to come. And behold, again the Lord stood by them; and the holy body having been received, he commanded that it be taken in a cloud into paradise: where now, [the body] rejoined to

---

8. See the summary in Adiaha Hunte, "Assumption of the Virgin by Pseudo-Melito," e-Clavis: Christian Apocrypha, *https://www.nasscal.com/e-clavis-christian-apocrypha/assumption-of-the-virgin-by-pseudo-melito/*. This work has been attributed to Bishop St. Melito of Sardis, but its authorship is given as "Pseudo-Melito." Indeed, no author was given by Pope St. John Paul II when he referred to this work in his General Audience of July 2, 1997: "The first trace of belief in the Virgin's Assumption can be found in the apocryphal accounts entitled *Transitus Mariae,* whose origin dates to the second and third centuries. These are popular and sometimes romanticized depictions, which in this case, however, pick up an intuition of faith on the part of God's People," *https://www.vatican.va/content/john-paul-ii/en/audiences/1997/documents/hf_jp-ii_aud_02071997.html/*.

the soul, [Mary] rejoices with the Lord's chosen ones, and is the enjoyment of the good of an eternity that will never end."[9] This is a very early and compelling account of the assumption.

In 1950, Pope Pius XII solemnly declared that "the Immaculate Mother of God, the ever-Virgin Mary, having completed the course of her earthly life, was assumed body and soul into heavenly glory" (MD 44). Before declaring the assumption of Mary into heaven a dogma, the pope called for a broad consultation in 1946, inquiring among bishops, clergy, and the people of God regarding the possibility and opportuneness of defining the bodily assumption of Mary a dogma of faith. In response, German theologian Ludwig Ott weighed in, arguing that it was possible that Mary had experienced death, not as a consequence of original sin, since in her immaculate conception she was free from it, a consequence of being human. Mary's dying, Ott said, would be in conformity with that of her Divine Son, who also experienced a human death. More than one thousand theologians concurred with Ott. When Pope Pius XII declared the assumption of Mary into heaven a dogma of faith, he stopped short of declaring that Mary did not die. The question whether Mary died or fell into a deep sleep before she was assumed into heaven therefore remains open (cf. MD 10–14).

In 1997, during his homily celebrating the Feast of the Assumption, Pope St. John Paul II reaffirmed what Pope Pius XII declared in 1950: "Today's liturgy sets before us the radiant icon of the Blessed Virgin who was taken up into heaven in the integrity of her body and soul. In the splendor of heavenly glory shines the One who, by reason of her humility, was made great in the sight of the Most High to the point that all generations

---

9. St. Gregory of Tours, "Eight Books of Miracles" in *The Faith of the Early Fathers*, vols. 1–3., translated by W. A. Jurgens, (Collegeville, MN: Liturgical Press, 1979), 3:306.

call her blessed (cf. Lk 1:48). Now, as Queen, she sits beside her Son in the eternal happiness of paradise and looks upon her children from on high."[10]

Presenting the dogma of the assumption here, Pope John Paul II (like Pope Pius XII) stopped short of saying that Mary did not die. To be free of original sin and its stain, as was Mary, is not the same as being in a glorified body. Jesus, too, was free of original sin and its stain but still experienced death. To claim that Mary did not experience physical death could be perceived as placing her above her son.

While addressing the assumption of Mary into heaven, we can hardly overlook the fact that Scripture depicts Elijah as being taken up into heaven without experiencing physical death. "As [Elijah and Elisha] continued walking and talking, a chariot of fire and horses of fire separated the two of them, and Elijah ascended in a whirlwind into heaven" (2 Kings 2:11). With reference to the words of Jesus, "No one has ascended into heaven except the one who descended from heaven, the Son of Man" (Jn 3:13), some have speculated that Elijah was taken up to a special place near God since only through the death and resurrection of Jesus could the just enter heaven.[11] However, several early theologians and Scripture scholars, including St. Cyril of Jerusalem and Blessed Theodoret of Cyrrhus, suggested that, as the latter put it, "although the great Elijah ascended, it was not into Heaven—but as if into Heaven." In the reading of these church fathers, what happened to Elijah was compared to ascending into heaven. It appears that they were following the Septuagint translation of the

---

10. Pope John Paul II, "Homily on the Feast of the Assumption of the Blessed Virgin Mary," August 15, 1997, 1, *http://www.vatican.va/content/john-paul-ii/en/homilies/1997/documents/hf_jp-ii_hom_15081997.html/*.

11. See Msgr. Charles Pope, "Were Elijah and Moses assumed into heaven Like Mary?" *Our Sunday Visitor*, November 17, 2020, *https://osvnews.com/2020/11/17/were-elijah-and-moses-assumed-into-heaven-like-mary/*.

Bible, which one translation states that "Elijah was taken up in the air *as* into heaven" (2 Kings 2:11; my italics).[12]

Once again, we recall the advice of St. Teresa of Jesus, who reminds us that we will never know everything concerning the things of God in this life and that believing is more important than knowing (cf. ST 29.3). Our human limitations remind us that many things of God are beyond comprehending while we are on this earth. Rather than our being disheartened, though, this should serve to heighten our anticipation of all that will be ours in the next life, where the experience of the fullness of God awaits us. For now, we can take comfort in knowing that one day, we too will be raised up like Mary for all eternity. While in this life, we look to our heavenly mother who embodies all that is right and holy and whose life remains a continuing testimony to the mysteries of God. Reassuring us of her role in our spiritual formation, the Vatican's Congregation for Catholic Education noted in 1988: "Everything about Mary—privileges, mission, destiny—is also intrinsically referable to the mystery of the Church. In the measure in which the mystery of the Church is understood the more distinctly does the mystery of Mary become apparent. Contemplating Mary, the Church recognizes its origins, its intimate nature, its mission of grace, its destiny to glory, and the pilgrimage of faith which it must follow."[13]

The words of the Vatican congregation remind us that to gaze upon Mary is like gazing into the life of the church. As the perfect contemplative, Mary provides a template for all who seek a deeper relationship with her son and with his body, the church.

---

12. See 4 Kingdoms 2:11 in *The Lexham English Septuagint*, Rick Brannan, Ken N. Penner, Israel Loken, Michael Aubrey, and Isaiah Hoogendyk, eds. (Bellingham, WA: Lexham Press, 2012).

13. Congregation for Catholic Education, "The Virgin Mary in Intellectual and Spiritual Formation," March 25, 1988, n. 20, *https://udayton.edu/imri/mary/m/magisterial-documents-the-virgin-mary-in-intellectual-and-spiritual-formation.php*.

INVITATION TO PRAYER

As pilgrims on the journey, we are blessed to have so perfect and loving a guide. Although Mary's earthly life is over, she remains ever vigilant, not only as our heavenly mother but as Queen of Heaven and Earth. Just as every good king shares his deepest plans with his Queen Mother, so Jesus shares his plan for us with Mary. We have no better advocate in heaven than Mary, whom we can salute as queen, even as we ask her to intercede for us.

HAIL, HOLY QUEEN

Hail, Holy Queen, Mother of Mercy, our life, our sweetness, and our hope.
To thee do we cry, poor banished children of Eve.
To thee do we send up our sighs, mourning and weeping in this valley of tears.
Turn, then, most gracious advocate, thine eyes of mercy toward us,
and after this, our exile, show unto us the blessed fruit of thy womb, Jesus.
O clement, O loving, O sweet Virgin Mary.

V. Pray for us, O holy Mother of God.
R. That we may be made worthy of the promises of Christ.

Almighty and everlasting God, Who by the working of the Holy Spirit didst prepare both body and soul of the glorious Virgin Mother, Mary, that she might deserve to be made a worthy dwelling for Thy Son, grant that we who rejoice in her memory, may, by her loving intercession, be delivered from present evils and from lasting death, through the same Christ our Lord.
Amen.

PART II

BLESSED VIRGIN MARY: MOTHER, MODEL, AND INTERCESSOR

10

Prayer:

Mary's Role in Our Journey Home

POPE FRANCIS HAS REFERRED TO MARY as the road we travel to God.[1] She who showed us by example the path to union with God now pleads for us before the throne of God, for we are her adopted children. With the words, "Woman, here is your son" (Jn 19:26), Mary's mantle of motherhood opened as wide as her son's arms as he hung on the cross. Her role as the Mother of God was without precedence and is never to be duplicated. Recognition of her favored status as Mother of God and our mother can be traced to the early years of Christianity, but it was during the Middle Ages that a more extensive library on the science of Mariology was developed. Saintly scholars such as Bernard of Clairvaux, Dominic, Bonaventure, Anthony of Padua, and, later, Louis de Montfort, contributed to the body of work on Mary that continues to evolve. Numerous encyclicals written about our Lady have inspired devotion among Catholics, but her role as

---

1. "[Mary] is the road that God travelled in order to reach us, and the road that we must travel in order to reach him": "Homily for the Solemnity of Mary, Mother of God," January 1, 2021, *http:/www.vatican.va/content/francesco/en/homilies/2021/documents/papa-francesco_20210101_omelia-madredidio-pace.html.*

intercessor and mediatrix reached doctrinal heights when Pope Leo XIII wrote:

> With equal truth may it be also affirmed that, by the will of God, Mary is the intermediary through whom is distributed unto us this immense treasure of mercies gathered by God. . . . Thus as no man goes to the Father but by the Son, so no man goes to Christ but by His Mother. . . . Those whose actions have disturbed their consciences need an intercessor mighty in favor with God. . . . Mary is this glorious intermediary; she is the mighty Mother of the Almighty. . . . Having chosen her for the Mother of His only begotten Son, He taught her all a mother's feeling that breathes nothing but pardon and love. Such Christ desired she should be, for He consented to be subject to Mary and to obey her as a son a mother. Such He proclaimed her from the cross when he entrusted to her care and love the whole of the race of man in the person of His disciple John. (OM 4)

Our imitation of Christ, then, begins with being a child of his own mother.

In bequeathing his mother to us before he died, Jesus gives us a mother, a teacher, and an intercessor. No human person accompanied Jesus, nor was united more closely with the Trinity, than Mary. While on earth, she embodied the fullness of the fruits and gifts of the Holy Spirit, which makes her the perfect guide to lead us to our home in the heart of God. Whether knowingly or unknowingly, this is the quest of every man, woman, and child, for we are all prodigal children who have left home, squandering the gifts that once belonged to us. Created in God's own image and likeness, we were given communion with God as our birthright until sin turned us out of our country of origin. Distraught and disoriented, we became slaves to gods of our own making, creating idols that left us seeking and searching for wholeness.

Only Mary was untethered by sin. As human nature's solitary boast, she is the perfect mirror of the tenderness of God's love, making her uniquely qualified to lead us to our home in the heart of God. Although the road is fraught with human failures and missteps, detours, and wrong turns, often as many dangers as delights, Mary reminds us that we are God's children and that somewhere in the latent recesses of our mind resides the memory of a time when we once walked with God. Deep within the storehouse of our soul, engraved in our heart, is the image of the invisible God, who breathed life into our soul and sustains us every moment of every day.

St. Augustine captured this basic truth when he proclaimed, "You have made us for yourself, O God, and our heart is restless until it rests in you."[2] It is well known that Augustine came to his conversion through the tireless intercession of his mother, St. Monica, who prayed for him unceasingly. If a natural mother could hold sway over the heart of God, how much more does God's own mother influence his response to sinners? In the parable of the Prodigal Son, Jesus told us that the father, who had been watching for the prodigal's return, ran out to meet him the moment he caught sight of him. Not only do we have a Father watching and waiting for our return; in Mary we also have a mother who keeps vigil with him, interceding even as she pleads with us to return to our home in the heart of God.

The tenderness of God's love is well documented in Scripture. In the words of the prophet, we are told, "Before I formed you in the womb I knew you" (Jer 1:5). Resonating with this secret knowing in our deepest center is the psalmist's prayer: "As a deer longs for flowing streams, / so my soul longs for you,

---

2. Augustine, *The Confessions of St. Augustine*, trans. John K. Ryan (Garden City, N.Y.: Image Books, 1960), I.1.

O God" (Ps 42:1). The yearning for God is an inherent part of our human nature. This has been corroborated by archaeologists who continue to unearth evidence that even the most primitive civilizations worshipped some sort of deity. Ancient philosophers, such as Plato and Socrates, believed in the existence of the soul, and religious storytellers from ancient civilizations captivated the minds and hearts of their people long before the one true God broke into the consciousness of human history.

Unlike the story of Adam and Eve, however, ancient theories are inconclusive, and religious myths end without the hope that is inherent in the Christian tradition. In those legends there is no promise of redemption, no hint of a God who would save sinners, no mention of a deity who allows for human free will, as in his cooperation with a virgin's fiat, nor is there a maternal presence to instruct and encourage persons when they stray. Only the triune God can restore hope to souls who seek the source of their deepest yearning where they find completion. Having been created in God's image, we were fashioned to live in communion with God and with one another, but sin created a chasm so deep and so wide that only God could bridge the divide. And so it happened: the Son of God came into the world incarnate of a woman, died, and rose from the dead. After ascending into heaven, he sent his Spirit as an Advocate, because God's love was such that he would not allow us to be orphaned. Ruth Burrows captures this wondrous miracle: "In a mystery we cannot fathom, God 'empties,' loses, Himself in bringing back to Himself, His estranged, lost children. And this is all the Father wants. This is the only remedy for His wound. God is no longer pure God, but always God-with-humanity-in-His-heart."[3]

3. Ruth Burrows, O.C.D., *Essence of Prayer* (Mahwah, N.J.: HiddenSpring, 2006), 74.

Clearly, from the beginning, union with God was and is always God's desire for us.

In a sermon on the Blessed Virgin Mary, St. Anthony of Padua compared the Blessed Mother to a rainbow. Citing Genesis, the saint wrote, "'I set my rainbow in the clouds to serve as a sign of the Covenant' (Gen 9:13). The rainbow is a sign of the peace and reconciliation, which the Virgin Mary, our mediatrix, effected between God and sinful man."[4] So highly did the saint esteem Mary that he claimed we have three Advocates: the Holy Spirit, Christ, and Mary.[5]

St. Anthony's supposition is in keeping with the divine tendency toward infinite generosity. When changing water into wine, Jesus provided more wine than the guests could possibly drink. After multiplying a few loaves and fish, not only were thousands of people fed, but twelve baskets of food remained. God's abundance can never be outdone, and Jesus's gift of his mother is one more example of God's infinite generosity.

As Queen of Heaven and Earth, Mary intercedes for people of every faith tradition—believers and non-believers alike. Just as the Word of God entered Mary's womb and bore fruit, so God desires the Word to be sown in every heart to bear fruit through the Holy Spirit. This happens in proportion to the degree that souls are willing to empty themselves. No one, after Jesus, exemplified this more perfectly than Mary, spouse of the Holy Spirit, whose virginal womb received the Word of God and changed the course of the world. But she is not alone. Throughout the centuries, saints bear witness to the transforming love of the Holy Spirit.

---

4. Anthony of Padua, *Seek First His Kingdom: An Anthology of the Sermons of the Saint*, ed. Livio Poloniato, O.F.M. Conv. (Padua: Edizioni Messaggero Padova, 1996), 78.

5. Anthony of Padua, *Seek First His Kingdom*, 76–79.

Graced self-emptying, the fruit of the Holy Spirit, prompted Francis of Assisi to stand naked before his earthly father and claim Lady Poverty as his bride. It transformed John of the Cross into a living flame of love, whose poetry has echoed through the ages. And it led Teresa of Jesus to leave a comfortable life in the Monastery of the Incarnation and embark on a path that would lead to hardships and obstacles of every kind. Yet in the end, they were victorious. As we look to the saints for inspiration, who better to lead us than Mary, Queen of All Saints? And so, we join our voices with the psalmist as we sing of Mary: "daughters of kings are among your ladies of honor; / at your right hand stands the queen in gold of Ophir" (Ps 45:9). This offers a perfect image for pondering the kingdom of God and Mary's place in it.

THE KINGDOM OF GOD WITHIN

When Jesus proclaimed that the kingdom of God was in their midst, he dismayed and angered the Jews in the synagogue at Nazareth (see Lk 4:16–30). It was not the message they expected, nor was it what they wanted to hear. They were hoping to be liberated from Roman rule, but now they were being asked to accept the poor and unclean who were not even worthy to enter the house of God. Who was Jesus to claim he was the promised one foretold by the prophet Isaiah? How could a carpenter's son assume so exalted a role? Unable to see beyond their own ignorance, they couldn't imagine a God who would champion the very people they despised. Yet, as outrageous as their thinking seems, we are not so different. Partial blindness and selective hearing have always been the bane of human existence, even for Christians as we stumble along the path the Master trod.

The human tendency to esteem those in power and chase after passing pleasures while hanging our hopes on man-made dreams is so embedded in the human condition that even people of faith barely notice the irony of it all. Infected with a spirit of entitlement, we take for granted necessities to which the poor will never gain access and then take pride in donating what we neither need nor can use, even as we slander our brothers and sisters and wage war in the name of God. The world is filled with blind guides, especially those that inhabit the inner room of our heart, which is why we need Mary to show us the way to her son.

Through her many apparitions, Mary has pleaded for her children to turn their hearts to God. Echoing the words of her son, she instructs us to fast and to pray. The Hebrew Scriptures testify to the importance of prayer and fasting as a means of conversion, and before embarking on his mission, Jesus entered the desert to fast and pray following his baptism by John. When Jesus's disciples were unable to cast out demons from a man's son, Jesus rebuked them, saying, "This kind can only come out through prayer" (Mk 9:29). When accompanying prayer, fasting adds leverage to our pleas to God.

Fasting can be from food, but it's also about denying ourselves in order to purify our heart so that God is our primary source of joy; it's what John of the Cross defined as "a privation and purgation of all sensible appetites for the external things of this world, the delights of the flesh, and the gratifications of the will" (A 1.1.4). This is the reason Mary pleads with us to pray and fast. She knows that only with God's grace are we able to choose God's will over our own. It's not because doing God's will is impossible, but that following it eventually takes us to Calvary, where even some of Jesus's closest friends were unable to follow. Ironically, the road, though arduous and steep, is concomitantly consoling and sweet, as evidenced in the life of Mary and in the experience of the saints who followed in her footsteps and who will form the subject of the rest of this chapter.

When St. Teresa instructed her nuns regarding prayer requests, she wisely indicated that suffering was to be expected. "If some of our requests are answered, I would consider well worthwhile the trials I have suffered in order to found this little corner, where I have also sought that this rule of our Lady and Empress be observed with perfection" (W 3.5). She continued, "Pay no attention to suffering that comes to an end" (W 3.6). Teresa gave herself to God through prayer. She willingly accepted the rigors and suffering when she insisted that her houses were not to have a designated income. As a result, she was rewarded with the wisdom of God, causing her to say, "These revelations helped me very much, I think, in coming to know our true country and realizing that we are pilgrims here below" (L 38.6). In her *Interior Castle*, she wrote, "Wouldn't it show great ignorance, my daughters, if someone when asked who he was didn't know, and didn't know his father or mother or from what country he came? Well now, if this would be so extremely stupid, we are incomparably more so when we do not strive to know who we are, but limit ourselves to considering only roughly these bodies. Because we have heard and because faith tells us so, we have souls. But we seldom consider the precious things that can be found in it, or who dwells within it, or its high value" (IC 1.1.2). This is self-knowledge in its most profound sense.

John of the Cross maintained that God's loving knowledge of himself is communicated to the soul in its deepest center. As persons of prayer can attest, shedding the fallacy of knowing prepares the soul to enter the night of unknowing. God does not duplicate the way he speaks to souls. Rather, he communicates his love according to each person's disposition and needs. To Teresa, he communicated himself as a king enthroned in the center of her soul, with her soul appearing to be like a castle, "made entirely out of a diamond or of very clear crystal in which there are many rooms, just as in heaven there are many dwelling places" (IC 1.1.1). John envisioned the journey to God as a dark night, through which, "fired with love's urgent longings" (A 1.1), he traveled unseen from a "house" that was stilled. Thérèse envisioned herself as a child who needed an elevator to climb to God, and because she was so weak, she needed the arms of Jesus to be her lift. Others might liken the experience of God to a drop of water that disappears into the ocean of God's love as they find themselves engulfed by a deep stillness where neither sunlight nor sound penetrate, where boundaries disappear, and the only sound is a symphony devoid of lyrics and melody.

It has been said that to *know about God* based on what others experience is to admire God, but that to *know God* is to fall on our knees in adoration. It was this type of knowing that led Peter, James, and John to lie prostrate at the sight of Jesus's transfiguration (see Mt 17:5). According to Matthew's gospel, Jesus told the disciples to tell no one, and indeed in Luke's gospel we read that they remained silent about their experience. Sometimes silence is the only appropriate response, as Mary intuited by pondering in her heart the ways of God, which she did not fully understand.

In the story of her life, St. Thérèse recalled how tormented she felt after she revealed the account of her healing through the smile of the Blessed Virgin. In talking about the experience to the nuns at the Carmel, after her sister Marie had told them of the cure, Thérèse was afflicted with scruples, worrying wrongly that she had lied, as the nuns were imagining something like an apparition (see S 67). As Thérèse matured, she understood that supernatural communications are by their very nature deeply intimate and therefore should only be disclosed cautiously to a spiritual guide, unless God sees fit to instruct the person otherwise. This may come about through obedience, as happened with St. Teresa and later with St. Thérèse, when each was asked to describe experiences of God that took place in the depths of their heart.

Supernatural disclosures could also be in response to a request or be an act of kindness, as was the case with John of the Cross who shared his poetry with others. His poetry and metaphors conveyed something of the essence of an experience, rather than offering definitive descriptions. Therefore, it should come as no surprise that the saint was asked to describe in prose the meaning of his poetry. In sharing their experience of God, mystics invite others to glean from them what they are able to learn from each reading. Like the horizon that is forever beyond our reach, insights and understanding of God's hidden communication relative to the soul's experience of God continues to evolve as souls learn to *know without knowing*. This is itself a grace, as John explained:

> I will never lose myself
> for that which the senses can take in here,
> nor for all the mind can hold,
> no matter how lofty,
> nor for the grace or beauty,
> *but only for I-don't-know-what*
> *which is so gladly found.* (P 12.9)

As these lines reveal so well, a mystic's uses of metaphors and poetry are like appetizers that encourage persons of prayer to persevere during times of aridity and darkness and that reassure them that heavenly food will follow. The ascent of the soul to God—what John of the Cross refers to as the "ascent of Mount Carmel"—takes place slowly and in stages, as God sees fit. We have, for example, two similar but slightly different experiences in the lives of two great biblical figures. We read that when

Moses asked to see the face of God, "[The Lord] said, 'You cannot see my face; for no one shall see me and live.' And the LORD continued, 'See, there is a place by me where you shall stand on the rock; and while my glory passes by I will put you in a cleft of the rock, and I will cover you with my hand until I have passed by; then I will take away my hand, and you shall see my back; but my face shall not be seen'" (Ex 33:20–23).

We can compare this with the experience of Elijah. After he had called down fire from heaven to consume the sacrifice to the Lord and slain the prophets of Baal, the word of the Lord came to him, as recorded in the following account from the First Book of Kings:

> He said, "Go out and stand on the mountain before the LORD, for the LORD is about to pass by." Now there was a great wind, so strong that it was splitting mountains and breaking rocks in pieces before the LORD, but the LORD was not in the wind; and after the wind an earthquake, but the LORD was not in the earthquake; and after the earthquake a fire, but the LORD was not in the fire; and after the fire a sound of sheer silence. And when Elijah heard it, he wrapped his face in his mantle and went out and stood at the entrance of the cave. (1 Kings 19:11–13)

As these last two passages show, mountains have long been considered places where persons encounter God. Moses encountered God on Sinai, Elijah on the same mountain, known also (as in the Elijah story) as Mount Horeb; Peter, James, and John witnessed the transfiguration of Jesus on Mount Tabor.

Like those who have traveled before us, we would prefer to remain on the mountaintop, but not even the mystics remained there. God gives souls glimpses of the supernatural, but these are never given solely for personal pleasure. While not all may be called to share their experiences of infused prayer in the way that many of the saints and spiritual teachers were, the fruits of supernatural prayer cannot be hidden. Moses and Elijah neither explained nor shared what took place in the depths of their soul, but the fruits of the divine encounters were evident in their lives. Supernatural or mystical encounters are less important than the fruit they bear. Jesus said to his followers: "Abide in me as I abide in you. Just as the branch cannot bear fruit by itself unless it abides in the vine, neither can you unless you abide in me. I am the vine, you are the branches. Those who abide in me and I in them bear much fruit, because apart from me you can do nothing" (Jn 15:4–5).

As in this passage, Jesus often used metaphors when speaking about the experience of God, yet his message was unmistakable to those who had ears to hear. Yet we know that not all who heard Jesus were able to accept his message, as was evident in the climate of unbelief in Nazareth that prevented Jesus from working miracles there or later when some of his followers walked away because his words were too difficult for them to believe (see Jn 6:66).

The faith of the people was essential to Jesus's ability to reveal the power that the Father had given him. For us, as with the people of Jesus's time, faith is the beginning of life in God. Jesus frequently told those whom he had cured that their faith had saved them. If faith is the starting point for a relationship with God, then prayer is the way to deepen it. Teresa noted that prayer is the entrance to our "interior castle." The more intimate and untethered our prayer becomes, the deeper our faith—until the time when signs are no longer needed and faith leads seekers along the path of unknowing. As John of the Cross explained: "For this reason the purer, simpler, and more perfect the general knowledge is, the darker it seems to be and the less the intellect perceives. On the other hand, the less pure and simple the knowledge is in itself, although it enlightens the intellect, the clearer and more important it appears to the individual, since it is clothed, wrapped, or commingled with some intelligible forms apprehensible to the intellect or the senses" (A 2.14.8). In this important passage, John presents the paradox that the less our intellect perceives, the more important and direct the knowledge of God. It is imperceptibly poured into us by God, which is why this is often referred to as "infused" prayer.

Regarding infused prayer, St. Teresa explained that those who have had the experience will understand. She admitted to finding it difficult to describe much of what she experienced. Her intention was not to advise her nuns to expect similar favors, but to help them understand the infinite nature of God's loving communication. Her goal was to reassure those who had experienced infused prayer that God can and does communicate his presence in extraordinary ways. She also wanted to instruct and to encourage those who had not experienced deepening stages of prayer never to stop seeking God who never stops seeking them.

John maintained that visions, locutions, and extraordinary experiences were not always reliable indicators of a person's relationship with God. St. Teresa would agree. In her concluding pages of the seventh dwelling places, Teresa emphasized that the reason for prayer is always good works (see IC 7.4.6), which bears out the words of Jesus, encountered earlier: "This kind can only come out through prayer" (Mk 9:29). And Teresa added, "The Lord doesn't look so much at the greatness of our works as at the love with which they are done" (IC 7.4.15). Indeed, not all are called to do great things, yet that does not lessen the importance of every good work, for "the Lord sees not as mortals see; they look on the outward appearance, but the Lord looks on the heart" (1 Sam 16:7). St. Thérèse is a good example of the way God sees. Only through the grace and providence of God could a young girl who entered a cloistered monastery at the age of fifteen become renowned the world over and named a Doctor of the Church and Patroness of the Missions. Perhaps a glimpse into her childhood can help us understand.

When Thérèse's sister Léonie decided she was too old to play with dolls, she came to Thérèse with a basket containing an assortment of doll's clothes as well as her own doll, and she asked Thérèse to choose what she would like. In characteristic fashion, Thérèse replied, "I choose all!" (S 27). Unbeknown to her at the time, the statement was a prophetic declaration of what would become her path to holiness. Following her Christmas conversion, Thérèse gladly accepted everything the Lord offered her, be it in the form of pleasure or pain. She liked to think of herself as "a little ball of no value" (cf. S 136) that the Child Jesus could play with or discard as he chose, which causes us to question: Where did this young woman, who suffered from neurosis and a strange, hallucinatory illness during her childhood years, find the strength to serve God with such courage and become one of the church's most popular saints? We needn't look far before we recognize Mary's role in this grace-filled development.

When breast cancer took her mother's life, Thérèse wrote that she sought consolation from the Mother of God. When she suffered her mysterious illness, after her sister Pauline entered the convent, it was to Mary's intercession that Thérèse attributed her healing. This is the episode referred to earlier, in connection with her scruples. In her autobiography, she described it as follows:

> Marie knelt down near my bed with Léonie and Céline. Turning to the Blessed Virgin and praying with the fervor of a mother begging for the life of her child, *Marie* obtained what

> she wanted. Finding no help on earth, poor little Thérèse had also turned toward the Mother of heaven, and prayed with all her heart that she take pity on her. All of a sudden the Blessed Virgin appeared *beautiful* to me, so *beautiful* that never had I seen anything so attractive; her face was suffused with an ineffable benevolence and tenderness, but what penetrated to the very depths of my soul was the "*ravishing smile of the Blessed Virgin.*" At that instant, all my pain disappeared. (S 65–66)

It is no surprise, given her love for Mary—and especially after such a powerful experience as this—that at significant moments during her life in Carmel, Thérèse entrusted herself to the care of the Blessed Mother, who was never far from her thoughts. When the day of her profession was delayed for eight months, she wrote, "The Blessed Virgin, nevertheless, was helping me prepare the dress of my soul; as soon as this dress was completed all the obstacles went away" (S 160). Thérèse's profession took place on September 8, the feast of the Nativity of Mary, just as she had hoped.

In every generation God raises up men and women to the heights of holiness, reminding us that we are all called to become saints. We may not all become canonized saints, but as the late Archbishop Dom Helder Câmara wrote: "In the last analysis, sanctity is nothing but the Lord. He invites us to share in his holiness. But this shared holiness is neither an entitlement to glory nor a privilege for exceptional souls, and much less a favor we want to offer God. It is an obligation for all of us from the moment, through Baptism, we receive sanctifying grace that makes us holy."[6] From this, we can see clearly that there is no

6. In Conrad De Meester, *With Empty Hands: The Message of St. Thérèse of Lisieux* (Washington, D.C.: ICS Publications, 2002), x.

doubt that we are called to holiness and that God himself gives us the means.

If holiness is our vocation, then prayer is the means that makes it possible. Like any relationship, communication is key. The more intimate the communication, the deeper and more intimate will the relationship be, and the same holds true for our relationship with God. The more we commune with God, the more God fills us with his light and love. Few saints set out to accomplish all they did in service of the Lord. They fell in love with God, and the deeper their love, the more they spent time in prayer, which eventually bore fruit in the world. No relationship can exist without communication, and when the one we communicate with is God, we can expect great things to follow because prayer changes the one who prays. Prayer changes tepid souls into devout souls who seek and follow in the footprints of the Master.

According to the *Baltimore Catechism*, we were created to know, love, and serve God in this world, and to be happy with him forever in heaven.[7] If knowing God is to love God, and to love God is to serve him, then the way we experience God's communication is less important than remaining faithful to prayer. The *Catechism of the Catholic Church* reminds us that the desire to pray is in response to God's initiative: "The wonder of prayer is revealed beside the well where we come seeking water: there, Christ comes to meet every human being. It is he who first seeks us and ask us for a drink. Jesus thirsts; his asking arises from the depths of God's desire for us. Whether we realize it or not, prayer is the encounter of God's thirst with ours. God thirsts so that we may thirst for him" (CCC 2560). As we can see, God communicates with us directly in prayer.

---

7. See *Baltimore Catechism No. 1*, Lesson First: On the End of Man, answer to question 6, *https://www.sacred-texts.com/chr/balt/balt1.htm*.

Or, as Sister Maria Boulding, O.S.B., writes, "Prayer moves us from knowing about God to knowing God; to knowing him through the direct lines of communication he has provided: faith and charity."[8]

Before he ascended into heaven, Jesus told his followers that he was going to the Father to prepare a place for them and that the Father's house has many dwellings. When the mother of James and John asked Jesus if her sons could sit one on the right and the other on the left of him when Jesus would come into his kingdom, she was told that she didn't know what she was asking. The same could be said of those who practice prayer, expecting to receive supernatural favors. Teresa warned her nuns that such desires would be the height of presumption. Only God knows what is needed for each person to become the person he or she is called to be. Just as no two people are completely alike, so no two people will have the same experience of God in prayer. John of the Cross explains: "Each runs along according to the way and kind of spirit and state God gives, with many differences of spiritual practices and works. They run along the way of eternal life, the way of evangelical perfection, by which they encounter the Beloved in union of love after their spirit has been stripped of all things" (C 25.4).

As John says so well here, we "run along the way of eternal life," and our role is to trust that if we do our part, the Father will run to meet us and celebrate our return home. The Paschal Lamb has given his life in anticipation of the heavenly banquet where we will dine in glory. In this life, we are but pilgrims journeying to the place that awaits us, the place where our mother, Mary, who is called "Gate of Heaven," is waiting with the Father to welcome us home.

---

8. Maria Boulding, O.S.B., *Prayer: Our Journey Home* (Ann Arbor, Mich.: Servant Books, 1979), 11.

INVITATION TO PRAYER

Over the centuries, numerous titles have been ascribed to Mary, but nowhere is there a more extensive collection of names and titles attributed to her than those contained in the Litany of Loreto. It has been prayed in the sanctuary of Loreto since the sixteenth century and remains a beloved tribute to Mary. This beautiful prayer invokes our Lady as mother, virgin, and queen, and also sets before us titles that symbolize her holiness and her exalted role in the church and among her children. When we consider Mary's privileged role as the woman who brought the Son of God into the world, what better way to honor her than by asking Holy Mary, Mother of God to intercede for us as we pray a portion of it (with others to follow in subsequent chapters):

HOLY MOTHER OF GOD, PRAY FOR US . . .
MOTHER OF CHRIST, PRAY FOR US.
MOTHER OF THE CHURCH, PRAY FOR US.
MOTHER OF MERCY, PRAY FOR US.
MOTHER OF DIVINE GRACE, PRAY FOR US.
MOTHER OF HOPE, PRAY FOR US.
MOTHER MOST PURE, PRAY FOR US.
MOTHER MOST CHASTE, PRAY FOR US
MOTHER INVIOLATE, PRAY FOR US.
MOTHER UNDEFILED, PRAY FOR US.
MOTHER MOST AMIABLE, PRAY FOR US.
MOTHER MOST ADMIRABLE, PRAY FOR US.
MOTHER OF GOOD COUNSEL, PRAY FOR US.
MOTHER OF OUR CREATOR, PRAY FOR US.
MOTHER OF OUR SAVIOR, PRAY FOR US.[9] AMEN.

---

9. For a presentation, with accompanying discussion, of the titles of Mary in this Litany, though without the words of prayer, see "Litany of Loreto in Context," *https://udayton.edu/imri/mary/l/litany-of-loreto-in-context.php*.

11

The Rosary:

Mary's Flower Garden

FEW SACRAMENTALS IDENTIFY Catholic religious practice as distinctly as the rosary. The beads are prayed with, can be seen hanging from cinctures on religious habits, dangle from rearview mirrors in automobiles, and are draped around the necks of devotees. However, the use of prayer beads is not unique to Catholics. Almost every religious tradition includes prayer beads to count prayers, mantras, or names for God. The repetition of words or prayers has long been used in striving to reach an elevated state of consciousness or to come closer to the divine. In the Catholic tradition, the word *rosary* derives from the Latin *rosarium*, meaning "rose garden" or "garland of roses"; and *bead*, though it is now used to refer to small, ball-shaped articles strung together on necklaces and strings of all kinds, actually has its origins in the context of the rosary and comes from the Anglo-Saxon word *bede*, meaning "prayer."

The use of beads for religious purposes is believed to have originated about twenty-nine centuries ago with Hinduism, but a recently discovered fresco among the ruins of the ancient Minoan civilization suggests that prayer beads were in use more than thirty-six hundred years ago. The practice of praying with beads was later adopted by Buddhists and then by Muslims.

St. Anthony of Egypt, who is credited with being the father of Christian monasticism, used stones to keep track of his prayers as early as the third century.

Desert fathers memorized the entire Psalter and prayed it daily, counting the psalms with stones while weaving baskets to support themselves. In the fourth century, St. Gregory of Nyssa created the "prayer rope" that used knots to keep track of recitations of the Jesus Prayer—"Lord Jesus Christ, Son of God, have mercy on me, a sinner"—and that remains a part of the spiritual practice of Eastern-rite Catholic and Eastern Orthodox believers today. Around two hundred years later, St. Columba, an Irish monk who converted half of Scotland's inhabitants to Christianity, created a string of one hundred and fifty beads, one for each of the psalms, which his monks prayed daily, though no repetition was involved. The practice was later adopted by Roman Catholic monastic orders. Monks unable to read or who did not have the Psalter memorized prayed the Lord's Prayer on each bead. Over time, praying the psalms was replaced with the repetition of the Hail Mary ten times, with each "decade" followed by the Our Father.[1]

Popular tradition attributes the practice of praying the rosary in its present form to St. Dominic, a tireless proponent of the rosary, who credited this devotion with the conversion of Albigensian heretics. According to tradition, the Blessed Mother appeared to St. Dominic and taught him to recite the rosary with the doxology preceding each Our Father. At the same time, Mary promised that all who faithfully recite the rosary would receive many graces, share in the light of God during their life, and receive a plenitude of graces at the moment of their death. Although the appearance of our Lady

1. See "Prayer Beads Worldwide: A Brief History," *https://culturetaste.com/blog/31_prayer-beads-worldwide-a-brief-history.html.*

to St. Dominic remains unsubstantiated by historical evidence, one biographer wrote: "If we remember the extraordinary power with which [the rosary] has been blessed, and its adoption through the universal church as the very alphabet of prayer, it is difficult for us not to believe it something more than a human invention, but rather a gift which came to us as the most precious token of the love of our dear mother. Although there is ample ground for belief, the details of any such revelation have not been preserved, leaving the date and manner in obscurity."[2] What matters most of all, though, is the faith with which we pray the rosary, as is the case with all prayer.

Some scholars say that St. Dominic encouraged his listeners to pray the rosary in private, to help them recall sermons he had preached on the mysteries of the rosary. Not unlike the use of stained-glass windows to catechize an illiterate population, the rosary served a similar purpose. While St. Dominic was alive—he died in 1221—fervor toward the rosary remained strong; but over the years, it was mostly forgotten and the flow of grace that accompanied it was therefore diminished. Two centuries later, while Europe was in the throes of the Black Death and the Western Schism, a renowned Dominican theologian, Alan de la Roche, wrote that he was reproached by the Lord for his failure to make the rosary better known. During the consecration of the Mass at which he was presiding, he said, he heard Jesus address him from the Host, saying, "You crucified Me once before by your sins. . . . You are crucifying Me again now because you have all the learning and understanding that you need to preach My Mother's Rosary, and you are not doing so. If you only did this, you could teach many souls the right path and lead them

---

2. Augusta Theodosia Drane, *The Life of Saint Dominic* (Charlotte, N.C.: TAN Books, 2011), 44.

away from sin—but you are not doing it and so you yourself are guilty of the sins they commit."[3]

Blessed Alan de la Roche said that following this rebuke from the Lord, he resolved to preach the rosary and was rewarded with an apparition by our Lady. She told him she had saved him from the great sins of his youth so that he could preach the rosary far and wide. Later, St. Dominic appeared to his protégé and told the friar that many sinners had been converted after he had returned to preaching the rosary. Known as the great "Apostle of the Holy Rosary," Blessed Alan wrote that he experienced a mystical marriage to the Blessed Virgin Mary. He explained that the Virgin placed a ring on his finger, draped a necklace made of her own hair upon him, and gave him a rosary.[4]

The history and development of the rosary from its origins is significant, because it offers an example of an ancient religious practice being adopted by Christian believers as a sound and fruitful expression of their own faith and relationship with Jesus and his mother. In addition, the graces arising from praying with these simple beads can make us think of Mary's son who changed water into wine and fed his followers by multiplying a few loaves and fishes from a young boy. In changing our simple offerings and understanding, God teaches us that when we offer to God what we have, the ordinary becomes extraordinary, the mundane sacred, and sinners and seemingly average people can become saints.

Pious tradition suggests that when Mary appeared to St. Dominic, she told him that the prayer beads were a powerful weapon to be used against existing heresies, as well as a tool to

---

3. St. Louis Mary De Montfort, *The Secret of the Rosary*, trans. Mary Barbour, T.O.P. (Bay Shore, N.Y.: TAN Books, 2009), 25.

4. De Montfort, 30.

be prayed with for the conversion of sinners. In our present culture, where war, disease, poverty, and racism exist amid the rise of secularization, the need to pray the rosary could not be more pressing. Mary continues to plead with us to turn our hearts to God and be converted—not once, but again and again. Sadly, many ignore what comes from the "Seat of Wisdom" who accompanied Jesus throughout salvation history and whom God chose for his own mother. The early-twentieth-century Carmelite author Fr. Gabriel of St. Mary Magdalene writes, "to anyone who wonders why so little is said about Mary in the Gospel, St. Thomas of Villanova replies: 'What more do you want? Is it not enough for you to know that she is the Mother of God? It would have been sufficient to say, *De qua natus est Jesus,* Jesus was born of her.'"[5] In that one phrase is contained all the mystery of the Mother of God.

A PERFECT UNION OF VOCAL AND MENTAL PRAYER

St. Dominic viewed the rosary as the perfect combination of vocal and mental prayer. The mysteries of the rosary were frequently the subject of his preaching, during which he instructed priests and laity to pray the rosary daily. He never viewed it as a simple prayer meant only for the uneducated. Considering her highly Christocentric approach to prayer, St. Teresa of Avila would agree with Dominic's view of the rosary as an aid to vocal and mental prayer. Teresa taught her nuns that vocal prayer must also be mental prayer: "I tell you that surely I don't know how vocal prayer can be separated from mental prayer if the vocal

---

5. Father Gabriel of St. Mary Magdalen, O.C.D., *Divine Intimacy,* trans. Discalced Carmelite Nuns of Boston (London: Baronius Press, 2008), 498–99.

prayer is to be recited well with an understanding of whom we are speaking to" (W 24.6). At one point she likened separating vocal prayer from mental prayer to a paralyzed person who has legs that do him no good. She noted that "to recite the Our Father or the Hail Mary or whatever prayer you wish is vocal prayer. But behold what poor music you produce when you do this without mental prayer. Even the words will be poorly pronounced at times" (W 25.3).

Teresa never recommended abandoning vocal prayer, even for those who had been brought to the highest stages of union. Counseling her nuns, she wrote, "Therefore, sisters, out of love for the Lord, get used to praying the Our Father with this recollection, and you will see the benefit before long" (W 29.6). In his introduction to The Way of Perfection, Kieran Kavanaugh writes, "The opening words of the Our Father lead [Teresa] into flights of her own unpremeditated prayer, and she teaches us to pray by praying herself. But the Our Father is always there to return to."[6] Teresa's appreciation for vocal prayer was also evident as she remained faithful to praying the Liturgy of the Hours, even reciting it with the nuns while they traveled across Spain in a covered wagon. Knowing how prone humans are to distraction during prayer, Teresa said she never went to prayer without a book on her lap as a prayer aid. Given her esteem for Mary, under whose patronage the order was founded, she surely made use of the rosary in a similar manner. The combination of vocal and mental prayer would have been very much in keeping with Teresa's teaching:

> To keep you from thinking that little is gained through a perfect recitation of vocal prayer, I tell you that it is very possible

---

6. Kieran Kavanaugh, O.C.D., "*The Way of Perfection* – Introduction," in *The Collected Works of St. Teresa of Avila*, vol. 2, trans. Kieran Kavanaugh, O.C.D., and Otilio Rodriguez, O.C.D. (Washington, D.C.: ICS Publications, 1980), 33.

> that while you are reciting the Our Father or some other vocal prayer, the Lord may raise you to perfect contemplation. By these means His Majesty shows that He listens to the one who speaks to Him. And it is His grandeur that speaks to the soul, suspending one's intellect, binding one's imagination, and, as they say. taking the words from one's mouth; for even though the soul may want to do so, it cannot speak unless with great difficulty. (W 25.1)

This is a most encouraging passage, showing us the potential for contemplation in every prayer.

It is impossible to appreciate fully the interweaving of human effort with divine grace. Unlike a patchwork quilt that defines various patterns, colors, and shapes, the human-divine partnership is a finely woven tapestry, its threads so closely interwoven that the intersection of human effort and divine grace are often indistinguishable. Perhaps this explains why we often fail to recognize God's presence in ordinary people and the events of life. Among the many children's stories that appeared in the 1930s, a poignant portrayal of Mary intervening in a young peasant girl's life reveals the human tendency toward blindness in this regard.

The story tells of a young teenage girl named Anna, the daughter of a poor widower who depended on his daughter to help care for her younger sister and brother and an infant orphaned after the child's parents died. One day, when Anna asked her father if she could have a new dress to wear to a festival, he explained that he didn't have money for such luxuries. Disappointed, she began to cry, which elicited laughter from her younger siblings. Distraught and angry, Anna lashed out at her father and told him she was tired of taking care of everyone and that he had no right to take in another child for her to look after. Storming out of the house, she ran until she found herself in front of the village church. Slowly she opened the door and went inside. Kneeling before the statue of the Virgin Mary, she prayed, "O Mother, your dress is so lovely. If only I could have such a dress, I too would feel like a queen."

Anna had hardly finished her prayer when she was transported inside the statue of Mary. After what seemed like hours, the door of the church opened, and she saw her twin siblings enter with the infant toddler in tow. They were dirty and the little one was crying. As they knelt before the statue of Mary, her sister Lizabeta took a string of beads from her pocket and placed them at Mary's feet. She told the Virgin she planned to give them to Anna, but she had run away, so she wanted Mary to have them if only she would bring Anna home. She wanted to tell Anna that she was sorry for laughing at her. Next, her brother Yakov placed a stick of candy at the Virgin's feet, apologizing for eating part of it. He was hungry since Anna wasn't home to prepare their supper. He asked the Blessed Mother to bring Anna home so the baby would stop crying. They were too small to feed him, and he was hungry. He told Mary that he loved Anna and wanted her to come home. Together they asked Mary to please help Anna not be so cross with them. Anna felt her heart sink. She wanted to apologize and comfort them, but she was unable to move her arms.

Shortly after they left the little church, Anna's father entered and, laying his pipe at the Virgin's feet, prayed to the holy Virgin to help Anna. "She is young and has so much responsibility. I want her to have a new dress, so I will stop smoking so I can buy one for her. Maybe this will show her how much I love her." Anna wanted to run to her father, throw her arms around him, tell him she loved him, and that she was sorry for what she had said, but again the Virgin's arms would not move. Only after her father left did Anna find herself once again in the pew. Awaking as if from a dream, she thanked the Blessed Virgin for helping her see how much she meant to her family and how much they meant to her. Anna raced home feeling like a queen because she had more than a new dress; she was able to do what even the Queen of Heaven could not do. She could throw her arms around her family and tell them that she loved them.[7]

We cannot expect God or Mary to do what we are able but unwilling to do. God does not force our hand. Deferring to our free will, God works most often through everyday life events and the process of human development. As Mediatrix of Grace, Mary does the same by inviting us to see the world through her eyes, while trusting us to respond as she would. When we see the world through the eyes of grace, people and the world around us look very different. It led John of the Cross to describe the world as a "sea of love." While we cannot ignore pain and suffering, ignorance, or lack of gratitude in our world, when we see as God sees, the needs of our brothers and sisters become our own. It's not within our capability to change people, nor is it always possible to change the environment or the circumstances in which we live, but we can entrust them to Jesus and his mother and then do what we can. As John of the Cross reminds us, "See that you are not suddenly saddened by the adversities of this world, for you do not know the good they bring, being ordained in the judgments of God for the everlasting joy of the elect" (SLL 64). In this way, we can accept through faith that God knows what he is doing, even if we ourselves cannot understand.

Jesus gave us his mother, and his mother gave us the rosary, not as a last resort but as a first response. While meditating on the mysteries of the rosary, we are awakened to God's way of seeing one another and the world. Reflecting on the life of Jesus and Mary

---

7. Adapted from a story by Caryll Houselander for The Children's Messenger, in *Caryll Houselander: Essential Writings,* ed. Wendy M. Wright (Maryknoll, N.Y.: Orbis Books, 2005), 52–58.

challenges us to reevaluate priorities and order our lives in keeping with gospel values, while deepening our relationship with God.

The life of Saint Titus Brandsma, a Carmelite priest and martyr, is an example of how hearts can be changed through the power of the rosary amid horrendous circumstances. As a journalist and scholar of mysticism and philosophy, he took a stand against the Nazis when they invaded the Netherlands. Titus Brandsma's prophetic stance led to his being imprisoned in multiple prison camps where he was abused by the guards. According to numerous witnesses, the priest ministered tirelessly to his fellow prisoners throughout his internment. His peaceful and cheerful demeanor was a source of inspiration as he encouraged his fellow prisoners, administering the sacraments whenever possible. Despite his brutal treatment, Titus Brandsma prayed for his captors, urging others to do the same. When he was questioned by fellow prisoners as to why they should pray for those who were beating and mistreating them, he responded gently, "You don't have to pray for them all day long."[8]

When his breviary and finally his rosary were taken away, the priest fashioned a rosary for himself from small chips of wood. Prior to his being put to death at Dachau, he gave his handmade rosary to the nurse who was to administer the lethal injection that would end his life. The nurse happened to be a lapsed Catholic to whom he said, "What a poor girl you are. I pray for you a lot."[9] Later, the nurse told members of the Carmelite Order that Fr. Titus Brandsma had helped bring her back to the practice of her faith. A model of uncompromising resistance to evil, trusting in Divine Providence, the Carmelite martyr was a living example of

---

8. Boniface Hanley, O.F.M., "Titus Brandsma," *https://www.ewtn.com/catholicism/library/titus-brandsma-5906/*. See also Hanley, *No Strangers to Violence, No Strangers to Love* (Notre Dame, Ind.: Ave Maria Press, 1995).

9. Constant Dölle, *Encountering God in the Abyss: Titus Brandsma's Spiritual Journey* (Leuven: Peeters, 2002), 186.

the compassion of Christ to all who knew him. He was beatified as a martyr by Pope John Paul II in 1985 and canonized by Pope Francis on May 15, 2022.

Titus Brandsma saw the world through God's eyes. Just as children bear a resemblance to their natural parents, so when we see the world through the eyes of our Divine Father and heavenly mother, we become more like them in all our interactions. Like the saints who traveled the path to holiness, we are called to build the kingdom of God one day at a time. Knowing our weakness, Mary reassures us of her presence and aid. At Lourdes, she appeared with the rosary over her arm, and at Fatima and Medjugorje she asked the young visionaries to pray the rosary.

Although the apparitions at Medjugorje have not been approved by the Catholic Church, the fruits of millions of pilgrims who leave the site committed to praying the rosary suggest that something supernatural is at work. Countless conversions, large numbers of people flocking to the sacrament of reconciliation, along with miracles and an increase in vocations to the priesthood, have led the church to view Medjugorje in a more favorable light, and in May 2019 Pope Francis authorized diocesan and parish pilgrimages to Medjugorje, due to the abundant graces that have sprung from there.[10]

Still, we don't have to visit apparition sites to take Mary's message to heart. In a letter written from his prison cell in Scheveningen, dated January 27, 1942, Titus Brandsma wrote, "I am already quite at home in this small cell. . . . I am alone, certainly, but never was Our Lord so near to me. . . . Now he is my only refuge, and I feel secure and happy. I would stay here forever, if he so disposed. Seldom have I been so happy and

---

10. See Massimiliano Menichetti, "Pope Authorizes Pilgrimages to Medjugorje," Vatican News, May 12, 2019, *https://www.vaticannews.va/en/pope/news/2019-05/pope-authorizes-pilgrimages-to-medjugorje.html/.*

content."[11] These words are a testimony to the fact that the heart of God is our true home on earth and that we are never alone, not even in an isolated cell. Given his great devotion to the rosary, Mary, who promised to be with her children, was surely with Titus, her Carmelite son and brother, throughout his life, especially during his suffering while on earth.

A GARLAND OF ROSES

Instructions on the mechanics of praying the rosary can be found in numerous publications, so there is no need to duplicate here what is already available. However, the prayers that make up the rosary—the Apostles' Creed, Our Father, Hail Mary, and Glory Be—merit discussion. Just as catechumens and candidates profess their belief in the teachings of the Catholic Church prior to baptism and reception into the church, so through the rosary we enter the mysteries of God, beginning with a profession of faith. The Apostles' Creed contains a summary of the church's key beliefs, serving as a gateway to the mystery of God's love while expanding our understanding and deepening our love for the Trinity. As we reflect on the mysteries, the rosary opens the door to contemplation. When we pray the words, not as a task to perform but as a way to enter into the heart of God, God communicates to us Mary's role in the history of salvation, which shows us the great esteem and love God has for his mother. Pope Paul VI warned: "Without contemplation, the Rosary is a body without a soul, and its recitation runs the risk of becoming a mechanical repetition of formulas, in violation of the admonition of Christ:

---

11. Redemptus Maria Valabek, O.Carm., *Titus Brandsma: Carmelite Educator, Journalist, Martyr* (Rome: Carmel in the World Press, 1985); see also "The Last Days of Titus: Letters Written in Prison," *https://www.ewtn.com/catholicism/library/last-days-of-titus--letters-written-in-prison-5607/*.

'In praying do not heap up empty phrases as the Gentiles do; for they think they will be heard for their many words'" (MC 47). This echoes, in its own way, the teaching of St. Teresa that vocal prayer must be joined with mental prayer and that it can simultaneously be contemplative prayer.

When praying the rosary, it isn't necessary to focus on every word of the Our Father, Hail Mary, and Glory Be. The quiet rhythm that accompanies the repetition of the words gradually becomes recollective and quiets the heart, allowing us to rest in the presence of God. With our mind cleared of distractions, we are better able to focus on the mysteries of our Lord's life. In keeping with St. Teresa's approach to prayer, we simply place ourselves at the Lord's feet within the setting of each mystery and become aware of his presence in the event. Teresa instructed her nuns to turn to the Lord frequently throughout the day, but her advice is also good counsel when praying the rosary: "I'm not asking you now that you think about Him or that you draw out a lot of concepts or make long and subtle reflections with your intellect. I'm not asking you to do anything more than look at Him. For who can keep you from turning the eyes of your soul toward this Lord?" (W 26.3). This gaze is at the heart of contemplation.

Since little effort is required for repeating prayers that are as familiar to us as our own name, the words flow fluently from our lips. In this way, the rosary facilitates our ability to be present to Jesus just as he is present to us. When our mind wanders, we gently return to the scene of the mystery. With our mind focused on God, the prayers rooted in Scripture fall from our lips in sweet praise of God. Every Hail Mary is a prayer of thanksgiving to God for the miracle of the incarnation and a love song to our Lady. St. Jerome considered the truths contained in the Hail Mary so sublime and so wonderful that neither human beings nor angels could fully understand them. Holding the Hail Mary in great esteem, Thomas Aquinas is said to have preached on this prayer for forty consecutive days. If esteemed theologians found such tremendous food for thought in the Hail Mary, we can be sure that when it is prayed reverently, God will take us where only God can.

If the salutations to Mary by the angel Gabriel and Elizabeth were wondrous enough to inspire the church's prayer, what more could be said about the prayer that came from Jesus's own lips? In *The Way of Perfection*, Teresa devoted sixteen chapters to discussing the Lord's Prayer. As a testimony to its efficacy, she wrote, "I marvel to see that in so few words everything about contemplation and perfection is included; it seems we need to study no other book than this one. Up to now the Lord has taught us the whole way of prayer and contemplation, from the beginning stages to mental prayer, to the prayer of quiet and to that of union" (W 37.1). From this we can understand why Teresa's treatment of the Our Father is a whole treatise in itself—indeed, probably the best ever written.

As for the Glory Be, there could be no more profound tribute to the Most Holy Trinity. Although it is positioned at the end of each decade, Pope St. John Paul II wrote:

> Trinitarian doxology is the goal of all Christian contemplation. For Christ is the way that leads us to the Father in the Spirit. If we travel this way to the end, we repeatedly encounter the mystery of the three divine Persons, to whom all praise, worship and thanksgiving are due. It is important that the Gloria, the high-point of contemplation, be given due prominence in the Rosary. . . . Far from being a perfunctory conclusion, [the Gloria] takes on its proper contemplative tone, raising the mind as it were to the heights of heaven and enabling us in some way to relive the experience of Tabor, a foretaste of the contemplation yet to come. (RVM 34)

This is an important reminder that the rosary is not just a Christocentric prayer but a trinitarian one as well.

Pope John Paul II made it known that the rosary was his favorite prayer. In the 2002 apostolic letter, which he devoted to the prayer, he wrote, "From my youthful years this prayer has held an important place in my spiritual life. . . . The rosary has accompanied me in moments of joy and in moments of difficulty. To it I have entrusted any number of concerns: in it I have always found comfort" (RVM 2). This has surely been true for countless people throughout the ages.

In the aftermath of the Second Vatican Council, some assumed that Mary had been reduced to a less prominent role in the church, but nothing could be further from the truth. In fact, the council reaffirmed the church's special love for Mary and reiterated her importance as Mother of God and mother of all of humanity: "Mary's function as mother of humankind in no way obscures or diminishes this unique mediation of Christ, but rather shows its power. All the Blessed Virgin's salutary influence on men and women originates not in any inner necessity but in the disposition of God. It flows forth from the superabundance of the merits of Christ. . . . Therefore the Blessed Virgin is invoked in the Church under the titles of advocate, helper, benefactress, and mediatrix" (LG 60, 62).

As we can see from this passage (and as we have seen throughout the ages), understanding and appreciation for the role of Mary in our life and in the life of the church continues to evolve. This should come as no surprise. When plumbing the depths of mystery, the journey of the human-divine relationship never ends. As if God becoming man through the consent of a mere human being was not enough, the Son of Man died so that we might live. We cannot enter the mystery of the triune God without beholding the mysteries of God, and we cannot enter the mysteries of God without entering through his mother.

As the Mother of God and our mother, Mary is the gateway to divine life. In concluding the chapter on Mary, the council fathers added:

> The entire body of the faithful pours forth urgent supplications to the Mother of God and of people that she, who aided the beginnings of the Church by her prayers, may now, exalted as she is above all the angels and saints, intercede before her Son in the fellowship of all the saints, until all families of people, whether they are honored with the title of Christian or whether they still do not know the Savior, may be happily gathered together in peace and harmony into one People of God, for the glory of the Most Holy and Undivided Trinity. (LG 69)

The prayer of the rosary, so humble and simple, is yet a sublime means of pouring forth "urgent supplications" for the church and the world, now and through the ages.

INVITATION TO PRAYER

The word rosary means "garland of roses" and has been called by St. Louis de Montfort a "tool," a "weapon in his apostolic work," and a "veritable school of Christian life."[12] His use of symbols to describe the rosary is an example of the power of metaphor and symbolic language to represent more than a literal description can convey. Similarly, through the use of artistic imagery, the Litany of Loreto bestows on Mary an exquisite array of images that describe her role in the church and in the world. With this verbal portrait of Mary in mind, we invoke her intercession and pray:

Continued

12. De Montfort, *The Secret of the Rosary*, 7.

INVITATION TO PRAYER *Continued*

Mirror of justice, pray for us.
Seat of wisdom, pray for us.
Cause of our joy, pray for us.
Spiritual vessel, pray for us.
Vessel of honor, pray for us.
Singular vessel of devotion, pray for us.
Mystical rose, pray for us.
Tower of David, pray for us.
Tower of ivory, pray for us.
House of gold, pray for us.
Ark of the covenant, pray for us.
Gate of heaven, pray for us.
Morning star, pray for us. Amen.

12

Keeping Vigil with Mystery

Among the many titles that honor Mary, none illustrates her contemplative nature more perfectly than the title "Mystical Rose," from the Litany of Loreto. The Merriam-Webster dictionary defines *mystical* as "having a spiritual meaning or reality that is neither apparent to the senses nor obvious to the intelligence."[1] A rose, on the other hand, is immediately apparent to the senses of both sight and smell. Long associated with love, beauty, life, death, and rebirth, the rose is an apt symbol for the woman whom God raised up to partner with Jesus as he saved the world through his life, death, and resurrection. In a most singular way, Mary is the bride who sings, "I am a rose of Sharon, / a lily of the valleys" (Song 2:1), to whom her spouse responds, "As a lily among brambles, / so is my love among maidens" (Song 2:2). Unlike Elijah, who encountered God at the entrance to a mountain cave, this highly favored Flower of Carmel held God in her arms, marveling as she nursed him and secure in knowing: "With great delight I sat in his shadow, / and his fruit was sweet to my taste" (Song 2:3).

Surely there can be no better guide than heaven's own Mystical Rose to lead earthly pilgrims through the mysteries

1. *Merriam-Webster's Collegiate Dictionary*, 11th ed. (Springfield, Mass.: Merriam-Webster, 2008), s.v. "mystical."

bestowed upon the world by the triune God. She who pondered in her heart all that was beyond knowing is a model of selfless humility, trusting in the ways of the Lord. As a song that is sung throughout Scripture, our Lady teaches us about Love to whom she is espoused, who overshadowed her, and to whom she gave birth. In gifting us with the rosary, Mary invites us to keep vigil with mystery, uniting the words that fall from our lips with her song that has echoed through the ages, "My soul magnifies the Lord, / and my spirit rejoices in God my Savior" (Lk 1:46–47).

It is no secret that people have long been fascinated by the unknown. Mystery books line shelves in libraries and bookstores, while television and movie scripts ignite imaginations, sprinkling clues that transform readers and viewers into amateur sleuths. However, unlike mysteries that are couched within the pages of crime novels and on-screen storylines, divine mysteries are not problems to be solved, but doctrines to be embraced through faith. Signs and events that surround them may seem in some ways to be clues, but rather than leading to certitude, they invite believers to ponder what neither science can prove nor the senses can confirm. To help navigate these uncharted waters, Mary, Star of the Sea, steers us through the storms of life because when left to our own devices, we, like Job, become victims of our own ignorance.

According to Scripture, Job was a faithful servant of God who insisted that he had done nothing to warrant the hardships that left him conflicted. Thinking as human beings do, he couldn't understand why he had fallen on hard times, declaring to his friends,

> I am innocent,
>   and God has taken away my right;
> in spite of being right I am counted a liar;
>   my wound is incurable, though I am without transgression.
> (Job 34:5–6)

As Job laid out his case before his friends, God listened patiently. Throughout the line of questioning by Job's friends, who insisted he must have done something to offend God, the righteous man refuted their accusations. Finally, when the time was right, God responded to Job's dilemma, not with answers but with more and different questions:

> Where were you when I laid the foundation of the earth?
> Tell me, if you have understanding.
> Who determined its measurements—surely you know!
> Or who stretched the line upon it?
> On what were its bases sunk,
> or who laid its cornerstone
> when the morning stars sang together
> and all the heavenly beings shouted for joy? (Job 38:4–7)

The questions continued on and on until, finally, Job was brought to his knees and declared:

> I have uttered what I did not understand,
> things too wonderful for me, which I did not know. . . .
> I had heard of you by the hearing of the ear,
> but now my eye sees you. (Job 42:3, 5)

Job's response was full of awe, because these powerful questions had confronted and overwhelmed him with the mysteries of God.

After hearing God's questions, Job was humbled and cried, "Therefore I despise myself, and repent in dust and ashes" (Job 42:6). Pride, complaint, and doubt in God's benevolence altered his relationship with God, which needed to be put in right order. When, like Job, we lose sight of the "I and Thou" that is the basis of trust in our relationship with God, then we, like

Adam and Eve, make ourselves equal to God. But such foolishness exists only in our minds. In response, the Son of God came to save us from ourselves. There were no human witnesses when God created the world, but when, through the life, death, and resurrection of his Son, God created the world anew, not only were there witnesses, but God commissioned mortal beings to carry out the work he had begun.

Descending from heaven, God became one of us by entering the womb of a woman, thus creating a marriage between heaven and earth. Unlike Job, we need no longer despise ourselves. Through the incarnation, humankind was recreated in God's own image as foretold by the psalmist: "

> You have made them little lower than God,
> and crowned them with glory and honor.
> You have given them dominion over the works of your hands;
> you have put all things under their feet. (Ps 8:5–6)

The conundrum of the divine-human relationship is as mysterious as it is glorious. It explains even as it confounds, and it defies human logic. Martin Buber, best known for his revival of mystical Hasidism, theorized, "Moments of the *Thou* appear as strange and lyric and dramatic episodes, seductive and magical, tearing us away to dangerous extremes, loosening the well-tried context, leaving more questions than satisfaction behind them, shattering security—in short, uncanny moments we can well dispense with."[2] This expresses well the elusiveness of God and the confusion with which we might always have approached him, were it not for the incarnation.

In becoming human, God reconsecrated all that sin had desecrated and drew all things to himself (see Eph 1:10). In

---

2. Martin Buber, *I and Thou*, trans. Ronald Gregor Smith (New York: Macmillan, 1956), 31–32.

Called to Communion, Joseph Ratzinger noted that when Christ rose from the dead, he existed in a new form of bodiliness, and the "uncrossable frontier of my 'I' is left wide open because Jesus himself has first allowed himself to be opened completely."[3] The moment we enter into a conversation with God, we enter into mystery; this understanding caused Martin Buber to warn his readers to "take care, not to understand this conversation with God."[4] God's speech is more than words: it is the Word of God who became flesh, a mystery beyond human understanding.

Consequently, it should come as no surprise that the apostles and those closest to the Lord while he was on earth did not understand what he was trying to teach them. Only in retrospect did they realize that Jesus had to die so that he could rise from the dead. Only after their hearts were set aflame were they able to accept in faith what had eluded them days earlier. And only after the coming of the Holy Spirit were they ready to die, knowing that they would rise with Christ.

God communicated his love for humankind by injecting mystery into human history so that the human-divine encounter would remain not as a single historical event but as an ongoing reality, which keeps us searching for happiness and wholeness that can only be found in God. We can never fully understand the mysteries of God in this life, but through prayer and by the grace of God divine mysteries are opened to us in stages. As Mediatrix of Grace, Mary invites us through her rosary to ponder the events of Jesus's life, so infused with mystery that to reflect on them once is never enough. Not everyone can receive the Eucharist every day or read Scripture

---

3. Joseph Ratzinger, *Called to Communion: Understanding the Church Today*, trans. Adrian Walker (San Francisco: Ignatius Press, 1996), 37.

4. Buber, *I and Thou*, 136.

daily, but the rosary is always available, and by praying it every day as Mary requested at Fatima, we enter into the mysteries that have set the world aright.

Like the child who tells his mother to read him a favorite bedtime story over and over, Mary delights in hearing her children pray the rosary, reflecting on the events in the life of her son again and again. In return, she guides our journey into mystery, taking us where angels fear to tread, because hidden beneath the veil of her gentle demeanor reside the power and perseverance of a courageous warrior. Teresa warned her nuns that whenever Satan sees souls turning to God, he will try to dissuade them. We need the protection of a fearless warrior, and who better than the woman whose unconditional obedience to God crushed the head of the serpent? Teresa cautioned, "If the devil, especially, realizes that [the soul] has all it needs in its temperament and habits to advance far, he will gather all hell together to make the soul go back outside [the interior castle]" (IC 2.1.5). Consequently, Mary's help is needed not only during times of temptation, but even following times of graced favors when fear and self-doubt may tempt us to abandon prayer.

When Queen Esther grew faint with fear before the king, he touched her with a golden scepter, permitting her to speak to him, and she said, "I saw you, my lord, like an angel of God, and my heart was shaken with fear at your glory" (Add Esth 15:13). Her words bring to mind Teresa's attesting to the fact that when souls are carried away during ecstatic rapture or flight of the spirit, the spirit seems to go forth from the body, though it is clear that this person is not dead (see IC 6.5.7). Now it is we who stand in need of the intercession of the Queen of Heaven who reigns over her children on earth and entreats the help of Christ in protecting us against our enemies. Mary's charity, purity, and virginal integrity could be her royal scepter, as she who has been called "House of Gold"[5] stands at God's right hand arrayed in robes of gold.[6] While Esther's physical beauty captivated the Persian king, it is Mary's interior beauty and purity that captivated the King of Heaven. Just as Esther grew in wisdom and courage when needed, risking even her life for the salvation of her people, so Mary, who is called "Seat of Wisdom," surrendered her life, holding nothing back. After her assumption into heaven, Mary's status was elevated to that of universal queenship. Although Mary is a Jewish woman by birth, she is intercessor for all the people, not just for one nation or race as was Esther. As the mother of Jesus, Mary is mother of all the world's children. As "Comfort of the Afflicted," she invites us to turn to her son. She is both Golden Rod and Scepter of Power, who prepares us to encounter the divine splendor for which contemplative souls long. Desiring the protection of this royal mother, St. Anselm prayed, "O beautiful to gaze upon, lovely to contemplate, delightful to love, whither do you go to evade the breadth of my heart? Lady, wait for the weakness of him who follows you; do not hide yourself, seeing the littleness of the soul that seeks you!"[7] In these words, we can sense the childlike soul of St. Anselm, reaching out to his Blessed Mother.

Just as earthly mothers hold out their arms to their children, encouraging them to take that first step, so Mary holds out the rosary to enable us to learn about the great mysteries of God. Although we may never fully understand them, Mary invites us to enter in and ponder the love of a God who sent his Son to

---

5. This title, as well as "Seat of Wisdom" and "Comfort of the Afflicted," are taken from the Litany of Loreto.

6. See Entrance Antiphon, Mass of the Queenship of Mary (August 22), *The Roman Missal*, Third Typical Edition (Washington, D.C.: USCCB), 2011. 934; cf. Ps 45:9.

7. Sister Benedicta Ward, S.L.G., ed., *Prayers and Meditations of St Anselm with the Proslogion* (London: Penguin, 1973), 115.

die for us so that we might enter heaven as adopted children of God. Mary grew into her role as Queen of Heaven, from the moment the Word of God entered her womb in Nazareth until her son rose from the tomb on Easter morning. As we travel the road to Christian maturity, we have in Mary a perfect guide, and we are most secure when we allow her to lead the way.

MYSTERIES OF THE ROSARY

The fifteen events that comprise the three sets of mysteries known as the Joyful, Sorrowful and Glorious Mysteries were formulated in the sixteenth century. At about the same time, the Glory Be, a most glorious tribute to the Trinity, was prescribed to follow each decade of ten Hail Marys. In 1569, Pope Pius V officially approved this form of the rosary, which would exist for the next four centuries.[8] And in 1571, he instituted the feast of Our Lady of the Rosary. Catholics around the world prayed these three sets of mysteries until 2002, when Pope St. John Paul II added the five Luminous Mysteries, or Mysteries of Light. The reason for the addition was to help Catholics enter more fully into the life of Christ as they prayed the rosary. The abrupt transition from the Joyful Mysteries to the Sorrowful had excluded Jesus's public ministry, which is crucial to our understanding of the life and teachings of Jesus. In his apostolic letter introducing the Luminous Mysteries, John Paul II wrote:

> To bring out fully the Christological depth of the Rosary it would be suitable to make an addition to the traditional pattern which, while left to the freedom of individuals and communities, could broaden it to include the mysteries of Christ's public ministry between his Baptism and his Passion. In the course

8. In his papal bull *Consueverunt Romani Pontifices* (September 17, 1569), *https://www.papalencyclicals.net/pius05/p5consue.htm/*.

> of those mysteries we contemplate important aspects of the person of Christ as the definitive revelation of God. Declared the beloved Son of the Father at the Baptism in the Jordan, Christ is the one who announces the coming of the Kingdom, bears witness to it in his works and proclaims its demands. It is during the years of his public ministry that the mystery of Christ is most evidently a mystery of light: "While I am in the world, I am the light of the world" (Jn 9:5). (RVM 19)

In this way, we are drawn into the heart of the gospels, contemplating the light of God's glory in the person of Christ.

For those who might wonder if praying the rosary—with its meditation on the episodes of the life of Jesus—contradicts the teachings of John of the Cross that call for purifying the appetites of both sense and spirit during prayer, the answer is a resounding "no." The Carmelite mystic did not entirely negate the senses as a gateway to God. Explaining that the faculty of discursive imagination and the external senses are goods pertinent to the interior senses, he wrote, "Whenever spiritual persons, on hearing music or other things, seeing agreeable objects, smelling sweet fragrances, or feeling the delight of certain tastes and delicate touches, immediately at the first movement direct their thought and the affection of their will to God, receiving more satisfaction in the thought of God than in the sensible object that caused it, and find no delight in the senses save for this motive, it is a sign they are profiting by the senses and the sensory part is a help to the spirit" (A 3.24.5). This insightful passage explains well how the senses and the spirit can be perfectly united in love of Christ through the prayer of the rosary.

Surely, there can be no higher use of the imagination than to meditate on the events of Christ's life while praying the words of the rosary. Current spiritual practices regarding "centering prayer" recommend using a mantra, a candle, or the breath as a means of emptying the mind of external distractions. However, neither Teresa nor John placed much emphasis on method or technique. They were more concerned with a person's interior disposition. Placing too much emphasis on external methods may lead to the misconception that infused prayer, which Carmelites refer to as contemplation, is the result of human effort rather than a gift from God. Drawing from Eastern traditions, some teachers of "centering prayer" suggest that in choosing a mantra, persons should choose a neutral word such as *be* or *still*, so as to avoid inadvertently directing the mind toward God. To such advice I can almost hear Teresa saying, "Nonsense!" She disapproved strongly (and sadly) of the idea that "images. . . . referring to the humanity of Christ" might be seen as "an obstacle or impediment to the most perfect contemplation" (L 22.1).

Given Teresa's Christocentric approach toward prayer, she would have said that imagining Mary during the nativity, gazing at Jesus in the Garden of Olives during his agony, or kneeling with Mary at the foot of the cross places people of prayer on firm ground. If union with God is our goal, then why would anyone *not* strive to direct their gaze toward God? In this regard Teresa writes, "This Lord desires intensely that we love Him and seek His company, so much so that from time to time He calls us to draw near Him. And His voice is so sweet the poor soul dissolves" (IC 2.1.2). Clearly, it is not up to the person praying to decide how and when God speaks to the soul. Teresa noted that the Master's voice may be heard while listening to a sermon, reading a spiritual book, or living in the midst of trials. To this we could add praying the rosary, which is one of many means through which the Lord may choose to speak to souls.

In describing souls in the second dwelling places, Teresa was referring to people who are just beginning the journey toward union with God. Yet, when it comes to understanding the mysteries of God, we are always beginning. For like the horizon beyond which we can never see, so the mysteries of God are always beyond our gaze. When we approach the mysteries of the rosary with the mindset of Job, who admitted he did not know what he was talking about or understand things too wonderful for him, our hearts are open to the counsel of John of the Cross who insisted that "souls must go to God by not comprehending, rather than by comprehending, and they must exchange the mutable and comprehensible for the Immutable and Incomprehensible" (A 3.5.3). John reassures us that our apprehending of natural thoughts and knowledge does not prevent God from infusing his light and love into souls any more than a window prevents the sun from shining through (see A 2.14.9). In fact, persons in the dark night who are unaware of God's hidden light entering the soul receive the greater gift. This doesn't mean that we should set aside knowledge that comes to us through the intellect. John drew on his extensive knowledge of Scripture, which permeated his life, guided his understanding, and helped him formulate into words what he experienced in prayer. Not all are called to be theologians or are schooled in Scripture, but everyone can take comfort in the words of Pope John Paul II, who referred to the rosary as the "School of Mary" (RVM 1, 14, 43). And as students at this school, we sit at the feet of our mother while listening to her tell us stories about her son.

ROSARY: COMPANION AND GATEWAY TO CONTEMPLATION

It is widely known that Mother Teresa of Calcutta prayed the rosary during almost every free moment. As she traveled around the world doing the Lord's work, she was rarely seen without rosary beads in hand. She was seen praying the rosary in airports, on board trains, and while waiting for meetings to begin. She often invited Father Leo Maasburg, who traveled with her, to join her in praying the rosary. According to this priest, Mother Teresa was a woman of few words, not prone to chitchat. When she was not ministering to the poor or engaged in business concerning the order she founded, she was speaking to God, her fingers moving along Mary's garland of roses, or else kneeling with her hands pressed to her forehead. Mother Teresa, when asked about prayer, she would often comment, "Prayer gives a clean heart and a clean heart can see God, can talk to God and peace comes."[9]

In his book about Mother Teresa, Leo Maasburg explained that Mother Teresa did not teach complicated prayer techniques. She simply reminded people that we must make the effort and be conscious of what we are doing when we pray.[10] According to Mother Teresa, "Listening is the beginning of prayer, and what we listen to is the voice of God."[11] God speaks in the stillness of a listening heart, so anything that awakens us to a deeper love of God is prayer not of our own doing, but of God's. Therefore, it can rightly be called infused prayer, even when we are unaware of what is taking place.

Teresa and John of the Cross would surely agree with Mother Teresa's approach to prayer. In a culture that prides itself on multitasking, many pray the rosary while driving, walking, rocking an infant, or doing housework. These times are commendable, since they enable us to engage in conversation with God. However, when we consider Jesus's teaching that when we pray, we are to go to our inner room and close the door (see Mt 6:6), then setting time aside solely to pray while meditating on the mysteries is a more excellent way to pray the rosary. It

---

9. Mother Teresa of Calcutta, *The Writings of Mother Teresa of Calcutta*, Mother Teresa Center. Used with permission.

10. Leo Maasburg, Mother *Teresa of Calcutta: A Personal Portrait*, trans. Michael J. Miller (San Francisco: Ignatius Press, 2011), 81.

11. Mother Teresa of Calcutta, *The Writings of Mother Teresa of Calcutta*, Mother Teresa Center. Used with permission.

is natural to be easily distracted while we are engaged in other activities. Focusing on God within the context of such profound mysteries requires intentionality and undivided attention. In making ourselves fully available to the Holy Spirit who prays through us, we become more accessible to mystery, opening the door to the inflow of God's grace. It may happen that we are granted a deeper understanding of the mysteries of God while meditating on them, or God may lead us into his presence where words and images disappear while he communicates to the soul in secret. But no matter what our experience of God may be, we can be sure that God is listening and gives us what we need at just the right time and in exactly the right way.

John of the Cross wrote extensively about prayer that takes place in the silence of our hearts, but I don't believe he meant that one form of prayer excludes the practice of another. It seems to me that praying the rosary pleases our Lord because it is an act of obedience to his mother who asks us to do so. When Sister Lucia, one of the visionaries at Fatima, who became a Carmelite nun, was asked why Mary told her that we are to pray the rosary every day, she responded that she had never asked Mary that question; but she offered her own explanation, saying, "To pray the Rosary is something everybody can do, rich and poor, wise and ignorant, great and small." And along with the Mass, the rosary "is the most pleasing prayer we can offer to God and one which is most advantageous to our own souls. If such were not the case, our Lady would not have asked for it so insistently."[12] Remembering that Mary herself calls us to this prayer is not just an encouragement but an invitation to respond with love.

---

12. Joseph Pronechen, *The Fruits of Fatima: A Century of Signs and Wonders* (Manchester, N.H.: Sophia Institute Press, 2019), 138–39; see also Pronechen, "Why Does Our Lady of Fatima Call Us to the Daily Rosary?" Catholic Exchange, May 4, 2021, *https://catholicexchange.com/why-does-our-lady-of-fatima-call-us-to-the-daily-rosary/.*

The more we pray the rosary, the more Mary opens our eyes to the wonders of God's immeasurable love. When keeping vigil with our heavenly mother, life's obstacles may not disappear, but when we entrust them to Mary, peace fills our soul. Responding to her invitation to pray the rosary, Mary takes us by the hand and together we enter mystery, only to discover that mystery has entered us. Then we find it easy to believe what Jesus told us when he said, "Those who love me will keep my word, and my Father will love them, and we will come to them and make our home with them" (Jn 14:23). We are entering God, and God is entering us.

INVITATION TO PRAYER

Each time we pray the rosary, we stand at the threshold of mystery; but rather than tremble in fear, we are invited to gaze in wonder as we recall the fiat that set in motion events that would change the world. When the God of the universe entered the womb of a young virgin, the mystery of the incarnation became real. And as the seed of God was planted in a woman, whose magnificent sense of emptiness was such that it took God to fill it, angels bowed in deference to the maiden of Nazareth who would bear God's son. As beneficiaries of this marriage between heaven and earth, we turn to Mary with grateful hearts, and extolling her virtues we pray:

HOLY VIRGIN OF VIRGINS, PRAY FOR US . . .
VIRGIN MOST PRUDENT, PRAY FOR US.
VIRGIN MOST VENERABLE, PRAY FOR US.
VIRGIN MOST RENOWNED, PRAY FOR US.
VIRGIN MOST POWERFUL, PRAY FOR US.
VIRGIN MOST MERCIFUL, PRAY FOR US.
VIRGIN MOST FAITHFUL, PRAY FOR US. AMEN.

13

The Joyful Mysteries

When only five decades of the rosary are prayed on a given day, St. John Paul II recommended praying the Joyful Mysteries on Mondays and Saturdays.[1] He also suggested that we take a few moments to ponder each mystery before beginning the Our Father. Amid distractions vying for our attention, we ask Mary to lead the way, for as keeper of this gate into mystery, she asks for surrender, not determination, since it is the Holy Spirit who prays in us. Mindful that we are standing on holy ground, we enter unshod, for only the meek and humble of heart can tread the land that once bore heaven's footprint. Yet as we trust the process, the steady rhythm of the prayers quiets the mind and empties the heart as mystery beckons. With the help of the Holy Spirit, new insights emerge and our appreciation for it deepens, no matter how often we pray the rosary.

THE ANNUNCIATION

As we reflect on the Joyful Mysteries, the presence of suffering, hidden within each joyful event, is as striking as it is

1. See RVM 38. Before the Luminous Mysteries were added, the Joyful Mysteries had traditionally been prayed on Mondays and Thursdays.

confounding. But rather than this detracting from Mary's experience of joy, her participation in the price that God paid to save sinners reveals a phenomenon that contemplative hearts understand. St. Thérèse described her own experience of the paradox: "In spite of this trial which has taken away *all my joy,* I can nevertheless cry out: '*You have given me DELIGHT, O Lord, in ALL your doings.* For is there a *joy* greater than that of suffering out of love for You? The more interior the suffering is and the less apparent it is to the eyes of creatures, the more it rejoices You, O my God!'" (S 214). As Thérèse shows here, suffering does not have to take away our joy. And when it is lived for God, suffering can even *increase* our joy.

This insight of Thérèse testifies to the presence of a twofold miracle contained within each mystery of the rosary. The first miracle took place more than two thousand years ago, within the context of time when God became incarnate of the Virgin Mary and lived among a sinful race. The second miracle is ongoing and takes place in the hearts of those who pray. While reflecting on the miracles of the past, hearts are opened to embrace the miracles of the present, within the context of daily life. Just as the world was changed when the Word of God entered Mary's womb and God revealed himself, so those who echo Mary's fiat, when the Word of God enters their soul, become partners in God's self-revealing work. Humbled before the presence of God, we are challenged to see as God sees and to respond by reflecting his presence to the world around us.

Mary's espousal to the Holy Spirit did not circumvent the "I and Thou" of her conversation with God;[2] it defined it. Her self-identity as the obedient handmaid of the Lord was rooted in God—this humble King who came down from heaven to dwell as a tiny embryo in the womb of a young girl. How incredible!

2. See Buber, *I and Thou*, 136, discussed in the previous chapter.

Yet, as Caryll Houselander exclaimed, "How consistent it is with the incredible compassion of God that His Christ, the Immortal Child, should be conceived by the power of the Holy Spirit in the body of a child. That a child should bear the Child who would redeem the world."[3] Is it any wonder, therefore, that Jesus said to his followers, "Unless you change and become like children, you will never enter the kingdom of heaven" (Mt 18:3)? If God humbled himself and became a child, how could we expect to do less? In becoming the mother of the Christ,

> [Mary] was not asked to do anything herself, but to let something be done to her. She was not asked to renounce anything, but to receive an incredible gift. She was not asked to lead a special kind of life, to retire to the temple and live as a nun, to cultivate suitable virtues or claim special privileges. She was simply to remain in the world, to go forward with her marriage to Joseph, to live the life of an artisan's wife, just what she had planned to do when she had no idea that anything out of the ordinary would ever happen to her . . . The whole thing was to happen secretly. There was to be no announcement and God was so jealous of His secret that He even guarded it at the cost of His little Bride's seeming dishonor.[4]

This gift, this secret, at the heart of Mary's life, has great implications for our own lives, and it leads us to reflect on God's choice of the ordinary as a privileged place for his creative action.

How could it be that God chose someone whose life was as ordinary as Mary's to become his mother? As we ponder the mystery, we reflect on our own ordinary life. What might God be asking of us in the secret of our heart? It may take us by surprise even as it fills us with joy. When we are unaware of what

3. Houselander, *The Reed of God*, 33.

4. Houselander, *The Reed of God*, 33.

God has planned for us, we can delight in the unexpected, for when God speaks in the silence of our heart, we instinctively know that whatever is revealed in secret is to be cherished. St. Thérèse may have been pondering such hidden surprises in her life when she wrote, "The little flower finds the dew with which she was filled so delightful that she would be very careful not to exchange it for the insipid water of praise" (S 206). In effect, she was speaking of the joy within the hidden life.

There is a deep joy that resides within the cloak of anonymity, for the language of the Bridegroom is too intimate to be spoken in the marketplace. Suffice it to say that not all privileged souls are hidden behind cloister walls. Most are housed within the walls of the domestic church, building the kingdom, unaware that they are being led deeper and deeper into the heart of God. Parents feeding and clothing, educating and forming their children in virtue are flowers that water the garden of souls when their actions are motivated by their love for God. Writing a check to feed the hungry, supporting a friend through a crisis, baking a cake for the church bazaar seem insignificant; although they go mostly unnoticed, God sees what is done in secret and rewards us accordingly. Like Mary, we carry within us the God who waits patiently for us to re-incarnate him in the world, whenever and wherever life takes us. Awakened by the power of God's love, we realize that everything in life is a potential birthing center where the world is being created anew in the image and likeness of God.

THE VISITATION

Scripture tells us that after Mary conceived Jesus, she went with haste to the hill country of Judea to help Elizabeth who was pregnant. Mary's sense of urgency to be of assistance to her aging kinswoman exemplifies what happens when the Word of God is welcomed and embraced by souls. The fruits of such encounters cannot be contained. Rooted in the life-giving communion of the Trinity, these souls are called forth, as John of the Cross explained: "Devout souls run along by the youthful strength received from the sweetness of your footprints, that is, run from place to place in many ways. Each runs along according to the way and kind of spirit and state God gives, with many differences of spiritual practices and works. They run along the way of eternal life, the way of evangelical perfection, by which they encounter the Beloved in union of love after their spirit has been stripped of all things" (C 25.4). These last few words are particularly important as John urges us to detachment that leads to freedom.

As spouse of the Holy Spirit, Mary was not impeded by human attachments. Her freedom makes her the perfect model for pilgrim souls as they journey toward union with God. Either we go forth and bear fruit, or we turn in upon ourselves, an act that St. Augustine defined as sin. To turn in on oneself is to turn away from God, which corrupts the soul, resulting in a miscarriage of God's abundant love and mercy.

Going forth like Mary means sharing Christ with family and friends, strangers and neighbors, coworkers in the workplace and in the vineyard of the Lord. It means being open to the gifts of those around us, rejoicing and praising God for their ability to proclaim the presence of Christ in our midst. Petty jealousies and gossip have no place in the Lord's vineyard. When we are mindful that we carry Christ within us, we are at once mindful of our unworthiness and find ourselves asking, "How is it that my Lord should come to me?" Or the soul might respond like St. Teresa who, when describing the Master's presence, wrote, "His voice is so sweet that the poor soul dissolves at not doing immediately what he commands. Thus, as I say, hearing his voice is a greater trial than not hearing it" (IC 2.1.2). Still others, more attuned to the voice of God, may echo Mary's *Magnificat* or the words of John of the Cross as they go forth singing:

Following your footprints
maidens run along the way;
the touch of a spark,
the spiced wine,
cause flowings in them from the balsam of God.
(C stanza 25, Redaction B)

There is a lightness of step in this rejoicing and a readiness to go swiftly to wherever God calls.

When reflecting on the visitation of Mary to Elizabeth, we usually direct most of our attention toward the two saintly women. However, as a silent bystander to all that unfolded, Zechariah was surely moved as the mother of the Messiah came to his wife's aid. What were his thoughts as he reflected on the trusting disposition of Mary, so different from his own response to the angel Gabriel? Confounded by the announcement that his wife would conceive in her old age and bear a son, Zechariah had asked for proof. Consequently, he was struck mute, sentenced to nine months of silence. Yet somewhere during that solitary night, Zechariah experienced the transforming love of God. Mary's sole purpose for visiting was to aid Elizabeth, but the graced presence of the Messiah, concealed in the womb of the Virgin Mother, surely helped turn the aging Zechariah from doubter to believer, from pessimist to prophet.

No sooner had his tongue been loosed than Zechariah gave voice to the hymn of praise that has been sung by the universal church wherever the *Benedictus* is prayed. In acknowledging the fulfillment of a promise, Zechariah recognized in his own son a foretaste of what was to come. Enlightened by the Holy Spirit, he praised God because the time had arrived when God would transform the past into an ever-present reality. In raising up a mighty Savior, God fulfilled his promise to Abraham, broke into human history in the person of his Son, and restored hope to a fallen race. Zechariah envisioned the coming of interior freedom, enshrined within the will of every person for all time. His prophecy—"that we, being rescued from the hands of our enemies, / might serve him without fear" (Lk 1:73)—did not mean that we would not be persecuted, but that we need not *fear* persecution. Once we are freed from the bondage of sin, the gates of heaven will be opened, and death will be no more, for not even the gates of hell can prevail against what God has ordained.

This was the reality to which Zechariah gave witness. He understood that in the tender compassion of God, the dawn from on high was about to break upon the world and shine on those who dwell in darkness and the shadow of death. Zechariah's prophetic hymn, prayed every morning by the church, promises that we will be guided—though never forced—to run toward the dawn of a new day, along the path of peace. The choice is ours, but we are never alone.

Just as Mary came to the aid of Elizabeth, so she, our mother, comes to our aid as model and intercessor. An example of perfect faith, hope, and charity, Mary leads us through her earthly encounters with God, reminding us that Jesus's presence remains with us. She reassures us that voices that were once organs of selfishness and sin can become instruments of celebration and kindness when we allow the Holy Spirit to guide us. The incarnation and Mary's visit to Elizabeth are no longer bound by constructs of time; they continue as ongoing realities, repeated in the lives of ordinary people who, like Mary, go forth seeking to do the will of God without counting the cost.

THE NATIVITY OF THE LORD

According to human standards, few things about the birth of Jesus suggest a fitting entrance into the world by the Son of God. Not everything surrounding Jesus's birth was bathed in light and love. The rigors of travel over dusty roads during the final days of Mary's pregnancy, the closing of doors as Joseph sought shelter, and the birthing of the Son of God in a cave where animals dwelt seem scandalous. Yet for the poor, such hardships were part of everyday life. In choosing to identify with the marginalized and homeless, God transformed everyday heartaches and disappointments into occasions of grace. Intuiting as much, Mary abandoned herself to circumstances beyond her control, confident that God would complete the work he had begun in her when she lent her womb for God's son to grow within her.

And so it was that, just as the Word of God entered Mary's womb in secret, so God entered the world in silent wonder with only Mary and Joseph invited to share the Father's joy. What blessed irony that as the marriage between God and humanity had begun, the world slept on. We might wonder: What were Mary's thoughts on that wondrous night as she gazed upon her son? As she drew the Child Jesus to her breast, did she understand that it was her own blood that was flowing through the veins of God? And could she have known that the song that filled her heart would echo through the centuries? This song of her heart, this interior movement of joy, has inspired saints and mystics like John of the Cross to exclaim:

> For he would make himself
> wholly like them,
> and he would come to them
> and dwell with them;
> and God would be man
> and man would be God. (R 4)

We can only respond with grateful awe to God coming to us and making us, as it were, his equals.

As angels' voices filled the nighttime sky over the shepherds' field, not even the prophets could have imagined that God would send a heavenly choir to so unlikely a place. But in reversing the effects of sin, God also reversed the way sinners were to think. He began by clothing himself in poverty and choosing the least important in the eyes of the world to be his first witnesses, because only the poor in spirit would be humble enough to welcome the infant God into a world blinded by sin.

Who were these shepherds, chosen to worship the Son of God? Were they Jews? Had they heard about a promised messiah? And did they wonder why they were chosen? All we know is that when they entered the humble abode, something deep within their soul resonated with what they saw, impelling them to fall on their knees before the newborn King. We don't know what became of the shepherds in the years that followed this epiphany. Having felt the presence of God, could they ever forget what they had experienced? Did they persevere in prayer, keeping watch over their heart with the same care they exercised over their sheep? For some helpful insights, we can turn to the writings of Teresa and John.

St. Teresa reminds us that the newly converted turn instinctively to prayer, but to continue with a life of prayer requires vigilance and perseverance. She noted that God frequently consoles those in the beginning stages of prayer by appealing to their senses, but the real test lies in persevering once the consolations end. In writing about prayer in the beginning stages, Teresa warned those in the second dwelling places against a false sense of security, noting: "they still don't have the determination to remain in this second stage without turning back, for they don't avoid the occasion of sin" (IC 2.1.2). To turn away from sin, something more is needed.

Prayer can't exist in a vacuum. Therefore, the efficacy of prayer is proven within the challenges and demands of everyday life, where seeking the will of God is paramount. Teresa cautioned against relying on consolations during the early stages of prayer, despite the natural tendency to do so. She considered it "an amusing thing that even though we still have a thousand impediments and imperfections and our virtues have hardly begun to grow—and please God they may have begun—we are not yet ashamed to seek spiritual delights or complain about dryness" (IC 2.1.7). Further on, she explained that "the whole aim of any person who is beginning prayer should be that he prepares himself with determination and every possible effort to bring his will into conformity with God's will" (IC 2.1.8). And John of the Cross offered a similar warning: "When evening comes, you will be examined in love. Learn to love as God desires to be loved and abandon your own ways of acting" (SLL 60). He also warned against judging others: "Because the virtues you have do not shine in your neighbor, do not think that your neighbor is not precious in God's sight for reasons that you have not in mind" (SLL 62). Both these saints are urging us to virtue and to see as God sees, to will as God wills.

All are precious in God's sight. Mary welcomed the shepherds, and she praised God for his love for all people, especially the poor and the marginalized, in her *Magnificat.* She rejoiced because God came to free us from the bondage of prejudice. When Mary held the infant God in her arms, she could not have known what the future would hold. Yet, as the spouse of the Holy Spirit, the mother of Jesus, and the most-pure daughter of the Father, Mary's every thought, word, and action mirrored the love within the Most Blessed Trinity. It was the love relationship with the triune God that drew her to surrender her life to God through perfect obedience.

Therefore, it should come as no surprise that in obedience to Mosaic Law, which required every male infant to be circumcised, Mary witnessed the first shedding of her son's blood. As the handmaid of the Lord, Mary fulfilled her responsibility as an observant Jewish woman and faithful servant of God. Yet, this was no ordinary circumcision. The ritual identified the Son of God as a member of the Jewish race, fulfilling the words of the prophet Zechariah who proclaimed: "On that day, the Lord will shield the inhabitants of Jerusalem so that the feeblest among them on that day shall be like David, and the house of David shall be like God" (Zech 12:8). What emotion must have filled the heart of Mary as she looked on this weak and feeble child who was God himself!

THE PRESENTATION OF THE LORD IN THE TEMPLE

Forty days after the wondrous night of Jesus's birth, Mary and Joseph entered the temple in Jerusalem for her purification and to dedicate their son to God according to the law of Moses, as was written: "Every firstborn male shall be designated as holy to the Lord" (Lk 2:22; cf. Ex 13:2, 12). As Mary ascended the temple steps, was the song in her heart in concert with the psalmist's words: "I will walk with integrity of heart / within my house" (Ps 101:2)? And did the event remind her of her own presentation in the temple when she was three years old? According to the apocryphal *Protoevangelium of James*, Mary was brought to the temple at that age. "And the priest received her, and kissed her, and blessed her, saying: The Lord has magnified your name in all generations. In you, on the last of the days, the Lord will manifest His redemption to the sons of Israel. . . . And when she was twelve years old . . . Joseph . . . took her into his keeping [and] said to Mary: Behold, I have received you from the temple of the Lord; and now I leave you in my house. . . . The Lord will protect you."[5]

---

5. Alexander Roberts, James Donaldson, and A. Cleveland Coxe, eds., *Protoevangelium of James*, trans. Alexander Walker, *Ante-Nicene Fathers* 8 (Buffalo: Christian Literature Publishing Co., 1886), rev. and ed. for New Advent by Kevin Knight, 7–9,. *https://www.newadvent.org/fathers/0847.htm.*

The temple was revered by Jews as the place where they could encounter God; within was located the sacred inner sanctuary known as the holy of holies. If Mary did in fact grow up at the temple as the *Protoevangelium of James* suggests, then in a sense God's home had been Mary's home, so it may have felt as if she was returning to the home of her childhood. Now she was returning as a married woman and mother, aware of all that God had accomplished in her. Yet there was nothing about Mary or Joseph that would cause others to take notice. The Gospel of Luke tells us that their sacrificial offering, "according to what is stated in the law of the Lord," was "a pair of turtledoves or two young pigeons" (Lk 2:24). The prescribed offering for this occasion would have been an unblemished lamb, but it was acceptable for the poor who could not afford the cost of such an offering to offer instead two turtle doves or pigeons. More than an offering of the poor, the offering that Mary and Joseph brought carried a symbolic meaning. In the Hebrew Scriptures, the dove symbolized peace of the purest kind. Although Mary did, of course, observe the prescribed Jewish customs, there was no real need for her to undergo the required purification, since she was the most-pure vessel of God, who is the source of all purity. Once again, the poverty of God was on display, but only for privileged souls such as Anna and Simeon, who were granted the grace to see. If Mary grew up in the temple, it's possible that she recognized the holy pair. If so, she would have rejoiced at seeing familiar faces. Although she would have been happy for them to share in her joy regarding the birth of her son, she could not have expected Simeon to recognize the infant in her arms as the long-awaited Messiah.

How astounded Mary must have been when "Simeon took [Jesus] in his arms and praised God, saying, 'Master, now you are dismissing your servant in peace, according to your word; for my eyes have seen your salvation'" (Lk 2:28–30). Nor could she have anticipated that he would follow the proclamation with an address to her, adding: "This child is destined for the falling and the rising of many in Israel, and to be a sign that will be opposed so that the inner thoughts of many will be revealed—and a sword will pierce your own soul too" (Lk 2:34–35). Then Anna also began to praise the child.

The events of that day surely remained in Mary's mind as she pondered these things in her heart, not only after they left the temple but in the days that followed. Yet as the life of this holy couple unfolded, it wasn't long before the sword that the prophet had predicted pierced Mary's soul for the first time. No sooner had the wise men departed, after worshipping Jesus, than Joseph was told to take Mary and Jesus and flee with them to Egypt.

Fearing for their son's life, their obedience was swift. Though visible only to the Father, Mary's acceptance of the uncertainty that lay ahead surely rose like incense before the throne of God, its sweet perfume endearing her all the more to the Father. And yet surely not lost on them was the irony that they were told to seek refuge in the land where their ancestors were enslaved, and after kings had traveled from afar to adore Jesus. As Mary held Jesus to her breast, her arms the only protection against the cold night air, her world was expanding along with her understanding that God's ways are not our ways.

The flight of the Holy Family should give us pause. Our world is not so different from the world of Mary and Joseph. Surrounded by darkness, they were called to hold fast to the light. Mary and Joseph lived in a world inhabited by sinners, and yet they held fast to the belief that their son would change the world. As they left behind the world they knew and traveled to Egypt, they unknowingly became the first missionaries to carry Christ to a foreign land. Before the evangelist proclaimed that "the light shines in the darkness, and the darkness did not overcome it" (Jn 1:5), the Holy Family gave witness to it.

As the first fruits of prayer send contemplatives into the marketplace, we cannot close our ears to the voice of Rachel, weeping for her children, as millions of children are destroyed in their mother's womb. Nor can we ignore the plight of immigrants, victims of hatred and violence or intolerance and bigotry. But as much as the sins of others may sadden us, we cannot ignore our own sins as we travel the path to union with God. John of the Cross warned, "Do not rejoice vainly, for you know how many sins you have committed and you do not know how you stand before God; but have fear together with confidence" (SLL 76). He is giving voice to the essential attitude of trust in God's mercy, to which we could add the gospel lesson: do not set yourself up as judge.

St. Bernard of Clairvaux offered a similar precaution, advising his monks to approach the Lord by imagining they were kissing the wounds on Jesus's feet. He counseled them to look upon one foot as God's mercy and the other as his justice, lest they sin by presumption.[6] Only humility can reconcile the tension between mercy and justice, and who better to guide us along the path toward union with God than the humble virgin of Nazareth? She who bore the Light of the World in her womb remains a beacon of hope for all who long for communion with God. In the last few weeks of her life, Elizabeth of the Trinity wrote the following tribute to Mary: "There is one who knew this gift of God, one who did not lose one particle of it, one who was so pure, so luminous that she seemed to be the light itself: '*Speculum justitiae* [Mirror of justice].' One whose life was so simple, so lost in God that there is hardly anything we can say about it. '*Virgo Fidelis*': that is, Faithful Virgin, 'who kept all these things in her heart.' She remained so little, so recollected in God's presence, in the seclusion of the temple, that she drew down upon herself the delight of the Holy

6. See Bernard of Clairvaux, *Sermons on the Song of Songs*, 26–27.

Trinity." (HF 39). This is the greatness of the mystery taking place in the temple, in the soul of Mary.

THE FINDING OF THE CHILD JESUS IN THE TEMPLE

The joy and relief that Mary and Joseph experienced when they found Jesus does not negate the pain they experienced as they searched for him for three days and three nights. They were physically and mentally exhausted, and the roller coaster of emotions was evident in Mary's reprimand to her son. As they searched and inquired after Jesus along the way, the full weight of human emotion came to bear on Mary's heart. Imagining each negative response to their queries, we might consider what our own response would be to the question, "Have you seen Jesus?" Would a shrug of the shoulders reveal a lack of concern? Does Jesus's presence go unnoticed amid our preoccupation with personal agendas, possessions, and projects? And are we too busy to notice Jesus in the people we encounter along the way? The Master warned, "No one can serve two masters; for a slave will either hate the one and love the other, or be devoted to the one and despise the other. You cannot serve God and wealth" (Mt 6:24). These words could well apply to us if we answer with indifference or no longer make seeking God a priority.

This choice between God and idols was the underlying premise that guided John of the Cross in his approach to union with God. Unless we seek God by way of the ascent and the dark night, we could be looking for God in all the wrong places. Nothing can take the place of seeking, finding, and receiving Jesus through prayer and the sacraments. Just as Mary and Joseph sought Jesus with great urgency, so we must continue the search by spending time in prayer. When our search seems to go unrewarded, Mary teaches us by example that the best response, when faced with what we cannot comprehend, is to ponder the ways of God in the silence of our heart.

Scripture tells us that Jesus spent three days with religious leaders and was asking them questions. Was it to gain information or to make them think? It seems unlikely that he was looking for answers, since Matthew says that all were amazed by his wisdom. Throughout his ministry, Jesus asked questions of his followers. He wanted them to seek and find, not simply to be told what they must do to gain eternal life; and so it is with us. We come to understand the ways of God by seeking in prayer what God chooses to reveal to us in the silence of our hearts.

The journey toward union with God involves both joy and suffering, but it also entails going forth. As with Mary who traveled to the hill country of Judea, to Bethlehem, to Egypt, and to and from Jerusalem, not once but multiple times, prayer prepares us to meet the challenges of life. Mary's journeys were the fruit of her contemplative spirit. In response to God's will, her travels took her beyond natural inclinations, as it will be for all who follow Jesus.

Those who embark on the pilgrimage to their deepest center cannot do so without embracing the cross. We do not have to look far, since each person's life contains sufficient challenges through which to become saints. Regardless of our state in life, Mary's principles of discipleship are universal. When Elizabeth of the Trinity wrote her extraordinary spiritual treatise "Heaven in Faith," it was for her sister who was married with children. Although she spoke from her experience as a nun, she believed it was just as relevant for those "living in the world." This holy nun's experiences were rooted in the gospels, which is where we meet Mary, humble wife and mother who became a model for all who seek union with God. As one biographer has written: "Elizabeth could see in Mary what life in Christ meant, of what her own calling as a contemplative involved. Mary was one who responded perfectly to what God asked of her. In other words, she was the perfect 'Praise of Glory,' the ideal to which Elizabeth herself aspired."[7] As Elizabeth could see, to imitate Mary is ultimately to imitate Christ.

The more aligned our will is to the will of God, the more Christlike we become and the more our suffering becomes our joy. Mary's life was interspersed with joy and sorrow, like the life of every person. She entered the dark night, relying only on the flame that burned within her heart to light the way, and she invites us to do the same. Through the centuries, Mary's fiat has resounded within the life of contemplatives. She remains the personification of "absolute trust in God, trust which will not set us free from suffering, but *will* set us free from anxiety, hesitation, and above all from *fear* of suffering. Trust which makes us willing to be what God wants us to be, however great or how ever little that may prove to be."[8] This is the trust that says the "yes" that is Mary's fiat.

INVITATION TO PRAYER

If *joyfulness of heart* is "the undiminished sense you have that God is with you,"[9] then Mary is surely the one most qualified to show us what it means to have a joyful heart. From the moment the Word of God entered her womb, she would have experienced the continuous presence of Emmanuel, filling not only her soul but her body with unspeakable joy. Despite the trials and suffering that accompanied her throughout her life, Mary's soul overflowed with the joyful assurance that God was with her. As a gift of the Spirit, joy can also be ours, to the

Continued

7. Moorcroft, *He Is My Heaven*, 148.

8. Houselander, *The Reed of God*, 52.

9. Archimandrite Aimilianos, *The Way of the Spirit: Reflections on Life in God*, trans. Maximos Simonopetrites (Athens: Indiktos Publishing Co., 2009), 136.

INVITATION TO PRAYER *Continued*

extent that we are open to receive it. Reflecting on the event that filled Mary with the joy that is beyond all telling, we can lift our hearts to her as we pray the traditional prayer, nearly a millennium old, known as the Angelus:

V. The Angel of the Lord declared unto Mary.
R. And she conceived of the Holy Spirit.

Hail Mary, full of grace,
The Lord is with thee;
Blessed art thou among women,
And blessed is the fruit of thy womb, Jesus.
Holy Mary, Mother of God,
Pray for us sinners,
Now and at the hour of our death. Amen

V. Behold the handmaid of the Lord.
R. Be it done unto me according to thy word.

Hail Mary, etc.

V. And the Word was made Flesh.
R. And dwelt among us.

Hail Mary, etc.

V. Pray for us, O holy Mother of God.
R. That we may be made worthy of the promises of Christ.

Let us pray.

Pour forth, we beseech Thee, O Lord, Thy grace into our hearts, that we, to whom the Incarnation of Christ Thy Son was made known

INVITATION TO PRAYER *Continued*

BY THE MESSAGE OF AN ANGEL, MAY BY HIS PASSION AND CROSS BE BROUGHT TO THE GLORY OF HIS RESURRECTION. THROUGH THE SAME CHRIST OUR LORD. AMEN.[10]

---

10. Although the Angelus has traditionally been said three times daily, at 6:00 a.m., noon, and 6:00 p.m., it can be prayed anytime, privately or with others.

14

The Luminous Mysteries

When Pope John Paul II proclaimed 2002 to be a "Year of the Rosary," he added five new Luminous Mysteries to the existing fifteen mysteries of the rosary (see RVM 19). At the time, he explained that their purpose was to fill in the years between the finding of Jesus in the temple and his agony in the garden. However, in assigning them to be prayed on Thursdays, they might seem misplaced. Yet further reflection reveals that the Mysteries of Light do more than add to the chronology of events in Jesus's life. They illuminate them. Just as the period of mystagogy follows the reception of the sacraments for the newly received into the Catholic Church, so the Luminous Mysteries shine a light on the events of Jesus's life in a way that can be appreciated only in the light of the paschal mystery.

THE BAPTISM OF JESUS

> Now when all the people were baptized, and when Jesus also had been baptized and was praying, the heaven was opened, and the Holy Spirit descended upon him in bodily form like a dove. And a voice came from heaven, "You are my Son, the Beloved; with you I am well pleased." (Lk 3:21–22)

The question that often arises regarding the baptism of Jesus is: Why would Jesus, who was without sin, ask to be baptized? Theologian Gerhard Lohfink offers one possible insight, suggesting that Jesus could have been a follower of John, at least for a short time. Like all the prophets of Israel, John spoke severely and without compromise, calling the Israelites to repent and be baptized. Therefore, Jesus, as a possible follower of John, or at least supportive of his mission, would accede to John's directive. There was, however, a distinct difference between the preaching of the prophets of old and John's preaching, which Jesus clearly understood. In being baptized, Jesus was already acting on behalf of his Mystical Body in anticipation of the church he would establish. Lohfink goes on to explain: "The Baptizer's words were received into the New Testament, and therefore they apply also to every Christian and to the church, just as they applied to Israel at the time. If the church does not repent and turn back, the judgment of which the Baptizer once spoke will come upon it even today."[1] In this way, Jesus was leaving us an example and a challenge to conversion, while carrying us within him as he turned toward the Father on our behalf.

Departing from the tradition of the Hebrew prophets, John warned the Jews that being an ancestor of Abraham was not enough to save them: "Bear fruits worthy of repentance. Do not begin to say to yourselves, 'We have Abraham as our ancestor'; for I tell you, God is able from these stones to raise up children to Abraham" (Lk 3:8). John's decision to baptize in the River Jordan, which the Israelites had to cross to get to the Promised Land, suggests that he was preparing the Jews for a new exodus. Warning his followers that God's judgment was upon them,

---

1. Gerhard Lohfink, *Jesus of Nazareth: What He Wanted, Who He Was*, trans. Linda M. Maloney (Collegeville, Minn.: Liturgical Press, 2012), 27–28.

John issued a call to repentance that was a mandate both to the Jews collectively and also to each person individually. All have sinned, and therefore all must repent and be baptized to be part of the exodus that would carry them into the future. Through his baptism, Jesus not only entered the new exodus: he became the new Moses who would take upon himself the sins of the people and lead them to freedom.

In entering the waters of the Jordan, Jesus initiated his journey on behalf of his people. Hearing the cry of the Israelites, Jesus looked beyond their sins and saw in the people God's own image. As Bridegroom of the new Israel, which through the marriage bed of the cross would become the church, Jesus was aware of the pleas of the bride that had echoed through the ages in the Song of Solomon, crying out on Israel's behalf:

> I am black and beautiful,
> O daughters of Jerusalem,
> like the tents of Kedar,
> like the curtains of Solomon.
> Do not gaze at me because I am dark,
> because the sun has gazed on me.
> My mother's sons were angry with me;
> they made me keeper of the vineyards,
> but my own vineyard I have not kept! (Song 1:5–6)

This poignant lament is one of the many emotions of the bride in the Song of Songs, a book that evokes the intense yet fleeting encounter between the people and God.

Throughout the centuries, the people of God had been unfaithful, and the prophets had not spared their words in depicting them as an unfaithful bride (see Hos 2:1–13; Ezek 16:38). But although at times the bride had turned away from

God, God could not turn away from her. Thus, he sent his Son as Bridegroom, setting the stage for what would be a turning point for the chosen people. Jesus saw Israel, when rebellious, as the harlot bride, whom he would redeem so that she could emerge from the waters of baptism as a "rose of Sharon, / a lily of the valleys" (Song 2:1). The baptism of Jesus was the beginning of the fulfillment of the promise to restore humankind to its original dignity, which would be accomplished through the death and resurrection of the Son of God.[2] The sole reason for the Baptist's preaching was to bear witness to the Bridegroom. Therefore, when he baptized Jesus and the Father proclaimed Jesus his beloved Son while the Holy Spirit hovered over him in the form of a dove, John's mission ended and Jesus's mission began.

Following his baptism, Jesus adopted John's eschatology, meaning that now God was acting through the person of his Son, whose appearing marked the end of the old and the beginning of a new covenant that would last for all eternity. Just as the institution of the Eucharist at the Last Supper was celebrated in anticipation of the sacrificial offering on Calvary, so through Jesus's baptism the sacrament of baptism was instituted in anticipation of his death and resurrection.

Immediately after being baptized, "Jesus was led up by the Spirit into the wilderness to be tempted by the devil. He fasted forty days and forty nights, and afterward he was famished" (Mt 4:1–2). Jesus, like every human being, was subject to temptation, for although baptism takes away sin, it does not eliminate the consequence of sin, which is part of the human condition. Through prayer and fasting, Jesus overcame temptation, teaching

---

2. In the Garden of Eden, God said, "See, the man has become like one of us, knowing good and evil; and now, he might reach out his hand and take also from the tree of life, and eat, and live forever" (Gen 3:22).

us by example that all who follow him must enter through the narrow gate, which John of the Cross called the "dark night of sense." Here the soul is despoiled and denuded and is increasingly grounded in faith which is foreign to the senses (see A 1.1.4). "To undertake the journey to God the heart must be burned with the fire of divine love and purified of all creatures. Such a purgation puts the devil to flight, for he has power over people through their attachment to temporal and bodily things" (A 1.2.2). These words show how vitally important it is to enter upon the journey to freedom and detachment.

All who travel the path to union with God must endure this purgation. Only Mary, who was free from temporal attachments and whose will was continuously united with the will of God, chose the narrow gate without exception, for she willed only what God willed. It was a habitual choice, throughout her life, following from the purgation that was affected all at once through her fiat, leading to what we might call a "continuous fiat." Her singular purity from the moment of her conception, reflected in this continuous fiat, predisposed her to heaven's light. As the wise and faithful Virgin, she stands by the door of the banquet hall lighting the path for all who journey toward union with the Bridegroom of souls. A beacon of hope, Mary leads us to heaven's gate through which we enter to gain admittance to her son. The motto "To Jesus through Mary," first proclaimed by St. Louis de Montfort, is more than a pious dictum; it is a reality grounded in the mystery of the incarnation of the Son of God through the consent of the Virgin Mary.

THE WEDDING AT CANA

> On the third day there was a wedding in Cana of Galilee, and the mother of Jesus was there. Jesus and his disciples had also been invited to the wedding. When the wine gave out, the

> mother of Jesus said to him, "They have no wine." And Jesus said to her, "Woman, what concern is that to you and to me? My hour has not yet come." His mother said to the servants, "Do whatever he tells you." (Jn 2:1–5)

The church ascribes great importance to the wedding celebration at Cana where Jesus performed his first miracle. Jesus's presence at the wedding is viewed as a "confirmation of the goodness of marriage and the proclamation that thenceforth marriage will be an efficacious sign of Christ's presence" (CCC 1613). Church teaching, which regards marriage as an encounter with Christ through the sacrament of matrimony, is a sacred union between one man and one woman who are to multiply and bear fruit. More than a sign of God's presence within the marital union of the couple, the sacrament of matrimony is a sign of the eternal covenant between God and his people where Jesus, the Bridegroom of souls, awaits union with his bride. Whether knowingly or unknowingly, each soul is a bride waiting to be transformed in God through love, according to the measure that the soul seeks and receives divine communication, both hidden and revealed, in accordance with God's plan.

Concerning the wedding celebration in Cana, it is noteworthy that at that time, wedding celebrations usually lasted seven days. It would have been extremely shortsighted on the part of the groom for the wine to run out too soon. Obviously, there was more to the account of the miracle than providing wine for the wedding guests. When Jesus stepped into the role of the groom, his first miracle did more than transform water into wine: it was a sign of the transformation that was to come when he would be lifted up on the cross.

That the miracle took place "on the third day" hints at the resurrection which took place on the third day, and Jesus addressing Mary as "Woman" suggests that he saw his mother's role extending beyond concern for the wedding guests to embracing the entire human race. Just as Eve invited Adam to partake of the forbidden fruit, so Mary invited Jesus to partake in the miracle signifying the paschal mystery that would lead to the reversal of the sin of Adam and Eve. Despite Jesus's raising what seemed like an objection, he complied with Mary's request, as she seemingly knew he would, since she immediately told the servants to do whatever Jesus said they were to do.

Similarly, the dialogue between Jesus and Mary alludes to the tension between the "not yet" and the "now." This seeming paradox, first announced in the Prologue of John's gospel, accompanied Jesus throughout his public life. Renowned Scripture scholar Francis Moloney noted that the fullness of God's gift, announced in the person of Jesus Christ through the incarnation, was the beginning, but that the miracle at Cana was the "now": "The transformation of water into wine . . . is the first act of the Word in the world and a type of the transformation that is to come. Perhaps it is the grace beyond grace, the messianic wine of being that replaces the inferior wine of the Torah, which is appropriate only to becoming."[3]

In line with this explanation, the words and actions of Jesus and Mary are eschatological, demonstrating that God provides for his people now and in the yet to come, but this is not without their cooperation and participation. The gospel account of the wedding at Cana reflects the values of the Mosaic Law: the obedience of the servants to Mary and Jesus, even Jesus's complying with his mother's request—all these things illustrate the importance of obedience to the law and to the will of God. Jesus said, "Do not think that I have come to abolish the law or the

3. Francis J. Moloney, S.D.B., *The Gospel of John*, Sacra Pagina 4 (Collegeville, Minn.: Liturgical Press, 1998), 69.

prophets; I have come not to abolish but to fulfill. For truly I tell you, until heaven and earth pass away, not one letter, not one stroke of a letter, will pass from the law until all is accomplished" (Mt 5:17–18). The law is not an entity unto itself, for along with the law comes the grace of obedience.

Abiding by the commandments and the laws of the church is the most obvious form of obedience to God's will, but we are also called to obey those who speak in God's name. Priests vow obedience to their bishop, consecrated men and women pledge obedience to their superiors, and couples promise to love, honor, and obey their spouse. When obedience is viewed as an act of listening to the voice of God, it is duly recognized as a help in discerning God's will, not a sign of servitude. When the words of St. Paul regarding marriage—that wives should obey their husbands and husbands are to love their wives as Christ loves the church—are interpreted as they were meant, the fullness of their covenantal relationship is experienced. Through respectful and prayerful listening to their spouse or to those in authority, persons become who God is calling them to be as a sign of God's covenant with his people.

The servants followed Jesus's directive to fill the jars with water and then take some of it to the chief steward. Despite being unaware of the transformation that had taken place, they obeyed and were surprised by what Jesus had done. As Scripture says, "Jesus did this, the first of his signs, in Cana of Galilee, and revealed his glory; and his disciples believed in him" (Jn 2:11). The disciples were amazed by what they had seen, and they believed; but later, Jesus reprimanded those who look for signs saying, "You faithless generation, how much longer must I be among you? How much longer must I put up with you?" (Mk 9:19). After the resurrection when Thomas demanded proof, Jesus appeared to him and showed him his wounds, but added, "Blessed are those who have not seen and yet have come to believe" (Jn 20:29).

Mary never asked for a sign prior to carrying out the will of God, nor did the servants demand proof before complying with Jesus's command. Likewise, those who practice prayer (which also involves listening to God) are called to believe in the absence of sensory satisfaction. Being open to where God is leading the soul is about believing without seeing. According to John of the Cross, both prayer and virtue are tested and strengthened in what he referred to as the passive night of sense:

> The conduct of these beginners in the way of God is lowly and not too distant from love of pleasure and of self. . . . God desires to withdraw them from this base manner of loving and lead them onto a higher degree of divine love. . . . God does this after beginners have exercised themselves for a time in the way of virtue and have persevered in meditation and prayer. For it is through the delight and satisfaction they experience in prayer that they have become detached from worldly things and have gained some spiritual strength in God. This strength has helped them somewhat to restrain their appetite for creatures, and through it they will be able to suffer a little oppression and dryness without turning back. (N 1.8.3)

It is clear from this passage that while our perseverance in prayer is very necessary, the actual work of transformation is carried out by God.

John of the Cross compares this stage to a mother who rubs bitter herbs on her breast to wean her child, so that it will accept solid food. Similarly, the all-loving God takes beginners where they would not go on their own, so that they can advance in love and remain faithful to prayer despite the dryness and aridity that accompany it. As the Mystical Doctor points out, "The more a person seeks some support in knowledge and affection the more the soul will feel the lack of these, for this support cannot be supplied through these sensory means" (N 1.10.5). For the work of God takes place in concealment, especially when we have been weaned away from dependence on what we can know through our senses or the intellect.

In this way, souls are led to depend on God rather than on what can be accomplished by their own effort. Through the effects of such secret divine communication, Mary became a vehicle of God's divine action. Similarly, in the absence of seeing that the water would be changed into wine, the servants trusted and were surprised by the superior quality of this new wine. According to John of the Cross, trusting despite "aridities and voids" is the "means to the knowledge of both God and self" (N 1.12.6). Although Mary could not herself produce more wine, she trusted that Jesus would provide it, though she didn't know how he would do it. God acts on the soul in a similar manner, for beginners, previously unable to overcome certain vices, find that God accomplishes in them what they were unable to accomplish through their own efforts.

THE PROCLAMATION OF THE KINGDOM

> And he came to Nazareth, where he had been brought up; and he went to the synagogue, as was his custom, on the Sabbath day. And he stood up to read; and there was given to him the book of the prophet Isaiah. He opened the book and found the place where it was written, "The Spirit of the Lord is upon me, because he has anointed me to preach good news to the poor. He has sent me to proclaim release to the captives and recovering of sight to the blind, to set at liberty those who are oppressed, to proclaim the acceptable year of the Lord." And he closed the book, and gave it back to the attendant, and sat down; and the eyes of all in the synagogue were fixed on him. And he began to say to them, "Today this Scripture has been fulfilled in your hearing." And all spoke

> well of him, and wondered at the gracious words which proceeded out of his mouth; and they said, "Is not this Joseph's son?" . . . When they heard this, all in the synagogue were filled with wrath. And they rose up and put him out of the city, and led him to the brow of the hill on which their city was built, that they might throw him down headlong. (Lk 4:16–22, 28–29)

As we see from this reaction, if the "not yet" and the "now" were a source of subtle tension at the wedding in Cana, the proclamation by Jesus that the reign of God was "now" went from subtle to explosive. That the long-awaited prophecy was fulfilled through the son of a carpenter was more than the people of Nazareth could bear. Their initial surprise quickly turned from denial to anger. How could this man, whom they assumed to know so well, proclaim that he was the long-awaited one of Israel? It was more than preposterous. It was blasphemous, and he had to be put to death. Gerhard Lohfink explains that the people did not understand that Jesus lives in full union with the Father, and that, therefore, for Jesus the time was *now*. The theologian points out: "When God comes he does not come halfway but entirely. And God does not come at just any time, even in the immediate future; God comes today. We simply do not do justice to Jesus's message if we talk as if God gives his *basileia* [kingdom] but not entirely at the moment; as if he caused it to dawn, but only bit by bit; but only in anticipation. . . . The unconditional 'today' that Jesus proclaims is grounded in his unrestricted participation in the eternal 'today' of God."[4] In this way, the "now" partakes of eternity, the fullness of time.

It was the "now" of the reign of God that the people were not ready to accept, because it required setting aside previous

4. Lohfink, *Jesus of Nazareth*, 34.

notions about the kingdom of God and the Messiah. Jesus's version of the reign of God was that of a humble God who cared for the poor, the crippled, and the blind. His was not an earthly kingdom, but one where love and compassion reign, which was not consistent with their version of a kingdom. Jesus came preaching more than repentance: he came preaching a revolution of the heart, and the time was now. Not surprisingly, the crowd responded the way the Israelites had often dealt with prophets whose message was not what they wanted to hear: they killed the messenger. And so they wanted to push Jesus off a cliff.

In rejecting the proclamation that the reign of God was "now," the people didn't have to change their thinking or their behavior. They could continue to look to the future for a messiah who would conform to their image of a savior. Since they were not ready to open their hearts to the presence of God in their midst, Jesus slipped away unseen and performed few miracles there (see Mt 13:54–58). We are not so different from the people of Nazareth when the message we hear is not to our liking or in agreement with our thinking. And yet, despite our aversion to the narrow gate and our failure to understand and trust, God doesn't give up on us. In his Word and in the teaching of his church, we perceive the paradox of the "now" and "not yet": the kingdom already here among us (see Lk 17:21) and still to come (see Lk 11:2).

As people of faith, though imperfect, we believe that the reign of God is both present and coming, which gives us the courage to pray, "Thy kingdom come." Seeds sown in the soul at baptism are sealed with the gifts of the Holy Spirit through the sacrament of confirmation. Thus, endowed with the courage to declare publicly the presence of God in our midst, we resolve to follow the example of Jesus—though not without a struggle, which makes prayer an imperative. St. Teresa attested to this when writing about her early life. She confessed, "Though I continued to associate with the world, I had the courage to practice prayer. . . . Though we are always in the presence of God, it seems to me the manner is different for those who practice prayer for they are aware that He is looking at them" (L 8.2). When our faith perceives that this is so, it adds an intensity to our relationship with God and reminds us of the help he is giving us continually.

Teresa insisted that God willingly disposes himself to souls who practice prayer, so that even amid temptations, sins, and failures, God gives to souls who practice prayer the grace to persevere. Though unseen, the gifts of the Holy Spirit, which we receive through the sacrament of confirmation, prepare us for the interior warfare that is part of life. Just as Jesus slipped away from the crowd, unseen and unharmed, so we are assured of God's presence acting through supernatural grace that is invisible. The grace of God surrounds us all day, every day. When we turn to God in prayer, trusting in his presence, we are able to rejoice, knowing that God is with us. Most often we comprehend the magnitude of graces received only in retrospect, causing us to lift our voice and echo the refrain, "I was blind, but now I see."

Mindful of God's presence "now" and "yet to come," Mary continues to plead for us even as she pleads with us to pray for the conversion of sinners. Considering all that we know about this gentle woman—who asks, but never demands—can anyone ignore her plea? Can we continue to put off until tomorrow what we can do today? And can we ignore St. Paul's words: "[God] says, 'At an acceptable time I have listened to you, and on a day of salvation, I have helped you.' See, now is the acceptable time; see, now is the day of salvation" (2 Cor 6:2)? The kingdom of God is with us *today*.

THE TRANSFIGURATION

The transfiguration of Jesus on Mount Tabor is recorded in all three Synoptic Gospels, which all report that Jesus was transfigured before Peter, James, and John; that his garments became dazzling white; and that Elijah and Moses appeared conversing with him. Matthew describes the face of Jesus as shining like the sun. In words that are similar in all three gospels, Peter says to Jesus, "Lord, it is good for us to be here; if you wish, I will make three dwellings here, one for you, one for Moses, and one for Elijah" (Mt 17:4). Peter was so enamored by the experience that he wanted it never to end, until the voice of the Father was heard, saying, "This is my Son, the Beloved; with him I am well pleased; listen to him!" (Mt 17:5). Then, not unlike Elijah when he encountered the Lord on Mount Horeb (see 1 Kings 19:13), the three men hid their faces.

In keeping with the Old Testament tradition that revered mountains as places where the prophets encountered God, the transfiguration of Jesus took place on a high mountain, held by tradition to be Mount Tabor. But the appearance of Moses and Elijah conversing with Jesus did more than validate Jesus's teachings as a continuation and fulfillment of the prophecies of old. It signaled the beginning of something new. In choosing only three of the twelve apostles to witness his glorification, Jesus demonstrates that God chooses people according to his plan, not according to a person's merit. James and John would soon be overheard seeking places of honor in the kingdom: "Grant us to sit, one at your right hand and one at your left, in your glory." And Jesus would say to them, "You do not know what you are asking. Are you able to drink the cup that I drink, or be baptized with the baptism that I am baptized with?" (Mk 10:37–38). Jesus knew that the three men didn't understand what they had witnessed, which explains why he instructed them to remain silent about the transfiguration. Only after the death and resurrection and the coming of the Holy Spirit would they understand and appreciate the significance of what they had been privileged to experience and would drink from the same cup that Jesus was speaking about.

This explains Teresa's deference when trying to explain supernatural favors which God grants to souls. Knowing that all attempts to explain them would fall short, she concluded that the experience would only be understood after a person received them. Although faith is imperative in the journey toward union with God, knowledge of God and of self is often gleaned through life experience, which is a process that is indispensable and occurs over time. Like the apostles who could understand the transfiguration only after Jesus's death and resurrection, the process of conversion and transformation is most often understood only after the veil of darkness has been lifted.

John's sketch of Mount Carmel, drawn after his imprisonment as a result of his reform of the Carmelite Order, serves as a guide for all who embark on the path to union with God through prayer. Just as Peter, James, and John fell to the ground when they heard the Father's voice, so the effects of God's hidden communication in the soul, though unseen, expose the pride and sinfulness of those who stand in the light of God. The response is to fall on one's knees in adoration. It has been said that knowing *about God* inspires us but that *knowing God* causes us to fall on our knees in adoration.

Whether a soul is brought to the night of sense or the night of spirit, the result is an increase in humility and a deepening desire to follow the path toward union with God. During the night of sense, the soul must gradually set aside thoughts of building tents, like Peter on Mount Tabor, as if people can capture God's favors by their own efforts and then hold onto them. The "goods of heaven"—which John of the Cross glosses on his sketch of Mount Carmel as glory, joy, knowledge, consolation, and rest—are given most completely when we no longer depend on them or cling to them.

Just as the transfiguration was followed by Jesus predicting his crucifixion, so those who heed the Father's words enter the night of spirit where there will be no shortage of crosses to bear. As they experience brief glimpses of what John of the Cross termed "*I-don't-know-what*" (P 12), they are led by way of darkness to conform their will to the will of God as they follow the path to Calvary. Souls transformed in God through love remain with Mary at the foot of the cross, as an ongoing experience of their participation in God through suffering.

For disciples of Jesus, the cross no longer stands on Calvary but is embedded in the trials and tribulations of life. After recognizing the passing nature of all things and relationships, souls—who no longer cling to these things and who commit their sufferings to Christ—experience a solitary wound, which our Savior endured out of love for us. Then the soul's cry is no longer the mournful coo of the turtledove seeking its mate, but the sweet sound of the nightingale calling from within the cleft of the mountainside. Unseen and hidden in the shelter of God's wing, she finds solace, for "no one looked at her" (C 40.1) because "her soul is detached and withdrawn from all things" (C 40.1). Further on, John writes that in this state "the senses discontinue their natural operations" (C 40.6). And he adds, "The bride sets all this perfection and preparedness before her Beloved, the Son of God, with the desire that he transfer her from the spiritual marriage, to which he desired to bring her in this Church Militant, to the glorious marriage of the Triumphant" (C 40.7). John's words here are the climax of his *Spiritual Canticle* and represent a lofty state which few have experienced, but to which we all can aspire.

Peter, James, and John could not understand all that had taken place during the transfiguration, but they would learn the full meaning of the event they witnessed over time. After the coming of the Holy Spirit, they devoted themselves to building the kingdom, and in the end they gave their lives for it. Peter and James surrendered their lives as martyrs, and John lived out his sentence in exile as he awaited the glorious marriage of the church triumphant.

THE INSTITUTION OF THE EUCHARIST

Without the Eucharist, there would be no church. The Eucharist is the summit, the mountaintop, where bread and wine are infused with divine life. The action by the priest, who prays to the Father to send down the Spirit like dewfall from heaven to sanctify the offerings of bread and wine that they may become the Body and Blood of Christ, constitutes the most trinitarian reality that mortals can encounter on earth. In his lengthy poem about the Trinity, John of the Cross portrays this eucharistic marriage banquet as a preordained gift from the Father to the Son. In words that are both tender and inspiring, the Carmelite poet imagines a loving dialogue that took place between the Father and the Son when the world was created:

> "My Son, I wish to give you a bride who will love you.
> Because of you she will deserve to share our company,
> and eat at our table, the same bread I eat,
> that she may know the good I have in such a Son;
> and rejoice with me in your grace and fullness."
> "I am very grateful," the Son answered;
> "I will show my brightness to the bride you give me,
> so that by it she may see how great my Father is,

> and how I have received my being from your being.
> I will hold her in my arms and she will burn with your love,
> and with eternal delight she will exalt your goodness." (R 9.3)

This "same bread," spoken of by the Father in this dialogue, points to the soul's sharing in the divine nature through the Eucharist, while the words of the Son express a union of love between Jesus and the soul.

Although the liturgy of the Eucharist is most often referred to as a sacrifice and banquet in remembrance of the Last Supper and Jesus's death, it is also a commemoration of the incarnation. During the eucharistic celebration, the priest offers bread and wine to the Father, transforming them into the Body and Blood of Christ, which is made possible through the marriage of God with humanity. Transcending human limitations of time, the triune God responds to words from mere mortals, just as God responded to Mary's fiat more than two thousand years ago. The God who is beyond all knowing comes to earth again and again, this time in the form of bread and wine—a mystery that takes place at every Eucharist. Just as in Nazareth, when the Holy Spirit came upon Mary and the power of the Most High overshadowed her, Christ comes to earth while saints and angels gather around the altar bowing before the mystery that is taking place.

Unworthy though we are, we respond, "Amen," and like Mary, with whose fiat our salvation was set in motion, we acknowledge that we believe without seeing, and we continue the mission that Jesus began. Mary's unfathomable gift is our unfathomable mandate, for in receiving Christ we are also being sent. Like Mary, we must acknowledge our mission and go forth, for if only the bread and wine are transformed during the sacred liturgy—that is, if we are not transformed as well—the world will remain unchanged. The mandate to be transformed, which began with our initiation into the common priesthood at baptism, continues as we go forth to build the kingdom of God. Mindful of the church's responsibility to spread the Good News, the priest sends the faithful forth to be Christ to the world at the end of every Mass.

Few have captured the magnitude of the mystery of transubstantiation as beautifully as John of the Cross, who spent hours before the Blessed Sacrament pondering his own priestly vocation. He declared that if God had not given him special grace to contemplate this trinitarian mystery, he would have been unable to do so and still live. Thus inebriated by Love's embrace, the Carmelite friar wrote:

> This eternal spring is hidden
> in this living bread for our life's sake,
> *although it is night.*
> It is here calling out to creatures;
> and they satisfy their thirst, although in darkness,
> *because it is night.* (P 8.9–10)

John is writing here of the mystical streams of grace from the Trinity which flow into our soul in the Eucharist.

To look beyond the bread we eat and the wine we drink and see the Body and Blood of Christ is to enter the night of ineffable love where sensory images disappear. The flow of eucharistic grace is communicated to the soul in secret and to the degree that the soul is properly disposed to receiving it. In one of his mystagogical sermons, St. Augustine instructs us to "be what you can see, and receive what you are."[5] It is a difficult task. But as members of

---

5. Saint Augustine, *The Works of St Augustine: A Translation for the 21st Century,* ed. John E. Rotelle, O.S.A., trans. Edmund Hill, O.P., vol. III/7, *Sermons 230–272B on Liturgical Seasons* (Hyde Park, NY: New City Press, 1993), 298.

the Body of Christ, when we receive Jesus's Body and Blood, we become a living sacrament and a sign of Christ in our midst.

When partaking of the Eucharist, we are called to recognize our own hunger and the hunger of all people, both spiritual and physical. We are called to respond to the famine of those starving for love, of those who go to bed hungry, and of those who thirst for justice. We can no longer turn away from the empty stares of those who live without love or hope, struggling to survive in a world of endless war, violence, and persecution. As the Body of Christ, we cannot be complacent in the face of growing disparity between the rich and the poor, for as St. Paul wrote, "If one member suffers, all suffer together with it; if one member is honored, all rejoice together with it. Now you are the Body of Christ and individually members of it" (1 Cor 12:26–27). The Eucharist binds us together as nothing else can.

We cannot take lightly the sacrament of Eucharist, lest we become like Judas who, after receiving the bread dipped in the blood of Christ, left the Upper Room—after which, Scripture says, "it was night" (see Jn 13:30). As sacrament and sign, we are called to be light for the abused, the betrayed, and the broken. When we bring our gifts to the altar, we must be prepared to allow Jesus to take us in his hands and, after lifting us to the Father, bless us, break us, and pass us around in imitation of the Christ whom we receive.

How we live this is unique to each person. Within each parish community, as in the universal church, we see distinctly different gifts that each person is given with which to feed the Body of Christ. Not all can be martyrs, preachers, or reformers. Most, like Mary, live their lives quietly, going lovingly about the ordinary duties of their state of life. Yet in offering their lives in union with Jesus, every thought, word, and deed can be transformed into food for the entire Body of Christ. This was at the heart of the spirituality of St. Thérèse, who rejoiced after she discovered "that if the Church had a body composed of different members, the most necessary and most noble of all could not be lacking to it, and so I understood that the Church *had a Heart and that this Heart was BURNING WITH LOVE. I understood it was Love alone* that made the Church's members act" (S 194).

This impassioned statement was the result of much searching on Thérèse's part to find her true vocation. She discovered that her vocation was *love*—and that since God is Love, we who receive him have thus been given the means to be like him. Ever mindful of our weakness, we can turn to Mary, Mother of God and Mother of Love, to become the person that Jesus is calling us to be. But regardless of our chosen path in life, what matters is not what we do but how we love, for as John of the Cross warned, "When evening comes, you will be examined in love. Learn to love as God desires to be loved and abandon your own ways of acting" (SLL 60). There is no means more powerful than living the Eucharist: the surrender of self in union with Christ and receiving the embrace of God's love.

INVITATION TO PRAYER

During a vision to St. Gertrude the Great, Mary said to her, "One may not call my sweet Jesus my only Son, but my firstborn, for I have conceived Him as the firstborn in my womb, but after Him, or rather through Him, I have conceived all of you, so that you are His brothers and my children and in Him I have taken you into the heart of my motherly love."[6] In a statement about Mary, quoted by the Second Vatican Council, St. Augustine spoke of Mary as truly "the mother of the

Continued

6. St. Alphonsus Liguori, *The Glories of Mary*, trans., Eugene Grimm (Brooklyn: Redemptorist Fathers, 1931 [Victory Missions reprint, c. 1980]), 48.

INVITATION TO PRAYER *Continued*

members of Christ," since she "has by her charity joined in bringing about the birth of believers in the church, who are members of its head."[7] Devotion to the Blessed Virgin under the title "Our Lady of Help," or "Our Lady of Succor," began at the start of the fourteenth century in the Church of St. Augustine in Palermo, Sicily.[8] And so, confident of our Lady's loving concern, we come to her and pray, addressing her once again by her esteemed titles from the Litany of Loreto:

Health of the sick, pray for us.
Refuge of sinners, pray for us.
Solace of migrants, pray for us.
Comfort of the afflicted, pray for us.
Help of Christians, pray for us. Amen.

---

7. St. Augustine, *De Sancta Virginitate*, 6, quoted in LG 53.

8. See "May 13—Our Lady of Help," *https://www.augustinian.org/saints-1/may-13/*.

15

The Sorrowful Mysteries

TRADITIONALLY WHEN ONLY FIVE DECADES of the rosary are prayed, the Sorrowful Mysteries are assigned to Tuesdays and Fridays. While it may seem as though the Sorrowful Mysteries don't apply to the Mother of God, her silent witness throughout Jesus's passion and death testifies to the salvific role of *interior* martyrdom. In honor of Mary's self-emptying alongside that of her son on Calvary (see Phil 2:7), the church has designated a liturgical feast, Our Lady of Sorrows, which is celebrated on September 15.[1]

While not all are called to physical martyrdom, suffering is part of every life and has a role to play in the ongoing salvation of the world, for it is a participation in the sufferings of Christ by the members of his Mystical Body.[2] In his apostolic letter on the Christian meaning of human suffering, St. John Paul II explained another important aspect: "Suffering, which is present

---

1. Aptly, this feast occurs alongside that of the passion of her son: the feast of the Triumph of the Cross, celebrated one day earlier.

2. As Edith Stein explains succinctly: "To suffer and to die is the lot of every human being. But if [one] is a living member of the Body of Christ, then [one's] own suffering and death receive redemptive power through the divinity of the Head."Edith Stein, *The Mystery of Christmas: Incarnation and Humanity*, trans. Sister Josephine Rucker, S.S.J. (Darlington, England: Darlington Carmel, 1985), 16.

under so many different forms in our human world, is also present in order *to unleash love in the human person*, that unselfish gift of one's 'I' on behalf of other people, especially those who suffer. The world of human suffering unceasingly calls for, so to speak, another world: the world of human love; and in a certain sense man owes to suffering that unselfish love which stirs in his heart and actions" (SD 29). In this sense we can truly say that suffering is transformative. And it may lead us to carry our cross generously, alongside Christ and in union with him, for the sake of the world.

Few have endured what Mary experienced through her interior participation in Christ's passion and death. For just as her son was lifted high upon the cross, so his mother's unfailing love has been lifted high by the church as a perfect example of redemptive suffering that has guided her children through the ages.

THE AGONY OF JESUS IN THE GARDEN

> [Jesus] said to them, "I am deeply grieved, even to death; remain here, and stay awake with me." And going a little farther, he threw himself on the ground and prayed, "My Father, if it is possible, let this cup pass from me; yet not what I want but what you want." (Mt 26:38–39)

Just as Jesus began his public ministry by going off alone into the wilderness to fast and pray, so when the final hour of his life on earth was approaching, he again sought solace in the company of his Father. In the sacred space within the depths of Jesus's soul, where not even his closest friends could enter, the Son of God laid bare his soul, placing his fears and anguish before his Father. With the encumbrances of his humanity closing in, the ever-humble Son of God fell on his knees and lay prostrate before the Father. Having donned the hubristic humanity of the people he came to save, Jesus prayed to the Father, even as evil lurked in the shadows of his midnight hour.

Satan, having failed in his attempt in the desert, sought to deal death's blow to the Christ in the midst of his final agony. In the desert, Jesus had fought the tempter's wiles with the Word of God. Now Jesus's only words were pleas to the Father to take the cup of suffering from him. Yet, ever mindful of his mission, Jesus wished only to remain faithful to the Father's will. During this night, so different from every other night, Jesus felt the inner strength that had sustained him throughout his earthly life slowly ebb away. The same body that radiated glory on Mount Tabor was now defaced in the shadow of sin and perdition; his garment, once dazzling white, was now drenched with sweat and blood, tying his humanity to the vulnerability of the prophets of old.

When Elijah pleaded with God to let him die in the wilderness, God sent an angel with food and drink to strengthen him for the journey ahead (see 1 Kings 19:5–8). When Moses, overcome by fear, asked God, "Who am I that I should go to Pharaoh, and bring the Israelites out of Egypt?" (Ex 3:11), God reassured him, promising that "I AM WHO I AM" (Ex 3:14) would be with him. In a similar way, Jesus's agony was mitigated by the Father who sent an angel to strengthen him for his passion and crucifixion. Could the discussion that took place on Mount Tabor, when Jesus was seen talking with Elijah and Moses about "his exodus that he was going to accomplish in Jerusalem" (Lk 9:31), also have been one of reassurance? Did the Father, knowing that the hour of his son's crucifixion was drawing near, send Israel's two great prophets to reassure him that he would not be alone?

When the burden seemed too great for Moses and Elijah to bear, the Father intervened, and he did the same when the sins of the entire human race bore down upon his son. "And there appeared to him an angel from heaven, strengthening him" (Lk 22:43). As Jesus's bloodied sweat drenched the earth like tears crying out from a world drowning in sin, heaven intervened as it does for every person who follows Jesus to Calvary. How else can we explain the courage of countless martyrs who went to their death singing hymns of praise with heroic resolve? How does one account for the valor of St. Teresa Benedicta of the Cross, the Discalced Carmelite nun who was martyred at the hands of the Nazis? Like Jesus, who roused his disciples by saying, "Get up, let us be going. See, my betrayer is at hand" (Mk 14:42), the Carmelite nun, knowing death was imminent, turned to her sister Rosa and said, "Come, Rosa. We're going for our people."[3] This was consonant with Edith's unfailing courage, right to the end.

Despite the heroic courage of martyrs going to their death, embracing suffering does not eliminate the pain. God's grace is sufficient to endure whatever suffering accompanies death, whether it be through martyrdom or natural causes, a fact that is illustrated perfectly in the account of the final hours of St. Thérèse. On the morning of her death, St. Thérèse pointed to the statue of the Blessed Virgin and said to her sisters, "Oh! I prayed fervently to her! But it is pure agony; there is no consolation!" (S 269). Later that day, the prioress said that God might prolong Thérèse's agony a little longer. And the saint's response? "Well, all right! Ah! I would not want to suffer a shorter length of time" (S 271). Thérèse's words, so full of courage, might also put to rest false assumptions that souls brought to the spiritual marriage participate continuously in the glory of Christ and therefore do not experience pain in all its intensity. In truth, and as a spiritual parallel to physical suffering, the final stage of union could

---

3. Waltraud Herbstrith, O.C.D., *Edith Stein: A Biography*, trans. Father Bernard Bonowitz, O.C.S.O. (San Francisco: Ignatius Press, 1992), 180.

be more accurately described as a participation in the agony of Christ. In describing her suffering, even in this exalted state, St. Teresa wrote: "The presence [of God] is almost continual, except when a lot of sickness weighs down on one. For it sometimes seems God wants one to suffer without interior consolation, but never, even in its first stirrings, does the will turn from its desire that God's will be done in it. The surrender to the will of God is so powerful that the soul wants neither death nor life, unless for a short time when it longs to die to see God" (ST 65.9). Teresa wrote these words the year before she died, when she had already reached the stage of the mystical marriage.

As the perfect contemplative, Mary was the first person to experience the mystical marriage as a meeting place where her pain was united with the blood of Christ. Although she did not suffer with Christ physically, her suffering was a martyrdom that was *interior*, mirroring the agony of Jesus in the Garden of Gethsemane.

THE SCOURGING OF JESUS AT THE PILLAR

From the time Jesus was arrested until Pilate ordered him to be scourged, he was betrayed, denied, and paraded before the high priest and religious leaders like a sheep led to the slaughter. Rather than a swift execution, the Lamb of God was bound, interrogated, slapped, and accused of blasphemy before being scourged at the pillar.

The proceedings of those intent on Jesus's death took place in secret, like so many sins committed under the cover of darkness. The plan of Jesus's execution, conceived in secret, was unveiled in the judgment hall of Pilate as religious leaders were unknowingly fulfilling the Lord's earlier prediction when he warned: "Beware of the yeast of the Pharisees, that is, their hypocrisy. Nothing is covered up that will not be uncovered, and nothing secret that will not become known. Therefore whatever you have said in the dark will be heard in the light, and what you have whispered behind closed doors will be proclaimed from the housetops" (Lk 12:2–3). The passion of Jesus would bring the secret machinations of his enemies into the light of day.

Unlike Adam and Eve, who hid their nakedness after they sinned, Jesus, who was sinless, allowed himself to be stripped of his garment, his sacred humanity exposed to the soldier's whip. No longer could the ugliness of sin be denied or the effects of humanity's sin on the Body of Christ be refuted. Whether knowingly or unknowingly, sins committed, no matter how secretly, wound the world. Sins of physical, sexual, verbal, and emotional abuse committed behind closed doors were laid bare in the wounded body of Jesus. Sins of violence and indifference, of greed, lust, and pride cried out to heaven even as pieces of metal bit into the flesh of the Son of God.

Sins of religious superiority and cultural and ideological divisions didn't begin with the Pharisees, nor did they end there. Human history is rife with examples of racial, religious, and ethnic warfare. As one group blames the other and justifies ideologies that dominate and enslave victims, the divide exposes double standards and duplicity, inflicting wounds that continue to bleed. Only when we gaze upon the suffering Savior can we recognize our own culpability, causing us to exclaim with St. Teresa, "O Lord, how we Christians fail to know you! What will that day be when You come to judge . . . ?" (IC 6.9.6). Here, Teresa was writing about the fright that can accompany a vision of Jesus when he reveals himself as friend, but she then goes on to exclaim, "Oh, daughters, what will it be like when He says in so severe a voice, *depart you who are accursed by My Father*?" (IC 6.9.6; cf. Mt 25:41). This is the insight that sprang from Teresa's self-appraisal after she had glimpsed what it is to stand before the majesty of God.

While honest self-appraisal incriminates, it also frees us to stand in the truth, as with Nathaniel, of whom Jesus said, "Here is truly an Israelite in whom there is no deceit!" (Jn 1:47). To be without deceit is to be transparent, honest, and sincere, rather than two-faced or duplicitous. Nathaniel's virtue enabled him to see Jesus as the Messiah. When, like Nathaniel, we stand in the presence of Truth, we cannot deny that Jesus was bound to a pillar, scourged, mocked, and beaten because of our sins. And while this is our shame, it is also our hope, for we are no longer idle witnesses standing outside the Christ. As members of his Body, we are within him, and he is within us. Therefore, we have no cause to be critical or indifferent toward others, to lose patience or resent being humbled or inconvenienced. As members of the Mystical Body of Christ, we, too, are called to participate in his sufferings in whatever way we are called and according to God's will for us.

Mary's perfect surrender bound her unconditionally to the pillar of God's will. Explaining Mary's role in Christ's death, theologian Father William G. Most noted: "Now since all perfection lies in positively willing what God wills whenever we know His positive will, it is clear that Mary was called on to positively will that her Son die, die then, die so horribly. She had to will this in spite of a love for her Son so great that 'only God can comprehend it.' . . . So in willing the death of her Divine Son, it is clear that her suffering was such that 'no one but God could comprehend it.'"[4] As this passage shows so insightfully, Mary was united so closely to God that this would have created an inner loneliness, for the world could not understand the depth of her love.

---

4. William G. Most, "The Blessed Virgin Mary: Her Privileges and Relation to Christ and His Church," from *The Basic Catholic Catechism* (1990), *https://www.ewtn.com/catholicism/teachings/blessed-virgin-mary-her-privileges-and-relation-to-christ-and-his-church-210/*. The words quoted by Most are from Pope Pius IX, *Ineffabilis Deus*.

She who gave Jesus his physical body became a secondary victim of sin. Like her son who came not to condemn but to save sinners, Mary is a sign of God's mercy, holding within her heart the wounds of the world. In donning the mantle of motherhood for the sake of the world, she instructs us to take courage and amend our lives. We pray to Mary to intercede for us so that we may be freed from the slavery of sin and find strength in Jesus's words: "Do not fear those who kill the body but cannot kill the soul; rather fear him who can destroy both soul and body in hell" (Mt 10:28). Yes, we are to fear the Lord—but with that fear that is a gift of the Holy Spirit: it means being afraid to sadden the Father who gave us his only Son.

JESUS IS CROWNED WITH THORNS

> They clothed him in a purple cloak; and after twisting some thorns into a crown, they put it on him. And they began saluting him, "Hail, King of the Jews!" They struck his head with a reed, spat upon him, and knelt down in homage to him. (Mk 15:17–19)

The horror of Jesus being mocked as he was hailed "King of the Jews" cuts deep into the soul, even as his silence serves as an indictment against words spoken in anger or in retaliation. The purple cloak, representing kingship, blasphemously placed on Jesus's shoulders, has forever altered our image of a messianic kingship. The color purple long associated with royalty, luxury, and high office has become liturgically synonymous with penance. Priests don purple vestments during the season of Lent and wear a purple stole when they receive penitents for the sacrament of reconciliation; during Holy Week, Christ's corpus is covered in purple.

As the ignominy of Jesus continued, the One whom before every knee should bend became the victim of a drunken revelry.

Kneeling before the Savior of the world, soldiers struck his face and fashioned for his head a crown of thorns that dug deeply into his scalp. Through it all, Jesus's silent dignity became a deafening proclamation of his Sermon on the Mount. His humble demeanor, etched deep in our hearts, has become the personification of what it means to be poor in spirit, meek and merciful. Surely, no one could hunger for righteousness, long for peace, or love one's persecutors with the intensity of the Prince of Peace.

Mindful of all that our Savior has done for us, we stand in the shadow of his quiet surrender, and we can no longer justify our wrongdoings or defend ourselves when misunderstood. Duly convicted, we resolve to add our silence to that of Jesus and his mother, so that our pain, no matter how slight, may become an occasion of grace. Lest we doubt the transformative merit of our smallest actions, St. Thérèse shows us how remaining silent when criticized can lead to holiness. During a recreation period, one of the nuns misjudged Thérèse's slow response to the prioress's request. Not knowing that Thérèse deliberately slowed her response so that the other sister could perform a task that she would have enjoyed carrying out, this sister misjudged Thérèse, who writes: "The sister . . . said: 'Ah! I thought as much, that you were not going to gain this pearl for your crown, you were going too slowly.' Certainly, the whole community believed I had acted through selfishness, and I cannot say how much good such a small thing did to my soul, making me indulgent toward the weaknesses of others" (S 221). Thérèse not only accepted unjust criticism but also gained understanding of those whose weakness makes them liable to be criticized through no fault of their own.

How easy it is to lash out at those who hurt us or whose perspective is different from our own. How quickly we point to the splinter in our neighbor's eye while ignoring the beam in our own. St. Thérèse struggled with the same tendency. Describing one of the nuns in community who had the "faculty of displeasing me in everything in her ways, her words, her character, everything seems very *disagreeable* to me" (S 222), Thérèse was able, with the grace of God, to transform her dislike for this nun into an occasion of grace: "I set myself to doing for this sister what I would do for the person I loved most. Each time I met her I prayed to God for her, offering Him all her virtues and merits. . . . I wasn't content simply with praying very much for this sister who gave me so many struggles, but I took care to render her all the services possible, and when I was tempted to answer her back in a disagreeable manner, I was content with giving her my most friendly smile, and with changing the subject of the conversation" (S 222–23). This is a marvelous example of charity that could do so much for the people we encounter, as well as for ourselves as we seek to grow in virtue and kindness.

Thérèse's little way of spiritual childhood requires a great deal of interior strength and fortitude. One of the desert fathers offers an example of the discipline such effort requires. A young spiritual seeker proudly told the desert *abba* that he had bitten his tongue until it bled so that he would not respond to a fellow pilgrim in anger. Expecting to be praised for his fortitude, he was dismayed when the elderly hermit told him that only when the tongue bleeds without having been bitten is a person's anger sufficiently restrained.

Perhaps this is the reason Mary's words in Scripture are few. As the embodiment of virtue, she went about doing the will God in silence, a perfect mirror of the meek and humble heart that her son exhibited before his persecutors.

JESUS CARRIES HIS CROSS

Jesus's encounter with the holy women of Jerusalem and with Simon of Cyrene, who was recruited to help Jesus carry his cross on his way to Calvary, is recorded in Scripture. There is no mention of a meeting between Jesus and his mother along the road, but her presence at the foot of the cross suggests that she would have been in the crowd that followed her son to his crucifixion. As Jesus's first disciple, Mary, who accompanied Jesus throughout his life, would surely have been with him on the journey toward his death.

We can only wonder what her thoughts were as her heart was being torn asunder. When the wood of the cross pressed into the flesh on Jesus's shoulder, did she recall the wood of the manger that held her son during those first days of his life? Did she long to draw him to her breast and comfort him, to dry his tears as she had done when he was a child? When he fell, did it take every ounce of restraint not to help him up as she had done when he was learning to walk? And when their eyes met, did her silence communicate the love that was in her maternal heart?

While such questions might be the musing of ordinary hearts, when Mary looked into the eyes of Jesus and he gazed into hers, their thoughts were not of this world. They understood the mission before them, and their meeting bound them ever more closely to the will of the Father. John of the Cross may have intuited the essence of their bond when he wrote of the exchange between the bride and the Bridegroom:

> Our bed is in flower,
> bound round with linking dens of lion,
> hung with purple,
> built up in peace,
> and crowned with a thousand shields of gold.
> (C stanza 24, Redaction B)

Commenting on this stanza, John writes, "By the 'den of lions' [the bride] understands the virtues possessed in this state of union with God, for dens of lions are very safe and protected against all other animals. . . . And the soul herself, united with him in these same virtues, is also like a strong lion because she receives the properties of God" (C 24.4).

Here, John is intuiting this bond in terms of great strength. And yet there is vulnerability, for who but someone whose soul was in God could know that God's suffering causes flowers to bloom? Who but a bride could see in the crown of thorns a royal diadem or recognize in Jesus's bruised and bloodied humanity a new Adam? And who but Mary could know that Jesus's cross would become the key that would open the gates of heaven?

When Mary looked upon her son, did she know that his blood-stained garments would be regarded as a royal canopy adorning his sacred flesh? As the wine of salvation flowed from his wounds, did she understand that the myrrh gifted to him when earthly kings knelt in quiet adoration was a prophetic gesture? Despite the jeers and tears of the crowd, the eyes of the new Adam and the new Eve lingered in a holy gaze as they read each other's soul. Each recognized in the other a crown of gold, even as their hearts broke and their bodies grew faint—offering hope to pilgrims whose pain often seems too great to bear.

How many parents have drawn solace from this sorrowful mother while they kept vigil at the bedside of their dying child? How many hearts does Mary hold within her own, to whom she whispers, "This is not the end, but a new beginning for your child's life?" Through every avenue of life, Mary accompanies us as she accompanied her son. She walks with those who are persecuted, the disenfranchised, and with those who advocate for victims of violence and injustice. Although few of her words have been recorded, she never stops teaching and reassuring her children from heaven. She invites us to draw near the cross, reassuring us of her son's love when we are weighed down by our sins. She soothes her children, kissing wounds that continue bleeding, pleading to the Father in the name of her Son with whom she reigns as Queen of Heaven. Our "Tower of Ivory" remained strong, beautiful, and unmovable in the face of danger. How blessed we are to have her for our mother, this "Refuge of Sinners" and the personification of the bride in the Song of Songs who says:

> Daughters of Jerusalem,
> come out.
> Look, O daughters of Zion,
> at King Solomon,
> at the crown with which his mother crowned him
> on the day of his wedding,
> on the day of the gladness of his heart. (Song 3:10–11)

This is the song of hope that Christians hold in their hearts when, like Simon of Cyrene, they are tempted to ask why they should help Jesus carry his cross; when, like the holy women, our tears flow at the sight of Jesus even as we fail to realize our culpability; when we hear the voice of Mary as she laments and instructs as we travel the road from exile to return. Through his poetry, John of the Cross lays bare our own misery, even as he offers hope, speaking here in the person of a captive of Babylon (see Ps 137):

> O Daughter of Babylon,
> miserable and wretched!
> Blessed is he
> in whom I have trusted,
> for he will punish you
> as you have me;
> and he will gather his little ones
> and me, who wept because of you,
> at the rock who is Christ
> for whom I abandoned you. (P 10)

Yes, when Jesus died on the cross, he drew all to himself (see Jn 12:32), gathering us, "his little ones," together.

THE CRUCIFIXION AND DEATH OF OUR LORD

No words can assuage the depth of our misery when we gaze at the crucifix. Reflecting on Mary at the foot of the cross, we, like the psalmist of old, acknowledge our guilt as we cry out:

> Wash me thoroughly from my iniquity,
> and cleanse me from my sin.
> For I know my transgressions,
> and my sin is ever before me.
> Against you, you alone, have I sinned,
> and done what is evil in your sight. (Ps 51:2–4)

This is the perhaps the most fitting disposition we can embrace before the cross.

The ancient text—ever ancient, ever new—reminds us that we are all God's people. The story of the Israelites is our story, because knowingly or unknowingly, we all seek to return to the place of our origin in the heart of God. Ransomed from captivity, we have been reborn from the root of Jesse, a branch from the cross of death that has sprung forth as the tree of life. The serpent's pole of Moses is now transformed into the scepter of the King. There is no longer Greek or Jew, male or female, saint or sinner, because all have been saved through the blood of the cross.

Who can explain the totality of mystery that salvation holds as seeming contradictions give way to the mercy of a God who is beyond knowing? How do we account for Etty Hillesum, once a professed atheist, experiencing an intimate encounter with God in a Nazi camp amid the most appalling human conditions? How could it be that so unlikely a candidate penned a prayer that remains a testimony to the universality of God's love and mercy? Three months before she was put to death, an entry in a letter reveals what God was doing through her when she wrote:

> You have made me so rich, oh God, please let me share out your beauty with open hands. My life has become an uninterrupted dialogue with You, oh God, one great dialogue. Sometimes when I stand in some corner of the camp, my feet planted on earth, my eyes raised toward Your heaven, tears sometimes run down my face, tears of deep emotion and gratitude. At night, too, when I lie in my bed and rest in You, oh God, tears of gratitude run down my face, and that is my prayer. Things come and go in a deeper rhythm, and people must be taught to listen; it is the most important thing we have to learn in this life. . . . The beat of my heart has grown deeper, more active and yet more peaceful, and it is as if I were all the time storing up inner riches.[5]

The fruits of suffering in union with God are evident from this moving passage, full of vibrancy and love.

Mahatma Gandhi gave his life for his people through peaceful resistance, and as he fell to his death at the hand of an assassin's bullet, his last words, "Ram, Ram," ("God, God"),[6] give credence to God's universal embrace. As Jesus took his last breath, it was the Roman soldier at the foot of the cross who declared, "Truly this man was God's Son!" (Mk 15:39). When Thérèse prayed for an imprisoned murderer to repent of his crime, she knew her prayer had been answered when she read in the paper that he had

---

5. Etty Hillesum, *An Interrupted Life and Letters from Westerbork* (New York: Henry Holt, 1996), 332.

6. Richard Cavendish, "The Death of Mahatma Gandhi," *History Today* 58:no. 1 (January 2008), *https://www.historytoday.com/archive/months-past/death-mahatma-gandhi/*.

reached out and kissed the priest's crucifix moments before he was executed (see S 100). The good thief who was promised paradise by Jesus is but one more example that God does not see as humans see. Rather, he looks at the person, and seeing himself in the soul he created, he cannot turn away. And his Spirit guides us "more surely than the light of noon" (N stanza 4).

To look at Jesus on the cross is to gaze into the heart of God and allow him to transform us into the image of his Son. It gives credence to the words of St. Thomas More, who blessed his executioner because he was sending him to God. Not all are called to die as martyrs, nor do all people die in transports of love like Francis of Assisi, who sang a hymn of praise to "Sister Death" as he lay dying. And yet everyday countless souls face death with steadfast faith and quiet abandonment, holding on to the image of Jesus who with arms outstretched welcomes them home.

Jesus died the way he lived. His last words were a testimony to his life and teachings. In union with the will of the Father, he surrendered his life to save sinners. In his thirst for souls, he forgave his persecutors, promised paradise to the good thief, bequeathed his mother to the world, and cried out to God. Then, as he drew his last breath, he proclaimed his mission finished and surrendered his spirit to the Father in the same way he had surrendered his will throughout his life.

Everything we need to learn about life can be learned at the foot of the cross, and who better to teach us than Mary, who remained with her son until the end? After Jesus was taken down from the cross, he was placed in her arms, an image that has been immortalized through the Pietà. It seems likely that this image may have inspired John of the Cross when he wrote:

> Upon my flowering breast,
> which I kept wholly for him alone,
> there he lay sleeping,

and I caressing him
there in a breeze from the fanning cedars.

When the breeze blew from the turret,
as I parted his hair,
it wounded my neck
with its gentle hand,
suspending all my senses. (N stanzas 6–7)

This is the last time that Mary held in her arms the son she had borne and loved so much.

Joining the funeral procession, Mary watched as her son was committed to a borrowed tomb. Once again, the poverty of God was on full display. Like the cave that served as Jesus's first home, his final resting place was hewn from the womb of the earth. The seed had been sown, the Lamb slain, and heaven and earth fell silent. For three days, the only sound was that of Rachel weeping for her children, until the day when the earth quaked and the glory of the Lord was born anew and death was no more.

INVITATION TO PRAYER

Many parents who have had the tragic misfortune of burying a child to whom they had given life have said that the death of their child was the most painful experience they had ever known, even causing some to wish they could have given their life so their child might live. As Mary stood at the foot of the cross, it seems possible that she may have had similar thoughts. And yet despite the wound her son's death inflicted on her soul, her unity with God was able to reconcile within herself the paradox of redemptive suffering as she joined her interior suffering with what her son had endured physically. Although the interior suffering that our

Continued

INVITATION TO PRAYER *Continued*

sorrowful mother experienced on Calvary is impossible to imagine, I find these words of John of the Cross most comforting: "I know that nothing else is so beautiful, / and that the heavens and the earth drink there, / *although it is night*" (P 8.3). Several prayers have been written in honor of our Sorrowful Mother; below is one that has been attributed to St. Bonaventure, a thirteenth-century Franciscan friar, scholar, priest, and Doctor of the Church who had a tender devotion to the Blessed Mother.

PRAYER TO OUR LADY OF SORROWS

(*Attributed To St. Bonaventure*)

O most holy Virgin, Mother of our Lord Jesus Christ,
by the overwhelming grief you experienced
when you witnessed the martyrdom,
the crucifixion, and the death of your divine Son,
look upon me with eyes of compassion,
and awaken in my heart a tender
commiseration for those sufferings,
as well as a sincere detestation
of my sins, in order that,
being disengaged from all undue affection
for the passing joys of this earth,
I may sigh after the eternal Jerusalem,
and that henceforward all my thoughts
and all my actions may be directed
towards this one most desirable object:
Honor, glory, and love to our divine Lord Jesus,
and to the holy and immaculate Mother of God.
Amen.

16

The Glorious Mysteries

THE GLORIOUS MYSTERIES ARE PRAYED on Wednesdays and Sundays.[1] However, in keeping with the liturgical season, the Joyful Mysteries are often prayed on Sundays during the season of Advent and the Sorrowful Mysteries on Sundays during Lent. The Glorious Mysteries take on an obvious mystical dimension, since they pertain to the post-resurrection days and years in the lives of Jesus and Mary. When Jesus was raised from the dead, his body was transformed. Not only was he no longer subject to death, but he was no longer constrained by the limitations that bind human beings to their temporal bodies, as was prophesied through Isaiah:

> See, the former things have come to pass,
> and new things I now declare;
> before they spring forth,
> I tell you of them. (Isa 42:9)

And Revelation, echoing Isaiah, takes up the message: "See, I am making all things new" (Rev 21:5; cf. Isa 43:19). For these are the new times after the resurrection of Jesus.

1. Before John Paul II's RVM, the Glorious Mysteries were prayed on Saturdays also.

THE RESURRECTION OF OUR LORD

Although numerous post-resurrection appearances by Jesus to his followers are well documented in Scripture, there is no mention of Jesus appearing to his mother after he rose from the dead. However, as mentioned in a previous chapter, Jesus told St. Teresa that after he rose from the dead, he appeared to his mother to console her because of all she had suffered. The Venerable Mary of Agreda received this revelation of the encounter between Jesus and his mother: "Christ, our Savior, arisen and glorious in the company of all the saints and patriarchs, made His appearance. The ever-humble Queen prostrated herself and adored her Divine Son; and the Lord raised her up and drew her to Himself . . . the glorious body of her Son so closely united itself to that of His purest mother that He penetrated into it or she into His."[2] This vision, speaking of the closest union between Mary and her son, provides much nourishment for contemplation.

The mystic further saw that during the visitation by our Lord, Mary was transformed and caught up in the beatific vision, participating in the triumph of the Lord as she had participated in his passion. Inebriated with the wine of love and charity, "she held sweet converse with her Son concerning the mysteries of His passion and glory."[3] After Jesus left her, Mary surely would have remained serene and tranquil. Subject to the divine will, she lived in union with God as Mother of the Church, interceding with Christ on behalf of a race wounded by sin. Consequently, the pain of the church remains the pain of the Virgin Mother, whose tears mingled with the blood of her son who won for us the gift of salvation.

---

2. Mother Mary of Agreda, *The Mystical City of God*, 453.

3. Mother Mary of Agreda, *The Mystical City of God*, 454.

Having witnessed all that her son had suffered during his passion and crucifixion, Mary's pain was as profound as it was piercing, as holy as it was hidden. Were it not for mystics who revealed what hearts hidden in the depths of God's love endure, we would never understand the extent of Mary's interior suffering. St. Teresa, as we have seen, was given to perceive this in a vision of the visit of Jesus to his mother (see ST 12:1, 3). And through his poetry, John of the Cross offers a glimpse of what transpires in souls who are united with God spiritually, even as they languish from corporal separation as did Mary while she remained on earth. In describing his own ineffable experience, John discloses what might have been in the soul of Our Lady of Sorrows as he wrote:

> Lift me from this death,
> my God and give me life;
> do not hold me bound
> with these bonds so strong;
> see how I long to see you;
> my wretchedness is so complete
> *that I die because I do not die.* (P 5.7)

Teresa echoed John's heartfelt cry when she wrote, "The soul dies with the desire to die" (IC 6.11.9). Since the soul is one with the will of God, it cherishes the pain, for it cannot do otherwise, as the saint explained: "The soul feels that the pain is precious; so precious—it understands very well—that one could not deserve it. However, this awareness is not of a kind that alleviates the suffering in any way. But with this knowledge, the soul suffers this pain very willingly and would suffer it all its life, if God were to be thereby served; although the soul would not then die once but be always dying, for truly the suffering is no less than death" (IC 6.11.6). We are here at the heart of a mysticism of suffering, which does not desire suffering for its own sake but so as to be united with Christ.

St. Teresa also described this suffering as a great gift given by God to fortify souls, preparing them to suffer in imitation of, and in union with, Jesus. She reminded her nuns that those closest to Jesus endured the greatest trials, as clearly evidenced in Mary, who was more united with him than anyone. Some might wonder, then, if it was necessary for Mary to continue to suffer after what she had already endured at the foot of the cross. However, Mary's suffering was not a purification but a means of fuller union with God; her suffering was a deeper participation in the suffering of Christ for the salvation of others. Teresa recognized the merit in such suffering and counseled her nuns not to discount the effect of love on others when souls suffer who are united with God. "This fire in you enkindles their souls" (IC 7.4.14), she wrote, for love cannot be content and is gladly willing to suffer for the sake of the salvation of others. She explained: "I have already told you that the calm these souls have interiorly is for the sake of their having much less calm exteriorly and much less desire to have exterior calm. What, do you think, is the reason for those inspirations (or to put it better, aspirations) . . . ? Is it so that those outside might fall asleep? No absolutely not! That the faculties, senses, and all the corporeal will not be idle, the soul wages more war from the center than when it was outside suffering with them, for then it didn't understand the tremendous gain trials bring" (IC 7.4.10). This is great encouragement, for when we are in the midst of trials, we can grow interiorly and our prayer will become all the more powerful.

Although Teresa often disavowed her theological expertise, it was all the more perceptive and profound as it came from experiential knowledge. She clearly exhibited a profound understanding of redemptive suffering in which souls, in union with God, lead others to holiness by means of their own suffering. As St. Paul declared, "I am now rejoicing in my sufferings for your sake, and in my flesh I am completing what is lacking in Christ's afflictions for the sake of his body, that is, the church" (Col 1:24). No one was positioned to participate in Christ's sacrificial offering to the Father as intimately as Mary. As Mother of the Church, she was never exempt from suffering. As mother of Jesus, she was privileged to share in the life, suffering, and death of her son in an extraordinary way, a favor that St. Alphonsus Liguori described in his tribute to the life of a soul espoused to Jesus:

> She does not seek pleasure, has no wishes or will of her
> own; the will of
> her sweet spouse is the soul's pleasure and desire of the soul,
> who is the bride of Christ.
>
> And since suffering is the best sign which, more than love,
> can reassure the beloved,
> the spouse who desires to show all her love, accepts gladly
> all suffering and pain.[4]

Before every such generous bride, who gladly accepts pain so as to show her love, the heart of God must be deeply moved.

THE ASCENSION OF OUR LORD

Forty days after Jesus rose from the dead, he gathered his disciples around him on Mount Olivet and, after promising to send the Holy Spirit, departed from them as Luke records in Acts: "As they were watching, he was lifted up, and a cloud took him out of their sight. While he was going and they were gazing

4. St. Alphonsus Liguori, "The Life of the Spouse," in *O God of Loveliness: The Poetry of St Alphonsus*, ed. Patrick Corbert, C.S.s.R. (Strathfield, N.S.W.: St. Pauls Publications, 2017), 63.

up toward heaven, suddenly two men in white robes stood by them. They said, "Men of Galilee, why do you stand looking up toward heaven?" (Acts 1:9–11). While this account of the ascension of the Lord has long been a familiar part of the Christian imagination, we rarely consider what it must have been like to experience this event.

According to some psychologists, when a person is surprised by an event, the brain experiences a type of "brain freeze," paralyzing its ability to process or implement an immediate response. The duration, though brief, triggers something in the brain that causes human beings to generate extreme curiosity in an attempt to figure out what is happening. Finally, the surprise changes the way a person, event, or relationship was perceived, leading the person to question how the change will affect them personally.[5]

This surely explains the reason why Jesus's disciples remained fixed in place, gazing up into the heavens when Jesus was taken from them until an angel directed them to return to Jerusalem. According to Scripture, they returned to the Upper Room, but given what they had just witnessed, their astonishment would naturally lead to questions about their immediate future. What were they to do? What did Jesus's leaving mean for them and what was their role in the kingdom that Jesus had proclaimed? Once again, their lives had been unexpectedly turned upside down, and with the Master gone, they were unable to move beyond personal concerns. After the resurrection, they assumed Jesus would remain with them, but now that he was gone, their hopes were suddenly dashed.

In the absence of Jesus's physical presence, it would have been natural for the apostles to turn to Mary for answers to their

---

5. See Kristen Meinzer and T.J. Raphael, "Here's What Happens after 'Surprise,'" *The Takeaway* radio program, April 2, 2015, ***https://www.pri.org/stories/2015-04-02/heres-what-happens-after-surprise/***.

questions. After all, no one knew and understood Jesus better than his mother. As we know from Scripture (see Acts 1:14), her response was to join them in prayer, perhaps reminding them of all that Jesus had taught them. Her strength and patience would have guided them amid questions and clouded thinking as she encouraged them to trust in the wisdom of God. In preparing them for the coming of the Holy Spirit, she may have echoed Gabriel's words, "Do not be afraid"—because they, too, had found favor with God. Her trust in God as she waited with the apostles, praying and pondering in the silence of her heart the many changes that had occurred since Jesus had risen from the dead, served as an example for the men who once again had entered unchartered waters.

When Jesus appeared to Mary Magdalene, his cryptic language had suggested that things were different now than before Jesus had died. His words—"Do not hold on to me, because I have not yet ascended to the Father. But go to my brothers and say to them, 'I am ascending to my Father and your Father, to my God and your God'" (Jn 20:17)—were unexpected. This cautionary warning was strange and difficult to understand. The previous familiarity between Jesus and his closest friends had changed, but that wasn't all that was new. Before his death and resurrection, when addressing the apostles, Jesus called them "friends"; now he referred to them as "brothers." They were more than friends; they were now family.

Beginning with the resurrection, Jesus's relationship with his followers took on a mystical dimension. His ascension into heaven marked the transition from a sensory perception of his presence on earth to one that could be realized only through the eyes of faith. Helping them to make the leap from seeing to believing was Mary, as St. Teresa Benedicta of the Cross explained, "Congregated around the silently praying Virgin, the emergent church awaited the promised new outpouring of the

Spirit that was to quicken it into inner clarity and fruitful outer effectiveness. . . . The Virgin, who kept every word sent from God in her heart, is the model for such attentive souls in whom Jesus's high priestly prayer comes to life again and again."[6] Here, the Carmelite saint draws us right into the praying heart of the Blessed Virgin.

Did the nine days that Mary spent with the apostles in the Upper Room provide an opportunity to share the events surrounding the infancy narratives? Could this have been the source for the narratives that eventually made their way into the gospels? We have no way of knowing for sure, as Pope Benedict pointed out, "We have to keep in mind the limit of all efforts to know the past: We can never go beyond the domain of hypothesis, because we simply cannot bring the past into the present. To be sure, some hypotheses enjoy a high degree of certainty, but overall we need to remain conscious of the limit of our certainties."[7] This is where faith is a surer guide than speculation, and even more enriching as it helps us to penetrate the mystery.

While it is impossible to know how those who gathered in the Upper Room understood the events that had taken place, one Scripture scholar, Gerhard Lohfink, points out, "They could only have understood them in the sense that now, with Jesus, the time of 'messianic salvation' had come." But although the word "messianic time" does not appear, Lohfink notes that "the *Psalms of Solomon* describe the messianic time as follows: 'Happy are those who shall live in those days, to see the good things of Israel that God shall accomplish in the congregation of the

---

6. Edith Stein, *The Hidden Life: Essays, Meditations, Spiritual Texts*, The Collected Works of Edith Stein IV, L. Gelber and Michael Linssen, eds. (Washington, D.C.: ICS Publications, 1992), 12–13.

7. Ratzinger/Benedict XVI, *Jesus of Nazareth: From the Baptism in the Jordan to the Transfiguration*, xvii.

tribes' (Ps Sol 17:44)."[8] Indeed, this directs the heart with joy to the coming of Christ.

If the apostles associated Jesus's coming with the end times, it's no wonder that they and first-century Christians thought that Jesus's second coming and the end times were imminent. Not knowing what to expect would have heightened their fear as they gathered together, watching and praying for the Holy Spirit whom Jesus had promised would come.

THE DESCENT OF THE HOLY SPIRIT

When the Holy Spirit descended on the apostles in tongues of fire, fear was dispelled, and the apostles, fortified by the Holy Spirit, emerged from the Upper Room with a sense of mission. Their work had begun. As the nascent church, they would continue Jesus's mission to build the kingdom by turning darkness into light, sadness into joy, and ordinary bread and wine into the Body and Blood of Christ. And death would be no more. The event, which is celebrated as the birthday of the church, is a permanent testimony to the power of God to transform sinners into saints: "And suddenly from heaven there came a sound like the rush of a violent wind, and it filled the entire house where they were sitting. Divided tongues, as of fire, appeared among them, and a tongue rested on each of them. All of them were filled with the Holy Spirit and began to speak in other languages, as the Spirit gave them ability" (Acts 2:2–4).

These tongues of fire that appeared over the apostles were an outward manifestation of what was taking place within the deepest center of their souls. Although the descent of the Holy

8. Lohfink, *Jesus of Nazareth*, 318. The *Psalms of Solomon* are an apocryphal book containing eighteen religious songs or poems, written in the first or second century BC. The seventeenth song, in particular, quoted here by Lohfink, has traditionally been attributed to Solomon.

Spirit at Pentecost is an exceptional moment of grace in the life of the church, it has dynamics in common with the moments of grace in which we are under the action of the Holy Spirit, and to these we can perhaps apply the insight of John of the Cross: "For what we are explaining about the activity of the Holy Spirit within [the soul] is something far greater than what occurs in the communication and transformation of love. This latter resembles glowing embers; the former is similar to embers that are not merely glowing but have become so hot that they shoot forth a living flame" (LF 1.16). This imagery is uncannily close to the tongues of fire, and John's words remind us that our own immersion in prayer can be itself a kind of Pentecost.

With the coming of the Holy Spirit on that first Pentecost, the apostles were transformed interiorly by a force so sublime that, according to Scripture, the external manifestation became visible as tongues of fire for all to see. The same men who had been frightened and confused became bold proclaimers of the word of God, not by their own power but through the power of the Holy Spirit. Their love had been purified, erasing fear of death. Now enlightened, they understood that the church was not only a militant body but a triumphant body. Impelled by the Spirit, they went forth proclaiming the kingdom of God, which had been accomplished through the dying and the rising of Jesus Christ. No longer self-absorbed, they gave little thought to their own safety or to self-aggrandizement. Like the prophet Elijah, they were consumed with zeal for the Lord God of hosts or, as St. Teresa said of her own transformation, "now it was time that she consider as her own what belonged to Him and that He would take care of what was hers" (IC 7.2.1). John of the Cross revealed similar sentiments in poetic verse when he wrote:

O lamps of fire!
in whose splendors

> the deep caverns of feeling,
> once obscured and blind,
> now give forth, so rarely, so exquisitely,
> both warmth and light to their Beloved. (LF stanza 3)

There is a gentleness in John's description. The "lamps of fire" that emanate warmth and light are not as dramatic as the tongues of fire, yet are no less powerful, for the Holy Spirit is at work in the soul.

Scripture is silent about Mary during and after the coming of the Holy Spirit. Yet we cannot doubt the interior work of the Holy Spirit taking place within her heart and in the hearts of all the baptized. As Teresa Benedicta of the Cross tells us:

> The work of salvation takes place in obscurity and stillness. In the heart's quiet dialogue with God the living building blocks out of which the kingdom of God grows are prepared, the chosen instruments for the construction forged. The mystical stream that flows through all centuries is no spurious tributary that has strayed from the prayer life of the church—it is its deepest life. When this mystical stream breaks through traditional forms, it does so because the Spirit that blows where it will is living in it, this Spirit that has created all traditional forms and must ever create new ones. Without him there would be no liturgy and no church.[9]

This very beautiful passage makes us aware that we, too, may open ourselves to the action of the Spirit—this "mystical stream," our "deepest life."

Who can account for the multitude of conversions that have transformed sinners into saints throughout the ages? It would

9. Stein, *The Hidden Life*, 15.

be impossible except for the ongoing activity of the Holy Spirit! Regarding his own awakening to the Holy Spirit, Thomas Merton wrote that upon entering the chapel at the Trappist monastery in Gethsemani, Kentucky, he found the presence of God palpable, and with a certitude he could not explain he felt as though he had entered the center of the universe. Throughout the Mass he felt the presence of the Holy Spirit. Recalling his experience, he wrote:

> The eloquence of this liturgy was even more tremendous, and what it said was one cogent, tremendous. truth: this church, this court of the Queen of Heaven, is the real capital of the country in which we are now living. This is the center of all the vitality that is in America. This is the cause and the reason why the nation is holding together. These men, hidden in the anonymity of their choir and their white cowls, are doing for their land what no army, no congress, no president could ever do as such: they are winning for it the grace and the protection and the friendship of God.[10]

Even the nature of Merton's experience—being overwhelmed with awe and wonder and admiration—is a hallmark of an encounter with the Holy Spirit.

The activity of the Holy Spirit at Pentecost was not a once-and-done event but remains an ongoing testimony to the presence of God within the Mystical Body of Christ. Every moment, every day, the Spirit of God breathes through men and women who live in the world but are not of the world. It bears witness through priests and religious whose lives burn like sanctuary lamps within the church reminding all that Christ is present. It beats in the heart of the elderly, the sick, the disabled, whose

---

10. Thomas Merton, The *Seven Storey Mountain: An Autobiography of Faith* (New York: Harcourt, 1998), 356.

prayers, pain, and sacrifices, offered for the good of the church, rise like incense before the throne of God. And it runs like a stream through the heart of the domestic church in parents who nurture and guide their children in the faith. All are called to share in this redemptive process: saints and sinners, the young and the old, the rich and the poor, you and me. Because, as St. Teresa Benedicta writes, "All authentic prayer is prayer of the church. Through every sincere prayer something happens in the church, and it is the church itself that is praying therein, for it is the Holy Spirit living in the church that intercedes for every individual soul 'with sighs too deep for words.' This is exactly what authentic prayer is, for 'no one can say "Jesus is Lord" except by the Holy Spirit'"[11]

This church—thus animated from within by the Holy Spirit—is the new Jerusalem, the bride of Christ, united with the Bridegroom who sacrificed his life for his bride. The paschal mystery is the recapitulation of the wedding of Adam and Eve, for all that was wrong with the world has been set in right order.

THE ASSUMPTION OF MARY INTO HEAVEN

There is no mention in Scripture of Mary being assumed into heaven, but Pope Pius XII noted that many have recognized a foreshadowing of it in Psalm 132, which he cited when he proclaimed the assumption of Mary a dogma of the church. Psalm 132 celebrates the ark of the covenant being brought by David to the temple in Jerusalem: "Arise O Lord and go to your resting place, you and the ark of your might" (Ps 132:8). Since Mary, who carried the Son of God in her womb, is the ark of the new covenant, some have seen the words of the psalmist as prefiguring Mary's assumption. Just as David transferred the ark to its rest in

11. Stein, *The Hidden Life*, 15; cf. Rom 8:26; 1 Cor 12:3.

the Jerusalem temple of old, so now Jesus, the true son of David, brings Mary, the new ark of the covenant, to her final resting place in heaven (See MD 26). These words are actually profoundly Carmelite, as they speak of a mutual indwelling—God in us, we in God—while we wait to be united with him in heaven.

The assumption of Mary into heaven is significant because it prefigures the final resurrection of the just who will be reunited with their bodies. Like Mary, these souls will enjoy the fullness of the beatific vision of God. When the Sadducees questioned Jesus regarding the resurrection of the dead, he explained that after the resurrection, those who die will no longer eat or drink, marry or be given in marriage, for they shall live like angels (see Mt 22:23–30). On this subject, Brant Pitre points out, "Jesus is assuming that one of the primary reasons for marriage is procreation, in order to continue the human race. After the resurrection, death will be no more, so there will no longer be a need for offspring. Earthly marriage, bound up as it is with death through procreation, is a temporary part of 'this age' or 'this world'; it will have no place in the 'that age,' the age of the bodily resurrection."[12]

In line with this account, Christians believe that human marriage is a sign of the heavenly marriage that awaits us when we will be united with Christ the Bridegroom of our soul. Only the spotless Virgin was deemed worthy to be assumed into heaven body and soul, but her assumption into heaven remains a sign of what is to come for all the just. Christian tradition affirms that she was lifted up by God and admitted to the supernatural realm of heaven. Surely the soul of Mary, who is the fairest flower of our race, was like perfumed incense rising to the throne of God.

Although we stand in awe of our Blessed Mother, we remain hopeful that one day we too will know the realization of the

12. Pitre, *Jesus the Bridegroom*, 132.

fullness of our being and be united with the heavenly Bridegroom for all eternity. As pilgrims on the journey, we look to Mary, chosen for our sakes for Christ's first coming, to clear the path and lighten our way, so that we may be found worthy when Christ comes again.

We give thanks to God for giving himself to us through a mere human being and for appointing Mary to reign as the most perfect exemplar as the bride of Christ. Throughout the ages, works of art have proclaimed her glory, and rightly so. From the moment of her conception, we can imagine Mary clothed in her customary blue mantle of purity—pure and blue like the water that immerses and purifies our broken humanity in the sacrament of baptism. Thus, her nature is so sinless that her purity pervades and penetrates her entire being and all her actions. Nothing in this bride is corruptible. In her person is revealed the infinite majesty of God, for when God created his mother, she became the manifestation of the fullness of his grace. The reflection of eternal light, Mary is the spotless mirror of God working in and through her to further our understanding of God's own glory. In return, Mary was so consumed with love for God that it would seem that her death was a death of one wounded by the cauteries of burning love. Though she was assumed into heaven unseen by mortals, she was identifiable to souls who, enkindled by the living flame that consumes but does not burn, cry out:

> I went out seeking love
> and with unfaltering hope,
> I flew so high, so high,
> that I overtook the prey. (P 11.6)

As John of the Cross shows so well, our essential quest must be love. From there, we can surrender ourselves to God in complete trust, knowing that the God who is Love will raise us up.

THE CORONATION OF MARY AS QUEEN OF HEAVEN AND EARTH

Although Mary is mother of all peoples and her queenship extends to every nation, the title "queen" honors her Jewish roots. It's not readily apparent to most Christians today why Mary is called queen since she is not the spouse of Christ the King. However, as Edward Sri points out: "In the ancient Near East, the woman sitting on the throne in the kingdom was not the King's wife, but the king's mother. Kings in this period had large harems. King Solomon, for example, had seven hundred wives and three hundred concubines (see 1 Kings 11:3). It would have been impossible to bestow the queenship on a thousand women! Yet, while the king had multiple wives, he had only one mother; thus, the queenship was given to her."[13] Even in this world, a queen mother inspires dignity and awe as well as love.

For mortal human beings, it is impossible to imagine the jubilation that filled the heavens when Mary entered the celestial realm. Welcomed by the Father, embraced by her Son, and filled with the joy of the Holy Spirit, Mary was crowned Queen of Heaven and Earth, Queen of Angels, of all saints, martyrs, prophets, and patriarchs. Her threefold task as mother, teacher, and intercessor is accomplished through the divine will of the Most Blessed Trinity. When, from the cross, Jesus said, "Here is your mother" (Jn 19:27), he gifted us with more than a woman who would offer us her maternal care. He bequeathed to us the spouse of the Holy Spirit. Mary's gifts exceeded those of all the angels, saints, prophets, and apostles. While so many of these others, through human weakness, hesitated before taking up their mission, Mary surrendered herself totally and unconditionally. How blessed we are to have for our mother God's own mother!

---

13. Edward Sri, *Praying the Rosary Like Never Before: Encounter the Wonder of Heaven and Earth* (Cincinnati: Franciscan Media, 2017), 145.

As we are her children, our task is to shape the image of Mary that we carry in our hearts to reflect the role that God has designed for her from the beginning of time, which is that of Mother of God, Mother of the Church, and mother of the children of God. The more we learn of Mary, the more we are in awe of the wondrous gift that God has given to us in her. As St. Teresa Benedicta explains:

> Like a spore from which new cells stream continually, [Mary] was to build up the living city of God. This hidden mystery was revealed to St. John as he stood beneath the cross with the Virgin Mother and was given over to her as her son. It was then that the church came into existence visibly; her hour had come, but not yet her perfection. She lives, she is wedded to the Lamb, but the hour of the solemn marriage supper will only arrive when the dragon has been completely conquered and the last of the redeemed have fought their battle to the end. . . . All who want to be married to the Lamb must allow themselves to be fastened to the cross with him. Everyone marked by the blood of the Lamb is called to this and that means all the baptized.[14]

This is our destiny: to be the bride of Christ the Lamb (see Rev 19:7–8).

All have been saved through the death and resurrection of Jesus and invited to the wedding feast of the Lamb, but only those who are properly attired, whose robes have been cleansed in the blood of the Lamb, will be admitted to the eternal banquet hall (see Matt 22:11–12; Rev 7:14). The requirement should not be off-putting, since Scripture reassures us that Jesus has won our salvation and is eagerly waiting to bathe us in his light and love. "Listen! I am standing at the door, knocking; if

---

14. Stein, *The Hidden Life*, 98–99.

you hear my voice and open the door, I will come in to you and eat with you, and you with me" (Rev 3:20). The golden age of the church's evangelization is now; this is the acceptable time for every generation to turn away from sin, for Scripture says, "At an acceptable time I have listened to you, / and on a day of salvation I have helped you" (2 Cor 6:2). We are never alone: it is the desire of Jesus that we may be with him (see Jn 17:24).

No, we are not orphaned children of God. We have both a mother and a Father. Our Father accepts us as his own adopted children. Our mother intercedes on our behalf. Mary presents each of us to the Father like a bride with her dowry. We are this dowry—the humanity she shares with her son in his incarnation, purchased by her son on the marriage bed of the cross, cleansed by the blood of her son—a perfected offering that God accepts from her son as a new covenant.

Over the centuries, our dear Lady has come to earth, her children drawing her down just as, we might say, her fiat drew God from heaven. Our disposition ought to be guided by the word of God, expressed here by St. Paul: "There is no restriction in our affections, but only in yours. In return—I speak as to children—open wide your hearts also" (2 Cor 6:12). This is the disposition that, we could say, attracts toward us the heart of the Trinity.

Throughout the history of the church, Mary has appeared to her children, pleading for them to convert and turn their hearts to her son who loved them unto death. The fruits of her apparitions continue to this day, as people are converted, return to the sacraments, and experience physical and spiritual healing. Although apparitions are not part of the deposit of faith, why would anyone—given Mary's privileged position within the church and salvation history—be dismissive of a message that ought to strengthen our faith since it comes from the Queen of Heaven and Earth? Regarding apparitions, the renowned Mariologist Father René Laurentin wrote:

> Their function is not to complete the gospel in which Christ revealed all that is necessary for our salvation. Rather their function is to recall, to remove the scales from our eyes, to reopen our ears, to actualize the gospel, to insert it into our times and show, once more, its power to underline its own life-giving values. Thomas Aquinas held that apparitions have more to do with hope than faith. They shape the future. They bring the gospel to life in a prophetic manner in new historical and geographical situations. These tangible signs, in proclaiming the immediacy, the presence, the familiarity and the power of the gospel, bring these gospel powers to life.[15]

The learning and authority of this important theologian is a sure basis on which to let our heart soar toward the motherly intervention of Mary in our life while we remain rooted in gospel truth.

As Laurentin noted, Mary and Joseph enjoyed visions, as did Moses and Elijah, Peter and Paul, to name only a few. If these great saints needed help from on high, it seems presumptuous to assume that such help is no longer needed. Knowing our weakness, Mary offers us the rosary as a way to enter more deeply into the mysteries of her son and to learn of his mercy. Mindful of our penchant to stray, she has also given us the brown scapular as a protection from the powers of darkness. Ever vigilant, our mother never tires of drawing us to her son. She labors unceasingly so that we may hear the word of God and keep it.

That we may all be united through him as one family is Jesus's deepest desire. During his final discourse, one of his last prayers to the Father was for us, as he pleaded, "I ask not only on behalf of these [disciples], but also on behalf of those who will believe in me through their word, that they may all be one. As you, Father, are in me and I am in you, may they also be in us"

---

15. René Laurentin, *The Apparitions of the Blessed Virgin Mary Today* (Dublin: Veritas Publications, 1991), 19.

(Jn 17:20–21). We are all one family—the family of God with one Father and one mother, whose unconditional love and mercy never forsake us as they lovingly wait to welcome us home.

INVITATION TO PRAYER

Love in the abstract is not real. Until love is made visible and actualized toward someone or something, it exists only in the imagination as a self-serving or romantic notion. Real love will always have a sacrificial dimension, because it requires going out from ourselves to move toward another for the good of that person's spiritual or physical well-being. Mary's life, like that of her son's, was a continuous movement toward affirming, inspiring, and coming to the aid of the people she encountered. The humble virgin of Nazareth, who reigns now in heaven, is highly esteemed because her love for God and humanity has surpassed that of all the angels and saints. Once again, we turn to the Litany of Loreto as we honor the queenship of Mary, and pray:

Queen of Angels, pray for us.
Queen of Patriarchs, pray for us.
Queen of Prophets, pray for us.
Queen of Apostles, pray for us.
Queen of Martyrs, pray for us.
Queen of Confessors, pray for us.
Queen of Virgins, pray for us.
Queen of all Saints, pray for us.
Queen conceived without original sin, pray for us.
Queen assumed into Heaven, pray for us.
Queen of the most Holy Rosary, pray for us.
Queen of families, pray for us.
Queen of peace, pray for us.[16] Amen.

16. See chapter 10, footnote 9.

17

The Brown Scapular of Our Lady of Mount Carmel

ONE OF THE GIFTS OF THE HOLY SPIRIT, regarded as a gateway to the transcendent God, is the gift of wisdom. Sought by contemplatives and imbued with feminine traits in Old Testament Wisdom literature, it's not surprising that one of the Scripture readings for enrollment in the scapular of the Blessed Virgin Mary is from chapter 8 of the Book of Proverbs. Part of the body of Wisdom literature, the text refers to the mystery of salvation but has also been understood with reference to the Blessed Virgin Mary, the "Seat of Wisdom."

I love those who love me,
 and those who seek me diligently find me.
Riches and honor are with me,
 enduring wealth and prosperity.
My fruit is better than gold, even fine gold,
 and my yield than choice silver.
I walk in the way of righteousness,
 along the paths of justice,
endowing with wealth those who love me,
 and filling their treasuries. (Prov 8:17–21)

Although these words may be read as an apt description of Mary, it is important to remember that she is not God. She has been singularly honored as the highest and most-pure member of the human race, but the church does not regard her as co-redemptrix.[1] On the vigil of the Solemnity of the Annunciation in 2021, Pope Francis used the occasion to clarify any misconceptions that might be unresolved in this regard, given that the title has been attributed to her in a devotional context. He explained, "Jesus extended Mary's maternity to the entire Church when He entrusted her to his beloved disciple shortly before dying on the cross. From that moment on, we have all been gathered under her mantle. . . . [Mary,] as the mother to whom Jesus entrusted us, 'enfolds' us all; but as a Mother, not as a goddess, not as co-redeemer: as a Mother. . . . But let us be careful: the beautiful things that the Church, the saints, say about Mary, take nothing away from Christ's sole Redemption. He is the only Redeemer."[2] Here, Pope Francis is giving us a sound theological perspective, but his words are no less beautiful than the titles he refers to: Mary is our mother, and we have all been gathered under her mantle.

Mary's mantle of motherhood is a metaphor that describes her maternal love for all God's children, but the brown scapular of Our Lady of Mount Carmel is a specific and concrete development of the idea. It's a sacramental that involves a blessing of the scapular and enrollment into a spiritual confraternity (a loosely organized association or movement). Enrollment is open to any member of the church, and this can be carried out by a priest or any authorized person. This sacramental is often referred to as simply "the brown scapular," and enrollment welcomes into the Carmelite family all who wear it and practice the

1. See chapter 8 above.

2. Pope Francis, "General Audience," March 24, 2021.

spirituality of the order. According to the instruction issued by the Carmelite provincials of North America: "A priest or authorized person enrolls people in the Brown Scapular only once. A cloth Scapular can be substituted by a scapular medal after enrollment. Medals have on one side the image of the Sacred Heart of Jesus and on the other, the image of Mary.[3] The scapular holds us to live as authentic Christians in line with the teachings of the Gospel, to receive the sacraments, to profess our special devotion to the Blessed Virgin, which should be expressed each day, at least by saying the Hail Mary three times."[4]

Initially, the scapular was an apron worn over the shoulders to protect the brothers' habits while they were working. But over time it became a regular part of the Carmelite habit and was given a spiritual meaning, representing Mary's maternal protection of the brothers. Later, a devotional scapular developed for the laity, consisting of two small pieces of dark brown cloth, preferably plain, joined by a cord or ribbon and worn over the shoulders with one square falling in the front and the other on the back.[5]

To better appreciate the role of the brown scapular within the Carmelite Order and the church, it's important to view it with an eye toward the history of the order. According to a document published by provincials of the order in 2000, "the scapular is a symbol of filial and grateful recognition of the mission that the Most Blessed Trinity willed to confide to

---

3. Congregation for the Doctrine of the Faith, "The Scapular Medal," *https://www.ewtn.com/catholicism/library/scapular-medal-2105/*.

4. North American Provincials of the Carmelite Orders, *The Scapular of Our Lady of Mount Carmel: Catechesis and Ritual* (Washington, D.C.: ICS Publications, 2000), 8.

5. See North American Provincials of the Carmelite Orders, *The Scapular of Our Lady of Mount Carmel*, 6–7.

Mary in the history of salvation."[6] By wearing the scapular, we are turning to Mary as our mother—mother of Christ and of his Mystical Body.

The Carmelite Order, which had its beginnings in about 1200 with a group of men living in community on Mount Carmel, was first known as the Brothers of the Blessed Virgin Mary of Mount Carmel. The chapel they constructed for liturgical and communal prayer was named in honor of Mary, and they looked to Mary as the personification of purity, goodness, and service to Jesus Christ. Inspired by the prophet Elijah, who stood before the face of God and was zealous for the Lord, they devoted their lives to prayer and service. Vowing allegiance to Jesus Christ under obedience to a rule of life written by Albert, Latin patriarch of Jerusalem, the brothers were never strictly an eremitical community. Although union with God through prayer was their primary focus, certain historical documents demonstrate the hermits' apostolic activity. For instance, by 1229 the prior of the community was given apostolic authority to dispense canonical censures incurred by repentant apostates.[7]

As the Crusades intensified and their lives were increasingly at risk, the brothers eventually migrated to Europe, where they became known as Carmelites. Some settled in Cyprus, others in Sicily, France, and England. In addition to the existing challenges of seeking recognition as a religious order, divergent locations and situations threatened their unity. Those who struggled with adapting to the environment of the church in the West argued that the Carmelites were losing their contemplative character. Others maintained that even Elijah and Elisha, though

6. North American Provincials of the Carmelite Orders, *The Scapular of Our Lady of Mount Carmel*, 14.

7. See Joachim Smet, O.Carm., *The Mirror of Carmel: A Brief History of the Carmelite Order* (Darien, Ill.: Carmelite Media, 2011), 7.

they lived primarily in the desert, ventured out into towns and villages among the people, performing miracles and calling the Israelites to reform their lives. While one group accused those desiring a more eremitical life of being out of touch with the mendicant orders of Europe, the other countered that without a life of prayer, preachers were ignorant of matters they were teaching. Despite internal tensions, they remained faithful to the contemplative spirit as their primary vocation, while sharing with others the fruits of their contemplative prayer.

Amid a climate of internal strife, St. Simon Stock, possibly prior general at the time, solicited help from Rome in 1247 to have certain points of the rule clarified and amended. Pope Innocent IV appointed two Dominicans to work on this. After just a month, it was ready, and the rule was approved by the pope that year. Unfortunately, while approval of the rule led to the most welcome recognition of the Carmelites as an order, it also exacerbated existing tensions, leading some to oppose what they regarded as a weakening of the rule. It was during this period of discord—on July 16, 1251, in Cambridge, England, (or Aylesford, according to some sources)—that the Blessed Virgin, holding the Child Jesus, appeared to St. Simon. In her hands was the Carmelite scapular, which she extended to the friar with the words: "This shall be a privilege for you and for all Carmelites, that whoever dies clothed in this . . . shall be saved."[8]

During the centuries that followed, the authenticity of the vision and message to St. Simon Stock came into question. However, since the history of the apparition can be traced to fourteenth-century documentation, Mary's appearance and promise were deemed credible. Consistent with teachings within the

8. Peter-Thomas Rohrbach, O.C.D., *Journey to Carith: The Story of the Carmelite Order* (Washington, D.C.: ICS Publications, facsimile of 1966 Doubleday edition), 67–68.

order it has been preached by Carmelites to the faithful through the centuries. As Peter-Thomas Rohrbach, O.C.D., has written:

> St. Simon's vision occupies a preeminent position in the history of the Carmelite Order, and it profoundly influenced its fortunes. It took place at the nadir moment in the Order's migration to the West, and helped re-establish its pride and confidence in itself, providing a tangible symbol of Carmel's original tradition and continuing relevance. . . . The scapular also helped the Order gain prestige in the medieval world of Europe. And it increased the Order's sphere of influence by eventually incorporating millions of lay people throughout the centuries into the Carmelite family.[9]

Indeed, the brown scapular has also been recognized by popes.

A story circulated in the fifteenth and sixteenth centuries that the fourteenth-century Pope John XXII extended and expanded Mary's promise regarding the scapular in a 1322 papal bull following a vision he received from the Blessed Mother. According to this claim, Mary told him that on the Saturday following their death, she would come to the aid of souls in purgatory who had been wearing the scapular at the time they died. This became known as the "Sabbatine Bull." But there is no extent copy of the bull or confirmation that it in fact ever existed, and in 1613 the Holy See declared the alleged appearance of Mary to Pope John XXII to be unfounded and admonished the Carmelite Order for preaching the doctrine.[10]

However, numerous popes have approved of and promoted the brown scapular. In the mid-nineteenth century, Pope Pius IX said, "This most extraordinary gift of the Scapular . . . from

---

9. Rohrbach, *Journey to Carith*, 73.

10. For more on the distinction between the Sabbatine privilege and the spurious "Sabbatine Bull," see Smet, *The Mirror of Carmel*, 183–85.

the Mother of God to Saint Simon Stock . . . brings its great usefulness not only to the Carmelite family of Mary, but also to all the rest of the faithful who, affiliated to that family, wish to follow Mary with a very special devotion."[11]

Pope John Paul II frequently spoke and wrote of his devotion to Mary and his love of Carmelite spirituality. In a message written to the Carmelite family on the seven hundred fiftieth anniversary of the bestowal of the scapular to St. Simon Stock, the Holy Father expressed his filial love for the Order of Carmel and its role in deepening Marian spirituality. In a letter to the general superiors of the Discalced Carmelites (O.C.D.) and the Carmelites of the Ancient Observance (O.Carm.), he cited words from the enrollment: "Those who wear the Scapular are thus brought into the land of Carmel, so that they may 'eat its fruits and its good things' (cf. Jer 2:7), and experience the loving and motherly presence of Mary in their daily commitment to be clothed in Jesus Christ and to manifest him in their life for the good of the Church and the whole of humanity."[12] We can see from this the great love of John Paul II for Mary—an experiential knowledge in which he feels her presence.

That Pope John Paul II held Mary in great esteem is well documented through his encyclicals and copious other teaching and preaching, and his personal devotion to her was reported widely. Therefore, it came as no surprise that in the same letter he wrote, "I too have worn the scapular of Carmel over my heart for a long time! Out of my love for our common heavenly Mother, whose protection I constantly experience, I hope that this Marian year will help all the men and women religious

---

11. Rohrbach, *Journey to Carith*, 74.

12. Pope John Paul II, "Message of John Paul II to the Carmelite Family," March 25, 2001, n. 5, *https://www.vatican.va/content/john-paul-ii/en/speeches/2001/march/documents/hf_jp-ii_spe_20010326_ordine-carmelo.html/*.

of Carmel and the devout faithful who venerate her with filial affection to grow in her love and to radiate to the world the presence of this Woman of silence and prayer."[13]

CURRENT CATECHESIS ON THE BROWN SCAPULAR

As often happens in the absence of proper understanding, sacramentals that are of considerable value can fall by the wayside or, worse yet, be reduced to objects of superstitious practice. Wishing to correct misconceptions regarding the brown scapular, Carmelite provincials in the United States, both the Discalced and the Ancient Observance, directed in 2000 the publication of a booklet (quoted several times above) about its nature and history. The document provides sound catechesis regarding both the brown scapular and the Carmelite family.

As noted by the Carmelite provincials, the brown scapular is not a guarantee of heaven. It is a sign of life with Mary in allegiance to Jesus Christ that includes frequent participation in the Mass and reception of the Eucharist, regular meditation on the Scriptures, and praying the rosary or at least part of the Liturgy of the Hours every day, along with the practice of Christian virtues in imitation of Mary. The brown scapular is a powerful sign of Mary's quiet, unfailing love and serves as a reminder of her ongoing presence in our lives. Although Mary's presence and love for Carmelites is unique in its own way, and she is often pictured wearing the Carmelite habit, her loving presence is not exclusive to Carmelites. Her maternal love for all is demonstrated, in part, by the Carmelite Order's welcoming into the Carmelite family not only the religious men

---

13. Pope John Paul II, "Message of John Paul II to the Carmelite Family," n. 6.

and women of the order and aggregated institutions, but also the secular/lay order (also known as the Third Order); members of public associations and confraternities of Our Lady of Mount Carmel, such as active communities of the Scapular Confraternity; those who have been invested in the scapular, practice the order's spirituality, and have been granted some association with the order; those who wear the scapular out of devotion, practice the order's spirituality, but have no formal association with the order; and those who are committed to the Marian character of Carmelite spirituality but use outward forms other than the brown scapular to express this devotion.[14] The inclusive nature of this list speaks of the great Marian outreach of Carmel.

THE PROPHETIC AND INCLUSIVE NATURE OF CARMEL

The spirit of Carmel is essentially contemplative and prophetic. The Virgin Mary, whose spirit exemplifies the interior life of Carmel, is understood by all who follow her into the dark night of faith. Perhaps therein lies the secret of the widespread appeal of Carmelite spirituality. In Mary we discover the mantle that offers a double portion of the spirit of Elijah, her mediation extending beyond ordinary human limits.

Just as the family of Carmel has roots that can be traced back to the Hebrew Scriptures, with the account of Elijah, so the writings of Teresa of Jesus and John of the Cross have guided Carmelites and all who desire a deeper relationship with God through the centuries. Their insight regarding the deepening stages of prayer serves as a guide for religious communities

---

14. North American Provincials of the Carmelite Orders, *The Scapular of Our Lady of Mount Carmel*, 2–3.

and laity alike. Their works are numbered among those of the great Spanish literary authors, poets, mystics, and Doctors of the Church. They turn up on the shelves in secular bookstores and are quoted in homilies. Their teachings are universal because they speak to the heart's deepest longing for union with God, in whom rests the source of happiness and wholeness. Carmelite spirituality speaks to humanity's need to love and to be loved; it expresses and plumbs the depths of the truth that when, at last, disordered affection for all else disappears, all that remains is a deep longing for God.

Whether or not Carmelite spirituality in general, or the brown scapular in particular, can be adopted by non-Christians, we might look to how Elijah befriended the widow of Zarephath (see 1 Kings 17:7–16), and Elisha formed a friendship with the Shunamite woman, whose son he raised from the dead (see 2 Kings 4:8–37). These were signs of what was to come in the person of Jesus Christ. As Elijah stretched out his body, lying on the dead body of his friend's son, the boy's life was restored. This can be seen as a prototype of Jesus, whose body was stretched out upon the cross to breathe life into the children of God. Elijah's bequeathing a double portion of his spirit to Elisha was the forerunner of discipleship, a prototype for Carmelites, who under the mantle of contemplation shoulder the scapular of apostleship. Imbued with the spirit of Elijah, who was awakened by the angel and told, "Get up and eat, otherwise the journey will be too much for you" (1 Kings 19:7), Carmelites, knowingly and unknowingly, instruct all seekers of truth in the practice of interior prayer. Much like the angel who was sent to Elijah, they are messengers who provide spiritual food to strengthen seekers for the journey ahead.

More than a symbol, the brown scapular is a way of life and a sign of maternal protection gifted to us by the Blessed Mother. The precious Flower of Carmel stands before the face of God, like Elijah (see 1 Kings 17:1), on behalf of all her children and, in a special way, for all who seek union with God through prayer. As mother of Christians and Jews, the baptized and unbaptized, Mary joins her voice to the voice of the Father who asks,

> Can a woman forget her nursing child,
> or show no compassion for the child of her womb?
> Even these may forget,
> yet I will not forget you. (Isa 49:15)

Mary as mother and as the perfect disciple points the way to Christ, and so we can be assured that the love she has for all her children will lead them to closer union with Christ and his church.

Mary draws us under her mantle and invites her devotees to be clothed in the scapular of Carmel as a reminder of her ongoing protection. She invites us to pray the rosary, counsels us to fix our gaze on God, and instructs us to do whatever he tells us. Although the rosary can be seen as a form of vocal prayer, it neither lessens nor contradicts the practice of prayer for Carmelites. The lives of Teresa and John of the Cross, characterized by contemplative prayer, also testify to the importance of vocal prayer. In writing about vocal prayer, Teresa focused on the two most common vocal prayers, the Our Father and the Hail Mary, both rooted in Scripture. This is how one writer describes Teresa's approach: "Instead of emphasizing what was distinctive about mental prayer, Teresa made the claim that the distinction between mental prayer and vocal prayer are actually unimportant, saying 'Mental prayer isn't determined by whether or not the mouth is closed' (Ltr 218. 2). In her defense of mental prayer, Teresa broadened the definition of mental prayer so that it became an essential part of the ordinary life of prayer."[15] Teresa's important linking of vocal and mental prayer provides us with an encouraging starting point for praying the rosary.

How could anyone who seeks union with God not wish to follow the example of Carmel's own mother and sister in faith? For Mary is the epitome of divine union, personifying what John of the Cross taught about the spiritual marriage: "In that sweet drink of God, in which the soul is imbibed in him, she most willingly and with intense delight surrenders herself wholly to him in the desire to be totally his and never to possess in herself anything other than him. God causes in this union the purity and perfection necessary for such a surrender. And since he transforms her into himself, he makes her entirely his own and empties her of all she possesses other than him" (C 27.6).

This is a state in which there is complete union of wills, and it can be applied preeminently to Mary in her relationship with God—with her son during his life on earth, and with the divine Persons in prayer.

Mary is both gift and gateway to contemplative prayer. To heed her call to pray the rosary daily and to be clothed with the scapular of Carmel is to open our soul to prayer by keeping vigil with mystery. As the familiar words fall sweetly from our lips, the deliberate rhythm of the rosary quiets needless anxieties and allows the mystery of God's love to unfold. In the shadow of Christ's passion and death, hearts are pierced as if by a sword that brings both pain and delight. Holding firm to

---

15. Tara K. Soughers, "Seeking Wisdom in Common Vocal Prayers: Teresa of Ávila's Response to the Banning of Vernacular Books," in Mary Frohlich, R.S.C.J., ed., *Carmelite Wisdom and Prophetic Hope: Treasures Both New and Old*, Carmelite Studies, vol. 11 (Washington, D.C.: ICS Publications, 2019), 292.

Christ's rising, they who remain watching and waiting by the tomb will hear the Master call them by name. Then, old wine skins, no longer able to contain new wine, bursts—and all who drink freely are sent forth. Time and place no longer matter, for they cannot contain the Word who became man.

Ordained from the beginning of the world, the Word became flesh and returned to the Father, the divine mission accomplished. God became human, and that human-divine person became bread. O blessed irony! How could it be that God, whom the universe could not contain and now disguised as bread for the world, is contained in tabernacles made by human hands to be consumed by mere mortals, so that human persons could become like God? When he was accused of blaspheming, Jesus answered, "Is it not written in your law, 'I said, you are gods'?" (Jn 10:34; cf. Ps 82:6). To which we could add that in the Eucharist, we not only become like God but share in God's own life. Truly, it is one of the greatest mysteries of all.

This is the legacy, the prophecy, and promise that each of us holds within the secret of our heart as we await Love's embrace. The meeting happens at a time not of our choosing, nor is it dictated by method or merit. Transcending time and space, mystery dwells among us, its meeting tent pitched on a mountaintop within the human heart, waiting to set souls aflame. It is that mystical space within us, like the experience of the first Carmelites who, after leaving the Holy Land, carried Mount Carmel within them—loving "the solitude of this mountain *with a view to contemplating* heavenly things."[16]

16. From the *Rubrica Prima* (1281), in Kees Waaijman, O.Carm., *The Mystical Space of Carmel: A Commentary on the Carmelite Rule*, trans. John Vriend (Leuven: Peeters, 1999), 3.

INVITATION TO PRAYER

During Jesus's life on earth, he excluded no one from his kingdom. What he required was that everyone believe in him and in the Father who sent him. Jesus healed the Roman centurion's servant (see Mt 8:5–13) and the Canaanite woman's daughter (see Mt 15:21–28), praising both the military officer and the foreign woman for their faith. Through the many miracles that Jesus performed, the presence of God was made visible through him as he reached out and touched many people when he healed them. As people began to recognize him, "they sent word throughout the region and brought all who were sick to him, and begged him that they might touch even the fringe of his cloak; and all who touched it were healed" (Mt 14:35–36). Jesus used the humblest means to show his love and mercy. In a similar manner, Mary has extended a small brown scapular as a means of spiritual healing and protection for all who wear it and believe in her power to protect and intercede for us. And so, in gratitude for the role that Mary has played in salvation history and continues to play in the church, we place our petitions before Our Lady of Mount Carmel.

FLOS CARMELI (FLOWER OF CARMEL)

(Thirteenth-century hymn to Our Lady attributed to St. Simon Stock)

Flower of Carmel, tall vine, blossom-laden;
splendor of heaven, childbearing, yet maiden;
none equals thee.

Mother so tender, whom no man didst know,
on Carmel's children thy favors bestow;
Star of the Sea!

Continued

INVITATION TO PRAYER *Continued*

STRONG STEM OF JESSE, WHO BORE ONE BRIGHT FLOWER,
BE EVER NEAR US, AND GUARD US EACH HOUR,
WHO SERVE THEE HERE.

PUREST OF LILIES, THAT FLOWERS AMONG THORNS,
BRING HELP TO TRUE HEARTS THAT IN WEAKNESS TURN
AND TRUST IN THEE.

STRONGEST OF ARMOR, WE TRUST IN THY MIGHT,
UNDER THY MANTLE, HARD PRESSED IN THE FIGHT,
WE CALL TO THEE.

OUR WAY, UNCERTAIN, SURROUNDED BY FOES,
UNFAILING COUNSEL YOU OFFER TO THOSE
WHO TURN TO THEE.

O GENTLE MOTHER, WHO IN CARMEL REIGNS,
SHARE WITH YOUR SERVANTS THAT GLADNESS YOU GAINED,
AND NOW ENJOY.

HAIL, GATE OF HEAVEN, WITH GLORY NOW CROWNED,
BRING US TO SAFETY, WHERE THY SON IS FOUND,
TRUE JOY TO SEE.

Epilogue

Having accompanied Mary as she is portrayed in Scripture and through the mysteries of the rosary, some might wonder what more can be said about this blessed lady. But such musings are imprudent, for no matter how much is said or written about the Mother of God, her portrait will always remain incomplete. No woman has been the subject of as many artistic renderings as the virgin of Nazareth, and yet she remains shrouded in mystery. Countless attempts by artists to capture on canvas what saints and mystics have depicted in poetic verse are mere products of artistic speculation, leading to the conclusion that Mary is no ordinary woman.

Referred to in Scripture as the woman clothed with the sun (see Rev 12:1–17), she who circles the globe gathers her children as eagerly as the Israelites once gathered manna from Sinai's desert floor. Akin to the burning bush, her heart was set aflame with the fire of God's love, forever burning but never consumed. She who dwelt beyond Satan's reach was sent as dew upon the earth that ushered in a new dawn. As heaven's purest fleece, she lent her womb to become the loom where the divine shuttle wove flesh and blood, bone and sinew to create the seamless garment that would clothe her son with a nature that was both human and divine.

In surrendering her will, Mary became one with the breath of God, awakening a sleeping world to the divine presence in its midst. During her earthly life, humankind remained largely indifferent to the miracle that God had sent to earth. More than two thousand years later, the handmaid of the Lord continues to be sent, traveling the roads her son trod in search of souls in order to lead them to Christ. This loving lady cares for the sick, ministers to the sorrowful, and instructs children and scholars alike. As the weaver of wisdom amid a people whose hearts have left their home in search of a lost identity, this dear lady comes bearing gifts—not of gold, frankincense, and myrrh, but of faith, hope, and charity.

The immaculate conception, whose flower of virginity remained intact, is human nature's solitary boast. Having no wish to rule haughtily from on high like some distant queen, aloof and foreboding, she spreads her mantle before us and welcomes us into its abundant folds. Rather than her assumption and coronation ending her role on earth, they expanded it and extended it to the farthest corners of the globe. No longer held bound by time and place, Mary is mother of all.

In Guadalupe, she appeared as an Aztec maiden. At Lourdes and Fatima, she came as a European, in Kenya as an African, and in Akita she came as a Japanese woman. No longer identified with one country, Mary belongs to every country. She is a cause of joy for races and religions alike. Muslims honor her, Jews esteem her as the mother of a great teacher, and unbelievers are won over by her. According to a Harvard professor who was a self-proclaimed atheist, Mary appeared to him and it changed his life. He is now a Catholic, attends Mass daily, and witnesses to the extraordinary beauty of the Mother of God.[1]

According to Buddhism, the heart sutra teaches that "form is emptiness and emptiness is form." From a Christian

---

1. See "Atheist Harvard Prof Says Supernatural Vision of Our Lady Led Him to Catholicism: She Was 'Indescribably Beautiful,'" December 2, 2019, *https://www.churchpop.com/2019/12/02/atheist-harvard-prof-says-supernatural-vision-of-our-lady-led-him-to-catholicism-she-was-indescribably-beautiful/*.

perspective, we could say that emptiness took form when the Virgin Mary, who was empty of anything that was not of God, consented to be the mother of Jesus. One with the Father's will, Mary was espoused to the Holy Spirit and the Word became flesh, a form that was both human and divine. This is but one more reason why many proponents of interreligious dialogue view Mary as a bridge for people of faith.

This is not to say that Mary is God. She is not! But through her espousal with God, she and God became one. In this, Mary is the personification of the words of John of the Cross who may have had Mary in mind when he wrote: "Having been made one with God, the soul is somehow God through participation. Although it is not God as perfectly as it will be in the next life, it is like the shadow of God. Being the shadow of God through this substantial transformation, it performs in this measure in God and through God what he through himself does in it. For the will of the two is one will, and thus God's operation and the soul's are one" (LF 3.78).

Clearly, there was never a soul more intimately united with the heart of God than Mary. She who was conceived without sin remained sinless throughout her life. As such she is our model, but she is also our hope. Her motherly protection has served her children and the church throughout the centuries. As Our Lady of Mount Carmel, she stands before the face of God, is zealous for souls, and has led countless people, both within Carmel and outside of it, to her son. As a model for all who seek union with God, Mary is the perfect contemplative, the perfection of wisdom, and our beloved mother. When we call upon Mary, she leads us to Jesus, and when we call upon Jesus, he directs us to his mother who, together with her spouse, the Holy Spirit, teaches us how to become fully human.

This thrice-favored bride of Love is uniquely positioned to hear our prayer. Only of her can it be said: she is daughter of the

Father, mother of the Son, and spouse of the Holy Spirit. And she is our mother, too.

O Mary, conceived without sin, pray for all who have recourse to thee!

Appendix 1

Questions for Reflection

CHAPTER 1 Nazareth: *Preparing The Way For Christ's Coming*

When the angel told Mary she would conceive in her womb and bear a son, she responded by asking how this would be accomplished.

- What does Mary asking how her pregnancy would come about tell you about making informed decisions? When faced with important decisions, how do you typically approach them? What does Mary embracing the will of God teach you about the virtue of obedience in your own life?

Mary identified herself as "the servant of the Lord" (Lk 1:38).

- How do you typically identify yourself when asked? Do you tend to identify yourself by your role in life, by your relationships, or by what you do? What does this tell you about how you see yourself? How might your self-identity affect your relationship with God? How can knowledge of God affect your self-identity?

CHAPTER 2 A Town of Judah: *Crossing a Threshold*

According to Scripture, Mary "went in haste" (Lk 1:39) to help Elizabeth.

- Who in your family or neighborhood might benefit from a helping hand from you? When you become aware of someone in need, what is your first response? How can you, like Mary, bring Christ to others? What are some ways you've done this in the past? How has helping others impacted you and your relationship with God?

When Mary entered the house of Zechariah, the infant in Elizabeth's womb leapt for joy in recognition of Christ.

- How might God be inviting you to be Christ to others in new ways, perhaps in your neighborhood or parish community? What is the mission that God has called you to embrace? Has it changed over the years, and if so, how?

CHAPTER 3 Bethlehem: *The Birth of Jesus*

Mary traveled to Bethlehem and gave birth to Jesus in a cave, away from family and friends.

- What does this tell you about Mary's commitment to her husband? How does the example of Mary speak to you in your life today? What does it say about the importance of the "domestic church"? During the course of your life, was there a time when you were asked to sacrifice the comfort of the familiar for the unknown? How did you feel and what was your response?

The first people whom God invited to worship the infant Jesus were lowly shepherds who had no significant status among the Jews.

- What does this tell you about how God views people? When you think about Christian community, who are the first people that come to your mind? What might this tell you about the way you view people? Is there someone that you may be ignoring or avoiding because of their status in the community, parish, or neighborhood? How can you remedy this?

CHAPTER 4 Distant Lands: *Offering a Light to the Nations*

Mary welcomed the magi, even though they were unexpected and were strangers from a foreign land.

- What does the presence of Mary at the end of their journey tell you about the role she plays in your faith journey? What in the journey of the wise men resonates most with your own faith journey? What difficulties or challenges have you encountered along the way? What has been your response? Who has been a star that has guided you toward God? Has there been a time in your life when God seemed distant or absent? How did you respond?

Mary and Joseph fled to Egypt to save Jesus from the slaughter by Herod, and became refugees is a foreign land.

- What opportunities have you had during your life to welcome strangers? How have you responded? Who is the stranger in your midst that could benefit from your reaching out to them? In the past, how has your giving been received? In what way have you been rewarded? How do these thoughts affect your thinking about refugees and people who are trying to gain access to the country where you live in order to escape violence, poverty, or persecution?

CHAPTER 5 Jerusalem: *Finding Jesus in the Father's House*

Mary and Joseph sought for Jesus for three days when he stayed behind in the temple.

- What does this tell you about the Holy Family and all that Mary suffered as she searched for Jesus? Have you had the experience of waiting for a child or a family member to return when you were not sure where they might have gone? If so, how did it make you feel? What was your response when the child or family member returned?

Upon finding Jesus in the temple, Mary reproached Jesus for the pain he had caused them.

- Has a child or a family member ever hurt you and then seemed to blame you for taking offense? How did that make you feel? What was your response? How can Mary's response help you work through hurt feelings?

CHAPTER 6 Cana: *Looking to Christ, the True Bridegroom*

When the wine was in short supply, Mary noticed and told Jesus about it.

- What does this tell you about Mary? What does it tell you about apostolic action as it flows from the contemplative life? Although it seemed as though Jesus was not interested, what does Mary's response tell you about the prayer of intercession?

Undaunted by Jesus's reply, Mary proceeded to say to the servants, "Do whatever he tells you" (Jn 2:5).

- What does this say about remaining faithful, even when things don't seem to make sense? What do Mary's words say to you about the importance of obedience? How do faith and obedience to God's will go hand in hand?

CHAPTER 7 Galilee: *God's Family Redefined*

Mary traveled with relatives to try to meet with Jesus, but Jesus used the occasion to define whom he considered his family.

- Mary's response to Jesus's words is not recorded in Scripture, so how do you think she might have felt? Have you ever found yourself in a situation where your suggestions or wanting to help someone have been rejected? How did it make you feel? Might this be an occasion to go deeper and see the merit of the situation?

Jesus told the crowd that those who keep his Father's will are his mother and sisters and brothers.

- What does this tell you about the family of God? Have you seen someone you know being excluded because they were not part of the Christian or Catholic family? How did it make you feel? How might God be calling you to be more inclusive?

CHAPTER 8 Calvary: *At the Foot of the Cross*

Mary followed Jesus to Calvary and remained at the foot of the cross until the very end.

- What does this tell you about Mary and the cost of discipleship? Can you think of a time when you remained faithful even when things seemed hopeless? Was there someone present who helped you get through the experience? What did they do that was most helpful to you during a time of crisis?

Before he died, Jesus gave us his own mother as his dying gift.

- In times of spiritual distress, has Mary been a help, and if so, in what way? How might your relationship with your own earthly mother affect your perception of and relationship with Mary?

CHAPTER 9 The Upper Room: *Mother of the Church*

Scripture informs us that Mary waited with the apostles in the Upper Room until the Holy Spirit was sent from heaven.

- What role do you think Mary might have played during that first Pentecost novena? Have you ever waited for something or someone, not knowing what to expect or how things would work out? How did you spend the time leading up to it? How did waiting affect you emotionally? What are some ordinary everyday occasions where you find yourself waiting? How do you react, and is there a way to make better use of the time?

When the Holy Spirit came upon the apostles in the Upper Room, Mary was present.

- What does Mary's presence there in the Upper Room and her role as Mother of the Church tell you about the role of women in the Church? How has that role changed over the years?

At that first Pentecost, Mary witnessed the apostles change from fearful men to bold proclaimers of the death and resurrection of Jesus.

- When you received the sacrament of confirmation, to what extent were you aware of the coming of the Holy Spirit in your life? How have you experienced the presence of the Holy Spirit in your life since then? How did it change you? How mindful are you of the presence of the Holy Spirit in your daily life? What might you do to increase your devotion to the Holy Spirit?

CHAPTER 10 Mary's Role in Our Journey Home

Life on earth is a daily journey toward the heart of God, our home for all eternity.

- What role has Mary played in your faith journey toward her son? Throughout her life, Mary remained faithful to the will of God even when she didn't understand the depth of all that was taking place. What has been your response when suffering, challenges, or disappointment have come your way? What in Mary's life might help or has helped you to place your trust in God?

CHAPTER 11 The Rosary: *Mary's Flower Garden*

The rosary is Mary's special prayer, a prayer that has been advocated by saints and preached by popes.

- When and how did you first hear about the rosary? Has it been part of your prayer life and, if so, what impact has it made on your appreciation of Mary? How has praying the rosary increased your appreciation for the mysteries of our faith? In what way can your familiarity with the prayers of the rosary facilitate your ability to reflect on the life of Jesus through Mary's eyes? What impact has meditating on the mysteries of the rosary had on your faith life?

CHAPTER 12 Keeping Vigil with Mystery

Mary's example shows us that faith is about believing without seeing or fully understanding the events of our life.

- Are there situations in your life or in your relationship with God where the only answer is no answer? How did Mary deal with times of unknowing in her own life? How can her example help you to take on faith what you may not understand?

Mary is the most perfect reflection of the goodness of God and his love for humanity.

- Is there one event in Mary's life that stands out for you as an example of her love for others? When do you find that it is most difficult to love others? What in Mary's life might help you to see people who are different or who have offended you as children of God?

CHAPTER 13 The Joyful Mysteries

As we follow Mary through the events that make up the five Joyful Mysteries of the rosary, there is also an element of sorrow.

- What does this tell you about life in general? Among the Joyful Mysteries, which one do you find the most relevant in your own life? How does joy differ from happiness? Can you have a joyful heart even when you are struggling or suffering?

Have you ever experienced such a time or known someone who seemed to have joy even in the midst of suffering?

Mary observed the Mosaic Law on purification even though she was sinless.

- What does this tell you about Mary and Joseph as observant Jews and about the importance of obedience to the laws of God? Have you ever been conflicted about the laws or teachings of the church? How can Mary's response to the joys and sorrows in her life be a source of inspiration for you?

CHAPTER 14 The Luminous Mysteries

Mary watched her son leave home to find John the Baptist, not knowing what Jesus's mission would entail.

- How do you think Mary might have felt? Have you watched someone you love (possibly a son or daughter) leave home to go off to college, live independently, or get married? How did you feel when they told you they were leaving? What was the most difficult part about watching them go?

During the wedding feast at Cana, Mary noticed that the wine was in short supply.

- What do Mary's words to Jesus tell you about her relationship with her son? What do you find most impressive about Mary during their exchange? Was there ever a time when you believed in someone even when their words or actions seemed to belie your trust?

CHAPTER 15 The Sorrowful Mysteries

Although in Scripture we read only of Mary's presence at the foot of the cross, we can assume with a fair amount of certainty that she followed her son along the road to Calvary.

- How have you been able to accompany someone who was seriously ill or perhaps was mistreated or subject to ridicule? How did you respond? How did it make you feel to see someone you love suffer?

Mary remained at the foot of the cross until the very end.

- Have you been at the bedside of a family member or of someone you loved who was dying? What was the most difficult part of that experience? What have you taken away from the experience? How did your presence make a difference? How important were words? How can Mary be a source of strength when you or a loved one might be facing death?

CHAPTER 16 The Glorious Mysteries

Mary was assumed into heaven, body and soul, and was crowned Queen of Heaven.

- How is Mary's being taken up to heaven a prototype for our own life in eternity? What does this tell you about the esteem God has for our physical bodies? How might this help us to better respect our own bodies?

The church honors Mary as Queen of heaven and earth.

- What does Mary's queenship mean to you personally? What does her role as queen and mother say about her influence as a powerful intercessor for her children and for the world?

CHAPTER 17 The Brown Scapular of Our Lady of Mount Carmel

The brown scapular is a sacramental, a physical sign that acknowledges the wearer's devotion to Mary as a member of the Carmelite family.

- When did you first learn about the brown scapular? How does being enrolled in the brown scapular honor Mary? What privileges do those who wear it enjoy? How is being enrolled in the brown scapular and a member of the Carmelite family different from being a member of the Carmelite Order? What responsibilities does enrollment in the brown scapular entail? How does having access to the Carmelite family through the brown scapular help you feel closer to Our Lady?

Appendix 2

Passages for *Lectio Divina* and Guidance For Readers

The following ten passages from Scripture are accompanied by passages from the writings of St. Teresa of Avila and St. John of the Cross that can be used for prayer and reflection. Whether you are alone or in a group, take time with one pair of passages on any given day. Each pair of passages focuses on a particular theme, and each quotation is introduced by being framed within the setting in which it was written. The following prayer aid may prove helpful to anyone not familiar with *lectio divina*:

First read the Scripture passage slowly, silently or aloud, pondering what comes to you from it. Next, as you close your eyes, allow the passage to sink deep within you, perhaps allowing a phrase that stands out in your mind to become one with your breath. Repeat it slowly; do not try to interpret its meaning or how it may apply to your life. *Lectio divina* is about allowing the word of God to speak to you, rather than you speaking to the word of God. After a few minutes, read the passage again slowly. Next, choose one word that resonates with you and repeat it slowly, as you inhale and exhale, mindful that it is the Holy Spirit who is praying through you.

Then, when you feel ready to move on, read the Carmelite passage that accompanies it, and follow the same process as when you read and prayed with the Scripture text. What phrase or word stands out for you that complements the phrase or word that captured your attention from the passage in Scripture? As the phrase and then the word become one with your breath, allow the silence to draw you in. As you open yourself to receive what God may wish you to take from this prayer practice, trust that even the absence of a message can be a message, inviting you to trust what John of the Cross calls "unknowing." You may wish to conclude this lectio divina session with an Our Father and a prayer of thanksgiving.

Making a mental note of the word or words that touched you in prayer and recalling them from time to time can serve as a gentle reminder of God's presence with you throughout the day.

PASSAGES FOR PRAYER

Self-knowledge

Mary's self-identification was rooted in her relationship with God, as was evident at the annunciation when she said, "Here am I, the servant of the Lord" (Lk 1:38).

In referencing the many rooms in each dwelling place in *The Interior Castle*, Teresa wrote, "Oh, but if it [the soul] is in the room of self-knowledge! How necessary this room is—see that you understand me. . . . Here it will discover its lowliness better than by thinking of itself" (IC 1.2.8).

Silence

After the shepherds paid homage to the Child Jesus, Scripture says, "Mary treasured all these words and pondered them in her heart" (Lk 2:19).

In writing about detachment, John of the Cross advocates setting aside all thoughts, even those concerning God, and writes, "It is better to learn to silence and quiet the faculties so that God may speak. For in this state . . . the natural operations must fade from sight. This is realized when the soul arrives at solitude in these faculties, and God speaks to its heart" (A 3.3.4).

Purpose of Contemplative Prayer

Upon hearing of Elizabeth's pregnancy, and after the angel left her, we are told that "Mary set out and went with haste to a Judean town in the hill country, where she entered the house of Zechariah and greeted Elizabeth" (Lk 1:39–40).

Teresa cautions her nuns not to practice prayer for their own pleasure and writes, "Let us desire and be occupied in prayer not for the sake of our enjoyment but so as to have this strength to serve" (IC 7.4.12).

Humility

After Elizabeth greeted Mary, she responded, "My soul magnifies the Lord, / and my spirit rejoices in God my Savior, / for he has looked with favor on the lowliness of his servant" (Lk 1:46-48).

In describing the effects that the prayer of union produces in the soul, Teresa writes, "Its [the soul's] humility is deeper because it sees plainly that through no diligence of its own did it receive that very generous and magnificent gift and that it played no role in obtaining or experiencing it" (L 19.2).

Trust

When Joseph was warned in a dream to flee to Egypt with Mary and Jesus to avoid the slaughter that Herod had ordered, Scripture says, "Then Joseph got up, took the child and his mother by night, and went to Egypt, and remained there until the death of Herod" (Mt 2:14–15).

In describing souls who seek comfort in the Lord alone, Teresa writes, "They place themselves under the protection of the Lord; they desire no other" (SS 5.3).

Faith

When Jesus remained behind in the temple, Mary and Joseph discovered their son was missing, and "they started to look for him among their relatives and friends. When they did not find him they returned to Jerusalem to search for him" (Lk 2:44–45).

In teaching about the importance of faith as the substance of things hoped for, John warns that faith occurs in the absence of knowing and writes, "For though faith brings certitude to the intellect, it does not produce clarity, but only darkness" (A 2.6.2).

Obedience

At the wedding feast at Cana, when Mary noticed the wine was in short supply, she said to the servants, "Do whatever he tells you" (Jn 2:5).

Offering advice on a number of topics, John counsels, "God desires the least degree of obedience and submissiveness more than all those services you think of rendering him" (SLL 13).

Family of God

When the crowd told Jesus that his mother and brothers wanted to speak to him, he pointed to his disciples and said, "Here are my mother and my brothers! For whoever does the will of my Father in heaven is my brother and sister and mother" (Mt 12:49-50).

In describing persons who are transformed in God through love, John of the Cross writes, "The will, which previously loved in a base and deadly way with only its natural affection, is now changed into the life of divine love, for it loves in a lofty way with divine affection" (LF 2.34).

Redemptive Suffering

The Gospel of John tells us: "Meanwhile, standing near the cross of Jesus were his mother, and his mother's sister, Mary the wife of Clopas, and Mary Magdalene" (Jn 19:25).

In writing about those who are going through the night of spirit, John of the Cross writes, "Their helplessness is even greater because of the little they can do in this situation" (N 2.7.3).

Indwelling Trinity

When one of his disciples asked Jesus how he would reveal himself to them, Jesus answered, "Those who love me will keep my word, and my Father will love them, and we will come to them and make our home with them" (Jn 14:23).

In counseling her nuns about interior prayer, Teresa writes, "All one need do is go into solitude and look at Him within oneself, and . . . with great humility speak to Him as to a Father" (W 28.2).

Glossary

GLOSSARY OF SPIRITUAL TERMS AS THEY APPLY TO MARY

The terms below, all of which appear in the book, are defined as they apply to Mary and to her relationship with God.

Ascent – In *The Ascent of Mount Carmel*, John of the Cross uses this term to describe the process of freeing oneself from sensory pleasures and satisfaction. We can't be certain how this process evolved within Mary, but we can assume that the intermittent movement by Mary toward God and by God toward her with ever-increasing intimacy continued during her formative years and culminated in the consummation of her union with the Holy Trinity during her spiritual marriage. The mutual self-giving of God to Mary and Mary to God would have continued as it played out through the events of her life.

Dark night of sense – In *The Dark Night*, John uses the term to describe the stage in the spiritual life when occasions or events occur that can assist in the process of detachment and purification. Mary had no need for purification since she was without sin. For her, the dark night of sense was a sign of her union with God as a pure offering of herself and would have been ongoing, most notably during those times when her detachment from the security of family, friends, and physical comfort was most evident. One event would have been when she left her home in Nazareth to travel to Bethlehem, knowing that the birth of Jesus was imminent. Another was when she and Joseph were told to flee to Egypt, a foreign land where they would be living with strangers in a non-Jewish culture. Other events would surely have included the three consecutive days and nights when Mary and Joseph searched ceaselessly for the Child Jesus when he had remained behind in the temple; the death of her husband Joseph; the day Jesus left home to begin his public ministry; and finally, his crucifixion, where she remained with Jesus until the end, regardless of the physical pain and danger it caused her.

Dark night of spirit – A term John uses to describe a more intense stage of purification, during which a person is deprived of any sense of intimacy with God and instead experiences a sense of being abandoned by God. Upon hearing Simeon's prophecy about the seven swords that would pierce her soul, the darkness of unknowing would have filled Mary's soul as she pondered what that meant in terms of her relationship with God. Similarly, as she searched anxiously for Jesus, the night of spirit would have encroached upon her, perhaps accusing her of negligence as the child God was missing. And yet, nothing would have cut as deeply into her soul as she stood by, helplessly watching her son mocked and beaten on the road to Calvary, where he was crucified. The words her son cried out—"My God, my God, why have you forsaken me?" (Mt 27:46)—surely eclipsed any sense of her communion with God as she was plunged into the darkness of abandonment that her son was experiencing as she beheld his crucified body.

Dwelling places – A metaphor that Teresa used in *The Interior Castle* to describe the soul as having seven dwelling places that persons enter, within themselves, as they experience stages of deepening prayer. Since Mary was free from sin, she would have experienced only the unitive stages of prayer. (See "Unitive way" below.)

Illuminative way – A stage that those who are proficient in prayer enter when they have been sufficiently purified, so that they are able to receive supernatural or infused prayer that illuminates their understanding as it deepens their journey toward union with God. It seems likely that Mary would have enjoyed such experiences of God during her early years, as they helped form her in the ways of God.

Infused contemplation – This term describes a supernatural experience of God that is given to a person by God—that is, from a source other than the person's own effort—whereby "God infuses himself into the soul" (LF 3.49). To experience infused contemplation is sheer gift, which Mary would surely have known, for from the moment of her immaculate conception, she was infused with knowledge of God. Her entire being was God's gift, not only to her but to the world, and it continued to deepen in her throughout her life.

Nuptial mystery of the cross – This has been referred to by St. Augustine as the "marriage bed of the cross," which is a metaphor used to describe the consummation of the covenant between God and his people as the Son emptied himself on the cross and gave his blood for the salvation of the world. Mary, as the bride of the Holy Trinity, having given her life to God in love, was privileged to participate in the salvific act of redemption as she stood at the foot of the cross on Calvary.

Purification and purgation – The process of self-emptying that leads to the self-surrendering that is needed to reorder the senses, making God's law of love the guiding principle behind a person's choices and decisions.

Purgative way – The way that beginners travel as they journey in prayer toward a deepening relationship with God. This would not have been part of Mary's experience as she did not need to be purified, and although she had free will, all her senses were ordered toward doing God's will.

Sensory appetites – The sensory part of human passions that can be obstacles to a person's spiritual growth. For Mary, the human senses were perfectly ordered so that they were always subject to the will of God; her every impulse was directed toward God, which meant she was completely relying on her relationship with God to motivate her actions. Yet she did not disdain the senses, as was evident when she noticed the wine was in short supply during the wedding feast. Rather, she took her concern directly to Jesus.

Spiritual betrothal – Just as persons who are engaged or betrothed have eyes and ears only for the one who has captivated their heart, so Mary, who was free from original sin, was focused entirely on God from her earliest years. Having been spiritually formed, first by her saintly parents, Anna and Joachim, and then—if the apocryphal *Protoevangelium of James* is accurate—by holy people at the temple where she lived from the age of three until around the age of twelve, Mary was receptive to every divine initiative. The words of Psalm 81 surely describe well her interior disposition toward God as she waited—unknowingly—for the Word of the Lord: "Open your mouth wide and I will fill it" (Ps 81:10).

Spiritual marriage – Mary's response to the angel Gabriel, "let it be with me according to your word" (Lk 1:38), was not only her consent to being the mother of the Messiah; it consummated Mary's spiritual marriage to God, so transforming her that she became "God by participation in God" (LF 2.34). This highest state of spiritual union between God and Mary took place only after she had reached a level of maturity that enabled her to respond to God's unceasingly emptying himself so that she could offer herself completely in return. "The angel said to her, 'The Holy Spirit will come upon you, and the power of the Most High will overshadow you; therefore the child to be born will be holy; he will be called Son of God'" (Lk 1:35). Mary's consent was informed, and her communion with God was real and visible throughout her life; she no longer lived for herself, but her every thought, word, and action were directed toward doing God's will. Although Mary is called "spouse of the Holy Spirit," her union involves the entire Trinity as described in the words spoken by the angel (see Lk 1:35). The church professes that there is *one God* in *three Divine Persons* (see CCC 253), which describes the mystery of the Holy Trinity. Therefore, through the spiritual marriage, Mary was in communion and in converse with all three Persons, as St. Teresa explains: "Here all three Persons communicate themselves to it [the soul], speak to it, and explain those words of the Lord in the Gospel: that He and the Father and the Holy Spirit will come to dwell with the soul that loves Him and keeps His commandments" (IC 7.1.6; cf. Jn 14:23).

Transverberation – Teresa described the experience of her spiritual marriage as one of both pain and pleasure, as though her entire being was being pierced through as if by a dart (see L 29.13). However, because Mary was sinless and free from even the stain of original sin, there was no veil of sin that God needed to penetrate when the Holy Trinity entered her soul. Therefore, Mary's spiritual marriage to God during the annunciation was one of pure and ecstatic joy. Her pain would come later, when the sins of others would pierce her heart, just as they pierce the heart of God.

Unitive way – A stage of prayer where more perfect souls may experience infused prayer that brings about a transformation of the person's will, uniting it ever more closely with the will of God. Depending on a person's disposition and God's will for such souls, it may culminate in the spiritual betrothal and finally the spiritual marriage, which Mary was privileged to experience. It is generally understood that few souls are brought to this level of perfection during their life on earth, though as we have seen through the lives of saints and holy souls, it can and does happen.

Bibliography

PRIMARY SOURCES

Elizabeth of the Trinity. *Complete Works of Elizabeth of the Trinity*, vol. 1. Trans. Sister Aletheia Kane, O.C.D. Washington, D.C.: ICS Publications, 1984.

John of the Cross. *The Collected Works of Saint John of the Cross*. Trans. Kieran Kavanaugh, O.C.D., and Otilio Rodriguez, O.C.D. Washington, D.C.: ICS Publications, 1991.

New Revised Standard Version Bible: Catholic Edition. New York: HarperCollins, 1989. *https://www.biblegateway.com/versions/New-Revised-Standard-Version-NRSV-Bible/*.

Stein, Edith. *The Hidden Life: Hagiographic Essays, Meditations, Spiritual Texts*. Trans. Waltraut Stein, Ph.D. Washington, D.C.: ICS Publications, 1992.

———. *The Mystery of Christmas: Incarnation and Humanity*. Trans. Sister Josephine Rucker, S.S.J. Darlington, England: Darlington Carmel, 1985.

———. *The Science of the Cross*. Trans. Josephine Koeppel, O.C.D. Washington, D.C.: ICS Publications, 2002.

Teresa of Avila. *The Collected Works of St. Teresa of Avila*. 3 vols. Trans. Kieran Kavanaugh, O.C.D., and Otilio Rodriguez, O.C.D. Washington, D.C.: ICS Publications, 1987, 1980, and 1985.

Thérèse of Lisieux. *Story of a Soul: The Autobiography of Saint Thérèse of Lisieux*, 3rd edition. Trans. John Clarke, O.C.D. Washington, D.C.: ICS Publications, 1996.

SECONDARY SOURCES

Aimilianos, Archimandrite. *The Way of the Spirit: Reflections on Life in God.* Translated by Maximos Simonopetrites. Athens: Indiktos Publishing Co., 2009.

Alaharasan, V. Antony J. *Home of the Assumption: Reconstructing Mary's Life in Ephesus.* Worcester, Mass.: Ambassador Books, 2002.

Albert, *The Rule of Saint Albert.* In *The Carmelite Rule.* Edited by Bruce Baker, O.Carm., and Gregory L. Klein, O.Carm. Totowa, N.J.: Catholic Book Publishing Company, 2000.

Alphonsus Liguori. *The Glories of Mary.* Edited and translated by Eugene Grimm. Brooklyn: Redemptorist Fathers, 1931; Victory Missions reprint, c. 1980.

———. "O God of Loveliness." In *Life of the Spouse.* Edited by Patrick Corbert. Strathfield, Australia: St. Pauls Publications, 2017.

Altemose, Charlene, M.S.C. *What You Should Know About Mary.* Liguori, Mo.: Liguori Publications, 1998.

Anthony of Padua. *Seek First His Kingdom: An Anthology of the Sermons of the Saint.* Edited by Livio Poloniato, O.F.M.Conv. Translated by Claude Jarmak, O.F.M. Padua: Edizioni Messaggero Padova, 1996.

Apostoli, Andrew, C.F.R. *Fatima for Today: The Urgent Marian Message of Hope.* San Francisco: Ignatius Press, 2010.

Augustine. *The Confessions of St. Augustine.* Translated by John K. Ryan. Garden City, N.Y.: Image Books, 1960.

———. *The Works of St Augustine: A Translation for the 21st Century.* Edited by John E. Rotelle, O.S.A. Translated by Edmund Hill, O.P. Vol. III/7, *Sermons 230–272B on Liturgical Seasons.* Hyde Park, NY: New City Press, 1993.

Barry, William, S.J. *Who Do You Say I Am? Meeting the Historical Jesus in Prayer.* Notre Dame, Ind.: Ave Maria Press, 1996.

Bernard of Clairvaux. "Sermon 2" in *Song of Songs I*. Vol. 2 of *The Works of Bernard of Clairvaux*. Translated by Kilian Walsh, O.C.S.O. Collegeville, Minn.: Liturgical Press, 2008.

Buzy, D., S.C.J., *Thoughts: Blessed Mary of Jesus Crucified* (*Mariam Baouardy*). Bethlehem, Palestine: Carmel of Bethlehem, 1997.

Catechism of the Catholic Church. Alexandria, Va.: Pauline Books & Media, 1994.

Chorpenning, Joseph. "St. Teresa's Presentation of Her Religious Experience." In *Carmelite Studies*, vol. 3: *Centenary of St. Teresa*. Edited by John Sullivan, O.C.D. Washington, D.C.: ICS Publications, 1984.

Cutri, Mary Paul, O.C.D. *Sounding Solitude: An Approach to Transformation in Christ by Love*. Washington, D.C.: ICS Publications, 2010.

De Fiores, Stefano and J. Patrick Gaffney, eds. *Jesus Living in Mary: Handbook of the Spirituality of St. Louis Marie de Montfort*. Bay Shore, N.Y.: Montfort Publications, 1994.

De Montfort, St. Louis Mary. *The Secret of the Rosary*. Translated by Mary Barbour, T.O.P. Bay Shore, N.Y.: TAN Books, 2009.

Drane, Augusta Theodosia. *The Life of Saint Dominic*. Charlotte, N.C.: TAN Books, 2011

Francis, Pope. *Evangelii Gaudium* (*On the Proclamation of the Gospel in Today's World*). November 24, 2013. *https://www.vatican.va/content/francesco/en/apost_exhortations/documents/papa-francesco_esortazione-ap_20131124_evangelii-gaudium.html/*.

———. *Gaudete et Exsultate* (*On the Call to Holiness in Today's World*). March 19, 2018. *https://www.vatican.va/content/francesco/en/apost_exhortations/documents/papa-francesco_esortazione-ap_20180319_gaudete-et-exsultate.html/*.

———. *Amoris Laetitia* (*The Joy of Love*). March 19, 2016. *https://www.vatican.va/content/francesco/en/apost_exhortations/documents/papa-francesco_esortazione-ap_20160319_amoris-laetitia.html/*.

Gabriel of St. Mary Magdalen, Father, O.C.D. *Divine Intimacy: Meditations on the Interior Life for Every Day of the Liturgical Year*. Translated by the Discalced Carmelite Nuns of Boston. London: Baronius Press, 2008.

Hennessy, Kate. *Dorothy Day: The World Will Be Saved by Beauty: An Intimate Portrait of My Grandmother.* New York: Simon & Schuster, 2017.

Houselander, Caryll. *Caryll Houselander: Essential Writings. Edited by Wendy M. Wright. Maryknoll, N.Y.: Orbis Books, 2005.*

———. *The Reed of God.* Notre Dame, Ind.: Ave Maria Press, 2006.

John Paul II. "Message of John Paul II to the Carmelite Family." Vatican, March 25, 2001. *https://www.vatican.va/content/john-paul-ii/en/speeches/2001/march/documents/hf_jp-ii_spe_20010326_ordine-carmelo.html/.*

———. *Redemptoris Mater* (*On the Blessed Virgin Mary in the Life of the Pilgrim Church*). March 25, 1987. *https://www.vatican.va/content/john-paul-ii/en/encyclicals/documents/hf_jp-ii_enc_25031987_redemptoris-mater.html/.*

———. *Rosarium Virginis Mariae* (*On the Most Holy Rosary*). October 16, 2002. *https://www.vatican.va/content/john-paul-ii/en/apost_letters/2002/documents/hf_jp-ii_apl_20021016_rosarium-virginis-mariae.html/.*

———. "Udienza Generale." January 28, 1987. *https://www.vatican.va/content/john-paul-ii/it/audiences/1987/documents/hf_jp-ii_aud_19870128.html/.*

Justin Martyr. "Dialogue with Trypho" in *Saint Justin Martyr.* Translated by Thomas B. Falls. Vol. 6 of *The Fathers of the Church.* Washington, D.C.: CUA Press, 1948.

Laurentin, René. *The Apparitions of the Blessed Virgin Mary Today.* Dublin: Veritas Publications, 1991.

Leo XIII, Pope. *Octobri Mense* (*On the Rosary*). September 22, 1891. *http://www.vatican.va/content/leo-xiii/en/encyclicals/documents/hf_l-xiii_enc_22091891_octobri-mense.html/.*

Lohfink, Gerhard. *Jesus of Nazareth: What He Wanted, Who He Was*. Translated by Linda M. Maloney. Collegeville, Minn.: Liturgical Press, 2012. © 2012, © 2015 by Order of Saint Benedict, Collegeville, Minnesota. Used with permission.

Manelli, Fr. Stefano M., F.I., *Blessed John Duns Scotus: Marian Doctor*. New Bedford, Mass.: Academy of the Immaculate, 2011.

Mary of Agreda, Mother, *The Mystical City of God: Popular Abridgment of the Divine History and Life of the Virgin Mother of God*. Translated by Fiscar Marison (Rev. George J. Blatter. Charlotte, N.C.: Saint Benedict Press/TAN Books, 2012.

Merton, Thomas. *Disputed Questions*. New York, N.Y.: Harcourt Brace & Company, 1985.

Moloney, Francis J., S.D.B., *The Gospel of John*. Sacra Pagina 4. Collegeville, Minn.: Liturgical Press, 1998. © 1998 by Order of Saint Benedict, Collegeville, Minnesota. Used with permission.

Mother Teresa of Calcutta. *The Writings of Mother Teresa of Calcutta*. Mother Teresa Center. Used with permission.

Murphy, Francis J., ed. and trans. *Listen to the Silence: A Retreat with Père Jacques*. Washington, D.C.: ICS Publications, 2005.

Nicholas of Narbonne. *The Flaming Arrow*. Vineyard Series 2. Translated by Michael Edwards. Durham, England: Teresian Press, 1985.

Nolan, Albert, O.P. *Jesus Before Christianity*. Maryknoll, N.Y.: Orbis, 1992.

North American Provincials of the Carmelite Orders. *The Scapular of Our Lady of Mount Carmel: Catechesis and Ritual*. Washington, D.C.: ICS Publications, 2000.

Otto, Rudolf. *The Idea of the Holy*. Translated by John W. Harvey. London: Oxford University Press, 1923.

Paul VI, Pope. *Marialis Cultus* (*For the Right Ordering and Development of Devotion to the Blessed Virgin Mary*). February 2, 1974. *https://www.vatican.va/content/paul-vi/en/apost_exhortations/documents/hf_p-vi_exh_19740202_marialis-cultus.html/*.

Paul-Marie of the Cross, O.C.D. *Carmelite Spirituality in the Teresian Tradition*, rev. ed. Translated by Kathryn Sullivan, R.S.C.J. Washington, D.C.: ICS Publications, 1997.

Peterson, Larry. "Mary's Death and Assumption: Beautiful Thoughts from the Saints." Aleteia. August 14, 2019. *https://aleteia.org/2019/08/14/beautiful-thoughts-from-the-saints-on-marys-death-and-assumption/*.

Pitre, Brant. *Jesus and the Jewish Roots of Mary*. New York, NY: Image, 2011.

———. *Jesus the Bridegroom: The Greatest Love Story Ever Told*. New York, N.Y.: Image, 2014.

Pius V, Pope. *Consueverunt Romani Pontifices*. September 17, 1569. *https://www.papalencyclicals.net/pius05/p5consue.htm/*.

Pius XII, Pope. *Munificentissimus Deus*. November 1, 1950. *https://www.vatican.va/content/pius-xii/en/apost_constitutions/documents/hf_p-xii_apc_19501101_munificentissimus-deus.html/*.

Pronechen, Joseph. *The Fruits of Fatima: A Century of Signs and Wonders*. Manchester, N.H.: Sophia Institute Press, 2019.

Protoevangelium of James. *https://www.newadvent.org/fathers/0847.htm*.

Ratzinger, Joseph/Pope Benedict XVI. *Jesus of Nazareth: From the Baptism in the Jordan to the Transfiguration*. Translated by Adrian J. Walker. San Francisco, Calif.: Ignatius Press, 2007.

———. *Jesus of Nazareth: The Infancy Narratives*. Translated by Philip J. Whitmore. New York, N.Y.: Image Books, 2012.

Rohrbach, Peter-Thomas, O.C.D. *Journey to Carith: The Story of the Carmelite Order*. Washington, D.C.: ICS Publications. Facsimile of 1966 Doubleday edition.

Smet, Joachim, O.Carm. *The Mirror of Carmel: A Brief History of the Carmelite Order*. Darien, Ill.: Carmelite Media, 2011.

Sri, Edward. *Praying the Rosary Like Never Before: Encounter the Wonder of Heaven and Earth*. Cincinnati: Franciscan Media, 2017.

Tindal-Robertson, Timothy. *Fatima, Russia and Pope John Paul II: How Mary Intervened to Deliver Marxist Russia from Atheism.* Still River, Mass.: Ravengate Press, 1991.

Vatican II. *Lumen Gentium* (*Dogmatic Constitution on the Church*). November 21, 1964. *https://www.vatican.va/archive/hist_councils/ii_vatican_council/documents/vat-ii_const_19641121_lumen-gentium_en.html/.*

von Speyr, Adrienne. *The Passion from Within.* Translated by Lucia Wiedenhöver, O.C.D. San Francisco: Ignatius Press, 1998.

West, Christopher. *Heaven's Song: Sexual Love as it was Meant to Be.* West Chester, Penn.: Ascension Press, 2008.

Biblical Index

About Us

ICS Publications, based in Washington, D.C., is the publishing house of the Institute of Carmelite Studies (ICS) and a ministry of the Discalced Carmelite Friars of the Washington Province (U.S.A.). The Institute of Carmelite Studies promotes research and publication in the field of Carmelite spirituality, especially about Carmelite saints and related topics. Its members are friars of the Washington Province.

The Discalced Carmelites are a worldwide Roman Catholic religious order comprised of friars, nuns, and laity—men and women who are heirs to the teaching and way of life of Teresa of Avila and John of the Cross, dedicated to contemplation and to ministry in the church and the world.

Information about their way of life is available through local diocesan vocation offices, or from the Discalced Carmelite Friars vocation directors at the following addresses:

Washington Province:
1525 Carmel Road, Hubertus, WI 53033

California-Arizona Province:
P.O. Box 3420, San Jose, CA 95156

Oklahoma Province:
5151 Marylake Drive, Little Rock, AR 72206

Visit our websites at:

www.icspublications.org and *http://ocdfriarsvocation.org*